Understanding American Federalism and Intergovernmental Relations

Concepts, Ideas, and Theories

Daniel Baracskay, Ph.D.
Carol M. Glen, Ph.D.
Neena Banerjee, Ph.D.
Nandan K. Jha, Ph.D.
Robert (Sherman) Yehl, Ph.D.

UNG
UNIVERSITY of
NORTH GEORGIA
UNIVERSITY PRESS
Blue Ridge | Cumming | Dahlonega | Gainesville | Oconee

I0121242

Understanding American Federalism and Intergovernmental Relations: Concepts, Ideas, and Theories is licensed under a Creative Commons Attribution-ShareAlike 4.0 International License.

This license allows you to remix, tweak, and build upon this work, even commercially, as long as you credit this original source for the creation and license the new creation under identical terms.

If you reuse this content elsewhere, in order to comply with the attribution requirements of the license please attribute the original source to the University System of Georgia.

NOTE: The above copyright license which University System of Georgia uses for their original content does not extend to or include content which was accessed and incorporated, and which is licensed under various other CC Licenses, such as ND licenses. Nor does it extend to or include any Special Permissions which were granted to us by the rightsholders for our use of their content.

Image Disclaimer: All images and figures in this book are believed to be (after a reasonable investigation) either public domain or carry a compatible Creative Commons license. If you are the copyright owner of images in this book and you have not authorized the use of your work under these terms, please contact the University of North Georgia Press at ungpress@ung.edu to have the content removed.

ISBN: 978-1-940771-99-1

Produced by:
University System of Georgia

Published by:
University of North Georgia Press
Dahlonega, Georgia

Cover Design and Layout Design:
Corey Parson

For more information, please visit http://ung.edu/university-press
Or email ungpress@ung.edu
Instructor Resources available upon request.

TABLE OF CONTENTS

CHAPTER 8: HOMELAND SECURITY AS A DIMENSION OF INTERGOVERNMENTAL RELATIONS   286

Carol M. Glen

Preface

We are pleased to offer this compilation of chapters which comprise important concepts, ideas, and theories in intergovernmental relations. So often, the notions of federalism, intergovernmental relations, and intergovernmental management are treated separately in the literature without attempting to draw out important connections between them, both in terms of theory and practice. This tends to neglect the many interrelated influences that have collectively shaped the evolution of our system of government. Consequently, this book seeks to broach this shortcoming by opting for a broader and more comprehensive approach, in which we explore the many *dimensions* of intergovernmental relations that have made it a facet of our nation's dynamic federal structure, and a significant impetus in the development of intergovernmental managerial techniques.

Our first chapter introduces federalism, intergovernmental relations, and intergovernmental management through conceptual and theoretical lenses to provide the foundational basis for successive chapters of the book. In particular, the concept of intergovernmental relations is understood as a term that more significantly encompasses the roles played by localities as a facet of federal structure. Intergovernmental relations has antecedents which are rooted in the founding days of the union, but which became more particularly developed and refined in twentieth-century American politics as the nation evolved away from patterns of dual federalism. As federal structure transitioned toward a more coordinated and cooperative structure to address the emergence of political, economic, and social issues that gave rise to newer policy and programmatic realms, intergovernmental relations provided a compelling need for techniques in intergovernmental management. This managerial side reflects the rise of operational and functional capabilities, and networks of interaction designed for policy and programmatic problem solving and decision-making across levels of government with an emphasis on outcomes. Using this as a springboard, chapters 2 through 5 examine the core political, legal, fiscal, and administrative dimensions of intergovernmental relations, which comprise both historical and contemporary influences that have shaped the evolution of American government over time. Chapters 6 through 8 subsequently extend these core dimensions to a more specialized treatment of the topic, with particular consideration of how collaborative networks, public education policy, and homeland security are illustrative of the multifaceted policy and programmatic dimensions of intergovernmental relations. In essence, our chapter themes help extend conceptualization and theory to practical applications that we hope will illustrate the many driving forces at play in the intergovernmental arena.

Each chapter begins with a listing of core learning objectives, followed by key terms that are introduced and relate to the exploration of various topics presented in the chapter. Chapter sidebars draw particular attention to concepts and provide useful definitions for terms that may otherwise be unfamiliar or confusing. Reflection questions appear at the conclusion of each chapter to help provide students with further opportunities to think about the many ideas they have been learning about, and to broach the often challenging divide that arises in applying their study of themes to important topics of discussion with other students in a more deliberative fashion. In addition, each chapter contains various illustrations, graphs, and examples to help enhance the learning process. Chapters 3 and 5, which examine the political and administrative dimensions of intergovernmental relations respectively, include an additional case study pertaining to COVID-19 and the Tenth Amendment, delving into how state and local governments initially reacted to and dealt with the rise of the public health crisis in early 2020 as a facet of American federalism. The spread of COVID-19 coincided with the writing of this book, and became an apparent exemplar to include given its significance and impact across the nation, and the global arena as a whole.

We like to think of this compilation of chapters as the beginning (or continuation) of your intellectual journey into the historical and contemporary events, transitions, and trends of intergovernmental relations as part of our ever-evolving federal system of government. We hope that the concepts and theories presented in this book will challenge you to think more analytically and critically of our nation's governmental structure, while the practical, real world applications that are presented will be beneficial in expanding your knowledge of the enduring importance of how intergovernmental management relates to your everyday professional endeavors. Learning and scholastic achievement have become a life-long process, and we are pleased to be a small part of your journey.

Acknowledgements

The authors of this book acknowledge and especially thank the many individuals who have diligently worked to make this work a reality. In particular, Angela Brodsky, the Open Education Resource (OER) Instructional Designer from eCampus at the University of West Georgia, was instrumental from day one forward in helping to align the many details and tasks necessary to proceed confidently toward publication. The project would not have been a possibility without the initial recommendation and enthusiasm provided by Christy Talley-Smith, Director of Curriculum and Instruction at eCampus. We also thank the numerous members of the University of North Georgia Press who worked on assorted stages of the project, and the many helpful comments provided by the various anonymous peer reviewers of the book, whose critiques helped to make this a stronger work that we are proud to offer to students of intergovernmental relations. As is often the case with major research projects, the path from beginning to end is often rigorous and demanding, though the process was eased by those whose efforts, advice, and expertise enhanced the final version of this timely book.

1

Introducing American Federalism, Intergovernmental Relations, and Intergovernmental Management: Historical, Conceptual, and Theoretical Foundations

Daniel Baracskay

LEARNING OBJECTIVES

- Demonstrate an understanding of how American federalism was established in the founding days and has evolved throughout our nation's history to include the coordination of activities across levels of government through what is referred to as intergovernmental relations.

- Demonstrate an understanding of how the related concept of intergovernmental management has become an aspect of intergovernmental relations in modern eras of American federalism as evidenced with collaborative partnerships between the public, private, and nonprofit sectors.

Figure 1.1: America Flags
Source: Unsplash
Attribution: Jakob Owens
License: Unsplash License

- Demonstrate knowledge of how metaphors of federalism historically have been used to illustrate changes in our nation's political structure and have also described changes in governmental structure.

- Demonstrate a basic understanding of how theory reflects many diverse perspectives for how federalism, intergovernmental relations, and intergovernmental management contribute to the complexities of American government.

- Demonstrate knowledge of how models of federalism and intergovernmental relations provide a base of foundational knowledge and also incorporate newer ideas like intergovernmental management into the field.

KEY TERMS

Anti-Federalists	Intergovernmental Management
Concurrent powers	Intergovernmental Relations
Confederation	Metaphors
Dillon's Rule	The Federalist
Federalism	Theory Building
Federalists	Unitary System
Home Rule	

1.1 INTRODUCTION

Federalism has been a regular feature of American government since the founding days of the union. Yet students often encounter considerable challenges in understanding its significance in American politics, let alone appreciating the ramifications that a federal structure has on organizational life and policy processes in the public sector. For several decades, political scientists have been expanding our understanding of the federalism concept, offering both similarities and differences in their efforts to clarify its meaning. From the broadest, most basic, perspective federalism refers to a system of government in which authority is distributed

> **Federalism**: a system of government in which authority is distributed across the national and subnational levels according to constitutional design.
>
> **Unitary system**: a system of government where authority is vested in the national government, and subnational levels like states, provinces, or other subdivisions may only exercise powers that are granted to them exclusively by the national government.

across the national and subnational levels according to constitutional design.[1] Taking this notion a step further, Samuel Beer conceptualizes federalism as involving a tiered pattern of intergovernmental interactions that include a juristic component that grants certain legal protections to territorial subdivisions. Beer grounds this concept in an assumption that states have certain rights and powers that are firmly rooted in the people or community.[2] Federal systems contrast unitary systems, where authority ultimately is vested in the national government and subnational levels, like states, provinces, or other subdivisions, that may only exercise powers granted to them exclusively by the national government. Unitary

---

1   Laurence J. O'Toole Jr., and Robert K. Christensen, eds., *American Intergovernmental Relations: An Overview* (Thousand Oaks, CA: Sage Publications, 2013), 3.
2   Samuel H. Beer, "The Modernization of American Federalism," *Publius* III, no. 2(fall 1973): 50–52.

governments are characteristic of most countries throughout the world and are most recognized in nations like France and Great Britain. As noted by political scientist Daniel J. Elazar, a key aspect of unitary structures is efficiency, whereby the organization of power revolves around maximizing control from the center over peripheral levels in the system.[3] In comparison to federal and unitary systems, confederations vest power in the states, with national powers being derived from the states and not the people. This was our nation's first system of government under the Articles of Confederation (ratified in 1781 and replaced by the U.S. Constitution ratified in 1789) and is also illustrated in modern times with the European Union.[4] This chapter is divided into several parts. First, this introductory section continues by defining and establishing two core concepts pertinent to our study of American and intergovernmental structure: intergovernmental relations (IGR) and intergovernmental management (IGM). From there, the chapter explores constitutional design and historical contexts, thus providing an appropriate springboard for an examination of eras in American federalism and the development of IGR. Afterward, the focus shifts toward an analysis of the relevant metaphors, theories, and models that have pervaded political science literature and help to illuminate how federal structure has evolved over time to accentuate national-state-local relations. Finally, the chapter offers concluding thoughts which tie together its main themes.

> **Confederations**: a system of government which vests power in the states, with national powers being derived from the states and not the people.

Figure 1.2: U.S. Constitution
Source: Pixabay
Attribution: Lynn Melchiori
License: Pixabay License

3   Daniel J. Elazar, "Contrasting Unitary and Federal Systems," *International Political Science Review*, 18, no. 3 (Jul. 1997): 243–244.
4   See Ronald K. Gaddie and Thomas R. Dye, *Politics in America, 2018 Elections and Updates Edition*, 11ᵗʰ ed. (New York, NY: Pearson, 2019), chapter 4.

1.1.1 Introducing the Concept of Intergovernmental Relations (IGR) as a Facet of Federalism

Much more is involved in understanding federal structure than identifying basic lines of authority. William H. Riker explains in his work on the origins and significance of federalism that a basic two-tiered structure of government is Federal by nature if the two levels rule the same land and people, each level exercises authority according to its jurisdiction, and there exists some guarantee that autonomy will be preserved within respective spheres of the system.[5] Autonomy is not unconditional, however, and complicating the political process are concurrent powers that are shared and exercised by both levels of government simultaneously and which promote a structure of interdependence.[6] These powers serve as both a restricting factor, which signifies that authority is divided, and a providing factor through developing means for facilitating cross-jurisdictional cooperation, which in modern times has been a necessity for building collaborative partnerships across sectors and organizations.

Federalism is closely correlated to the intergovernmental relations (IGR) concept, which encompasses a broader perspective where local governments, as created by their respective states, represent significant players in American politics. From the late-eighteenth through mid-nineteenth centuries, Dillon's Rule established the guiding doctrine for how power was divided between state and local governments. The rule was derived from an 1868 court case argued by Iowa Supreme Court Justice John F. Dillon, who formulated the legal basis upon which localities were only permitted those powers expressly granted by their respective states. However, Kevin B. Smith and Alan Greenblatt explain that changing political, social, and economic conditions in the nation gave rise to home rule, a counter-perspective where states granted considerably more freedom to localities with established charters in order to facilitate local decision making and the administration of core functions.[7] States with especially vibrant home rule traditions permitted localities

Concurrent powers: powers that are shared and exercised by both levels of government simultaneously which promote a structure where interdependence of action exists rather than separation.

Intergovernmental relations (IGR): a broader perspective where local governments represent significant players in our federal system and places less emphasis on autonomy and independence across levels of government in favor of greater cooperation and collaboration where various levels work together.

Dillon's Rule: the rule derived from an 1868 court case that provided the legal basis upon which localities were only permitted those powers expressly granted by their respective states.

Home Rule: a counter-perspective to Dillon's Rule where states granted considerably more freedom to localities with established charters in order to facilitate local decision making and the administration of core functions.

---

5   William H. Riker, *Federalism: Origin, Operation, Significance* (Boston: Little, Brown, 1964), 11.
6   Vincent Ostrom, *The Meaning of American Federalism* (San Francisco, CA: ICS Press, 1991), 7.
7   Kevin B. Smith and Alan Greenblatt, *Governing States and Localities*, 4th ed. (Los Angeles, CA: Sage, 2014), 365–367.

the autonomy to operate without interference from state officials, offering flexibility for communities to adapt the process of governance to their unique needs. Greater local autonomy was viewed as a pragmatic necessity in many respects as public policies became increasingly complex and local governments became responsible for larger, more developed infrastructures where service provisions were funded through corporate and residential taxes. Why are localities so important in the IGR equation? A simple response to this question lies in the sheer number of governments in the United States. As shown in the figure below, while there is one national government and fifty state governments, there are more than ninety thousand local governmental units in our nation, comprising both special and general purpose. There is considerable diversity in what role each structure performs in society and how they may interface with the state and national levels as part of the intergovernmental playing field.

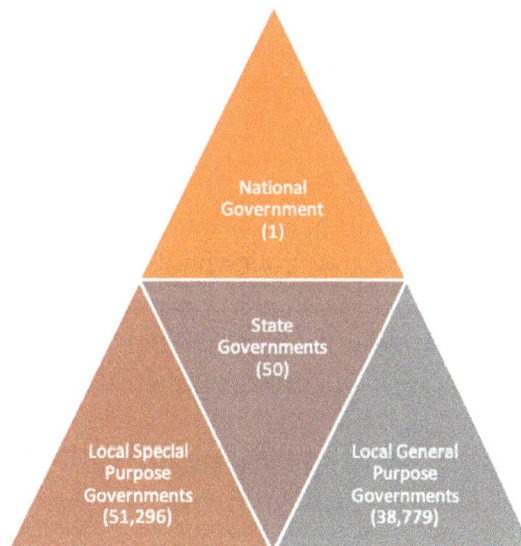

Figure 1.3: American Government Under a Federal Structure
Source: U.S. Census Bureau
Attribution: U.S. Census Bureau
License: Public Domain

With IGR, there is less emphasis on autonomy and independence across levels of government in favor of greater cooperation and collaboration where levels work together. The "relations" part of IGR has been of particular focus since the mid-twentieth century onward; in fact, the Conference of Mayors passed a resolution at its meeting in 1957 which requested that attention be devoted to developing several aspects of IGR more significantly, with particular emphasis on granting cities greater recognition and aid from the national government to maintain infrastructure and provide services to citizens. The conference also pressed to have cities be afforded greater representation in the legislatures of their respective states.[8] In his work "Intergovernmental Relations: An Analytical Overview,"

8   University of Chicago Press, "Intergovernmental Relations," *Social Service Review* 31, no. 4 (Dec., 1957): 442–443.

Deil S. Wright, in distinguishing the IGR concept from federalism, accentuates several features which highlight how activities and interactions occur between governmental units. First, IGR occur within the American federal structure and encompass considerably more activities than are typically associated with federalism alone. As chapter 6 will cover extensively, IGR provide a context by which relationships (e.g., cross-level, cross-sector, cross-organizational) are built. They incorporate and emphasize local governments as a unit of analysis more than traditional models of federalism. Second, IGR account for individualist perspectives more to provide consideration of how human behavior affects outcomes within the system. As chapters 7 and 8—which focus on public policies—will particularly show, Federalist perspectives alone do not adequately treat how social interactions are an aspect of organizational and policy processes. Third, IGR assume that interactions are ongoing occurrences which reflect patterns of behavior and activity that may be formal and/or informal in nature. As chapters 2, 3, and 5 will discuss in particular, IGR apply agreements, policies, regulations, statutes, court decisions, and other mandates which allow the political system to function. Fourth, intergovernmental perspectives accentuate the role that public officials play as actors in the system, particularly lending credence to the importance of mayors, council people, governors, legislators, and, of course, public administrators in states and localities. And fifth, Wright emphasizes that IGR also contribute to the significant role that policy holds in our system of government, which extends how economic, political, and social issues are handled beyond the traditional juristic focus that federal perspectives have when framing problems from legalistic angles.[9] Chapter 4 will explore the fiscal side of IGR in detail.

1.1.2 The Concept of Intergovernmental Management (IGM) as a Facet of Intergovernmental Relations (IGR)

A final important idea that is relevant to our introduction relates to organizational management, which has particular importance for public sector civil servants. As Michael McGuire maintains in his work, the "intergovernmental landscape" of the nation has come to represent a complex mixture of relationships that are not distinctively governmental or organizational in nature but that also include managerial dimensions that "transcend political boundaries."[10] In the literature of IGR, this trend is commonly referred to as intergovernmental management

Intergovernmental management (IGM): an approach which reinforces the cooperative nature of modern IGR contexts and focuses on problem solving, operational and functional capabilities, and the existence of networks of interaction as are common in the implementation of intergovernmental programs, cross-level policies, and generating organizational outcomes.

9   Deil S. Wright, "Intergovernmental Relations: An Analytical Overview," *The Annals of the American Academy of Political and Social Science*, 416 (Nov., 1974): 2–3.
10   Michael McGuire, "Challenges of Intergovernmental Management," *Journal of Health and Human Services Administration* 36, no. 2 (Fall 2013): 109.

(IGM) and is an important concept of modern organizational environments. IGM has applications rooted in the 1960s forward, with particular relevance to the practitioner side of governance. The origins of IGM are found, first, in management-driven approaches of the post-World War II era designed to bring about effective policy implementation; second, in a shift in federal structure over time to more cooperative power arrangements which emphasize the execution of vast numbers of intergovernmental programs; and, third, in an effort to professionalize the roles played by public managers and administrators and at all levels of government.[11] As later chapters will draw out, IGM focuses on problem solving, operational and functional capabilities, and networks of interaction which bring administrative professionals in the public sector together. Service delivery is a relevant aspect of managerial approaches, where there is a concentration on outputs, outcomes, and generating results. The administrative side of IGR has particular significance when considering how public sector management facilitates program creation and implementation which has widespread repercussions in our federal system. McGuire's supposition that the intergovernmental landscape reflects a variable and evolutionary structure also holds that managerial, service-based, and policy-driven aspects within the system continually challenge governments to find innovative approaches to solve complex problems in society.[12] This structure has made collaborative arrangements more popular in recent decades, as non-governmental organizations (NGOs) have increasingly partnered with the public sector, extending the intergovernmental context through multi-party resolutions to problems that elude simple answers. Though not official entities in the public sector, NGOs exist as nonprofit and private sector entities (e.g., humanitarian groups, interest groups, citizen groups, and other miscellaneous associations) which work collectively with other stakeholders to achieve a common mission or objective. From a managerial perspective, research has shown that an intergovernmental structure affords significant potential to benefit from cross-sector arrangements where partnerships, participation, collaboration, and the joining of participants together in networks facilitates democratic principles while inspiring innovative strategies.[13] Consequently, IGR perspectives take a broader view than federalism on how the American public interfaces with public agencies, societal organizations, and their respective communities as citizens of the nation, states, and localities in which they reside. These and other historical, conceptual, and theoretical foundations of our nation's federal structure and the landscape of IGR will be explored in greater detail below.

---

11 Deil S. Wright, "Federalism, Intergovernmental Relations," 170.
12 Michael McGuire, "Challenges of Intergovernmental Management," 109–110.
13 Daniel Baracskay, "Future Directions in Intergovernmental Relations," *Journal of Health and Human Services Administration*, 36, no. 2 (Fall 2013): 265–266.

1.2 CONSTITUTIONAL DESIGN AND HISTORICAL CONTEXTS

A brief overview of the founding era and an exploration of historical context provides a basic starting point for understanding our nation's federal system and, consequently, the path toward developing a structure for IGR. As Jack P. Greene notes, in "The Background of the Articles of Confederation," an atmosphere of suspicion and distrust toward the aggregation of power, along with a strong sense of individuality and a commitment to parochialism without the perceived need for centralized national power all made the prospects of forming a stronger continental union implausible until the late 1770s.[14] It was at this time that our nation's first system of government largely failed because power resided in the states rather than in a national government. An over-zealous commitment

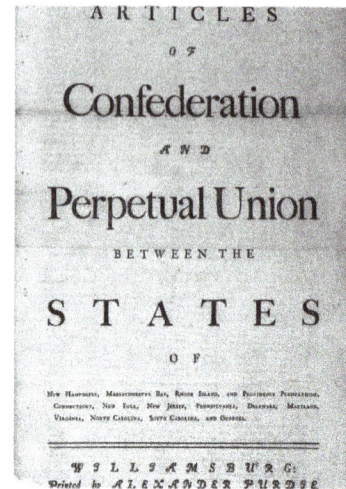

Figure 1.4: Alexander Purdie
Source: Wikimedia Commons
Attribution: Alexander Purdie
License: Public Domain

to decentralized power and state autonomy proved to be unworkable, and Congress experienced considerable difficulties in enforcing laws. James Madison, one of the Founding Fathers, James Madison, remarked at the time that significant monetary problems plagued the Treasury and there was little recognition that a nation existed.[15] Consequently, creating a federal structure became a fundamental theme at the Constitutional Convention of 1787, though the notion of IGR was relatively undeveloped, with localities lacking a clearly-defined role in the new republic.[16] The ratification of the U.S. Constitution required considerable bargaining and compromise, and ultimately the debate narrowed to supporters and opponents of the new republic. Those who supported a stronger, more centralized national government were known as *Federalists*, while those who maintained support for decentralizing power and having it reside in the states were referred to as *Anti-Federalists*.[17] Despite the many heated debates regarding how the new nation would be structured, a system of government emerged with significant guidance provided by a series of 85

> *Federalists*: those at the Constitutional Convention of 1787 who supported a stronger, more centralized national government.

---

14 Jack P. Greene, "The Background of the Articles of Confederation," *Publius* 12, no. 4 (Autumn, 1982): 25–26.

15 James Madison, *The Papers of James Madison*, vol. 9 (Chicago, IL: University of Chicago Press, 1975), 369.

16   As mentioned in the introduction, Federalism provides the context for IGR, and it was not until the twentieth century that the nation came to realize the need for cooperative approaches to Federalism which would inspire greater intergovernmental coordination. The basic notion for IGR was established early in our nation's foundation, but patterns of activity largely came to fruition in the post-World War II era as a venue for implementing the expanding number of intergovernmental programs.

17   Alison L. LaCroix, *The Ideological Origins of American Federalism*, (Cambridge, MA: Harvard University Press, 2010), 182–183.

essays authored by Alexander Hamilton, James Madison, and John Jay, a series originally known as *The Federalist Papers*. The essays were published from 1787 through 1788 and comprised both a theoretical and practical discussion of ideas relating to the general form and nature of government. A few select essays are relevant to understanding how American federalism was designed under the U.S. Constitution, paving the way for later developments in IGR and the management of cross-level programs.

Federalist 39 was authored by Madison and offered initial thought for establishing a republican form of government. Madison believed that this design most closely coincided with the aspirations of the Founding Fathers, with a republican form of government establishing an arrangement upon which all powers are directly or indirectly derived from the people.[18] It is important to note that Madison considered both the federal and national perspectives in *Federalist 39*, ultimately giving greater attention to the former. He envisioned that administration of the republic would be run by public officials who would hold office for a period of time reliant on good behavior and were representative of broader society rather than a privileged class, as was the case in many other nations at the time. Madison's idea was that a republican form of government would help to mediate the self-centered whims of tyrannical nobles through the delegation of powers, which he joined with his perspective on federalism.

As Martha Derthick notes in her book *"Keeping the Compound Republic,"* Madison reflected that the national government would have due supremacy in necessary matters but also spoke of a middle ground where states were regarded as "subordinately useful" in matters of less urgency.[19] Consequently, the powers of government were separated into branches with checks and balances and further divided across levels under a tiered-arrangement where the national and subnational levels co-exist simultaneously, each with their own spheres of authority and jurisdictions. While *Federalist 39* contended that the new structure of government was neither wholly federal nor wholly national, Madison tended to accentuate the concept of federalism over national perspectives, since the central government's jurisdiction was enumerated and connected to specific matters

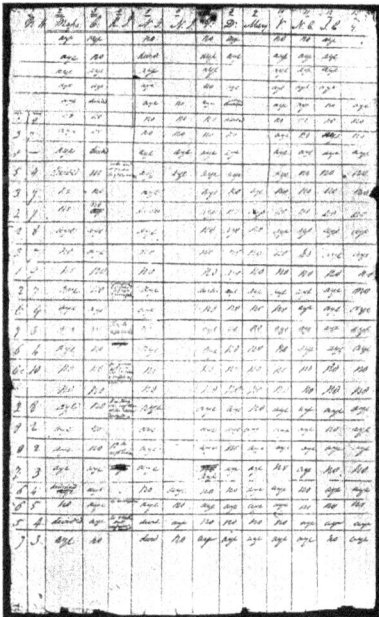

PHOTOGRAPH OF FIRST PAGE OF SECRETARY'S RECORD OF VOTES [1]

Figure 1.5: Reproduction of secretary's handwritten records of votes conducted at the U.S. Constitutional Convention of 1787, as published in Farrand's Records, Volume 1 (1911)

Source: Wikimedia Commons
Attribution: User "Tarmstro99"
License: Public Domain

---

18   James Madison, *The Federalist, No. 39*, ed. by Benjamin Fletcher Wright. (Cambridge, MA: Belknap Press of Harvard University Press, 1961), 280–283.

19   Martha Derthick, *Keeping the Compound Republic*, 1.

while at the same time leaving residual sovereignty and grants of power (particularly those not reserved under the Supremacy Clause) to the states. As Derthick notes, the Founding Fathers intended to create balance between centralization and decentralization within the government through mixing of the two.[20]

Further, in *Federalist 45*, Madison refers to the states as "constituent and essential parts of the federal government."[21] He continues with an explanation of how states represent a supply of funding for defense and the general welfare, and in *Federalist 46*, Madison contends that the federal government and the authority of the states are regarded as "different agents and trustees of the people" upon which the respective powers and purposes of each are grounded in the people's standing rather than in each governmental tiers' ambitions to enlarge their jurisdiction and status to the detriment of the others.[22] Madison, in fact, argued that the structure of Congress would reflect the prevalence of a "local spirit" in the country's political structure, more so than a "national spirit" would be able to attain over the vibrancy of state legislatures.[23] This concept implied a significant role for localities as part of the IGR equation, though it left this aspect of the federal system open to development and progress.

1.2.1 Eras of American Federalism and the Development of IGR

A federal structure emerged from the U.S. Constitution which also offered a degree of flexibility to respond to future political, social, and economic issues in the nation. American politics is anything but static, and federalism has evolved considerably over time based upon a vast array of influences. Though the above discussion of *The Federalist Papers* provides a brief synopsis of how our nation's government was formed, it is important to understand that shifts in authority over time have affected the

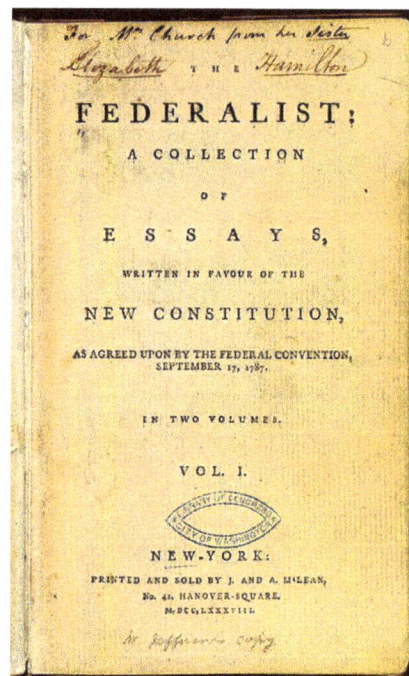

Figure 1.6: Title page of Publius (pseudonym) [Alexander Hamilton, John Jay, James Madison] (1788) *The Federalist: A Collection of Essays, Written in Favour of the New Constitution, as Agreed upon by the Federal Convention, September 17, 1787. In Two Volumes.* (1st ed.), New York, N.Y.: Printed and sold by J. and A. M'Lean, No. 41, Hanover-Square OCLC: 642792893. This copy is from the Rare Books and Special Collections Division of the Library of Congress.
Source: Wikimedia Commons
Attribution: Publius (pseudonym) [Alexander Hamilton, John Jay, James Madison]
License: Public Domain

---

20   Martha Derthick, *Keeping the Compound Republic*, 3.
21   James Madison, *The Federalist, No. 45*, ed. by Benjamin Fletcher Wright. (Cambridge, MA: Belknap Press of Harvard University Press, 1961), 327.
22   James Madison, *The Federalist, No. 46*, ed. by Benjamin Fletcher Wright. (Cambridge, MA: Belknap Press of Harvard University Press, 1961), 330.
23   James Madison, *The Federalist, No. 46*, 331.

nature of national-state-local relations along the spectrum of centralization-decentralization of power, prompting changes within the system. Political scientists have identified several eras of American federalism that have come to reflect periods of systemic change in how IGR have developed. Unfortunately, the political science literature lacks consistency in how each era has been referred to, though the same basic premises remain intact regarding certain qualities which characterize each era.

1.2.1.1 State-Centered, Dual, and Cooperative Federalism

Thomas Dye's classification system provides one of the clearer synopses in the field while permitting for variations in common themes and will be drawn upon in the discussion below, along with other relevant scholarship in the field.[24] In his work *Understanding Public Policy*, Dye characterizes the first era as being relatively state-centered (1787-1865), occurring after the adoption of the U.S. Constitution and enduring to the concluding days of the Civil War. In this era, many issues that lacked earlier precedents in the new nation were resolved at the state level. Localities were important in providing basic services to the people. Yet, this era was marked by judicial disputes on the supremacy of the national government, especially in the early days of the Union when the Anti-Federalists were active. After the Civil War, a period of dual federalism (1865-1913) followed, where the antebellum era gave way to a more hierarchical and centralized interpretation of the national government in American political structure. Loren Beth observes in her research on the U.S. Constitution that the Supreme Court largely established an eighteenth-century tradition where rulings assumed that the national government functioned according to enumerated powers which existed alongside of states' reserved powers but with both sets being relatively rigid and discrete.[25] States retained authority to decide domestic issues that were of local interest, but the pattern had become one in which the national government concentrated on delegated powers and the states focused on their respective areas under a "layer cake" system demarcated by considerable segmentation.

Yet, soon after the turn of the century, the duality of the national and state tiers gave way to an era of cooperation (1913-1964) which political scientists argued made the preceding layer cake vision of federalism unworkable (if clear layers had even existed), if not, at the very least, an obsolete design. Significant changes occurred in the nation stemming from the Industrial Revolution, the rise of the federal income tax (1913), the Great Depression, and the New Deal program, which provided public assistance, and contributed to the growing complexity of policy areas, shifting the focus from higher levels of autonomy between tiers to shared national-state responsibilities where localities also played a significant role in programmatic implementation as part of the IGR equation. From layer cake federalism to marble

---

24 Thomas R. Dye, *Understanding Public Policy*, 15th ed.(Boston: Pearson, 2017), 75–77.
25 Loren Beth, *The Development of the American Constitution 1877-1917* (New York: Harper and Row, 1971), 51.

Figure 1.7: Top left: The Tennessee Valley Authority, part of the New Deal, being signed into law in 1933. Top right: FDR (President Franklin Delano Roosevelt) was responsible for the New Deal. Bottom: A public mural from one of the artists employed by the New Deal's WPA program.

Source: Wikimedia Commons
Attribution: User "LordHarris"
License: Public Domain

cake federalism, a revisionist perspective offered by scholars like Morton Grodzins, Jane Perry Clark, and Daniel J. Elazar rejected preceding views of duality, such that American federalism was not one of "mutual independence," but rather existed in a state of "interdependence."[26] Consequently, the marble cake metaphor, in which there exists more of a blending and interconnection of governmental layers, came to replace the layer cake metaphor of federalism, which viewed governments as being largely separate and disconnected. Further, this era of cooperative federalism was a reaction to challenging times stemming from involvement in two world wars and intermittent economic downturns which gave local governments new importance in program delivery and the evolving structure of public administration. Edward S. Corwin notes that the preceding dual era of federalism had been "overwhelmed" such that there was a "remolding" of the federal system into a more cooperative framework. Yet, his article on "The Passing of New Federalism" raises doubt that cooperation translated into significant latitude for lower tiers to act through large grants of discretion, since New Deal era intergovernmental grant programs

---

26   Clifford Lee Staten, "Theodore Roosevelt: Dual and Cooperative Federalism," *Presidential Studies Quarterly*, vol. 23, (1) (Winter, 1993): 29–30.

reflected the means by which states were drawn into supporting actions that reinforced national policy priorities based upon shared responsibilities.[27] As mentioned above, the 1868 judicial case which established Dillon's Rule had previously created municipalities as "creatures of the state," such that they owed their existence and powers to state governments. Cooperative federalism reflected how localities had expanded exponentially in number as immigration produced significant population growth and people began amassing in cities for employment opportunities and to occupy residential dwellings. As the number of localities grew, this period not only signaled the closing of frontier life but also the progression toward having various levels of government interface under IGR to provide an expanding assortment of services to address the nation's increasing number of communities. The institutionalization of policy domains in areas inclusive of both defense and education, transportation, and public welfare necessitated the growth of public sector organizations at all levels of government, and also pointed toward the need for coordination and interaction between groups.[28]

1.2.1.2 Centralized Federalism, the New Federalism and Coercive Federalism

Eventually, the era of cooperative federalism transitioned into a more centralized form (1964–1980) when the national government took the lead in setting goals that were implemented downward in the system. The political scientist Michael D. Reagan declared in his book *The New Federalism* that the old style of federalism was dead and a new style had arisen, a new style which reflected the significant responsibilities and obligations that states had under a system of IGR. This assertion was both a political and pragmatic reflection of the growing trends in interdependence across levels of government.[29] President Lyndon B. Johnson initiated the Great Society program of 1964 to address priorities relating to pollution levels,

Judicial federalism: a term used to describe how the 1970s saw a marked increase in rulings by state court judges to safeguard rights not previously decided under the U.S. Constitution.

Representational federalism: view of American Federalism where the system is maintained through voting trends at the subnational level rather than through Constitutional provisions relating to the division of powers between levels.

education reform, public health, and urban decay, among others. National-state relations became more centralized, and states focused on responding to policy initiatives introduced at the national level that were tied to delegations of federal grant funding which had regulatory and procedural requirements. States, in essence, became the administrative tools by which important programs relating to welfare, Medicaid, housing, employment training, and environmental protection were implemented. Yet, states also protected their standing under periods of

27   Edward S. Corwin, "The Passing of Dual Federalism," *Virginia Law Review*, 36 (1) (February 1950): 23.
28   Thomas R. Dye, *Understanding Public Policy*, 75.
29   Michael D. Reagan, *The New Federalism* (New York: Oxford University Press, 1972), 3.

centralization by the federal government through the use of judicial rulings. The term "judicial federalism" has been used to describe how the 1970s saw a marked increase in rulings by state court judges to safeguard rights not previously decided under the U.S. Constitution, illustrating a newer aspect of federalism where civil liberties were expanded under state rulings.[30] State constitutions provided the basis for the expansion of rights which, over the course of two decades, became an embedded facet of American political culture and an indication that states occupied significant roles in shaping the system, particularly through judicial precedents.

Figure 1.8: President Lyndon B. Johnson signs the 1964 Civil Rights Act as Martin Luther King, Jr., and others, look on. The Civil Rights Act was part of the Great Society program which also aimed to eliminate racial injustice.
Source: Wikimedia Commons
Attribution: Cecil Stoughton
License: Public Domain

This trend in administrative and policy centralization (but with judicial protections occurring through state court decisions) continued until an era commonly referred to as new federalism (1980–1985) emerged to return power and responsibilities to state and local governments. President Ronald Reagan's devolution revolution was premised on the idea that big government from the New Deal era had taken its course; newer approaches should therefore replace top-heavy designs that accentuated centralized hierarchy to favor policy solutions at the subnational levels. The principle of devolving power downward in the system stemmed from the Nixon presidency as a facet of general revenue sharing, where state and local governments were allocated tax revenues collected by the national

30   Alan Tarr, "The Past and Future of the New Judicial Federalism," *Publius* 24, no. 2 (Spring, 1994): 63.

government with few strings attached in order to provide for policy implementation. Reagan implemented a broader and deeper version of Nixon's devolution strategy to diminish the power of the federal government and to place responsibility for many domestic programs in the hands of the states and localities. This, in effect, led to the consolidation of various categorical grants into broader block grants which were fewer in number, effectively bringing an end to general revenue sharing and resulting in a significant rise in the number of unfunded mandates (to be discussed in later chapters relating to fiscal and administrative aspects of American federalism). Grant funding was used to induce cooperation at the subnational level, and states that did not align with federal policies had funding withheld. Congressional strings were attached to funding through a "carrot and stick" routine, and states infrequently deviated from conditions placed on funding, given the dire state of budgetary resources. As David L. Chicoine asserts, a hallmark of the new federalism has been toward creating a "self-reliant fiscal environment" where the federal-state-local relationship has changed with the end of centralized models. In effect, the devolution of power rippled downward in the system with less funding to state governments, leading to fluctuations in local government aid over time. This consequence forced localities to find other ways to be self-sustaining, whether through changes in the tax burden, reductions in services, and/or inter-jurisdictional competition for more growth through economic development strategies.[31] Rural areas have particularly been at odds with reduced intergovernmental funding, having less capacity to attract residents and businesses into the area with tax enticements designed to bolster the economy. Larger metropolitan areas have more successfully absorbed the effects of lower funding levels, though they have been forced into difficult fiscally-driven decisions that have broad implications on their communities.

In 1985, a period of coercive federalism (1985–1995) occurred after the Supreme Court case Garcia v. San Antonio Metropolitan Transit Authority rendered a decision which permitted Congress the authority to directly legislate over the affairs of the state and local tiers. The Court ruled in favor of allowing Congress to order state and local governments to pay employees minimum wages, which contradicted earlier decisions that prevented Congress from legislating in such affairs. This, in effect, placed the burden of safeguarding state powers onto elected members of Congress and the president (subject to changes in election results) rather than grounding powers in the Reserved Powers Clause of the Tenth Amendment

Collaborative federalism: a style of federalism that makes coordination, partnerships, and networks an innate aspect of American politics and requires alternative approaches when developing policies and procedures due to the impacts such dynamics have on the law-making process.

Election politics: the idea that the direction of intergovernmental activity reflects rational choices by public officials who seek reelection by claiming credit while minimizing costs.

31   David L. Chicoine, "New Federalism and Rural America: Implications for Local Public Economies," *American Journal of Agricultural Economics* 70, no. 5 (Dec. 1988): 1089.

of the U.S. Constitution (which would produce longer term stability). The notion of "representational federalism" disregarded the constitutional division of powers between government levels in favor of having each respective state's population influence national structure through electing public officials. Consequently, this perspective views American federalism as being sustained through voting trends at the subnational level, where Electoral College votes granted to the states, the apportionment of representatives for House members based upon state population, and the allotment of two Senators irrespective of state size provide the means by which states and localities exercise power. Congress has particular relevance in legislating issues pertaining to subunits of government under representational federalism as related to the Garcia decision, which significantly changed how American federalism was perceived under two centuries of constitutional tradition that previously provided the basis for dividing powers between levels.[32]

1.2.1.3 Contemporary Perspectives on American Federalism and IGR

Figure 1.9: U.S. President George W. Bush greets tornado victims at Lafayette, Tennessee neighborhood on February 8, 2008, and assures them they will receive help from the government.
Source: Wikimedia Commons
Attribution: Chris Greenberg
License: Public Domain

Since the mid-1990s when political scientists dubbed federal structure as being "coercive" and driven by representational factors (rather than constitutional), there have been varying perspectives on how the system may be classified. Some political scientists continue to maintain that coercive federalism endures. For instance, Paul Posner makes the case in his article "The Politics of Coercive Federalism in

32   Thomas R. Dye, *Understanding Public Policy*, 76.

the Bush Era" that the George W. Bush presidency *proposed* a decentralized form of federalism through the use of grant consolidations for community development, super-waiver proposals, greater state flexibility for programs like Head Start and Medicaid, and other initiatives which drew in lower-tier support, as was the case with the War on Terror. However, Posner also contends that the Bush administration placed "very little capital" in the *actual* pursuit of decentralization plans and retreated from many initiatives which sought to give subnational levels of government a vibrant role in implementation. Posner identifies several areas where centralization and nationalization consolidated power around the federal government, inclusive of education programs, welfare, election politics, taxation policies, and homeland security.[33]

In departing from the notion of federalism being coercive, several political scientists have instead denoted a revitalization of federalism in the past twenty years, particularly in terms of multi-tiered responses to crisis situations. Whether this move represents a form of "New Age Federalism" that inspires introspection, innovation, and revitalization remains to be seen. Donald Kettl, for instance, contends in his article "The Transformation of Governance: Globalization, Devolution, and the Role of Government" that American government has transitioned from traditional structures and processes to embrace a more collaborative form of federalism which includes the roles that nongovernmental organizations (NGOs) play in public policy. Governments share authority not only across levels but also with other sectors inclusive of private companies and nonprofit organizations.[34] This idea coincides with the concept of IGM introduced above, where policy complexity, resource challenges, and the need to coordinate functions across levels and sectors have given rise to collaborative approaches which seek to bring together multiple actors and organizations for effective program execution. The New Deal era established a cooperative framework which was reformed through periods when recentralization efforts sought to reconsolidate power at the national level. Collaborative approaches to federalism build upon preceding frameworks like this, indicating that coordination, partnerships, and networks are an innate aspect of American politics and that this style, therefore, requires alternative approaches when developing policies and procedures due to the impacts such dynamics have on the law-making process. Kettl also notes that globalization and the rise of technologies like the Internet created rapid communication systems that permanently transformed the process of governance, elevating the stature of NGOs in all aspects of policy. Further, Jessica Bulman-Pozen contends in her research article "Executive Federalism Comes to America" that partisan polarization in Congress has made the legislative process arduous, putting the burden of action on executives at different levels of government. She refers to this structure as a form of "executive federalism" which holds a vibrant place in parliamentary systems

33   Paul Posner, "The Politics of Coercive Federalism in the Bush Era," *Publius* 37, no. 3 (Summer 2007): 392.

34   Donald F. Kettl, "The Transformation of Governance: Globalization, Devolution, and the Role of Government," *Public Administration Review* 60, no. 6 (Nov./Dec. 2000): 488.

and, within the American system, has allowed executives to become dominant actors at all levels of government. Today's complex environment necessitates that federal and state executives work outside of the intense partisan relationships that are indicative of Congress to, instead, bring about changes through federal and state laws that are conducive to achieving their political agendas more rapidly. This process has been the case with healthcare, climate change, and other policy domains which have significant implications for cross-level implementation.[35]

Craig Volden, on the other hand, offers a perspective that is less grounded in cooperative opportunities but that focuses more on a theory of intergovernmental competition. Federalism still follows a marble cake model, which assumes that the national government and lower tiers share policy responsibilities in providing goods and services. However, Volden's article "Intergovernmental Political Competition in American Federalism" argues that resource availability and concerns for efficiency (e.g., programmatic, organizational) drive basic assumptions on how the system operates. Federalism is significantly affected by election politics, such that the direction of intergovernmental activity reflects rational choices by public officials who seek reelection by claiming credit while minimizing costs. This credit-blame calculation requires a constant assessment of balancing public goods and services provision with raising taxes in order to maximize resource usage. It also helps to provide some explanation for how national spending patterns affect state level activities, particularly in terms of which level of government will assume a leadership role in programmatic areas where they are most competent and able to claim the most credit in the eyes their constituents.[36]

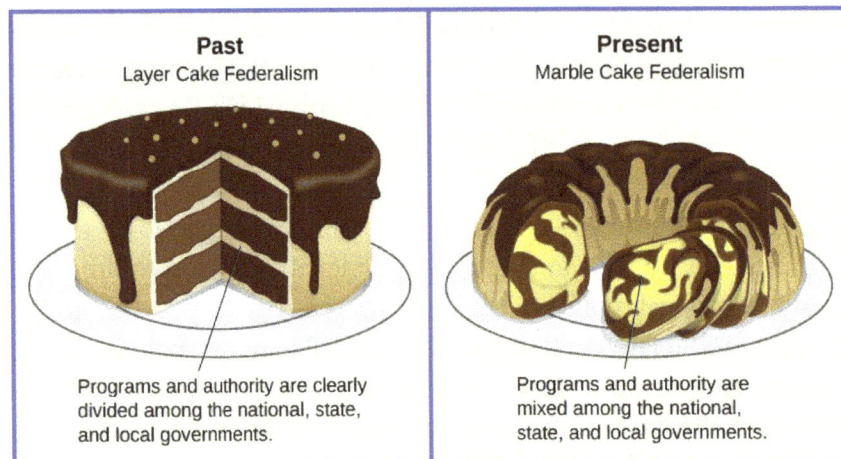

Figure 1.10: Morton Grodzins, a professor of political science at the University of Chicago, coined the expression "marble-cake federalism" in the 1950s to explain the evolution of federalism in the United States.
Source: *Texas Government 1.0*, OER Commons
Attribution: Austin Community College
License: CC BY-SA 4.0

35   Jessica Bulman-Pozen, "Executive Federalism Comes to America," *Virginia Law Review* 102, no. 4 (Jun. 2016): 954–955.
36   Craig Volden, "Intergovernmental Political Competition in American Federalism," *American Journal of Political Science* 49, no. 2 (Apr. 2005): 327–329.

As an extension of this line of reasoning, numerous studies accentuate the policy side of federalism and view it from the standpoint of intertwining policy networks. Thomas Anton, for instance, notes in his book *American Federalism and Public Policy: How the System Works* that, over time, policies have more commonly followed a joint strategy of implementation across levels of government. Given these policies' inherent complexities and the society-wide ramifications that their outcomes have in shaping large segments of American citizens' lives, a broader intergovernmental perspective is, therefore, necessary. Policies that originate at the federal level have considerable impact on state and local affairs, as is evidenced by health care, public assistance programs, the environment, and housing. Yet, they are also expensive from a resource perspective, where lower tiers have been forced to assume a greater share of the cost and execution sides of the process.[37] Competition for scarce resources and finding ways of "doing more with less" in light of budgetary constraints has become the standard in policy and programmatic processes.

The managerial perspective of federalism offers particular utility, since the policy cycle consists of patterns of behavior that lend themselves well to analysis and revision, thus allowing for programmatic and organizational adaptation. Programs are not static; rather, they adapt to changes in the environment, forcing public sector organizations to adapt as the principal executors of policies. Policy formulation also relates strongly to the existence of iron triangles (relationships between congressional committees, bureaucratic agencies, and interest groups), issue networks, and the existence of intergovernmental lobbies, comprising what Dale Krane refers to as a "policy soup" in a complex system of IGR and cross-organizational management and administration.[38] Robert Agranoff and Michael McGuire expound upon this facet of federalism in their exploration of management, specifically as it relates to the manner in which federal structure has evolved to where managers now interact with assorted governmental and nongovernmental organizations across several programs which are mandated in Washington but undertaken in multiple state capitols. In an environment of complex intergovernmental transactions, public sector organizations have been presented with a number of instruments which Agranoff and McGuire analyze. These tools include the following: top-down approaches, where the executive branch takes the lead with the enforcement of laws, rules, and regulations; the donor-recipient approach, which accentuates a shared administrative perspective where there is mutual dependence across levels; the jurisdiction-based approach, where local officials and public administrators pursue modifications and participants outside of their purview to help reinforce the strategic planning aspect of their entity; and the network approach, which brings together multiple entities inside and outside of government to pursue common joint actions which have the potential to produce

---

37   Thomas J. Anton, *American Federalism and Public Policy: How the System Works* (New York: Random House, 1989), 1–2.
38   Dale Krane, "American Federalism, State Governments, and Public Policy: Weaving Together Loose Theoretical Threads," *PS: Political Science and Politics* 26, no. 2 (Jun., 1993): 187.

beneficial outcomes for various stakeholders involved.[39] The top-down and donor-recipient perspectives are more established aspects of IGR, while the jurisdiction-based and network-based perspectives are newer facets of IGM. The figure below shows the primary features of each era in American federalism, including more recent perspectives.

Table 1.1: Eras of American Federalism

First Era	
• State-centered • Approximate period: (1787–1865)	• Significant importance held by states • Marked by judicial disputes on national supremacy
Second Era	
• Dual structure • Approximate period: (1865–1913)	• Hierarchical and centralized structure • "Layer cake" federalism with relatively separated tiers • Segmentation of powers Dillon's Rule (1868 Supreme Court case)
Third Era	
• Cooperative arrangement • Approximate period: (1913–1964)	• Shared national-state responsibilities • Localities played a greater role under IGR • Significant industrialization, urbanization, and population growth
Fourth Era	
• Centralization • Approximate period: (1964–1980)	• National government took the lead in setting broad policy goals implemented downward in the system • States were tied to federal grant funding with requirements for usage • States became the administrative tool for federal policies • Broader application of general revenue sharing and the use of categorical grants
Fifth Era	
• New federalism • Approximate period: (1980–1985)	• Devolution of power to lower tiers of government under the Reagan administration • State and local governments were given responsibility for many domestic programs • Significant increase in the number of unfunded mandates • Consolidation of categorical grants into block grants
Fifth Era	
• Coercive power arrangement • Approximate period: (1985–1995)	• Garcia v. San Antonio Metropolitan Transit Authority case gave Congress authority to legislate over the affairs of lower-tiered governments • Representative form of federalism where American federalism is a product of electoral voting patterns

39   Robert Agranoff and Michael McGuire, "American Federalism and the Search for Models of Management," *Public Administration Review* 61, no. 6 (Nov.–Dec., 2001): 671–677.

Sixth Era	
• Numerous competing perspectives on federalism • New Age federalism in which states consider new ways to innovate and respond to policy challenges • Approximate period: (1995–present)	• Segments of thought continue to favor coercive approaches which emphasize the ongoing nature of consolidating power at the national level despite promising lower tiers a greater role in the process • Parts of Federalist theory denote collaborative approaches which emphasize managerial coordination and partnerships across sectors and organizations • Some emphasis on competitive approaches which advance fiscal models of federalism and treat governments as rational actors seeking to maximize resources • Portions of the literature focus on patterns of behavior that regard the public policy making cycle as crucial to shaping American federalism • Most perspectives on federalism take into consideration the expanding nature of globalization and the influence of instantaneous communication systems

Source: Constructed by author from various sources. See in particular: Thomas R. Dye, *Understanding Public Policy*, 15th ed.(Boston: Pearson, 2017), 75–77; Michael D. Reagan, *The New Federalism* (New York: Oxford University Press, 1972), 3; Paul Posner, "The Politics of Coercive Federalism in the Bush Era," *Publius* 37, no. 3 (Summer 2007): 392; Donald F. Kettl, "The Transformation of Governance: Globalization, Devolution, and the Role of Government," *Public Administration Review* 60, no. 6 (Nov./Dec. 2000): 488; Thomas J. Anton, *American Federalism and Public Policy: How the System Works* (New York: Random House, 1989), 1–2; Robert Agranoff and Michael McGuire, "American Federalism and the Search for Models of Management," *Public Administration Review* 61, no. 6 (Nov.–Dec., 2001): 671–677.

1.3 METAPHORS, THEORIES, AND MODELS: FEDERALISM AND IGR

The introductory section of this chapter began by providing conceptualizations for federalism, IGR, and IGM and connected the concepts together, which allows us to proceed forward with examining how metaphors, theories, and models have been formulated to expand our understanding of the topic. The next several sections of this

Metaphors: figurative language that identifies certain traits as being associated with specific periods of, in this case, federalism, which also systematically tie to perspectives of IGR.

chapter briefly examine metaphor usage, theory building, and model construction as a means for understanding the development of IGR as an aspect of our nation's evolving federal structure. It is important to note that a significant part of theory and model building has involved the use of figurative language and metaphors, making these interrelated themes.

1.3.1 Exploring the Many Metaphors Inherent in Language and Description

It is unlikely that a political science student will be able to research federalism and IGR without finding metaphors. Early segments of this chapter referred to common metaphors that have been prevalent in political science literature, with examples including cooperative federalism, fiscal federalism, the new federalism, etc. These devices have value as descriptors of how our system of government has evolved over time (particularly in the period when they were offered), yet they have also been so varied and broad that it is easy to confuse their meanings. In his work "Metaphors, Models, and the Development of Federal Theory," William H. Stewart's analysis of figurative language identifies an extensive listing of metaphors for federalism, which also systematically tie to perspectives of IGR. In sifting through these many classification schemes, he uses a reductionist strategy to identify several categories comprising the following: analogical, attitudinal, configurative, functional, group-based, local-based, power-based, personalized, authority-driven, standardized, study-based, and a miscellaneous category.[40] In drawing upon these classifications, a few relevant points are worth noting. First, an implicit assumption of scholarship in the field is that federalism is an ever-evolving, rather than static, feature of American government. The political science literature commonly references *analogical metaphors* (particularly in introductory textbooks) to denote how federal structure has evolved from the founding days of the Union to what is characteristic of modern systemic attributes. From the era of relative autonomy and independence (state-centric) found in the initial era of federalism transpiring shortly after the Constitution was ratified, political scientists have offered numerous metaphors to signify the shifting of power and responsibility over time. As discussed in the above section, our system of government has progressed from relative independence to mutual interdependence across tiers demarcated by greater degrees of coordination, cross-jurisdictional authority, partnerships, and policy cooperation. Analogical metaphors have labeled this transition as fused federalism, hybrid federalism, interlocked federalism, intertwined federalism, picket fence federalism, spaghetti federalism, and twin-stream federalism, to name a few of the more popular adjectives.

Second—and related—as American federal structure has evolved over time, we have seen shifting attitudes both within government and across the public as to how the activities of government should transpire. From the perspective that assumed the national government would handle its sets of enumerated powers relatively independent from the states, to the attitude that policy complexity demands greater collaboration (or coercion to compel action, depending upon the nature of societal problems), we find that how federalism and IGR are approached both theoretically and pragmatically has changed considerably. *Attitudinal metaphors* have both positive and negative connotations which attempt to illustrate degrees of cooperation or compulsion in how the national government and states have interacted. From the standpoint of negative metaphorical labels, we find antagonistic federalism, coerced federalism, competitive federalism, cooptative federalism, imposed federalism, rigid federalism, and restrictive federalism denoting a more pessimistic perception of relations across levels. Optimistic appraisals, on the other hand, refer to bargaining federalism, compromise federalism, consensual federalism, consultative federalism, creative federalism,

---

40   William H. Stewart, "Metaphors, Models, and the Development of Federal Theory," *Publius* 12 (2) (Spring 1982): 21–24.

interdependent federalism, responsive federalism, and unifying federalism as reflecting a stronger sense of facilitating constructive relationships which promote the nation's interest under an attitude of intergovernmental harmony.

Third, societal changes in the twentieth century led to a more robust alignment of federal design to policy processes (particularly implementation) as public sector organizations and programs became institutionalized as facets of IGR (to be discussed in chapters 6, 7, and 8 in particular). In Stewart's conceptualization scheme, *configurative metaphors* and *functional metaphors* both represent categories which identify how the federal system has been organized and managed over time, particularly in terms of drawing in aspects of IGR that relate to agency, programmatic, and policy execution (chapter 5). Configurative metaphors have commonly surfaced to characterize asymmetrical federalism, horizontal federalism, matrix federalism, multidimensional federalism, and vertical federalism, among others. Functional metaphors have tied systemic attributes to structure with such designations as administrative federalism, judicial federalism, categorical federalism, fiscal federalism, instrumental federalism, and technological federalism. Fourth, a crucial aspect of American federalism rests in the nature of group interactions and how power reflects political agendas and priorities in society as part of the ever-changing dynamics of our shifting culture. For instance, *group-based* perspectives on federalism utilize adjectives like culture, public, social, sociocultural, cliental, ethnic, and religio-political. By contrast, local-based perspectives utilize figurative language which symbolize IGR as having a parochial dimension relating to areal, city, commonwealth, domestic, geographical, intrastate, neighborhood, urban, and regional aspects of federalism. As chapter 3 will explore in greater detail with the discussion of political dimensions, power-based and authority-driven relationships lead to changing group dynamics from the standpoint of influence and control. Metaphors such as dual federalism, balanced federalism, centralized federalism, centrifugal federalism, fragmented federalism, and peripheralized federalism are associated with the power side. Conversely, anarchist federalism, aristocratic federalism, capitalistic federalism, oligarchic federalism, representational federalism, and technocratic federalism comprise a segment of linguistic descriptors for the authority side. Finally, from the aspect of study and learning, many of the categorical metaphors indicated above attempt to capture the pragmatic side of how agencies operate, programs function, and policies are implemented. It is expected that academic conceptualizations may differ from practical characterizations, though common metaphors which attempt to bridge theory to practice have involved comparative federalism, epistemological federalism, methodological federalism, ontological federalism, philosophical federalism, and scientific federalism.[41] Students tend to grapple with the more abstract nature of metaphor usage and symbolism. However, theory building is grounded in conceptualization and guides practice, though it tends to complicate how students learn about the many facets of how federalism is regarded within the

---

41   William H. Stewart, "Metaphors, Models, and the Development of Federal Theory," *Publius*, 21–24.

field. The table below summarizes the several thematic headings just presented with linkages to metaphors in the field and examples that are commonly found.

Table 1.2: Themes, Emphasis, and Examples of Metaphors Used to Describe the Changing Nature of IGR under Federalism

Theme heading	Emphasis	Selected examples of metaphors used	How IGR is treated
1) Assumption that federalism is an ever-evolving, rather than static, feature of American government	Federal structure has evolved from the founding days of the Union to what is characteristic of modern systemic attributes	Analogical metaphors: fused federalism, hybrid federalism, interlocked federalism, intertwined federalism, picket fence federalism, spaghetti federalism, twin-stream federalism	IGR has developed into an implicit part of federal structure, inclusive of IGM as a micro-level perspective of managerial techniques which span tiers of government, programs, public organizations, and sectors of society to produce measurable policy outcomes
2) Shifting attitudes both within government and across the public regarding governmental activities	Variable perspectives shift from assuming the national government explicitly handles enumerated powers, to the public's expectation that policy complexity demands cross-level responses and greater calls for efficiency	Attitudinal metaphors: antagonistic federalism, coerced federalism, competitive federalism, co-optive federalism, imposed federalism, rigid federalism, restrictive federalism, bargaining federalism, compromise federalism, consensual federalism, consultative federalism, creative federalism, interdependent federalism, responsive federalism, and unifying federalism	IGR may be treated as an opportunity for governments to work together, or a possible detriment when competition and restrictions occur
3) Alignment of federal design with policy processes as public sector organizations and programs became institutionalized	Alignment strategies accentuate the policy aspects of multi-tiered implementation (rather than the preceding legal focus of federalism)	Configurative metaphors: asymmetrical federalism, horizontal federalism, matrix federalism, multidimensional federalism, and vertical federalism Functional metaphors: administrative federalism, judicial federalism, categorical federalism, fiscal federalism, instrumental federalism, and technological federalism	Metaphors identify how the federal system has been organized and managed over time, particularly in terms of drawing in aspects of IGR that relate to agency, programmatic, and policy execution

| 4) The nature of group interactions and how power reflects political agendas and priorities in society | Group-based perspectives on federalism are grounded in culture, public, social, sociocultural, cliental, ethnic, and religio-political factors | Power-based metaphors: dual federalism, balanced federalism, centralized federalism, centrifugal federalism, fragmented federalism, and peripheralized federalism

Authority-based metaphors: anarchist federalism, aristocratic federalism, capitalistic federalism, oligarchic federalism, representational federalism, and technocratic federalism | Local-based perspectives view IGR as having a parochial dimension relating to areal, city, commonwealth, domestic, geographical, intrastate, neighborhood, urban, and regional aspects of federalism |
| 5) There are both academic and practitioner-oriented dimensions to metaphor usage | Attempts to bridge theory developed by academics with practices by public administrators in the profession are more prevalent | Comparative federalism, epistemological federalism, methodological federalism, ontological federalism, philosophical federalism, and scientific federalism | Theory building is grounded in conceptualization and guides practice |

Source: Constructed by author based upon William H. Stewart, "Metaphors, Models, and the Development of Federal Theory," *Publius*, 5–24.

1.4 UNDERSTANDING THE DEVELOPMENT OF IGR THEORY

A number of points are important to considering the enlargement of theory over time. First, as Elazar notes in his book *American Federalism: A View From the States*, rather than there existing a clearly-defined separation between the national government and the states, there has been theoretical development regarding how intergovernmental frameworks have evolved to serve the American public through integrated administrative structures with overlapping jurisdictions.[42] The notion of partnership complements cooperation and denotes degrees of substantive and functional autonomy. Decision making and policy execution comprise pillars of activity which necessitate significant levels of attention and resource allocation. Second, Elazar reflects upon the notion of federal democracy as a reflection of democratic thought and republican government. The democratic perspective emphasizes the cultivation of partnerships between individuals and governments to attain justice and power sharing. Federalism establishes "a network of arenas within arenas" in order to foster political action, with some bases being larger or smaller representations than others, so as to reflect disparities of power that

---

42   Daniel J. Elazar, *American Federalism: A View From the States*, 3rd ed. (New York: Harper & Row, Publishers, 1984), 1–2.

relate to issues of significance and the activities pursued by actors responsible for decision making.[43]

Third, Corwin enhances our understanding of Federalist theory as the execution of tasks within each respective sphere. Reflecting the intergovernmental dimension which has evolved throughout our nation's history, levels of government each have their own associated political arrangements comprising separate branches (executive, legislative, judicial) with corresponding administrative systems for policy implementation, though the national government ultimately holds supreme authority over any conflicting assertions of state power.[44] In posing whether IGR augment or supersede federalism, Wright theorizes that both have implicit and explicit aspects that reinforce one another, with IGR largely comprising patterns and relationships not entirely expounded upon by examining federalism alone.[45] IGM subsequently encompasses the micro-level managerial aspects involved in coordinating programmatic and organizational resources so as to achieve positive outcomes.

1.4.1 Distinctions in Federalist and IGR Theory

In moving forward, we may note that several broad theoretical distinctions are particular to IGR and stand in contrast to Federalist theory alone. First, as introduced above, the U.S. Constitution was grounded in the perspective that a federal structure essentially focuses on the national-state relationship, whereas IGR more broadly reflect local linkages which are vital to policy execution and community preservation. In identifying the relevant inter-jurisdictional actors (units of analysis) and areas of focus for each tier, further distinctions may be drawn. For instance, federalism primarily involves a focus on elected politicians who behave in environments driven by partisanship and politics and where conflict is resolved through laws, court systems, and election cycles. The emphasis at this level is on broad missions and

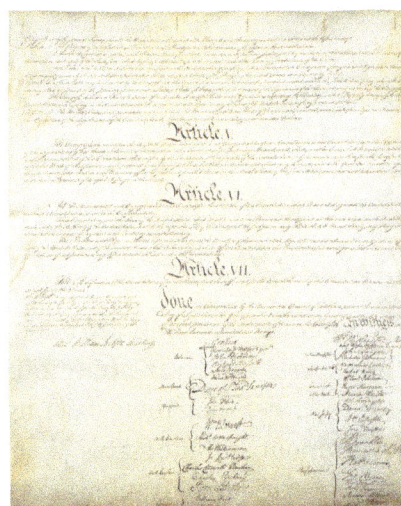

Figure 1.11: Page 6 of the U.S. Constitution.
Source: Wikimedia Commons
Attribution: National Archives and Records Administration
License: Public Domain

mandates which may be politically contentious, and public officials largely derive their powers from the use of sanctions and rewards. IGR, on the other hand, primarily address how general administrators (particularly at the state and local levels as units of analysis) affect the direction of policy, establish tradeoffs across

---

43   Elazar, *American Federalism: A View From the States*, 3.

44   Edward S. Corwin, "The Passing of Dual Federalism," 1–24.

45   Deil S. Wright, *Understanding Intergovernmental Relations*, 3rd ed. (Belmont, CA: Wadsworth Publishing Company, 1988), 36–37.

priorities, and utilize various perspectives from inside and outside government upon which to base decisions and activities. Competition for resources is resolved through markets, coalitions, and games played across levels to maximize the potential for positive outcomes, and policy coordination is a primary emphasis in generating favorable results. IGM is largely grounded on exploring organizations, programs, and public managers as units of analysis, which devote considerable attention to functions within their scope of operations pertaining to task and project completion and the procedures and methods utilized to realize outcomes. Disagreements are settled through bargaining and negotiation strategies, along with dispute settlement and coping tactics. Policy professionals largely concentrate on problem solving and implementation.[46]

A second theoretical distinction is found in how power and authority are regarded. As noted above, theories of federalism emphasize the significance of legal approaches to analyze systemic outcomes, such that laws (rather than people) justify the basis for action, comprising the footing for the justification and legitimacy of decisions. Federalist theory's legal emphasis of the national-state viewpoint suggests a more hierarchical arrangement for power relationships grounded in the supremacy clause in Article VI, Section 2 of the U.S. Constitution. This emphasis tends to ignore the human dimension in how decisions occur, where outcomes reflect the many informal relationships and activities inherent to public officials who have individual preferences and agendas of their own. IGR theory has focused more broadly on diffused power structures where there is a sharing of authority through cross-level arrangements. Intergovernmental activity accentuates the significant roles that state and local governments play in the American political system. Consequently, the dimensions of authority and use of power are mapped differently, such that federalism is primarily concerned with a structure which Wright refers to as "contingent hierarchy," which is grounded in national supremacy. By contrast, IGR represent "asymmetric orientations" where there is a perceived hierarchy but more latitude for working under less centralized conditions across tiers of government.

A third theoretical distinction involves the resolution of conflict, which is innate to authority and power usage. Under federalism, the jurisprudent approach is characteristic of how conflict resolution occurs, along with changes stemming from elections. This strategy is in contrast to IGR which approaches conflict resolution from the standpoint of market solutions, games, and coalition building. The former is grounded more in legalistic precedents and the latter in human actions which seek resolutions to conflict that may circumvent conventional channels. From an organizational perspective, bargaining, compromise, dispute settlement, and other forms of conflict management help to bring about resolutions to problems inherent in the use of power.

Fourth, as will be covered throughout this book, the policy process is the foundation upon which government focuses resources and other factors into

---

46   Deil S. Wright, "Federalism, Intergovernmental Relations," 172; 174.

generating outcomes that have broader ramifications for society. The literature on federalism has segments of perceptible linkages to policy issues from a strongly juristic perspective, while IGR has been more theoretically focused on policy making so as to integrate elements of the policy cycle into how each tier functions, particularly relating to the formulation and implementation stages. IGR theorists have linked their study of programs and initiatives to empirical findings in the realm of policy research to develop a more robust intersection of the two realms. This has the added benefit of drawing upon policy-choice approaches in lieu of legalism, where modes of inquiry revolve around analyzing decision-making as a reflection of utility-maximizing participants who seek to increase the chances of policy successes rather than failures. Such explorations have been an expanding facet of IGR theory building with empirical investigations (e.g., education, criminal justice, infrastructure, economic development) of state and local activities which point toward policy achievements and areas where programmatic revisions are needed.[47]

Finally, segments of IGR scholars have particularly highlighted that theory building in the realm of intergovernmental analysis has offered greater precision and utility in understanding the changing nature of federal structure. While Federalist theory is not displaced, newer approaches have significantly added to our understanding of the national-state-local system of authority which is in a constant state of flux due to a variety of influences. Wright contends that the literature of federalism has often been "muddied" by vague descriptions that parallel historical shifts in the system. By contrast, IGR provides a more systematic vision, since its usage is more refined and less vague yet also includes localities as a unit of analysis. This, in turn, provides a stronger sense of linkage across levels of government and public sector organizations which is conducive to examining how actors interrelate and affect the outcomes of policy areas.[48]

1.5 SELECTED EXAMPLES OF MODELS

Models represent how abstract concepts and ideas are applied to idealistic constructs which are designed to simplify real world complexities and enhance our understanding of challenging topics. In this case, they help to augment our knowledge of American political structure. Each model taken in isolation fails to perfectly capture the complex realities of federal structure. However, examining key attributes from several models aids in simplifying reality and helps students understand what roles public administrators and organizations play in our federal system of government. Several examples are presented below.

1.5.1 Beer's Model of Federalism and IGR

Beer's model is theoretically rich and directly links IGR to federalism as a facet of modernization. He argues that the term federalism is more ambiguous

---

47   Deil S. Wright, "Federalism, Intergovernmental Relations," 172–174.
48   Wright, *Understanding Intergovernmental Relations*, 36–39.

than IGR and has, in the past, embodied a familiar and simple means for referring to the intergovernmental relationships that exist under a federal structure.[49] Beer's analysis proceeds on the basis that federalism is instrumental to, though also contingent upon, such democratic values as liberty and equality. Accordingly, states

Modernization: an aspect of nation-building which created policy complexity and developed intricate and interdependent networks affected by significant strides in economic development.

have played a decisive role in the nation's development. Yet, he cautions against using federalism to model how change has occurred in the power structures between levels of government. Instead, modernization provides the principal means by which power shifts have occurred and is the focus of analyzing American political structure.

A period of nation-building occurred significantly after the Constitution was ratified, particularly as states were added to the Union over time. As this process occurred, IGR became an instrument of modernization reflecting the transition from an autonomous two-tiered design—exemplified under the dual federalism of the late eighteenth century through the early twentieth century—to a nation of significant trade, industry, and expanding government, where cooperative structure became more conducive to policy implementation. With modernization came policy complexity and the development of intricate and interdependent networks affected by significant strides in economic development. The nature of evolving intergovernmental dynamics is a function of many causes, from the advance of science and technology fueling the productive capacity of the modern economy, to expanding scales of interaction and growing demand for labor and mechanical innovation, to broader practices in interdependence reflecting labor specialization, expanding social structure, and a broader, more integrated role for organizations in society.[50]

Beer's model considers the growth of discrete groupings of political, spillover, class, and technocratic coalitions, either in pure or mixed forms, as having a permanent effect on structural change. The succession of change is cumulative.[51] While we cannot reverse the reigns of modernity, IGR help to frame how we view motivations, behaviors, and attitudes. Political structure and culture reflect incremental changes over time, though how we use instruments like IGR helps to shape future directions based on democratic principles where analytical models provide the means for evaluation and reorganization.

49   Samuel H. Beer, "The Modernization of American Federalism," 50.
50   Samuel H. Beer, "The Modernization of American Federalism," 57.
51   Samuel H. Beer, "The Modernization of American Federalism," 92.

Table 1.3: Summarizing Beer's Model of Federalism and IGR

Emphasis	Main ideas	Outcomes
• Directly links IGR to federalism as a facet of modernization • Focus is on the causes for systemic expansion • States have played a decisive role in the nation's development • The nature of evolving intergovernmental dynamics is a function of many causes	• The term federalism is more ambiguous than IGR • Modernization provides the principal means by which power shifts have occurred • Federalism is instrumental to, though also contingent upon, democratic values, such as liberty and equality	• IGR are used as a means for systematic analysis more so than being a practice in normative reflection • With modernization came policy complexity and the development of intricate and interdependent networks • Newer models of IGR take into consideration the expansion of large networks where collaboration and cooperation reflect the drive toward utility maximization as a facet of modernity

Source: Constructed by author based upon Beer, Samuel H. "The Modernization of American Federalism."
Publius III, no. 2 (fall 1973): 49–95.

1.5.2 Elazar's Models of IGR

Besides Beer's model of IGR and modernity, there have been other efforts to characterize changes in federalism based on the influence of intergovernmental approaches in administrative structure and policy implementation. Elazar's research, for instance, proposes a sequence of models—the matrix model, Jacobin model, and the managerial pyramid model— which exemplify how federalism has evolved over time with consideration of the important role played by IGR.[52] The matrix perspective on federalism is composed of arena and sub-arena networks which illustrate how powers are diffused and formulated around centers. Elazar divides the matrix into four quadrants comprising the judicial, legislative, and executive

Figure 1.12: Portrait of James Madison
Source: Wikimedia Commons
Attribution: John Vanderlyn
License: Public Domain

branches, along with supporting institutions. A noncentralized organizational structure reflects how powers exist in larger and smaller cells of the matrix. Cell magnitude does not reflect the degree of importance; rather, it delineates the

52   Elazar, *American Federalism: A View From the States*, 3–9.

separation of powers across branches of government and the interrelationship to supporting institutions which have a function in the policy process. Cross cutting the cells and quadrants are lines depicting the roles that the fifty states play and overlapping areas where the public is involved in the governmental process as a facet of democracy. This model reflects the thoughts of James Madison (American statesman and the Father of the Constitution) and Albert Gallatin (politician, diplomat, and secretary of the treasury). Both advanced considerable thought for establishing a federal structure based on intergovernmental relations.

By contrast, the Jacobin model is a more centralized ideal where power is concentrated around the core (national government), with less influence being entrusted to peripheral levels (states). Jacobinism was crafted during the French Revolution and later was expanded and revised by Karl Marx and other nineteenth century socialists. It views the nation as an organic entity where change is a natural byproduct of governmental activities reflecting societal trends. Jacobinism was an instrument for secular liberation and a means for attaining higher levels of organizational efficiency via centralized authority. Furthermore, it was based upon the perspective that dispersion of power extends greater latitude for potential abuse, which has a decisively anti-IGR tone where the role of localities is significantly downplayed. Jacobinism was introduced in the United States under the premise of liberalism in the mid-nineteenth century, in that it critiqued compact theory (a basis for Federalist thought) as having significant deficiencies. Instead, one of the leading proponents of Jacobinism at the time, Francis Lieber (a political scientist

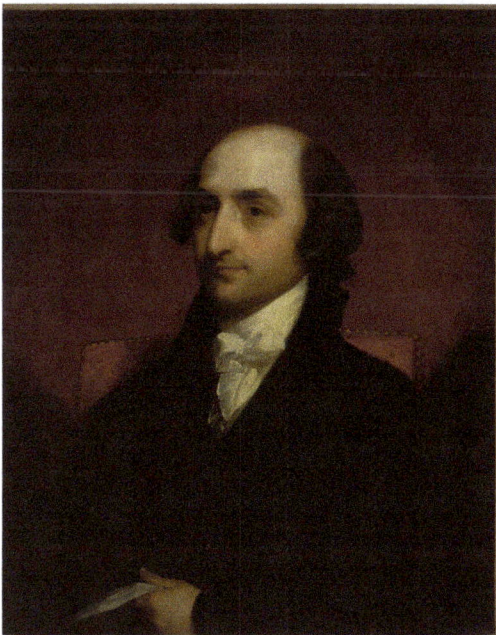

Figure 1.13: A portrait of Albert Gallatin.
Source: Wikimedia Commons
Attribution: Gilbert Stuart
License: Public Domain

Figure 1.14: Portrait drawing of 19th-century German American educator and political activist Francis Lieber.
Source: Wikimedia Commons
Attribution: Jacques Reich
License: Public Domain

at Columbia University), contended in his work, *On Civil Liberty and Self-government*, that a new perspective on nationalism grounded in the decision-making authority of the central government would result in national strength by having a single center from which political power could be exercised. This assertion was made during a time when the nation was becoming less isolated in world affairs, and Woodrow Wilson (the twenty-eighth president of the United States) also promoted the notion of having a single center of political power through Congress. According to Wilson's perspective, the national government should reflect a more solidified structure, as found in parliamentary systems, where the executive and legislative branches are aligned in unison. Therefore, they would not reflect original Federalist designs, where Congress represented delegates elected in states by their respective constituencies. Wilson's vision of a centralized government also contended that the administrative system should be more hierarchical with an emphasis on efficiency.

Elazar's third model mentioned above examines the broad theme of managerialism in federal structure, relating it to the spread of the Industrial Revolution in the late-nineteenth and early-twentieth centuries. Under the managerial pyramid model, elected officials have, over time, emulated the characteristics of autocratic rulers by seeking to establish a nation shaped by trade and industrial considerations. When they later sought national growth with the large and powerful corporations that emerged from the Industrial Revolution, they acted as imperial autocrats. Managerialism diverged from traditional models of federalism by focusing on the organization as a unit of analysis. Managerial philosophies intersected with divided power structures and levels of government to bring about efficiency in organizational operations. It was actually viewed as a means for displacing the traditions of authoritarian rule and introducing alternative, democratically-based approaches grounded in principles of scientific management which were imported from Europe into the United States. This philosophy still reflected hierarchical structures, though it included levels of government as part of the model and as a crucial aspect of managerialism. The micro-level focus of managerialism was more conducive to accepting intergovernmental perspectives in a political system comprising bottom, middle, and top layers, where efficiency in operations became a byproduct of calls for political neutrality. A decentralization of power in the hierarchy observes flows to lower levels from the top (to the states

Figure 1.15: President Woodrow Wilson (center) waves his top hat from the deck of USS George Washington (ID # 3018), as she steamed up New York Harbor upon the President's return to the U.S. from the World War I peace conference in France, 8 July 1919.
Source: Wikimedia Commons
Attribution: Naval History and Heritage Command
License: Public Domain

from the national government), meaning that public sector organizations represented a significant part of the policy equation.[53]

Table 1.4: Summarizing Elazar's Models of IGR

Emphasis	Main ideas	Outcomes
• The matrix model illustrates how arena and sub-arena networks affect how powers are diffused and formulated • The Jacobin model is a more centralized ideal where power is concentrated around the core • Under the managerial pyramid model, elected officials have emulated the characteristics of autocratic rulers by seeking to establish a nation that has been shaped by industry and corporations	• The matrix model comprises four quadrants including the judicial, legislative, and executive branches, and supporting institutions • Jacobinism views the nation as an organic entity where change is a natural byproduct of governmental activities reflective of societal trends • Managerialism diverged from traditional models of federalism by focusing on the organization as a unit of analysis	• Noncentralized organizational structure reflects how powers exist in larger and smaller cells of the matrix • Jacobinism was an instrument for secular liberation and a means for attaining higher levels of organizational efficiency via centralized authority • Managerialism intersected with divided power structures and levels of government to bring about efficiency in organizational operations and was viewed as a means for introducing principles of scientific management

Source: Constructed by author based upon Daniel J. Elazar, *American Federalism: A View From the States*, 3rd ed. (New York: Harper & Row, Publishers, 1984), 1–9.

1.5.3 Wright's Models of IGR

Wright's development of the coordinate-authority, overlapping-authority, and inclusive-authority models offers another comparison of federal structure and how IGR factor in (whether strongly or otherwise) that may be contrasted to the above discussion of Beer and Elazar's models. Wright's models essentially accentuate distinctions across the dimensions of power relationships and authority patterns. With the coordinate-authority model, IGR exists under well-defined and structured conditions where there are decisive boundaries separating the national government from the state level.[54] Local governments are treated as dependent actors that exist separate from the states, which differs from traditional theories of federalism that emphasize legalism as a mode of inquiry but tend to ignore programmatic and organizational influences, particularly at the local level. Dillon's Rule (see above) provides the basis for state-local interactions, such that localities comprise "creatures of the state" that may be created or abolished according to state discretion and that may exercise only powers expressly granted by the state.

---

53 Elazar, *American Federalism: A View From the States*, 3–9.
54 Wright, *Understanding Intergovernmental Relations*, 40–42.

The coordinate-authority model sees the relationships across levels of government as being independent, with an authority pattern described as autonomous. Cross-level interaction is tangential and occurs pragmatically as needed. In cases where the national government and state power conflicts, the Supreme Court becomes the deciding authority in maintaining boundaries between the two levels. The coordinate-authority model provides the clearest depiction of American federalism, from the time when the U.S. Constitution was ratified until approximately the early twentieth-century. As court decisions in the early 1900s began to exhibit less of an insular perspective that treated the levels of government as discrete spheres, the model started to show less promise in capturing the nature of American politics. Further, policy complexity, the need for greater programmatic coordination under conditions of uncertainty, the progression toward using cross-jurisdictional arrangements to respond to societal problems, and the expansion of the governance process by expanding numbers of actors both internal and external to government gave rise to academics questioning the utility of the coordinate-authority model.[55]

By contrast, Wright's inclusive-authority model[56] is framed around hierarchical authority patterns where there is dependence in power relationships. Local government is a smaller circle enclosed within state government, which is likewise an area enclosed under the national government. The area within each circular area represents a proportion of power under which that level of government exercises jurisdiction over a part of the system as a whole. In situations when the national government wants to expand its power, it reduces the area of power represented in the circles for state and local governments, or it enlarges its own circle while holding the other two circles constant. Wright relates this structure to game theory, where decision-making scenarios are largely driven by the desire for actors to maximize benefits and ensure they limit losses. Changes in the circular areas for the state and local governments are negligible and represent marginal victories for subnational actors competing for a piece of the pie under a hierarchical system. Consequently, IGR is grounded in a centralized form of federalism, which Wright asserts has been supported by the power-elite perspective where states and localities largely take their cues from national leaders.[57]

As it becomes clear that the coordinate-authority and inclusive-authority models offer diametrically opposing ideals, the overlapping-authority model is based upon a more interdependent assumption for power relationships and views authority patterns exemplified by bargaining across levels and organizations. The model is illustrated through a sequence of concentric circles that have overlying areas denoting power sharing. Local governments represent a sphere which overlaps with the national government and state governments. This model opposes having an enclosed circle representing state governments and another separated

55   Wright, *Understanding Intergovernmental Relations*, 40–43.
56   For a diagram and clear illustration of Wright's model, please see his book *Understanding Intergovernmental Relations*.
57   Wright, *Understanding Intergovernmental Relations*, 45–46.

circle for the national government, which stands apart under the coordinate-authority model, or a sequence of inner circles for the local and state governments which are but a proportional segment of the national government under the inclusive-authority model. The overlapping-authority model presents a moderate perspective that captures how conditions fall between the extremes of the two other models and holds the greatest relevance in contemporary perspectives on IGR. While sporadic systemic shifts have occurred toward centralization or hierarchy in American federalism, an overlapping perspective of IGR has broadest applicability in capturing how national, state, and local units interact simultaneously. It also denotes that extended periods of autonomy or single-jurisdictional activity, where subnational levels have significant degrees of discretion, are relatively confined and infrequent, and bargaining is crucial in producing shared outcomes.[58]

Table 1.5: Summarizing Wright's Models of IGR

Emphasis	Main ideas	Outcomes
• Under the coordinate-authority model, IGR exists under well-defined and structured conditions where there are decisive boundaries • The inclusive-authority model is framed around hierarchical authority patterns, where there is dependence in power relationships • The overlapping-authority model is based more upon interdependence and views authority patterns as being exemplified by bargaining rather than autonomy	• Under the coordinate-authority model, local governments are treated as dependent actors that exist separated from states • With the inclusive-authority model, local government is a smaller circle enclosed within state government—which likewise is an area enclosed under the national government; the area within each circular area represents a proportion of power • The overlapping-authority model presents a moderated perspective that effectively captures how conditions fall between the extremes of the two other models, as is most conducive to intergovernmental cooperation	• The coordinate-authority model sees the relationships across levels of government as being independent, and cross-level interaction is tangential, occurring pragmatically as needed • Under the inclusive-authority model, in situations when the national government wants to expand its power, it reduces the area of power represented in the circles for state and local governments, or it enlarges its own circle while holding the other two circles constant • The overlapping-authority model holds the greatest relevance in contemporary perspectives on IGR, and has broadest applicability in capturing how national, state, and local units interact simultaneously (also via practices in IGM)

Source: Constructed by author based upon Wright, Deil S. *Understanding Intergovernmental Relations*, 3rd ed. (Belmont, CA: Wadsworth Publishing Company, 1988), 40-49.

58 Wright, *Understanding Intergovernmental Relations*, 48–49.

1.5.4 Collaborative Models of IGR

As a more recent example, Agranoff and McGuire construct a jurisdiction-based model that looks at the managerial side of IGR rather than at applying a top-down or bottom-up approach, which has typically been associated with studies of American federalism in the past. Their model specifically considers the vitality of intergovernmental programs and assesses whether local managers are controlled by external forces or actors, are passive implementors, or are intergovernmental activists. In considering how jurisdiction-based considerations factor in, they question whether the conventional models of American federalism as being representative of a hierarchical and centralized system still apply with the national government taking the lead in policy making, or whether local actors have a larger role in a system of mutual interactions where there is an exchange of resources as players interact for mutual advantages.[59] Using data from a sample of cities, Agranoff and McGuire contend that a jurisdiction-based model effectively reflects trends in diversity within the system and newer approaches to public management. They reinforce that IGM has become fashionable as localities have taken a stronger role in the administration of federal initiatives and also in terms of satisfying state mandates. However, they have also been more challenged in terms of funding and financial assistance, and the plethora of regulations which originate at the federal level makes the intergovernmental process more intense, particularly in terms of competition with other localities and in functioning in interdependent environments. While principles of hierarchy and control have not endured in effectively capturing modern IGR contexts, neither have models that propose the wide extension of autonomy to local governments, which assume that a devolution revolution has permanently shifted power downwards in the system to inspire greater buy-in at the subnational levels.

Rather, a variety of forces ranging from fiscal awareness, the viability of state governments as proponents of intergovernmental programs, the expansion of federal flexibility to accommodate diverse local conditions, and alternative delivery arrangements that are tailored to complex problems all factor into the IGR equation. Agranoff and McGuire's model approaches intergovernmental activity from the standpoint of managerial techniques and organizational/programmatic mechanisms which facilitate policy successes and also respond to the unique needs of local jurisdictions. The model proposes three characteristics which drive managerial pursuits, inclusive of interdependence, strategic activity, and multiple actors.[60] Interdependency reflects the need to share resources and levels of expertise to achieve a mutually-beneficial outcome; strategy is the means by which barriers to action are minimized or removed; and numerous actors reflect the many ways that fragmentation necessitates synchronization across stakeholders to ensure policy success. Agranoff and McGuire's model provides empirical evidence that a large

---

59   Robert Agranoff and Michael McGuire, "A Jurisdiction-Based Model of Intergovernmental Management in U.S. Cities," *Publius* 28 no. 4 (Autumn 1998): 1–2.
60   Robert Agranoff and Michael McGuire, "A Jurisdiction-Based Model," 6.

number of cities do engage in considerable intergovernmental pursuits outside of their boundaries which necessitate some form of collaborative partnering. They also find that cities which exhibit stronger tendencies toward interdependence with other agencies and actors are more engaged in bargaining and intergovernmental activities. Intersectoral policy leadership and policy activity represent two of the greatest influencers of intergovernmental activity in the jurisdiction-based model.

Table 1.6: Summarizing Collaborative Models of IGR

Emphasis	Main ideas	Outcomes
• Represents a more recent example of a model that considers the vitality of intergovernmental programs and assesses whether local managers are controlled by external forces or actors, are passive implementors, or are intergovernmental activists	• The model questions whether the conventional models of American federalism are still representative of a hierarchical and centralized system or whether local actors have a larger role in a system of mutual interactions	• A jurisdiction-based model that effectively reflects trends in diversity within the system and newer approaches to public management

Source: Constructed by author based upon Robert Agranoff and Michael McGuire, "A Jurisdiction-Based Model of Intergovernmental Management in U.S. Cities," *Publius* 28 no. 4 (Autumn 1998): 1–20.

1.6 CONCLUSION

This chapter has introduced how federalism, IGR, and the related term IGM are conceptualized. Our discussion examined important historical aspects of how our nation was founded as a federal structure as a means for offering resolution to some of the most pressing deficiencies experienced under the Articles of Confederation. While a legalistic perspective dominated much of what occurred in American federalism from the nation's formation until the beginning of the twentieth century, there has always been some regard for the roles played by states in political structure, as well as the growing importance of localities in providing public goods and services. Though segments of the academic scholarship note that Federalist theory alone has not adequately encapsulated how significantly our system of government has evolved, IGR have provided supporting theoretical value in considering how policy complexity, the nature of human behavior and interaction, and the expanding nature of cross-level coordination along with cross-sector partnerships have come to illustrate our nation's modern federal structure. As an aspect of this structure, IGM has represented a contemporary and related segment of theory in the field that has advanced our understanding of federalism and IGR in new directions, focusing on the managerial and programmatic aspects of policy implementation. Having introduced these basic concepts and ideas, we are ready to proceed to an examination of the legal dimensions of IGR in the next chapter.

REFLECTION QUESTIONS

1. Consider several shortcomings that were apparent in the Articles of Confederation. As you read more about the history of the founding days of the Constitution, discuss how the framers specifically intended to resolve the preceding shortcomings by having a federal structure.

2. Select several examples of metaphors and discuss how these tools have helped to describe the nature of American Federalism and IGR in the time periods they originated from.

3. How has the concept of IGM reflected the modern context of IGR and the progression toward policy processes? In particular, what roles have collaboration and coordination played in the progression toward IGR and cross-sector arrangements to address complex and multifaceted policy issues?

4. Please discuss several distinctions in Federalist and IGR theory. Particularly, what are apparent areas where they contrast, and what are areas where they may complement each other?

5. How have models enhanced our understanding of Federalism and IGR? From the discussion in this chapter, which model seems to provide the strongest potential for describing our current system of government? Which model tends to be the weakest in offering a basis for systematic explanation?

BIBLIOGRAPHY

Agranoff, Robert, and Michael McGuire. "A Jurisdiction-Based Model of Intergovernmental Management in U.S. Cities." *Publius* 28, no. 4 (Autumn 1998): 1–20.

Agranoff, Robert, and Michael McGuire. "American Federalism and the Search for Models of Management." *Public Administration Review* 61, no. 6 (Nov.-Dec., 2001): 671–677.

Anton, Thomas J. *American Federalism and Public Policy: How the System Works.* New York: Random House, 1989.

Baracskay, Daniel. "Future Directions in Intergovernmental Relations." *Journal of Health and Human Services Administration* 36 no. 2 (Fall 2013): 252–269.

Beer, Samuel H. "The Modernization of American Federalism." *Publius* III, no. 2 (fall 1973): 49–95.

Beth, Loren. *The Development of the American Constitution 1877–1917.* New York: Harper and Row, 1971.

Bulman-Pozen, Jessica. "Executive Federalism Comes to America." *Virginia Law Review* 102, no. 4 (Jun. 2016): 953–1030.

Chicoine, David L. "New Federalism and Rural America: Implications for Local Public Economies." *American Journal of Agricultural Economics* 70, no. 5 (Dec. 1988): 1085–1090.

Corwin, Edward S. "The Passing of Dual Federalism." *Virginia Law Review* 36, (Feb. 1950): 1–24.

Derthick, Martha. *Keeping the Compound Republic: Essays on American Federalism.* Washington, D.C.: Brookings Institution Press, 2001.

Dye, Thomas R. *Understanding Public Policy*, 15th ed. Boston: Pearson, 2017.

Elazar, Daniel J. *American Federalism: A View From the States* 3rd ed. New York: Harper & Row, Publishers, 1984.

Elazar, Daniel J. "Contrasting Unitary and Federal Systems." *International Political Science Review* 18 no. 3 (Jul. 1997): 237–251.

Gaddie, Ronald K., and Thomas R. Dye. *Politics in America, 2018 Elections and Updates Edition* 11th ed. New York, NY: Pearson, 2019.

Greene, Jack P. "The Background of the Articles of Confederation." *Publius* 12, no. 4 (Autumn, 1982): 15–55.

Kettl, Donald F. "The Transformation of Governance: Globalization, Devolution, and the Role of Government." *Public Administration Review* 60, no. 6 (Nov./Dec. 2000): 488–497.

Krane, Dale. "American Federalism, State Governments, and Public Policy: Weaving Together Loose Theoretical Threads." *PS: Political Science and Politics* 26, no. 2 (Jun., 1993): 186–190.

LaCroix, Alison L. *The Ideological Origins of American Federalism.* Cambridge, MA: Harvard University Press, 2010.

Lieber, Francis. *On Civil Liberty and Self-government*, 3rd ed. Philadelphia, PA: J. B. Lippincott & Co., 1874.

Madison, James. *The Papers of James Madison,* vol. 9. Chicago, IL: University of Chicago Press, 1975.

Madison, James. *The Federalist No. 39,* ed. by Benjamin Fletcher Wright. Cambridge, MA: Belknap Press of Harvard University Press, 1961.

McGuire, Michael. "Challenges of Intergovernmental Management." *Journal of Health and Human Services Administration* 36, no. 2 (Fall 2013): 109–123.

Ostrom, Vincent. *The Meaning of American Federalism.* San Francisco, CA: ICS Press, 1991.

O'Toole Jr., Laurence J., and Robert K. Christensen, eds. *American Intergovernmental Relations: An Overview.* Thousand Oaks, CA: Sage Publications, 2013.

Posner, Paul. "The Politics of Coercive Federalism in the Bush Era." *Publius* 37, no. 3 (Summer 2007): 390–412.

Reagan, Michael D. *The New Federalism.* New York: Oxford University Press, 1972.

Riker, William H. *Federalism: Origin, Operation, Significance*. Boston: Little, Brown, 1964.

Smith, Kevin B., and Alan Greenblatt. *Governing States and Localities*, 4th ed. Los Angeles, CA: Sage, 2014.

Staten, Clifford Lee. "Theodore Roosevelt: Dual and Cooperative Federalism." *Presidential Studies Quarterly* 23 no. 1 (Winter, 1993): 129–143.

Stewart, William H. "Metaphors, Models, and the Development of Federal Theory." *Publius* 12, no. 2 (Spring 1982): 5–24.

Tarr, Alan. "The Past and Future of the New Judicial Federalism." *Publius* 24, no. 2 (Spring, 1994): 63–79.

University of Chicago Press. "Intergovernmental Relations." *Social Service Review* 31, no. 4 (Dec., 1957): 442–443.

Volden, Craig. "Intergovernmental Political Competition in American Federalism." *American Journal of Political Science* 49, no. (2) (Apr. 2005): 327–342.

Wright, Deil S. "Intergovernmental Relations: An Analytical Overview." *The Annals of the American Academy of Political and Social Science*. 416 (Nov., 1974): 1–16.

Wright, Deil S. *Understanding Intergovernmental Relations*, 3rd ed. Belmont, CA: Wadsworth Publishing Company, 1988.

Wright, Deil S. "Federalism, Intergovernmental Relations, and Intergovernmental Management: Historical Reflections and Conceptual Comparisons." *Public Administration Review* 50, vol. 2 (Mar.-Apr., 1990): 168–178.

2

Legal Dimensions of Intergovernmental Relations

Carol M. Glen

LEARNING OBJECTIVES

- Demonstrate an understanding of the constitutional origins of federalism's legal aspects, including Federalist and Anti-Federalist arguments, and how these elements influenced the direction of intergovernmental relations in the nation.

- Demonstrate knowledge of the Commerce Clause in the U.S. Constitution and the landmark legal decisions that have expanded and limited federal power based on that clause, thereby providing a more significant role at the subnational level.

- Demonstrate knowledge of the Spending Clause in the U.S. Constitution and the landmark legal decisions that have expanded and limited federal power based on that clause as a facet of expanding intergovernmental relations.

- Demonstrate an understanding of the significance of the 14th Amendment in shaping federal and state relations, especially in regards to civil rights.

- Demonstrate an understanding of the significant role played by the Supreme Court in determining the balance of power between the federal and state levels as a facet of intergovernmental relations under a federal structure.

KEY TERMS

Federalists

Anti-Federalists

Article III

10th Amendment

"Elastic Clause"

Supremacy Clause

Spending Clause

14th Amendment

"Horizontal Federalism"   Due Process Clause

Marbury v. Madison   Equal Protection Clause

Figure 2.1: Gold judge's gavel.
Source: Pixabay
Attribution: User "QuinceCreative"
License: Pixabay License

2.1 INTRODUCTION

The federal system in the United States allocates authority between the national level of government and the states, assigning separate decision-making powers to each sphere. It is based on the idea that the Union will be strengthened if, in the words of Chief Justice Hugo Black in *Younger v. Harris* (1971), states are "left free to perform their separate functions in their separate ways."[1] This division of authority imposes constitutional limits designed to prevent a concentration of power, especially at the federal level, which correspondingly has facilitated the advancement of intergovernmental relations over time. As Justice Salmon Chase explained in *Texas v. White* (1868), "The Constitution, in all its provisions looks to an indestructible Union, composed of indestructible states."[2]

The constitutional authority allocated to states is enshrined in the 10th Amendment. It stipulates, "The powers not delegated to the United States by the Constitution, nor prohibited by it to the States, are reserved to the States, respectively, or to the people." While this language appears to set clear limits on federal authority, federal power, in reality, has increased over time. Federal and state powers are established by the U.S. Constitution, but the interpretation of those powers is not. The federal judiciary, especially the Supreme Court,

1   *Younger v. Harris*, 401 U.S. 37 (1971), https://supreme.justia.com/cases/federal/us/401/37.
2   *Texas v. White* 74 U.S. (7 Wall.) 700 (1869), https://www.law.cornell.edu/supremecourt/text/74/700.

has had a significant impact on the interrelationship between the federal government and states, at times expanding federal power, at times imposing more limits. Consequently, the flexibility of American federalism has allowed for significant changes in federal-state relations over time as part of an evolving system of intergovernmental relations. This chapter examines the role played by the Supreme Court in balancing federal and state powers, beginning with a discussion of the constitutional origins of federal judicial authority. From there it explores the principal constitutional amendments that affect the legal dimensions of intergovernmental relations, including how these amendments have been interpreted by the Supreme Court. The chapter concludes with an overview of the current balance of power between federal and state governments as shaped by the federal judiciary.

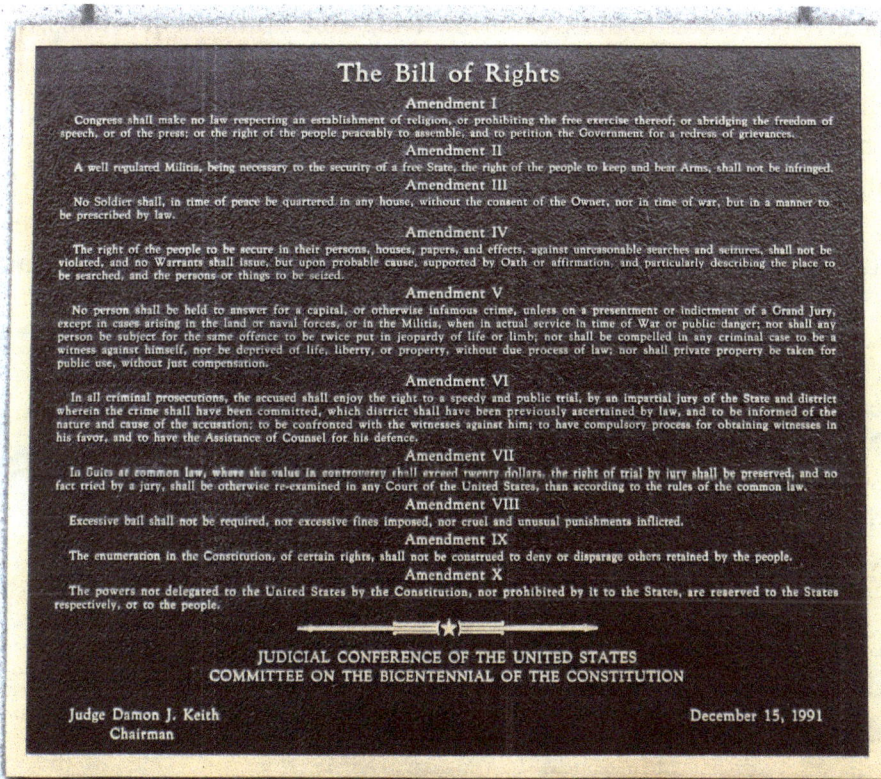

Figure 2.2: A Bill of Rights Plaque.
Source: Wikimedia Commons
Attribution: David Jones
License: CC BY 2.0

2.2 JUDICIAL FEDERALISM AND THE CONSTITUTION

The federal judicial branch of government was established by Article III of the U.S. Constitution. The first sentence of Article III states, "The judicial power of the United States shall be vested in one Supreme Court, and in such inferior courts as the Congress may from time to time ordain and establish." Congress quickly exercised this authority by expanding the federal court system through the Judiciary Act, signed into law by George Washington on September 24, 1789. The first bill ever introduced into the U.S. Senate, it established the multi-tiered federal judicial system that we know today, consisting of the Supreme Court, U.S. district courts, and U.S. circuit courts. Despite this extensive federal court system, Article III of the U.S. Constitution makes it clear that federal judicial power was never intended to be comprehensive. Judicial authority is limited to just a few "cases" or "controversies." Specifically, it is limited to those cases involving Constitutional questions, disputes between different states and citizens of different states, maritime law, and those involving foreign ambassadors and other foreign public ministers. The Supreme Court has original jurisdiction (meaning that cases can be introduced directly for resolution in the Supreme Court) only when foreign ambassadors and foreign public ministers are involved or when U.S. states are party to the dispute. In all other cases, the Supreme Court acts as the country's highest court of appeal.

> *Article III of the U.S. Constitution*: Established the judicial branch of the federal government, which includes the Supreme Court and lower courts created by Congress.
>
> *Judiciary Act*: Established the structure and jurisdiction of the federal court system. Signed into law by President George Washington on September 24, 1789.

Figure 2.3: Panorama of the west facade of United States Supreme Court Building at dusk in Washington, D.C., USA.
Source: Wikimedia Commons
Attribution: Joe Ravi
License: CC BY-SA 3.0

Since the authority granted by Article III covers only a small portion of all potential court cases, a system of state courts is needed to resolve the majority of disputes that fall outside of federal authority. The original 13 colonies each had their own court systems, and the Founding Fathers expected that this structure would continue under the new Constitution, but the Framers did not dictate how state court systems should be developed. Instead, such provisions are determined by legislation and the constitutions in each of the 50 states. The U.S. Constitution does, however, address legal relations between states. Article IV, Section 1 mandates that "Full faith and credit be given in each state to the public acts, records, and judicial proceedings of every other state." This clause requires that states recognize and honor the court judgments of other states. Often called "horizontal federalism," this clause was designed to acknowledge the independent authority of each state within a national legal system.

Figure 2.4: This is the first page of the Judiciary Act of 1789.
Source: Wikimedia Commons
Attribution: United States Congress
License: Public Domain

Debates concerning the appropriate balance between federal judicial authority and state judicial authority were evident at the founding of the Republic. Immediately following the Constitutional Convention in 1787, a series of essays representing supporters of a strong central government (Federalists) and opponents of strong centralized government (Anti-Federalists) were published. One prominent Anti-Federalist, who wrote under the pseudonym "Brutus," warned that the new federal government would "possess absolute and uncontrollable power, legislative, executive and judicial, with respect to every object to which it extends."[3] He later attacked the proposed federal judicial system specifically. In Essay 14, Brutus argued "the supreme court under this constitution would be exalted above all other power in the government, and subject to no control."[4] He added in Essay 15, "Perhaps nothing could have been better conceived to facilitate the abolition of the state governments than the constitution of the judicial."[5] Anti-Federalists warned that the new federal judiciary had too few limits placed on its power and that it would inevitably expand to encroach on the authority of state courts and threaten individual liberties.

By contrast, the Federalists were convinced that a strong national judicial authority would be required in order to keep the Union together. In a letter to Thomas Jefferson during October 1787, James Madison argued that the federal judiciary would protect against the "dangerous encroachment" of the states and "keep the states within their proper limits."[6] Madison was also concerned about

---

3   Brutus, *Essay No. 1,* October 18, 1787, in Herbert J. Storing, ed., *The Complete Anti-Federalist* (Chicago: The University of Chicago Press, 1981, 2:363–372.

4   Brutus, *Essay No. 14* March 6, 1788, *The Complete Anti-Federalist,* 2:363–372.

5   Brutus, *Essay No. 15* March 20, 1788, *The Complete Anti-Federalist,* 2:363–372.

6   James Madison, *Letter to Thomas Jefferson,* October 24, 1787.

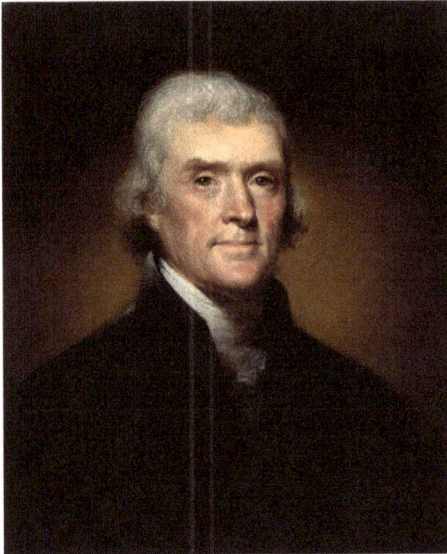

Figure 2.5: Thomas Jefferson.
Source: Wikimedia Commons
Attribution: Rembrandt Peale
License: Public Domain

Figure 2.6: Alexander Hamilton.
Source: Wikimedia Commons
Attribution: John Trumbull
License: Public Domain

the power of the legislative branch of government because "it alone has access to the pockets of the people."[7] He warned of the danger posed by popular factions who would seek to use the legislature to pursue their own interests contrary to the rights of other citizens. Over time, bolstered by the passions of constituents, the legislature would draw "all power into its impetuous vortex."[8] Believing legislative power to be the problem, Madison proposed federal judicial power as the solution.

The case for a strong federal judiciary was promoted even more explicitly by Alexander Hamilton. In Federalist Papers Nos. 78-83, Hamilton developed a new theory of judicial decision-making that gave Article III greater coherence and logic.[9] Hamilton begins with the premise that the judicial branch will be the weakest and "least dangerous" of the three branches of government. Unlike the executive branch, which controls the military, and the legislative branch, which controls taxes and spending, the judiciary's power is "merely judgement."[10] Hamilton argued that, given this inherent weakness, the judicial branch had to be protected from manipulation by the other two branches of government. To ensure an independent judiciary, he therefore proposed that "all judges who may be appointed by the United States are to hold their offices during good behavior."[11] From this perspective, judicial independence and impartiality go hand-in-hand and the purpose of both is to protect the rights of the people and guard the U.S. Constitution. Hamilton proclaimed that, in order to fulfill those obligations, it was essential that the judiciary be given the power of judicial review. Judicial review refers to the power of the Supreme Court to declare laws unconstitutional.

7   James Madison, *Federalist 48*, February 1, 1788, https://avalon.law.yale.edu/18th_century/fed48.asp.
8   James Madison, *Federalist 10,* November 23, 1787, https://avalon.law.yale.edu/18th_century/fed10.asp.
9   William M. Treanor, "The Genius of Hamilton and the Birth of the Modern Theory of the Judiciary" in *Cambridge Companion to the Federalist,* Jack Rakove and Colleen Sheehan eds. (Cambridge: Cambridge University Press 2020) 464–514.
10   Alexander Hamilton, *Federalist 78,* (May 28, 1788), https://avalon.law.yale.edu/18th_century/fed78.asp.
11   Alexander Hamilton, *Federalist 78.*

Hamilton was not the first to advocate for judicial review, but he provided the most complete justification for the doctrine at that time.[12] Anti-Federalists instead argued that judicial review would place the courts above the legislature, threatening popular sovereignty and individual liberty. Hamilton reasoned that it was required in order to ensure that the legislature continued to serve the U.S. Constitution, and, therefore, the people. Hamilton contended that "No legislative act, therefore, contrary to the Constitution, can be valid. To deny this, would be to affirm, that the deputy is greater than his principal; that the servant is above his master; that the representatives of the people are superior to the people themselves."[13] Hamilton viewed judicial review as a safeguard to protect the U.S. Constitution and individual liberties against the vacillations of temporary legislative majorities. He believed that judges would be more qualified than legislatures to decide on the constitutionality of laws, since "members of the legislature will rarely be chosen with a view to those qualifications." Legislatures would also be more likely to succumb to the influence of factions that could "stifle the voice both of law and of equity."[14]

Although the doctrine of judicial review is not explicitly mentioned in the U.S. Constitution, the power of the Supreme Court to declare legislative and executive acts unconstitutional was established in the landmark case *Marbury v. Madison* in 1803. Consequently, judicial precedents likewise wielded significant influence over the direction of intergovernmental relations over time. President John Adams appointed William Marbury as one of several dozen justices of the peace in 1801. Although the Senate confirmed all of these justices before President Adams left office, four of the commissions had not yet been delivered, including Marbury's. When the new president, Thomas Jefferson, assumed office, he ordered his Secretary of State James Madison to withhold the undelivered appointments, since they had been made by his political opponent. As a result, Marbury and others were unable to assume their posts. Marbury sued Madison to try to force him to deliver the commission. Writing for a unanimous court, Supreme Court Chief Justice John Marshall asserted that Marbury had a right to the commission but that the provision in the Judiciary Act (1789) enabling Marbury to bring his lawsuit was itself unconstitutional. Marshall maintained that the Judiciary Act had extended Congress' jurisdiction beyond what Article III, Section 2 had established. In declaring parts of the Judiciary Act unconstitutional, Marshall in effect established the principle of judicial review,

Marbury v. Madison (1803): A landmark Supreme Court case that established the principle of judicial review by declaring a federal law unconstitutional.

Supremacy Clause: Article VI, Paragraph 2 of the U.S. Constitution. It establishes that the federal law take precedence over state laws, and even state constitutions. It prohibits states from interfering with the federal government's exercise of its constitutional powers.

12   William M. Treanor 2020, 466.
13   Alexander Hamilton or James Madison, *Federalist 49*, February 5, 1788, https://avalon.law.yale.edu/18th_century/fed49.asp.
14   Alexander Hamilton, *Federalist 81*, June 25, 1788, https://avalon.law.yale.edu/18th_century/fed81.asp.

making it an embedded institutional feature of our nation's judiciary from that point forward.

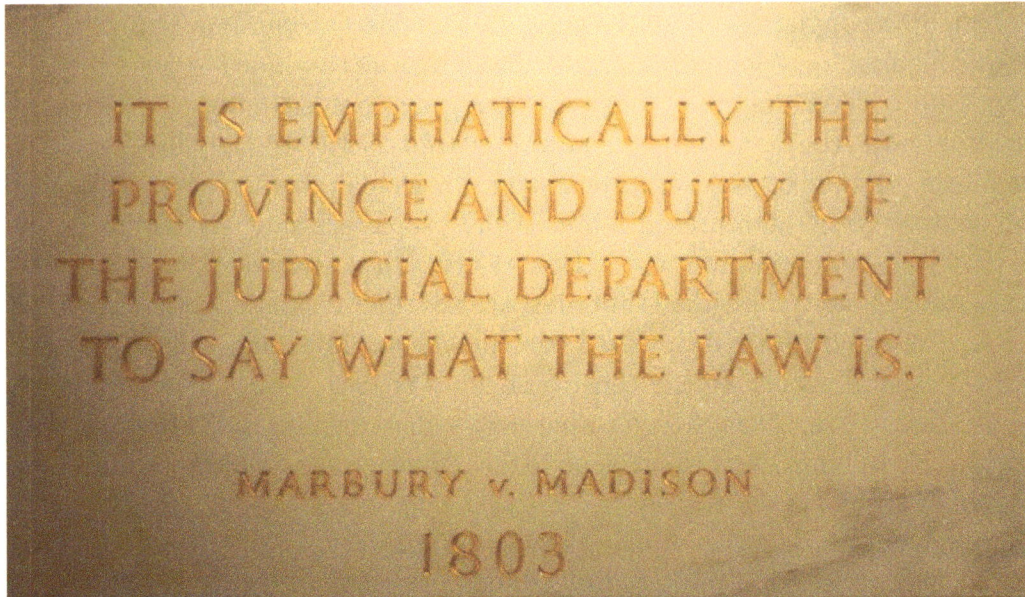

Figure 2.7: First Floor at the Statute of John Marshall, quotation from *Marbury v. Madison* (written by Marshall) engraved into the wall. United States Supreme Court Building.
Source: Wikimedia Commons
Attribution: User "swatjester"
License: CC BY-SA 2.0

The ruling in *Marbury v. Madison* echoed Hamilton's earlier arguments concerning judicial review and is widely considered to be one of the Supreme Court's most important opinions. Like Hamilton, Chief Justice Marshall argued that "a law repugnant to the constitution is void." Marshall also alluded to the Supremacy Clause of the Constitution (Article VI, para. 2) as justification for judicial review. The Supremacy Clause makes federal law the "supreme law of the land," thus prohibiting state governments from passing laws that conflict with federal laws, but it also places the U.S. Constitution above federal law. The Supremacy Clause prohibits enforcing laws that are in conflict with the U.S. Constitution.

Figure 2.8: Portrait of Chief Justice John Marshall, who opined *Marbury v. Madison* in 1803.
Source: Wikimedia Commons
Attribution: John Blennerhassett Martin
License: Public Domain

The power of the federal government is defined by the U.S. Constitution mostly under Article I, Section 8. Among other provisions, the federal government has the power to tax, borrow money, regulate interstate commerce, establish the rules for citizenship, establish a military, and declare war. These are known as enumerated powers and represent the principle that the federal government can only exercise powers explicitly granted to it in the U.S. Constitution. The 10th Amendment to the U.S. Constitution also establishes limits on federal power. It affirms that powers not delegated to the federal government, nor prohibited to the states, are reserved to the states, or to the people. In practice, however, federal enumerated powers have been interpreted broadly and court rulings over many subsequent decades have led to an expansion of federal government power. The justification for this expansion is found in the U.S. Constitution under what has become known as the "Necessary and Proper Clause," or the "Elastic Clause." Included at the end of Article I, Section 8, the clause grants Congress the power to make all laws "necessary and proper" to execute its enumerated powers. The Elastic Clause is the source of the vast majority of federal laws and has been described by legal scholars Gary Lawson and Neil S. Siegel as "the single most important provision in the Constitution."[15] The system of judicial federalism established by the Founding Fathers is therefore not static; the balance between federal and state authority has been molded by numerous legal interpretations and court opinions over many years, consequently shaping how intergovernmental relations have advanced as a facet of federal structure over time. Some of the most important Supreme Court decisions that have shaped federal and state powers are reviewed in the next section.

> **Necessary and Proper Clause**: Article I, Section 8 of the U.S. Constitution. Also known as the Elastic Clause. It gives Congress the authority to make all laws that are necessary and proper for carrying out its enumerated powers.

Figure 2.9: Article 1 of the U.S. Constitution.
Source: Pixabay
Attribution: User "WikiImages"
License: Public Domain

2.3 THE COMMERCE CLAUSE

The Commerce Clause refers to Article 1, Section 8, Clause 3 of the U.S. Constitution, which grants Congress the power "to regulate commerce with foreign nations, and among the several states, and with the Indian tribes." This legislation was designed to facilitate international trade and address problems related to interstate trade barriers. Prior to the Constitutional Convention, commerce was controlled in the original thirteen colonies by state legislatures who, in an attempt to protect their own interests, erected a series of

> **Commerce Clause**: Article I, Section 8 of the U.S. Constitution. Gives Congress the power to regulate international and interstate commerce.

---

15   Gary Lawson and Neil S. Siegel, "Necessary and Proper Clause," *Interactive Constitution* https://constitutioncenter.org/interactive-constitution/interpretation/article-i/clauses/754.

trade barriers. The overall effect of these actions, however, was to stifle interstate commerce and undermine economic growth. The Commerce Clause shifted the power to regulate commerce to the federal government, which enabled the establishment of a free trade zone among states and allowed the president to pursue international trade agreements. The prohibition against states discriminating in interstate commerce is called the Commerce Clause. While the following is not explicitly stated in the Constitution, legal interpretations have established that the Commerce Clause not only gives the federal government positive authority to regulate commerce, but also acts as a restraint on state action. The Commerce Clause, therefore, has a very direct impact on the balance of power between the federal government and the states.

Over the years, courts have interpreted the Commerce Clause both narrowly and broadly, often based on how the word "commerce" is defined. Should the term be limited to only trade in goods, or should it be interpreted to also include the production of goods and other economic activities? In *Gibbons v. Ogden* (1824), a case involving the regulation of steam boat operations in New York and New Jersey, the Supreme Court ruled that, under the Commerce Clause, the federal government had the authority to regulate navigation. In writing the majority opinion, Chief Justice John Marshall stated, "The power to regulate commerce, so far as it extends, is exclusively vested in Congress, and no part of it can be exercised by a State."[16] The ruling recognized that, because transportation is inextricably linked to interstate trade, federal authority takes precedence.

More than 100 years later, a similarly broad interpretation of the Commerce Clause was evident in *NLRB v. Jones & Laughlin Steel Corp* (1937). The question in this case was whether the National Labor Relations Board (NLRB) had the authority to order the reinstatement of employees of a Pennsylvania steel company who had been fired for engaging in labor union activities. Even though there was no direct interstate commerce, the dispute involved workers in only one state, the Supreme Court ruled that federal authority nonetheless took precedence, contending that "Although activities may be intrastate in character when separately considered, if they have such a close and substantial relation to interstate commerce...Congress has the power to exercise that control.[17] The Supreme Court opinion argued that, since the Jones and Laughlin Corporation conducted significant business outside of Pennsylvania, the company's attempts to limit labor union activities had the potential to significantly affect interstate commerce. This ruling signaled that federal courts were willing to employ a broad interpretation of the Commerce Clause even in seemingly local cases provided they have a link to interstate commerce. The broad understanding of the Commerce Clause was further reinforced in the years that followed; between 1937 and 1995, the Supreme Court did not invalidate a single federal law exercised under the

---

16   *Gibbons v Ogden*, 22 U.S. 1 (1824), United States Supreme Court, https://www.oyez.org/cases/1789-1850/22us1.

17   *NLRB v. Jones & Laughlin Steel Corp.*, 301 U.S. 1 (1937), United States Supreme Court, https://supreme.justia.com/cases/federal/us/301/1.

Commerce Clause.[18] Since then, however, the Supreme Court has, at times, offered both narrower and broader interpretations of federal authority with respect to commerce as illustrated in the two cases discussed below.

2.3.1 United States v. Lopez (1995)

The question before the Supreme Court in the *United States v. Lopez* (1995) case was whether the Gun-Free School Zones Act (1990) was constitutional under the Commerce Clause. The Act stipulated that it is a federal offence for any individual to possess a firearm in a school zone without authorization. The case involved a high school senior, Alfonzo Lopez, who was discovered carrying a concealed .38 handgun and five bullets into a high school in San Antonio, Texas. He was indicted by a federal grand jury, later found guilty, and sentenced to six months in prison and two years' probation. Lopez appealed his conviction on the grounds that schools are controlled not by the federal government but by state and local governments, so Congress had overstepped its authority. After several appeals, the case was heard by the Supreme Court during April 1995.

The federal government's case relied on the Commerce Clause to justify the Gun-Free School Zones Act. It argued that guns in schools lead to violence that can be harmful to the local economy. People would be less likely to travel to, and conduct business in, violent areas; also, gun violence undermines children's education. The government argued that, since a well-educated populace is required for a strong national economy, it had a compelling interest under the Commerce Clause to regulate guns in schools. In a 5-4 decision, the Court rejected the government's arguments, ruling that the Gun-Free School Zone Act was unconstitutional because it was not sufficiently related to interstate commerce. The majority opinion, written by Chief Justice Rehnquist, noted that "The possession of a gun in a local school zone is in no sense an economic activity that might, through repetition elsewhere, substantially affect any sort of interstate commerce." The Court found that Congress had exceeded its powers under the Constitution by enacting the Gun-Free School Zones Act. The opinion concluded, "To uphold the Government's contentions here, we have to pile inference upon inference in a manner that would bid fair to convert congressional authority under the Commerce Clause to a general police power of the sort retained by the States. This we are unwilling to do."[19]

The ruling in the *Lopez* case indicated that the Supreme Court was concerned about the expansion of federal power in relation to state power. The opinion specifically quoted Federalist No. 45 in which James Madison wrote that, in the U.S. Constitution, the federal government's enumerated powers are few and defined, while the powers that remain with state governments are numerous and indefinite. This decision broke with prior rulings that offered a more expansionist

18   Legal Information Institute, *Commerce Clause, Cornell Law School* https://www.law.cornell.edu/wex/commerce_clause.
19   *United States v. Lopez* 514 U.S. 549 (1995), United States Supreme Court, https://supreme.justia.com/cases/federal/us/514/549.

view of federal authority and which generally allowed the Commerce Clause to be used to limit state legislation. *U.S. v. Lopez* is a particularly significant case in that, for the first time in 50 years, the Supreme Court ruled Congress had overstepped its authority under the Commerce Clause.[20] The *Lopez* case was followed a few years later by another Supreme Court opinion that also struck down Congress's authority to legislate under the Commerce Clause. In *United States v. Morrison* (1999), the Supreme Court rejected parts of the Violence Against Women Act (1994) that allowed victims to sue their attackers in federal court. In this case, a student at Virginia Polytechnic Institute sued two football players at the school for alleged sexual assault under the Violence Against Women Act. The Court ruled that the Act's civil remedy was unconstitutional since gender-motivated crimes are unrelated to economic activity. According to the majority opinion, Congress exceeded its authority under the Commerce Clause in providing a private right of action under the Violence Against Women Act. The Court also noted that if the allegations were true, then under the federal system the remedy should be provided by the Commonwealth of Virginia, not by the United States.

2.3.2 Gonzales v. Raich (2005)

The *Lopez* and *Morrison* cases demonstrated that federal power under the Commerce Clause is not unlimited and that some local activities are beyond the reach of the federal government. However, in *Gonzales v. Raich* (2005), the Supreme Court again interpreted the Commerce Clause more broadly. In this case, California residents Angel Raich and her co-defendant Diane Monson used medical marijuana to relieve symptoms of a serious illness. Under state law in California, it was legal for them to do so since voters legalized medical marijuana in the 1996 Compassionate Use Act. The California law, however, conflicted with the federal Controlled Substances Act (CSA) (1970). While the Clinton Administration took the position that the medical use of marijuana was exempt from the CSA, the Bush Administration eliminated this exemption, thereby allowing the Drug and Enforcement Agency (DEA) to seize marijuana plants. When their plants were confiscated, Raich and Monson challenged the Controlled Substances Act, claiming that homegrown marijuana did not substantially affect interstate commerce; therefore, its seizure violated the Commerce Clause. Relying heavily on *Lopez* and *Morrison,* the Ninth Circuit Court of Appeals ruled that the government did not have the authority

Figure 2.10: A 2002 rally to legalize marijuana.
Source: Wikimedia Commons
Attribution: Bart Everson
License: CC BY 2.0

20   Bill of Rights Institute, *United States v. Lopez* (1995), https://billofrightsinstitute.org/e-lessons/united-states-v-lopez-1995.

Figure 2.11: Justice Sandra Day O'Connor.

Source: Wikimedia Commons
Attribution: Library of Congress
License: Public Domain

Figure 2.12: Justice Clarence Thomas.

Source: Wikimedia Commons
Attribution: U.S. government
License: Public Domain

to seize the plants under the Commerce Clause because the narrow class of activity in this case was neither commercial nor economic in nature. However, when the case reached the Supreme Court, that opinion was reversed.

The question before the Supreme Court was, does Congress have the power, under the Commerce Clause, to ban the cultivation and use of marijuana even when it is legal under state law? In a 6-3 majority opinion, the Court decided that Congress does have that right. They reasoned that, unlike the *Lopez* and *Morrison* cases—which did not involve interstate commercial activities—the cultivation of marijuana could affect the national market for marijuana. The Court noted, "Given the enforcement difficulties that attend distinguishing between marijuana cultivated locally and marijuana grown elsewhere, and concerns about diversion into illicit channels..."[21] Congress acted rationally and within its authority to seize the marijuana plants.

In a strongly-worded dissent, three justices criticized this ruling on the grounds that it represented a vast expansion of federal power into state affairs. Justice Sandra Day O'Connor argued that the ruling violated "one of federalism's chief virtues," that states have a right to act as social and economic laboratories without risk to the rest of the country. She maintained this to be especially true when, as in this case, there was no evidence that personal use of marijuana affected interstate commerce. Justice O'Connor wrote, "Whatever the wisdom of California's experiment with medical marijuana, the federalist principles that have driven our Commerce Clause cases require that room for experiment be protected in this case."[22] Similarly, Justice Clarence Thomas reasoned that, by allowing Congress the power to regulate non-

21   *Gonzales v. Raich* 545 U.S. 1 (2005), United States Supreme Court, https://supreme.justia.com/cases/federal/us/545/1.
22   *Gonzales v. Raich* 545 U.S. 1 (2005).

commercial intrastate activities, the Court has granted the federal government police power over the entire country that subverts the principles of federalism and dual sovereignty.[23] The *Gonzalez* case reminds us that, while Congress has limited enumerated authority, it can significantly expand power through the Commerce Clause. Another clause that has been used to expand federal authority since the founding of the Republic is the Spending Clause.

2.4 THE SPENDING CLAUSE

Article I, Section 8, Clause 1 of the U.S. Constitution is known as the Spending Clause, or General Welfare Clause. It reads in part as follows: "Congress shall have power to lay and collect taxes, duties, imposts and excises, to pay the debts and

> ***Spending Clause***: Gives Congress the power to raise taxes and spend for the "general welfare."

provide for the common defense and general welfare of the United States." This clause has been the focus of debate since the founding of the Republic, specifically over the meaning of "general welfare" and the extent to which federal spending can be limited. The Federalist Papers reveal a sharp divide on this question between Madison and Hamilton. For Madison, the Spending Clause authorizes Congress to spend money only in order to carry out its enumerated powers. Otherwise, he reasoned Congress would have unlimited power to spend on the general welfare, rendering its enumerated powers meaningless. By contrast, Hamilton interpreted this clause much more broadly. In his view, it grants Congress an independent power to provide for the general welfare, that is, to enact national laws designed to promote the general welfare of the United States. For Hamilton, federal spending would be constitutional if it is "general, and not local; its operation extending in fact, or by possibility, throughout the Union, and not being confined to a particular spot."[24]

Figure 2.13: A farmer in despair over the Great Depression, 1932.

Source: Wikimedia Commons
Attribution: Unknown
License: Public Domain

The first major test of the general welfare provision in the Spending Clause came much later in 1934 in *United States v. Butler*. The law in question was the Agricultural Adjustment Act (AAA), (1933) in which Congress taxed and set limits on some areas of agricultural production. The Act was part of President Franklin D. Roosevelt's New Deal program and was designed to limit overproduction of some crops in order to increase prices and restore the incomes of farmers during the Great Depression.

---

23   *Gonzales v. Raich* 545 U.S. 1 (2005).
24   Alexander Hamilton, *Final Version of the Report on the Subject of Manufactures* (5 December 1791), https://founders.archives.gov/documents/Hamilton/01-10-02-0001-0007.

The law was challenged on the grounds that crop production is a local activity that should rightfully be regulated by the states. The Supreme Court agreed with this argument, ruling that the AAA was unconstitutional; importantly, however, their opinion also recognized that Congressional spending authority is broad. The power of Congress "is not limited by the direct grants of legislative power found in the Constitution."[25] In other words, Congressional spending is not limited to only its enumerated powers. In this opinion, the Court affirmed the Hamiltonian view that the federal government has an expansive right to tax and spend for the general welfare of the country. The Court also went a step further by declaring that, for the most part, it is for Congress to determine what constitutes the general welfare. The ruling in the *Butler* case not only provided for an expansion of federal legislation under the New Deal but also significantly extended Congressional and federal power.[26] Since *Butler,* the Supreme Court has largely sided with Congress on the subject of spending for the general welfare such as in the case of *South Dakota v. Dole.*

2.4.1 South Dakota v. Dole (1986)

The *Butler* case laid the foundation for a series of subsequent legal opinions that firmly established federal authority to spend. Decades later, the Supreme Court was asked to decide whether Congress could go further and withhold a percentage of federal funds from states that refused to adopt a federal standard. In this case, the federal standard was to establish a minimum drinking age of 21. In *South Dakota v. Dole,* South Dakota challenged the 1984 National Minimum Drinking Age Act (NMDA), which stipulated that states refusing to raise their drinking age to 21 would receive 5% less money in federal highway funding. The Act was passed in response to highly publicized incidents of teen drunk driving injuries and deaths as well as to pressure from the powerful lobbying group Mothers Against Drunk Driving (MADD). In *South Dakota v. Dole,* the Supreme Court was asked to resolve constitutional questions related to the authority of the federal government under the Spending Clause, as well as the rights of states under the 21st Amendment. Under the 21st Amendment, which ended national prohibition, state legislatures had the right to regulate the sale of alcohol within their state.

Prior to the passage of the National Minimum Drinking Age Act, minimum legal drinking age requirements differed across states. This meant that teenagers could drive across state lines to legally purchase alcohol where the drinking age was lower. The goal of the legislation was to set a national drinking age standard and reduce teenage traffic fatalities. At the time the NMDA was passed, South Dakota permitted those who were 19 years of age to purchase drinks that contained up to 3.2% of alcohol. Since the NMDA required the Secretary of Transportation,

---

25   *United States v. Butler* 297 U.S. 1 (1936), United States Supreme Court, https://supreme.justia.com/cases/federal/us/297/1.
26   Herman J. Herbert, Jr., "The General Welfare Clauses in the Constitution of the United States", *Fordham L. Rev. 390* (1938), https://ir.lawnet.fordham.edu/flr/vol7/iss3/5.

Elizabeth Dole, to withhold federal highway funds from states that did not comply, South Dakota sued the federal government. The state challenged the constitutionality of the law, arguing that Congress had overstepped its authority under the Spending Clause and that it had also violated the 21st Amendment.

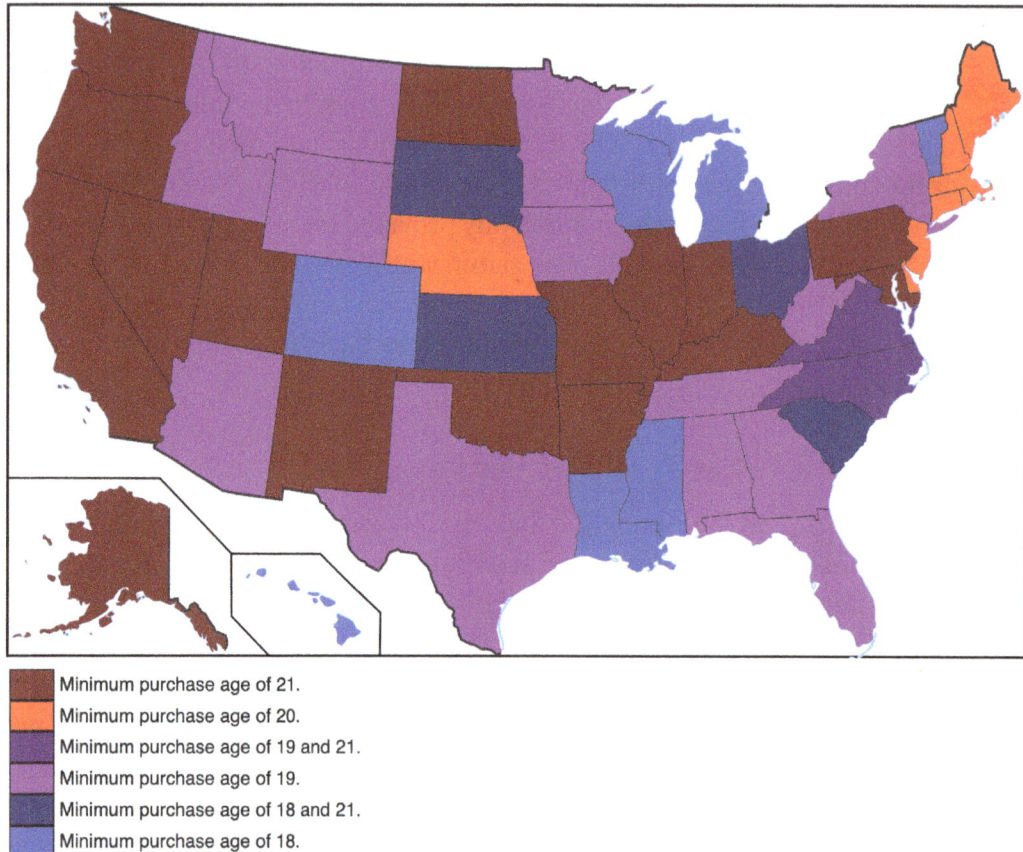

Minimum purchase age of 21.
Minimum purchase age of 20.
Minimum purchase age of 19 and 21.
Minimum purchase age of 19.
Minimum purchase age of 18 and 21.
Minimum purchase age of 18.

Figure 2.14: This map shows the various minimum age for purchasing alcohol in the United States in 1983. Teen drunk driving deaths spurred action by groups such as MADD (Mothers Against Drunk Driving) to educate youth on the dangers of drinking, as well as to successfully lobby for a rise in the minimum age to purchase and consume alcohol to 21 years of age.

Source: Wikimedia Commons
Attribution: User "Areatius"
License: CC BY-SA 4.0

In a 7-2 opinion, the Supreme Court rejected the South Dakota challenge. With respect to the Spending Clause, the Court referenced both the U.S. Constitution and the *United States v. Butler* case. It ruled that Congress has the power to place restrictions on the distribution of funds if certain conditions are met. The legislation in question must be in pursuit of the general welfare, the requirements of the law and the consequences of noncompliance must be clear, and the law must be related to a national concern. With respect to the 21st Amendment, the Court ruled that, by offering an inducement to states to implement a particular law, Congress acted indirectly under its spending authority. Provided that the inducement was neither designed to encourage states to act unconstitutionally nor was coercive, the law is constitutional. Chief Justice Rehnquist described the withholding of 5% of federal highway funds as a "relatively mild encouragement" and noted that South Dakota still had a choice as to whether or not it complied. Rather than lose federal funds, South Dakota did eventually choose to comply with the NMDA, as did every other state by 1988. Ultimately, *South Dakota v. Dole* set a precedent for Congressional spending authority by endorsing the use of federal financial inducements in the intergovernmental equation. It further clarified the line between federal and state power and had a significant impact on the country as a whole.

2.4.2 National Federation of Independent Business v. Sebelius (2012)

The *National Federation of Independent Business (NFIB) v. Sebelius* (2012) case also had the potential for a far-reaching and significant national impact and to shape the balance between federal and state power. The case revolved around a challenge to the Affordable Care Act (ACA) that was brought by the Obama Administration in 2010. The ACA sought to expand the coverage of health insurance to millions more Americans by requiring that most Americans have health coverage. This goal would be achieved by requiring employers with more than 50 employees to provide health insurance, expanding Medicaid, and mandating that individuals who are not covered by the previous provisions purchase government subsidized health insurance or face a penalty. Before and after its passage, the ACA was highly politicized and controversial.

Following the enactment of the ACA, 13 states challenged the law in district court. They were later joined by an additional 13 states and also by the National Federation of Independent Business and several individuals. The plaintiffs argued that the law was unconstitutional on three grounds: (1) the employer mandate undermines state sovereignty; (2) the expansion of Medicaid is coercive; and (3) the individual mandate was an overreach of Congressional authority under the Commerce Clause. After district and circuit courts found the individual mandate to be unconstitutional, the case was heard by the U.S. Supreme Court during March 2012. Since this was one of the most politically contentious cases in recent years, Americans eagerly anticipated the announcement of the Supreme Court's ruling in June of the same year.

The Supreme Court upheld parts of the ACA while rejecting others as unconstitutional. The employer mandate to provide healthcare was upheld as a valid exercise of Congressional authority under the Commerce Clause. Health insurance can have an impact on the mobility of employees, which consequently has an impact on interstate commerce. The Supreme Court, however, deemed the Medicare expansion provision as written to be overly coercive and unconstitutional. Under the ACA, states were required to expand the number of people covered by Medicaid. The federal government would cover 100% of the costs of this expansion for three years and 90% of the cost thereafter. However, if states did not comply with this provision, they would lose all federal Medicaid funds. The majority opinion noted that this consequence would represent a much greater financial loss than in the *South Dakota v. Dole* case and would give states little choice but to comply. At the same time, the Court did not invalidate Medicaid expansion entirely. Chief Justice Roberts stated that nothing in the opinion precluded Congress from offering funds for Medicare expansion, but "What Congress is not free to do is to penalize states that choose not to participate in that new program by taking away their existing Medicaid funding."[27] By the beginning of 2021, 38 states and the District of Columbia had adopted Medicaid expansion while 12 had not.

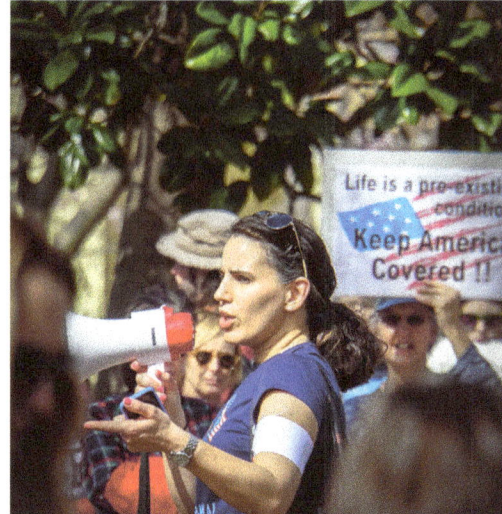

Figure 2.15: Rally in Support of the Affordable Care Act, at The White House, Washington, DC USA.
Source: Wikimedia Commons
Attribution: Ted Eytan
License: CC BY-SA 2.0

The most controversial aspect of the ACA was the individual mandate requiring all Americans to have health insurance coverage. The central question was whether the federal government had the authority to enforce this obligation on individuals and to impose financial penalties if they failed to comply. The lawsuits against the ACA focused on the Commerce Clause, claiming that Congress had overstepped its constitutional authority as provided by that clause. Before the case reached the Supreme Court, lower courts had rendered mixed judgments on this issue. Three district courts upheld the individual mandate, three struck it down, while two appellate courts agreed that the ACA was constitutional and one disagreed.[28] The Supreme Court agreed that the Commerce Clause does not give Congress the right to impose the individual mandate. The Court also recognized that, while the Commerce Clause gives the federal government the right to regulate commerce, it does not give Congress the right to compel it, noting, "to regulate individuals precisely *because* they are doing nothing would open a new and potentially vast domain to congressional authority."[29] Consequently, Congress cannot command individuals to buy health insurance.

The Supreme Court's rejection of the individual mandate under the Commerce Clause, however, did not render it unconstitutional. Rather, the majority of the Court recognized the individual mandate as constitutional under the Spending Clause. The Spending Clause gives the federal government not only the power to

---

27   *National Federation of Independent Business (NFIB) v. Sebelius* 567 U.S. 519 (2012), United States Supreme Court, https://supreme.justia.com/cases/federal/us/567/519.

28   Erika K. Lunder and Jennifer Staman, *NFIB v. Sebelius: Constitutionality of the Individual Mandate,* Congressional Research Service, September 3, 2012, https://fas.org/sgp/crs/misc/R42698.pdf.

29   *National Federation of Independent Business (NFIB) v. Sebelius* 567 U.S. 519 (2012).

spend but also to tax. When the individual mandate is viewed not as a penalty but as a tax, Congress has clear authority. Chief Justice Roberts wrote, "Those subject to the individual mandate may lawfully forgo health insurance and pay higher taxes, or buy health insurance and pay lower taxes. The only thing they may not lawfully do is not buy health insurance and not pay the resulting tax."[30] The Court's decisions regarding the ACA are extremely important. On the one hand, the Court concluded that the individual mandate is not justified under the Commerce Clause because, although Congress has the power to regulate commerce—what people *do*—it does not have the power to compel commerce—what people *do not do*.[31] On the other hand, the Court upheld the individual mandate under Congress' taxing powers. The Court also ruled that the penalty for not expanding Medicaid was not consistent with federalism, since the consequence was overly coercive. This meant that states could decide whether or not to expand Medicaid without fear of losing all Medicaid funding as a penalty.

Despite the Supreme Court ruling that most of the ACA is constitutional, legal challenges to the Act did not end. During 2017, Congress included a provision in the Tax Cuts and Jobs Act that reduced the individual mandate penalty to $0. In other words, if individuals choose to forego health insurance, they would not be fined. The elimination of this financial penalty opened the door to additional lawsuits that sought to overturn the entire Affordable Care Act. Recently, Texas and 17 other states were seeking to invalidate the ACA. They argued that the individual mandate is no longer a constitutional exercise of federal taxing power, since Congress has eliminated the dollar amount of the tax. On the other side of the argument were California and 19 additional states, the District of Colombia, and the U.S. House of Representatives, all of whom were defending the ACA. The Supreme Court heard oral arguments regarding this case during October 2020, and ruled on June 17, 2021 that the plaintiffs lacked standing. Essentially, this was a non-answer; the Court did not rule on the constitutionality of the ACA nor on the individual mandate.

2.5 THE 14TH AMENDMENT

Another significant source of Congressional power is the 14th Amendment to the Constitution. Numerous legal struggles over federal and state constitutional authority have been fought over the meaning and scope of this amendment. Passed in

> ***14th Amendment:*** Establishes citizenship rights and guarantees equal protections for all citizens under the law.

1866, Section 1 of the 14th Amendment guarantees citizenship rights, due process, and equal protection under the law. Along with the 13th Amendment, which outlawed slavery, and the 15th Amendment, which banned racial discrimination in

---

30   *National Federation of Independent Business (NFIB) v. Sebelius* 567 U.S. 519 (2012).

31   David J. Edquist and Jeffrey E. Mark, "Analysis: U.S. Supreme Court Upholds the Affordable Care Act: Roberts Rules?" *The National Law Review* March 8, 2021, Vol. XI, No. 67, https://www.natlawreview.com/article/analysis-us-supreme-court-upholds-affordable-care-act-roberts-rules.

elections, they are collectively known as the "Reconstruction Amendments" since they were enacted during the Reconstruction period after the Civil War. Together, these amendments dramatically altered the balance of power between the states and federal government in favor of the federal government by subjecting state authority over citizens to oversight by the federal judiciary or Congress.[32] Of the three, the 14th Amendment has had the most far–reaching legal and social consequences. The Supreme Court has interpreted the 14th Amendment to guarantee a wide array of rights against infringement by the states, and it has been cited in numerous civil rights cases for 150 years.

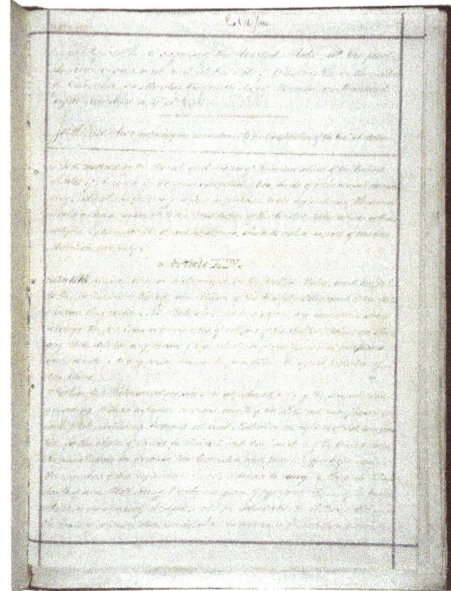

Figure 2.16: The 14th Amendment to the U.S. Constitution.
Source: Wikimedia Commons
Attribution: National Archives of the United States
License: Public Domain

2.5.1. The Due Process Clause

The due process clause of the 14th Amendment asserts that "No state shall make or enforce any law which shall abridge the privileges or immunities of citizens of the United States; nor shall any state deprive any person of life, liberty, or property, without due process of law." It mirrors the 5th Amendment which places similar obligations on the federal government. This clause has been used to guarantee fundamental rights that are not specifically enumerated in the U.S. Constitution.

In 1965, the Supreme Court heard the case *Griswold v. Connecticut*, in which an 1879 law that banned contraceptives was challenged. The Connecticut law not only outlawed the use of contraceptives but also forbade the promotion and provision of "any drug, medicinal article or instrument for the purposes of preventing conception."[33] The case was brought by a Yale Medical School doctor and the director of Planned Parenthood in Connecticut after they were fined for providing contraceptives to married couples. In a 7-2 opinion, the Supreme Court ruled that, although a right to privacy is not enumerated in the U.S. Constitution, one can be inferred from the rights that are enumerated. The Court used the Due Process Clause of the 14th Amendment, along with several other amendments, to effectively create such a right and declare the Connecticut law unconstitutional. The Court noted

> *Due Process Clause*:
> Found in the 5th and 14th Amendments to the U.S. Constitution. It states that no one shall be "deprived of life, liberty or property without due process of law."

32 Kenneth R. Thomas, *Federalism, State Sovereignty, and the Constitution: Basis and Limits of Congressional Power,* Congressional Research Service, September 23, 2013, https://fas.org/sgp/crs/misc/RL30315.pdf.
33 *Griswald v. Connecticut* 381 U.S. 479 (1965), United States Supreme Court, https://supreme.justia.com/cases/federal/us/381/479.

that the 14th Amendment protects individuals from arbitrary or capricious denials of their liberty and that there is a realm of family life the government cannot enter without substantial justification. This right to privacy became the foundation on which other reproductive rights cases were built, including *Eisenstadt v. Baird* (1972), which ruled that states cannot ban the use of contraceptives by anyone. In writing the majority opinion, Justice William J. Brennan, Jr. wrote, "it is the right of the individual, married or single, to be free from unwarranted governmental intrusion into matters so fundamentally affecting a person as the decision whether to bear or beget a child."[34]

The Supreme Court's assertion of a right to privacy set a precedent for the later, much more contentious, case *Roe v. Wade* (1973). Jane Roe (a fictitious name) brought a class action law suit challenging a Texas law that outlawed abortion. Roe's lawyers based their legal case on the word

> *Roe v. Wade (1973)*:
> Supreme Court ruling that the 14th Amendment incorporates a right to privacy, which includes a woman's right to choose abortion.

"liberty" contained in the Due Process Clauses of the 5th and 14th Amendments, arguing that the law violated Roe's right to privacy. While recognizing the "sensitive and emotional nature of the abortion controversy," the Court ultimately ruled in Roe's favor. The Court noted that the Due Process Clause of the 14th Amendment protects the right to privacy against state action and that a woman's right to choose an abortion falls within that right. At the same time, the Court recognized that states have a legitimate interest in protecting the health of pregnant women as well as the "potentiality of human life" so these interests should be weighed against the right to privacy. For that reason, the Court ruled that, while states could not regulate abortion during the first trimester of pregnancy, they could regulate it during the second trimester to protect maternal health and during the third trimester to protect potential life. The Court later modified this ruling in *Planned Parenthood of Southeastern Pa. v. Casey* (1992), which established the "undue burden" test. This meant that, under the 14th Amendment, the pregnant woman has a constitutional right to abortion and cannot be unduly burdened by state interference prior to the viability of the fetus.

2.5.2 The Equal Protection Clause

Like the Due Process Clause, the Equal Protection Clause of the 14th amendment has been cited in numerous court cases and has been used as a vehicle to guarantee fundamental rights. As a facet of intergovernmental relations, it declares that states shall not "deny to any person within its jurisdiction the equal protection of the laws." Ratified in 1868, the objective of this clause was to prevent states from discriminating against Black Americans. While some states continued to find ways to deny or curtail the civil rights of their citizens, the Supreme Court has, over time,

---

34   *Eisenstadt v. Baird*, 405 U.S. 438 (1972), United States Supreme Court, https://supreme.justia.com/cases/federal/us/405/438.

used the Equal Protection Clause to reinforce and extend protections to prohibit discrimination generally.

Despite later rulings that favored equal rights, however, a landmark Supreme Court case in 1896 held that racial segregation did not violate the constitution. The case *Plessy v. Ferguson* revolved around the question of whether a Louisiana law that required separate streetcars for white and Black passengers was constitutional. The Separate Car Act (1890) stipulated that white and Black passengers must travel in separate cars but that the cars should be equal in terms of facilities. Plessy, who was only 1/8 Black, tested the law by sitting in a whites-only car and was fined for doing so. In this case, the Supreme Court denied Plessy's appeal on the grounds that separate-but-equal laws did not imply the inferiority of Black people

Plessy v. Ferguson (1896): Supreme Court case that upheld the constitutionality of racial segregation under the "separate but equal" doctrine. This led to the enactment of numerous state laws that discriminated against black Americans.

Brown v Board of Education (1954): Supreme Court case that overturned Plessy v. Ferguson. The Court declared that the "separate-but-equal" doctrine violated the Equal Protection Clause in the 14th Amendment.

and, therefore, did not violate the equal protection clause. The Court also reasoned that the 14th Amendment was intended to protect civil rights, such as voting,

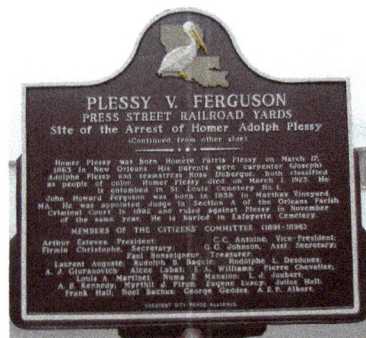

Figure 2.17: Back of the marker placed Feb. 12, 2009 recalling the arrest of Homer Plessy for violating Louisiana's segregationist 1890 Separate Car Act. His act of civil disobedience was planned by the Comité des Citoyens (Committee of Citizens) (1891-96). They financed Plessy's legal challenge. John Howard Ferguson, born in 1838 in Martha's Vineyard, MA., appointed judge in Section A of the Orleans Parish Criminal Court in 1892, ruled against Plessy in November, 1892.

Source: Wikimedia Commons
Attribution: User "Skywriter"
License: CC BY-SA 3.0

but not social rights, like sitting in a railroad car. The *Plessy v. Ferguson* opinion enshrined the "separate-but-equal principle" and opened the door to a plethora of "Jim Crow" state laws designed to restrict African American rights. This decision was not overturned until 1954.

The groundbreaking case that reversed *Plessy* was *Brown v. Board of Education* (1954). Oliver Brown brought this class action suit against the Board of Education in Topeka, Kansas. When Brown's daughter was denied access to an all-white elementary school, Brown's lawsuit claimed that schools for Black children were not equal to those for white children, therefore educational segregation violated the 14th Amendment's Equal Protection Clause. When it reached the Supreme Court for decision, the Court combined a total of five similar cases from other states and issued a unanimous opinion. Chief Justice Earl Warren wrote, "We conclude that, in the field of public education, the doctrine of 'separate but equal' has no place. Separate educational facilities are inherently unequal..." and affirmed that segregation deprives students' "...equal protection of the laws guaranteed by the Fourteenth Amendment."[35] The Court then remanded the case to lower courts to require compliance "with all deliberate speed." Although the ruling did not have an immediate effect, it laid the groundwork for the civil rights movement and established a precedent for other civil rights cases.

Two such cases involved the right to marry. In *Loving v. Virginia* (1967), an interracial couple challenged a state law that banned marriage between Blacks and whites, known as "antimiscegenation" laws. After marrying in Washington, D.C. in 1958, the couple returned to their home state of Virginia and were subsequently charged with unlawful cohabitation. They were sentenced to one year in prison, a sentence suspended on the condition that the couple would leave Virginia and not return together for at least 25 years. The couple returned to Washington, D.C. where they could live legally but later decided to sue in an effort to overturn the Virginia law. When the case reached the Supreme Court in 1967, the Court overturned the couple's conviction and invalidated laws prohibiting interracial marriage in 15 other states. The Court ruled that the Virginia

Figure 2.18: Interracial couple
Source: Unsplash
Attribution: Jakob Owens
License: Unsplash License

law violated both the Due Process Clause and the Equal Protection Clause of the 14th Amendment. The Court asserted that the law was based on racial discrimination and was designed to "maintain White Supremacy."[36] In a unanimous opinion, Chief Justice Warren also wrote, "we find the racial classifications in these statutes repugnant to the Fourteenth Amendment."[37]

A more recent case involving the right to marry is *Obergefell v. Hodges* (2015). In this case, same-sex couples in Michigan, Kentucky, Ohio, and Tennessee sued to overturn their states' laws that defined marriage as a union between one man and one woman. Federal District Courts in each

Obergefell v. Hodges (2015): Supreme Court ruling that the Due Process Clause in the 14th Amendment includes the right to marry for same-sex couples.

state agreed that denying same-sex couples the right to marry violated the 14th Amendment, but rulings in all of these cases were reversed by the Sixth Circuit Court of Appeals. When the case reached the Supreme Court in 2015, its 5-4 opinion declared that the 14th Amendment requires states to license a marriage between two people of the same sex and also recognize a marriage between two people of the same sex when their marriage was lawfully performed out-of-state.

---

35   *Brown v. Board of Education of Topeka*, 347 U.S. 483 (1954), United States Supreme Court, https://supreme.justia.com/cases/federal/us/347/483.
36   *Loving v. Virginia*, 388 U.S. 1 (1967), United States Supreme Court, https://supreme.justia.com/cases/federal/us/388/1.
37   *Loving v. Virginia*, 388 U.S. 1 (1967), fn. 11.

Figure 2.19: Same-sex marriage
Source: Unsplash
Attribution: In Lieu & In View Photography
License: Unsplash License

The Court explained that failure to do so would deny same-sex couples equal protection under the law. In strongly worded dissents, however, the minority rejected this view. Chief Justice Roberts argued that no prior decisions had changed the core meaning of marriage and that the majority's opinion conflicted with the right of religious liberty, while Justice Scalia attacked the majority opinion as "lacking even a thin veneer of law."[38] Today, several states and courts do not accept same-sex marriage as a settled issue. As of 2017, eight counties in Alabama and one county in Texas, for example, still refused to issue marriage licenses to same-sex couples.

Actions by some states to restrict civil rights is not universal, however. In recent years, state courts have increasingly relied on state constitutions to promote civil rights and liberties beyond what is guaranteed under federal law and the U.S. Bill of Rights. G. Alan Tarr points out that "the most recent development involving the exercise of state judicial power was the emergence in the early 1970s of the new judicial federalism."[39] This development initially occurred in reaction to changes in the composition of the Supreme Court. When Warren Burger replaced Earl Warren as Chief Justice in 1969, some feared that the new Court might erode some of the rights and liberties that had been gained. As a result, civil liberties groups began pursuing their cases in state courts, building their claims on protections contained in state constitutions. This trend has grown significantly over time to become a standard practice. From 1950 to 1969, there were only 10 cases in which state judges relied on state guarantees of rights to afford greater protection than was available under the federal Constitution, but between 1970 and 2020, they did so in more than 2,000 cases.[40] Today, the federal government sets constitutional minimum standards to ensure the protection of fundamental rights, though states can choose to build upon that base to provide additional protections for state citizens. New judicial federalism has, therefore, created substantial opportunities for state courts to develop their own bodies of civil-liberties law independently.[41]

38   *Obergefell v. Hodges,* 576 U.S. (2015), United States Supreme Court, https://supreme.justia.com/cases/federal/us/576/14-556.
39   G. Alan Tarr, "Judicial Federalism in the United States: structure, jurisdiction and operation" *Journal of Constitutional Research,* Vol. 2, No. 3 (September/December 2015).
40   G. Alan Tarr, *State Constitutional Rights Federalism,* Center for the Study of Federalism, https://encyclopedia.federalism.org/index.php?title=State_Constitutional_Rights_Federalism.
41   G. Alan Tarr, *State Constitutional Rights Federalism.*

2.6 CONCLUSION

This chapter has shown that, since the founding of the Republic, the federal judiciary has played a significant role in determining the balance of power between national and state governments. For most of its history, the Supreme Court has interpreted Congress' constitutional authority broadly and has generally ruled in favor of increasing that authority. Notwithstanding the 10th Amendment's clear purpose that powers not delegated to the national government in the Constitution are reserved to the states, the Supreme Court has expanded federal authority largely through its interpretation of the Commerce Clause, Spending Clause, and the 14th Amendment to the Constitution.

In recent years, however, the Supreme Court is reversing this trend by becoming more willing to place limits on federal power, thereby having an impact on the direction of intergovernmental relations. Beginning in the 1990s, with cases such as *United States v. Lopez*, the Court has acted to revive the vertical division of power within federalism by protecting state authority. This is not to say that the Supreme Court has overturned centuries of precedent responsible for enhancing federal powers but that there has been some degree of rebalancing in federal-state relations. This rebalancing has also been supplemented by trends toward new judicial federalism, which describes how state courts have become more active in protecting civil rights and liberties based on state law and state constitutions. So, while the role of the Supreme Court in shaping the legal aspects of intergovernmental relations remains pivotal, American judicial federalism continues to promote both national uniformity and state diversity in the administration of justice.[42] Chapter 3 will further explore the political dimensions of intergovernmental relations.

REFLECTION QUESTIONS

1. Debates concerning the role of the federal judiciary in the new Republic were contentious from the start. What were the main arguments presented by the Federalists and the Anti-Federalists?

2. Describe the landmark case, *Marbury v. Madison*. What is the significance of this case for the power of the federal judiciary?

3. The 10th Amendment asserts that powers not delegated to the national government are reserved to the states, but federal power has expanded under the Commerce Clause and the Spending Clause. Explain how this has occurred.

4. How have Supreme Court decisions promoted civil rights and liberties in the United States? Which parts of the U.S. Constitution have been used to protect those rights?

5. What is "new judicial federalism?" Describe Supreme Court opinions that illustrate this trend.

42   G. Alan Tarr, "Judicial Federalism in the United States: structure, jurisdiction and operation."

BIBLIOGRAPHY

Abrahamson, Shirley S. "State Constitutional Law, New Judicial Federalism, and the Rehnquist Court" *Cleveland State Law Review*, Vol. 51, Issue 3, Article 4, https:// engagedscholarship.csuohio.edu/cgi/viewcontent.cgi?article=1317&context=clevst lrev.

Bill of Rights Institute, *United States v. Lopez* (1995), https://billofrightsinstitute.org/e- lessons/united-states-v-lopez-1995.

Brutus, "Essay No. 1," October 18, 1787, in Herbert J. Storing, ed., *The Complete Anti-Federalist* (Chicago: The University of Chicago Press, 1981) 2:363–372.

Brutus, "Essay No. 14" March 6, 1788, in *The Complete Anti-Federalist*, 2:363–372

Brutus, "Essay No. 15" March 20, 1788, in *The Complete Anti-Federalist*, 2:363–372

Edquist. David J. and Jeffrey E. Mark, "Analysis: U.S. Supreme Court Upholds the Affordable Care Act: Roberts Rules?" *The National Law Review* March 8, 2021, Vol. XI, No. 67, https://www.natlawreview.com/article/analysis-us-supreme-court-upholds-affordable- care-act-roberts-rules.

Hamilton, Alexander or James Madison, *Federalist 49*, February 5, 1788, https://avalon. law.yale.edu/18th_century/fed49.asp.

Hamilton, Alexander, *Federalist 78*, May 28, 1788, https://avalon.law.yale.edu/18th_ century/fed78.asp.

Hamilton, Alexander *Federalist 81*, June 25, 1788, https://avalon.law.yale.edu/18th_ century/fed81.asp.

Hamilton, Alexander *Final Version of the Report on the Subject of Manufactures*, 5 December 1791, https://founders.archives.gov/documents/ Hamilton/01-10-02-0001-0007.

Herman J. Herbert, Jr., "The General Welfare Clauses in the Constitution of the United States", *Fordham L. Rev. 390* (1938), https://ir.lawnet.fordham.edu/flr/vol7/iss3/5.

Lawson, Gary and Neil S. Siegel, "Necessary and Proper Clause," *Interactive Constitution* https://constitutioncenter.org/interactive-constitution/interpretation/article-i/ clauses/754.

Legal Information Institute, Cornell Law School, *Commerce Clause*, https://www.law. cornell.edu/wex/commerce_clause.

Lunder, Erika K. and Jennifer Staman, *NFIB v. Sebelius: Constitutionality of the Individual Mandate*, Congressional Research Service, September 3, 2012, https://fas. org/sgp/crs/misc/R42698.pdf.

Madison, James, *Letter to Thomas Jefferson*, October 24, 1787. https://founders. archives.gov/documents/Jefferson/01-12-02-0274.

Madison, James *Federalist 10*, November 23, 1787. https://avalon.law.yale.edu/18th_ century/fed10.asp.

Madison James, *Federalist 48*, February 1, 1788, https://avalon.law.yale.edu/18th_

century/fed48.asp.

Tarr, G. Alan "Judicial Federalism in the United States: structure, jurisdiction and operation" Journal of Constitutional Research, Vol. 2, No. 3 (September/December 2015).

Thomas, Kenneth R. *Federalism, State Sovereignty, and the Constitution: Basis and Limits of Congressional Power*, Congressional Research Service, September 23, 2013, https://fas.org/sgp/crs/misc/RL30315.pdf

Treanor, William M. "The Genius of Hamilton and the Birth of the Modern Theory of the Judiciary" in *Cambridge Companion to the Federalist*, Jack Rakove and Colleen Sheehan eds. (Cambridge: Cambridge University Press 2020) 464–514.

century/fed48.asp.

3

Political Dimensions of Intergovernmental Relations

Neena Banerjee and Nandan K. Jha

Figure 3.1: Capital Hill
Source: Pixabay
Attribution: User "cytis"
License: Pixabay License

LEARNING OBJECTIVES

- Demonstrate knowledge of the key players involved in the American intergovernmental system responsible for developing and implementing public policy.

- Demonstrate an understanding of how multiple levels of governing units and interests engage in and exercise influence over each other in decision-making within the structure of the American intergovernmental network.

- Demonstrate knowledge of intergovernmental lobbying by subnational government interest groups to influence intergovernmental programs.

- Demonstrate knowledge of political parties' roles and the political system's influence on intergovernmental relations and policy management.

- Demonstrate an understanding of all the above political and intergovernmental elements in a practical sense by analyzing the public policy response to the Covid-19 pandemic.

KEY TERMS

Public Policy	Electoral College
Intergovernmental Programs	Interest Groups
Bureaucracy	Intergovernmental Lobbying
Policy Implementation	Conflict
Public Interest Groups	Politics
Political Parties	Covid-19
Political System	Congress
Courts	Elections

3.1 INTRODUCTION

Chapter 3 delves into how intergovernmental politics are conducted as a key dimension of IGR within the foundational structures of federalism, as described in Chapter 1, and the legal boundaries that a federal system operates in, a topic covered in Chapter 2. Understanding the scope and nature of intergovernmental relations politics has become paramount due to the growing levels of interaction between the federal and subnational governments in domestic policy making and public services provision. The major subnational actors include state legislatures, governors, state courts, state bureaucracies, local governments, and regional independent agencies. Private and nongovernmental agencies are also important players within the federal structure. While the distribution of power between the federal and subnational governments is determined and regulated by the U.S. Constitution, the actual dynamics of intergovernmental relations depend on subnational government

Politics: Politics in the context of intergovernmental relations in a federal system broadly refers to ongoing interactions among various levels of governments as they share the powers and responsibilities to decide policies in such a system. The nature and extent of power and influence exercised by various actors of intergovernmental politics often determine the outcome of a policy decision. Since various levels of governments may desire different outcomes from a policy decision, there is always potential for conflict when they engage with one another.

Figure 3.2: President Donald J. Trump participates in an agricultural roundtable with members of Congress and state governors, in the Cabinet Room at the White House, Thursday, April 12, 2018, in Washington, D.C.
Source: Wikimedia Commons
Attribution: Joyce N. Boghosian
License: Public Domain

policy prerogatives vis-à-vis the federal government. Furthermore, the degrees of collaboration or adversarialism that characterize relationships between national and subnational governments are often due to divergences in their policy prerogatives. Policy prerogatives are usually understood in terms of power, responsibilities, and resources that can be combined to capture the degree of authority available to regional governments and shape the territorial balance of power within a country. Nevertheless, neither constitutional structures nor new regional policy prerogatives are the sole determinants of intergovernmental relations dynamics. Informal institutions, such as subnational coalitions, interests, and local political clientelism, are particularly relevant to understanding the actual balance of power between national and subnational governments and among subnational levels. In recent years, policy disagreements have caused the federal government, and occasionally the president himself, to retaliate and take punitive actions against states for their decisions to go with policy preferences that diverge from the preferences of the federal government. As noted by Greg Goelzhauser and David M. Konisky (2020), such retaliation, which scholars have termed as "punitive federalism," involved the federal government's using its formal powers to punish states.[1]

Policy decisions in a federal system, therefore, are made in a complex and dynamic environment characterized by dispersed authority, overlapping jurisdictions, politics, rivalry, competition, cooperation, conflict, integration, and differentiation.[2] It is a complex arena where numerous actors try to leverage their influence over intergovernmental decisions through communications and networking with the goal of building the desired consensus and outcomes. Nevertheless, there are always disagreements and cross-purpose operations. Conflict is an expected and normal occurrence in IGR, and the federal Constitution provides a judiciary for moderating such conflicts. It is precisely because of the po-

Public policy: The term public policy refers to actions / inactions that are authorized by the government in addressing public problems / issues.

Conflict: It refers to situations characterized by various levels of governments having different expected outcomes from a policy decision and disagreements over the same when they engage with one another.

---

1   See Greg Goelzhauser and David M. Konisky, "The State of American Federalism 2019–2020: Polarized and Punitive Intergovernmental Relations." *Publius: The Journal of Federalism*, 50, no. 3 (2020): 311–343.
2   See Vincent L. Marando and Patricia S. Florestano, Intergovernmental Management in Naomi B. Lynn and Aaron B. Wildavsky (Eds.) *Public Administration: The State of the Discipline*. Chatham House Publishers (1990): 288.

tential for conflict that consultation, bargaining, negotiation, and compromise are vital aspects of IGR. Politics is at the heart of such interactions; therefore, the distribution and exercise of political influence on intergovernmental relations is an important topic to explore within IGR.[3]

The goal of this chapter is to discuss the political dimensions of IGR, including the roles, behaviors, and interconnections of many actors who have the power to influence decisions on intergovernmental programs. The chapter is organized as follows: First, we describe the various institutional actors involved with the intergovernmental system who develop and implement public policy and render administrative services. The mechanisms through which national and subnational governments, and interests, engage and exercise influence over each other to have an impact on intergovernmental programs is also explored. Next, we discuss the role of interest groups, with a special focus on government interest groups at the subnational levels and how they engage in intergovernmental lobbying. In the following section, we focus on the roles and influence of political parties on the political system in states and how these forces shape intergovernmental relations and policy management. Finally, we examine federal and subnational governments' response to the Covid-19 pandemic through the lens of intergovernmental relations politics.

3.2 INSTITUTIONAL ACTORS IN INTERGOVERNMENTAL POLITICS IN A FEDERAL SYSTEM

A federal system's intergovernmental politics involve many levels of political actors as these groups share the powers and responsibilities to decide policies; with power comes influence. The nature and extent of such influence exercised by various intergovernmental politics actors often determines policy decision outcomes. However, since various levels of government may desire different outcomes from a policy decision, there is always potential for conflict when they engage with one another. As noted by Elizabeth D. Frederickson, Stephanie L. Witt, and David C. Nice in *The Politics of Intergovernmental Relations*, the scope of conflict, including its size and extent, is determined by not only the number, type, and level of government actors but also the number of nongovernmental actors who are involved. Changes to the scope of conflict regarding a policy decision leads to corresponding changes in the balance of power among the different stakeholders whose engagement with one another can range from adversarial (when the scope of conflict grows) to collaborative (when the scope of conflict narrows). Thus, the institutional actors involved in intergovernmental politics seek out the scope of conflict and decision-making arenas most likely to produce a desired policy

---

3   See Elizabeth D. Frederickson, Stephanie L. Witt and David C. Nice, *The Politics of Intergovernmental Relations*, Third Edition, Birkdale Publishers (2016): 43–48.

decision.[4] Understanding who these institutional actors are at the national and subnational levels is therefore critical to developing a better understanding of the nature of influence they exert in policy decision-making in the domestic context.

Figure 3.3: Obama told a gathering of the nation's governors in the State Dining Room of the White House.
Source: Wikimedia Commons
Attribution: Pete Souza
License: Public Domain

3.2.1 Institutional Actors at the National Level

3.2.1.1 The Presidency/The Executive

The leadership and actions of the federal government's executive branch in creating intergovernmental programs has grown substantially with the emergence of an "executive-centered era."[5] As head of the executive branch, the office of the president is vested with enormous power to lead the federal government's legislative priorities. The Constitution clearly established the authority of the president to exercise legislative leadership on specific matters. As noted by James E. Anderson in Public Policymaking: An Introduction, the expansion of such authority in other policy domains, however, is accepted as a political necessity due to the fragmentation of authority in Congress, which prevents it from moving swiftly on legislative matters. On the other hand, Congress in the 20th century has largely looked to the

---

4   See Elizabeth D. Frederickson, Stephanie L. Witt and David C. Nice, *The Politics of Intergovernmental Relations*, Third Edition, Birkdale Publishers (2016): 44–45. Elmer Eric Schattschneider. "The semisovereign people." Hinsdale, IL: Drysdale Press (1975). Dan Wood. "Federalism and Policy Responsiveness: The Clear Air Case." *Journal of Politics*, 53: 851–859.
5   See James E. Anderson. *Public Policymaking: An Introduction*. Cengage Learning (2015): 53.

president to offer recommendations on legislative agendas and priorities. Presidents, for their part, have acted on such opportunities afforded by Congress to put forth preferred policies for the legislative body to authorize with varied amounts of success. The president usually leads the negotiation and bargaining efforts with Congress and is supported in this process by the executive office of the president comprising several agencies, including the Office of Intergovernmental Affairs, Office of Management and Budget, Council of Economic Advisors, National Security Council, and the Office of Policy Development, among several others.[6] While politics is a central feature of legislative bargaining between the president and members of Congress, numerous instances have occurred when the president has directly engaged with states and local governments to build support for their legislative priorities and pressure members of Congress to enact laws on such policies. Recent examples include President George W. Bush's engagement with multiple levels of government to push for bipartisan support in Congress for passage of the No Child Left Behind Act in 2001. President Obama, during his terms in office, directly engaged in intergovernmental relations politics to build support for the passage of his signature initiative, the

Intergovernmental programs: intergovernmental programs span federal, state, and local government. Such programs are generally created by the Congress as it is one key federal government institution that comprises elected members who represent state and local government interests at the national level.

Figure 3.4: President Joe Biden calls Texas Governor Greg Abbott

Source: Wikimedia Commons
Attribution: The White House
License: Public Domain

Affordable Care Act (known more colloquially as "Obamacare") in 2010. Finally, President Trump similarly relied on intergovernmental politics to build a coalition of state and local government agencies and interest groups to attempt to invalidate the ACA. A final verdict on the case rested with the U.S. Supreme Court. In June, 2021, the SCOTUS ruled that the challengers to the ACA lacked standing, which effectively threw out the lawsuit argued by 18 Republican state attorneys general and the Trump Administration.

Figure 3.6: Barack Obama signing the Patient Protection and Affordable Care Act at the White House

Source: Wikimedia Commons
Attribution: Pete Souza
License: Public Domain

---

6   United States Government Manual, 2020 available at Home Page (usgovernmentmanual.gov); James E. Anderson, *Public Policymaking: An Introduction*. Cengage Learning, 8th ed. (2015): 53–55.

Figure 3.5: First Cabinet of President Barack Obama
Source: Wikimedia Commons
Attribution: Chuck Kennedy
License: Public Domain

The Electoral College system shapes the direct engagement of presidents in subnational politics; it does so by creating strong incentives for presidential candidates, and sitting presidents facing reelection, to be sensitive to interests that are influential in highly populated, politically-competitive states. We cover the Electoral College system's influence, along with the topic of political parties on intergovernmental politics, in greater detail below.

3.2.1.2 The Congress

Congress is the architect of intergovernmental programs by virtue of its being the federal government's legislative branch. Members of Congress are a key force who make important decisions affecting how intergovernmental relations are conducted with various state governments.[7] The two primary roles that members of Congress perform are (a) to engage in the task of representing their constituents, and (b) to

Congress: It collectively includes the Senate and the House of Representatives of the legislative branch of the federal government. One key means by which the Congress influences politics in intergovernmental relations is by providing legislative backing to policies and programs.

---

7   See Aaron Wildavsky. *The Politics of the Budgetary Process* (2nd ed). Boston, MA: Little, Brown (1974). Elizabeth D. Frederickson, Stephanie L. Witt and David C. Nice, *The Politics of Intergovernmental Relations*, Third Edition, Birkdale Publishers (2016): 62–65.

Figure 3.7: Unofficial seal of the United States House of Representatives, based directly on the Great Seal of the United States. The official seal depicts the House side of the Capitol building, but this is still a commonly seen.
Source: Wikimedia Commons
Attribution: U.S. Government
License: Public Domain

undertake the political task of lawmaking.[8] Their work, therefore, has immense implications for state and local governments whose interests are generally addressed by members of Congress when drafting broad national policies. Between the two chambers of Congress, the Senate tends to be more attentive to the interests of the state governments than does the House of Representatives. Senators do so because they tend to be more powerful than those representatives in the House, where power primarily resides with the Speaker of the House and the House Majority leader. Unlike members of the House, who represent single districts within states, Senators represent entire states; consequently, they represent diverse constituencies requiring broader appeal to win reelection. Since two senators represent a whole state in Congress, they also have greater need

Figure 3.8: President Donald J. Trump welcomes Republican members of Congress Friday, May 8, 2020, to a meeting in the State Dining Room of the White House.
Source: Wikimedia Commons
Attribution: Shealah Craighead
License: Public Domain

8   Troy E. Smith. "Intergovernmental Lobbying: How Opportunistic Actors Create a Less Structured and Balanced Federal System" in Paul Posner and Timothy Conlan (Eds.) *Intergovernmental Management for the 21st Century*. Washington, DC: Brookings Institution Press (2008): 318.

for information to understand state-specific issues.[9] As Walter A. Rosenbaum illustrated in *Energy, Politics, and Public Policy*, when making important policy decisions, members of Congress—in both the House and the Senate—are not just motivated by their own values, policy preferences, and reelection prospects; they also try to balance competing political powers and pressures, local versus national interests, and complex choices involving loyalty towards their own parties or congressional leaders versus loyalty to power centers at the state and local levels.[10] These subnational governments also receive critical funding support from the federal government which allocates benefits in such areas as building highways, research facilities, and public buildings. Congress either decides or is involved in decisions concerning both funding amounts and restrictions to be placed on the recipients of federal funding and also in monitoring the usage of federal funds by subnational governments. Finally, using its oversight authority, Congress also monitors federal policies and programs such as Social Security, veterans' benefits, and regulatory or other programs that are implemented by the bureaucracy at the subnational levels.[11] Therefore, the work of Congress has enormous implications for whether subnational (state and local) interests are reflected in making intergovernmental programs.

3.2.1.3 The Federal Courts

The federal courts are also key players in creating intergovernmental programs. Through their powers of judicial review and statutory interpretation in cases that are brought before them, federal courts have historically played an important role in shaping the nature and content of intergovernmental programs. Furthermore, in matters pertaining to the allocation of powers between national and state governments, the federal courts have at times interposed when such powers were not clearly articulated or when questions on the permissibility of national or state governmental actions occasioned disagreements. A host of landmark Supreme Court federalism-related cases are noteworthy in this regard. These cases have involved the commerce clause, the necessary and proper clause, sovereign immunity, and preemptive cases. Federal courts' and, most importantly, the

> **Courts**: It refers to a decentralized system of judiciary as a third and co-equal branch of government in the US. It consists of both an individual state system of judiciary as well as federal court system at the national level. The federal courts are key players in the politics of creating intergovernmental programs. Through its powers of judicial review and statutory interpretation in cases that are brought before them, federal courts have historically played an important role in shaping the nature and content of intergovernmental programs. Furthermore, in matters pertaining to the allocation of powers between national and state governments, the federal courts have chimed in from time to time when such powers were not clearly articulated or when disagreements have emerged over the permissibility of actions taken by either the national or state governments.

9   Troy E. Smith. "Intergovernmental Lobbying: How Opportunistic Actors Create a Less Structured and Balanced Federal System" in Paul Posner and Timothy Conlan (Eds.) *Intergovernmental Management for the 21st Century*. Washington, DC: Brookings Institution Press (2008): 317.

10   Walter A. Rosenbaum. *Energy Politics and Public Policy*. CQ Press (1987): 51.

11   James E. Anderson, *Public Policymaking: An Introduction*. Cengage Learning (2015): 52.

Supreme Court's involvement in federalism cases, however, can incur criticism. Although held to the standard of being apolitical, judges in numerous instances have invoked judicial activism by deeply and willingly involving themselves in policy and dispute resolution politics between national and subnational governments. The fact that their party affiliation, policy preferences, and values are typically taken into consideration when they are selected, whether by appointment or election, also influences their decisions. Scholars who have studied federalism cases historically have examined pro-national or pro-state bias among justices and the decisions they have rendered. The inconsistency in leanings from the Supreme Court when rendering decisions on federalism cases has also contributed to widespread skepticism about the objectivity of high court.[12] These issues are discussed in greater detail in Chapter 2, which focuses on intergovernmental relations' legal dimensions.

Figure 3.9: Panorama of the west facade of United States Supreme Court Building at dusk in Washington, D.C., USA.
Source: Wikimedia Commons
Attribution: Joe Ravi
License: CC BY-SA 3.0

3.2.1.4 The Federal Bureaucracy

The administrative agencies at the federal level are influential actors in legislative and policy process politics. The inseparability of politics from administration is proverbial these days, though earlier scholars viewed administrative agencies solely as implementers of policy/legislation, acting only after the "political" branches of the government passed laws.[13] More

12   Stephanie Lindquist and Pamela Corley. *National Policy Preferences and Judicial Review of State Statutes at the United States Supreme Court.* Publius. 43 (2): 151–178. Christopher Shortell. *The End of the Federalism Five? Statutory Interpretation and the Roberts Court.* Publius. 42 (3): 516-537. Elizabeth D. Frederickson, Stephanie L. Witt and David C. Nice, *The Politics of Intergovernmental Relations*, Third Edition, Birkdale Publishers (2016): 128.
13   See James E. Anderson, *Public Policymaking: An Introduction.* Cengage Learning (2015): 57–58. Terry Moe. "The politics of structural choice: toward a theory of public bureaucracy" in Oliver E. Williamson (ed.)

recent theories of public bureaucracy highlight its political side. In *The Politics of Structural Choice: Toward a Theory of Public Bureaucracy*, Terry Moe noted public bureaucracies' roles as political entities with political goals. One can best understand the role of federal bureaucracy in making intergovernmental programs by analyzing the structure as a political exchange system between interest groups, politicians, and bureaucrats.[14] Moe argued that politicians represent their constituencies, which consist of both passive voters and active interest groups. Unlike most passive voters, interest groups are well informed about structural issues of interest. As a result, they are active participants in any political exchange. The role these interest groups play in the political exchange process determines the structural design of intergovernmental programs. The presence of multiple interest groups competing for a policy will also result in winners and losers in the political exchange process. Political compromise would ensure the losing side has a second opportunity to participate in the policy's design, which it opposed in the bargaining process. The losing side then uses this opportunity to create conflicting structures,

Bureaucracy: Bureaucracy implies government agencies that comprise appointed officials. Bureaucracies implement public policies that are enacted by the legislative agencies. They also actively engage in policymaking as part of their regular job duties that include exercising their powers of implementation, regulation, adjudication, and discretion.

Figure 3.10: U.S. Department of State Seal
Source: Wikimedia Commons
Attribution: United States Department of State
License: Public Domain

intending to damage the effectiveness of the policy once it gets implemented. Bureaucratic agencies talk to interest groups for a variety of reasons. Statutory obligations are a key reason that prompts agencies to talk to interest groups; however, in order to advance their mission, some agency personnel seek out these groups to gain their political support and gather information. The interest groups, for their part, approach bureaucratic agencies to gain legislative alliances, implementation benefits, and long-term working relationships.[15] As a result, bureaucratic strategy and interest group initiatives are interdependent in the policymaking process. Below, we discuss interest groups' roles regarding intergovernmental relations politics in greater detail.

Organization Theory: From Chester Barnard to the Present and Beyond, New York: Oxford University Press.
14   John E. Chubb, *Interest Groups and the Bureaucracy: The Politics of Energy*. Stanford, CA. Stanford University Press (1983). Terry Moe. "The politics of structural choice: toward a theory of public bureaucracy" in Oliver E. Williamson, ed., *Organization Theory: From Chester Barnard to the Present and Beyond*. New York: Oxford University Press (1990).
15   John E. Chubb, *Interest Groups and the Bureaucracy: The Politics of Energy*. Stanford, CA. Stanford University Press (1983).

Figure 3.11: U.S. Secretary of Defense Leon E. Panetta, right, and U.S. Secretary of State Hillary Rodham Clinton meet with Filipino Foreign Affairs Secretary Albert del Rosario and Filipino Defense Secretary Voltaire Gazmin at the State Department in Washington, D.C., April 30, 2012.

Source: Wikimedia Commons
Attribution: Glenn Fawcett
License: Public Domain

Figure 3.12: Vice President Kamala Harris delivers remarks to Department of Defense personnel, with President Joe Biden and Secretary of Defense Lloyd J. Austin III, the Pentagon, Washington, D.C., Feb. 10, 2021.

Source: Wikimedia Commons
Attribution: U.S. Secretary of Defense
License: CC BY-SA 2.0

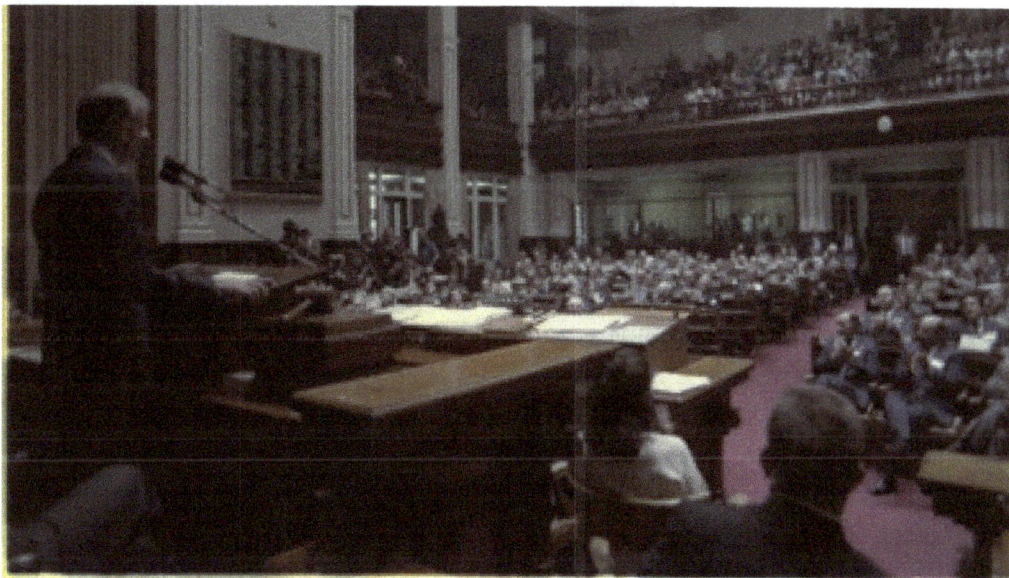

Figure 3.13: Jimmy Carter addresses the Georgia State Legislature at the Capitol in Atlanta, GA in 1979.

Source: Wikimedia Commons
Attribution: Unknown
License: Public Domain

3.2.2 Institutional Actors at the Subnational Levels

The states are important subnational actors who play influential roles in the federal system's operation. States' capacity to fulfill these roles and seek solutions to policy problems has been largely limited due to political and financial constraints.[16]

16   Ann O'M. Bowman and Richard C. Kearney. *The Resurgence of the States*. Englewood Cliffs, NJ: Prentice Hall (1986). Gary F. Moncrief and Peverill Squire. *Why States Matter: An Introduction to State Politics*. Lanham, MD: Rowan and Littlefield Publishers (2013). Elizabeth D. Frederickson, Stephanie L. Witt and David C. Nice, *The Politics of Intergovernmental Relations*, 3rd ed, Birkdale Publishers (2016): 121–161.

The cooperation and rivalry between the national government and the states, and between states themselves, create an evolving equilibrium that fundamentally shapes intergovernmental relations politics.[17] The U.S. Constitution sets the ground rules for national-state and inter-state relations in terms of sharing powers and responsibilities. However, lack of clarity in constitutional guidance on many key areas leaves room for disagreements between national and state governments and among state governments. As noted by Ann O' Bowman in her work *Trends and Issues in Interstate Cooperation*, disagreements also arise due to other factors, including disputes over policies, egos, personalities, reelection concerns of state and national officials, and states' self-interests when pursuing opportunities and resisting obstacles. Such disagreements over power and responsibilities are at the heart of IGR politics.[18] Scholars over the decades have analyzed the roles of state legislatures, executives, courts, and bureaucracies in managing intergovernmental disagreements. This chapter will explore their roles further below.

3.2.2.1 State Legislatures

State legislatures are at the forefront of intergovernmental politics. They largely determine the direction and nature of national-state, interstate, and state-local relationships ranging from being cooperative to adversarial. Historically, state legislatures have played an important role in supporting national policies whenever they found aligned interests or opposing ones due to disagreements over scope of authority or other disputes. The creation of the Interstate Highway System exemplifies cooperation between states and national government. On the other hand, conflict between the national government and states severely hindered the passage of civil rights legislation for various groups as well as school integration policy implementation and, more recently, the No Child Left Behind Act and the Affordable Care Act. State legislatures also are instrumental in determining the nature of interstate connections. States pursue self-interest, which dictates their decision to compete or cooperate with each other when tackling major problems. State officials determine the assessment of self-interest, officials including elected representatives in the state legislatures.[19] Finally, state legislatures also influence state-local relations. Local governments have only the powers clearly granted to them by the state legislatures, and local policies generally are subordinate to state policies. However, Home Rule and recent delegation of authority to local officials have allowed local governments to act without prior approval from state governments. At the same time, disagreements do arise between state and local governments due to political rivalries, state restrictions on local decision making,

17   Ann O'M Bowman, "Trends and Issues in Interstate Cooperation" in Lawrence O'Toole and Robert Christensen, eds., *American Intergovernmental Relations: Foundations, Perspectives, and Issues.* CQ Press (2013): 132.
18   Ann O'M Bowman, "Trends and Issues in Interstate Cooperation" in Lawrence O'Toole and Robert Christensen, eds., *American Intergovernmental Relations: Foundations, Perspectives, and Issues.* CQ Press (2013): 132.
19   Ann O'M Bowman, "Trends and Issues in Interstate Cooperation" in Lawrence O'Toole and Robert Christensen, eds., *American Intergovernmental Relations: Foundations, Perspectives, and Issues.* CQ Press (2013): 133.

and the controversial practice of redistricting by the state legislatures. Redistricting allows the majority party, who controls the process, to exaggerate and perpetuate its majority and so alter the flow of state transfers to local governments.[20] In this role, state legislatures are subjected to a major share of criticism directed at state governments in the larger context of IGR.

3.2.2.2 The Governors

State governors lead policy efforts and wear many hats, ranging among being the chief legislator, party leader, chief negotiator, ceremonial head, and crisis manager.[21] Before popular elections became widespread in the early 19th century, colonial governors were sometimes elected by state legislatures for tenure as short as two year terms, with limited or nonexistent veto power. Limited terms constrained the efforts of governors, who were thus unable to initiate the preparations needed to implement long-term programs. The term of governors has expanded since then, with 48 states (not including Vermont and New Hampshire) now having four year terms for governors.[22] The formal limits to their reelection (two term restrictions in most states) constrain governors from building long-term working relationships with leaders in the state legislators, which exacerbate the restrictions that the imposed term limits have on legislatures at the state level.[23] Finally, governors face additional restrictions in executing influence and control over policy initiatives and their implementation due to the widespread practice in many states of independently electing the heads of state executive agencies/bureaucracies. As a result, state executives do not owe their positions to the governors, and governors have limited control over the executive branch—a situation often resulting in disputes over policy priorities and coordination problems between the governors' offices and offices of other state executive agencies.[24] Despite these limitations, governors who are particularly popular with the public, and whose party holds a majority of seats in the state legislature, are well positioned to effect the success of policies at the subnational level by exercising leadership on policy and budgets.[25]

---

20   Elizabeth D. Frederickson, Stephanie L. Witt and David C. Nice, *The Politics of Intergovernmental Relations*, 3rd ed, Birkdale Publishers (2016): 217–218.

21   Thomas R. Dye and Susan A. McManus. Politics in States and Communities, 15th ed., Pearson (2015).

22   Elizabeth D. Frederickson, Stephanie L. Witt and David C. Nice, *The Politics of Intergovernmental Relations*, 3rd ed, Birkdale Publishers (2016): 140.

23   Alan Rosenthal, *The Best Job In Politics: Exploring How Governors Succeed as Policy Leaders*, Los Angeles, CA. Sage/CQ Press (2013): 33.

24   John A. Hamman. "Career Experience and Performing Effectively as Governor." *American Review of Public Administration*, 34, no. 2 (2004): 151–163, Gary F. Moncrief and Peverill Squire. *Why States Matter: An Introduction to State Politics*. Lanham, MD: Rowan and Littlefield Publishers (2013), Elizabeth D. Frederickson, Stephanie L. Witt and David C. Nice, *The Politics of Intergovernmental Relations*, 3rd ed, Birkdale Publishers (2016): 141.

25   Alan Rosenthal, *The Best Job In Politics: Exploring How Governors Succeed as Policy Leaders*, Los Angeles, CA. Sage/CQ Press (2013): 11, Thad Kousser and Justin H. Phillips. *The Power of American Governors: Winning on Budgets and Losing on Policies*. New York: Cambridge University Press (2012).

Figure 3.14: President Ronald Reagan, Nancy Reagan, and then Governor of Arkansas, Bill Clinton with Hillary Clinton in The Blue Room During a Dinner Honoring Nation's Governors on February 22, 1987.
Source: Wikimedia Commons
Attribution: White House Photographic Collection
License: Public Domain

3.2.2.3 State Courts

Courts are established to offer resolution to conflicts in society. In this role, they act as political institutions deeply involved in making public policy, comparable to the legislative and executive institutions.[26] Historically, federal and state courts have been involved in some of the most consequential policy decisions in the nation, including issues such as school integration, separation of church and state, voting rights, and the rights of women to obtain abortions. As Thomas Dye and Susan A. MacManus noted in *Politics in States and Communities*, in American politics the most important policy questions sooner or later reach the courts. State courts are particularly

Figure 3.15: Seal of the Supreme Court of Georgia
Source: Wikimedia Commons
Attribution: User "Fry1989"
License: Public Domain

important as they handle around 98% of all the nation's cases, especially the type of cases in which individual citizens are most likely involved. Although each court system is responsible for hearing certain types of cases, the interdependence of the court system is most visible in cases involving interpretations and implementation of principles laid out in the U.S. Constitution's Bill of Rights and 14th Amendment.[27] In the context of IGR, the states have periodically been recommended as the final

26   Thomas R. Dye and Susan A. McManus. *Politics in States and Communities*, 15th ed., Pearson (2015): 250.
27   Thomas R. Dye and Susan A. McManus. *Politics in States and Communities*, 15th ed., Pearson (2015): 250.

conflict arbiters over the national-state allocation of powers and responsibilities. As noted in the Federalist Papers Nos. 45 and 46, states and their citizens could oppose national policy or actions that create problems for a state using remedies such as "nullification," whereby states can declare the acts null and void due to constitutional violation by the national government, or through "interposition," whereby states can interpose themselves between the national government and the people of the state to block the national government from administering unconstitutional federal policies.[28] Although these possibilities have existed in theory, states have so far been unsuccessful in their efforts to invoke either of these two options, as the courts did not uphold them and because the Civil War effectively settled the nullification issues once and for all.[29] In addition to their roles in interpreting national policies, state courts also set the legal context of state-local relations by interpreting the state constitutional provisions pertaining to the relative authority of the state to its subgovernments. State constitutions generally assume that local governments are creatures of the states and receive their authority from state governments rather than directly from the people. Thus, local governments operate under a legal framework primarily based on state policies. Dillon's Rule, Charter Systems, Home Rule, Mandates, Incorporation, Annexation, and Consolidation are various mechanisms by which states shape the development and operation of local governments. These mechanisms are discussed in detail in Chapter 1. The state courts play an influential role when conflicts arise in state-local relations by offering resolutions to various disputes involving these various mechanisms of state influence on local governments.[30]

3.2.2.4 State Bureaucracies

Bureaucracies at the state and local levels are active players in IGR politics. In theory, bureaucracies implement policies only after legislative agencies enact them; in practice, however, bureaucracies actively engage in policymaking as part of their regular job duties, including exercising their powers of implementation, regulation, adjudication, and discretion.[31] In the last several decades, the growth of bureaucracies at all levels of government has increased as new offices are created to tackle such myriad issues as environmental protection, insurance and banking regulation, highway planning and construction, university governance, and school curriculum. Along with unprecedented growth, bureaucracies have seen increased professionalization through hiring more highly-educated employees with expertise in specific policy domains and advanced technical skills in applying

28 Alexander Hamilton, John Jay and James Madison, *The Federalist*. New York: Modern Library (1937), Parris N. Glendening and Mavis Mann Reeves, *Pragmatic Federalism*, 2nd ed, Pacific Palisades, CA: Palisades (1984): 55–57
29 Elizabeth D. Frederickson, Stephanie L. Witt and David C. Nice, *The Politics of Intergovernmental Relations*, 3rd ed, Birkdale Publishers (2016): 130.
30 Elizabeth D. Frederickson, Stephanie L. Witt and David C. Nice, *The Politics of Intergovernmental Relations*, 3rd ed, Birkdale Publishers (2016): 204–207.
31 Thomas R. Dye and Susan A. McManus. *Politics in States and Communities*, 15th ed., Pearson (2015): 224.

knowledge to appropriate bureaucratic actions. Even with advanced skills, however, compensation for bureaucrats at the state and local levels is lower than that of private sector employees in the same or similar positions.[32] Furthermore, a growing number of states now have at-will employment and are eliminating due-process protections to easily replace underperformers. However, opponents argue that such strategy makes bureaucracies vulnerable to political influence.[33] By allying with federal administrative agencies when pursuing federal objectives in states in return for federal grants, state bureaucracies become a powerful force in state politics and policymaking.[34]

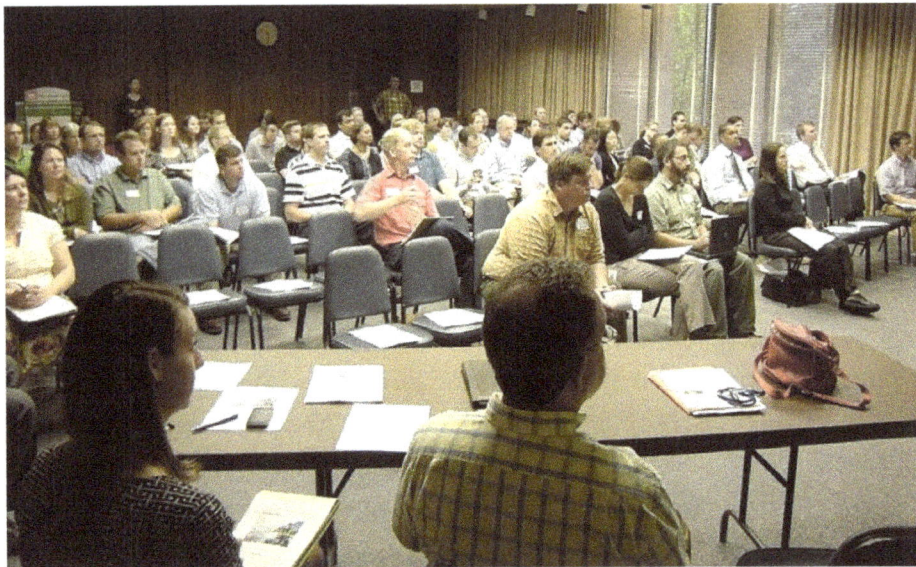

Figure 3.16: The Corps Savannah District issues permits under Section 404 of the Clean Water Act for any construction or development that involves the discharge of dredged or fill material into U.S. waters.

Source: Wikimedia Commons

Attribution: U.S. Army Corps of Engineers Savannah District

License: Public Domain

3.2.2.5 Regional Organizations

Over the years, regional organizations have been created to tackle problems that cover two or more states. These problems usually extend beyond individual states but are not nationwide in scope. These organizations are large enough to cover the area affected by the problem but not so large as to involve unaffected groups.[35] In describing regional organizations, Elizabeth Ferris and Daniel Petz noted in their work *In the Neighborhood: The Growing Role of Regional Organizations in Disaster Risk Management* that these organizations are established to cover the affected area without producing the excessive centralization that a completely

32   Thomas R. Dye and Susan A. McManus. *Politics in States and Communities*, 15th ed., Pearson (2015): 225.
33   Elizabeth D. Frederickson, Stephanie L. Witt and David C. Nice, *The Politics of Intergovernmental Relations*, 3rd ed, Birkdale Publishers (2016): 142.
34   Martha Derthick and Gary Bombardier, *Between States and Nation*, Washington DC: Brookings (1974).
35   Martha Derthick and Gary Bombardier, *Between States and Nation*, Washington DC: Brookings (1974).

national program might entail. While many of these organizations function under the direct influence of states, some operate under indirect state influence. These agencies are also the target of federal influence on matters that are under the agency's control. Notable examples of regional organizations include the Tennessee Valley Authority (TVA), Delaware River Basin Commission, and the various Regional Commissions for Economic Development. While some regional organizations have managed to accomplish more compared to others, a common roadblock they all encounter is suspicion from both national and state political actors concerning their true allegiance. Nationally, presidents and members of Congress fear these organizations as lobbying groups for state and local governments to extract federal resources. On their part, state government officials worry that regional organizations will be used to further federal objectives in the states and increase national control, thereby subjecting one state to undue influence from other participating states. States also fear that regional organizations have too much authority without comparable accountability and that these agencies will operate programs independently of similar state programs.[36]

3.2.2.6 Local Governments

The U.S Constitution does not mention local governments, which are regarded as creatures of the state governments with powers delegated to them by state constitutions or laws. A multitude of local governments (89,000 to be precise) operate under the legal control of states to provide citizens with numerous services, activities, and infrastructures ranging from schools to hospitals, libraries, ports, water, sewer, sports stadiums, and public safety services.[37] In addition to providing services, local governments are also responsible for collecting certain taxes and regulating its citizens. States vary in how they hold local elections of government officials whose functions, titles, and assigned responsibilities also vary greatly across the country. Although they operate under the legal control of states, local governments' counties, municipalities, special districts, and school districts exercise substantive autonomy and are, therefore, important players in the federal system. As Elizabeth Frederickson, Stephanie Witt, and David Nice noted in their work *The Politics of Intergovernmental Relations*, state governments are usually reluctant to exercise their legal authority over local governments who frequently exercise substantial political influence on state governments.[38] While state-local relations have remained mostly cordial over the years, disagreements or conflicts have occurred between state and local governments—of large cities particularly—over matters of grant mandates, political rivalries, and state-imposed restrictions on local decision-making. Direct demands for state intervention in local policy

---

36   Elizabeth Ferris and Daniel Petz. "In the neighborhood: the growing role of regional organizations in disaster risk management." Brookings Institution Press (2013). Elizabeth D. Frederickson, Stephanie L. Witt and David C. Nice, *The Politics of Intergovernmental Relations*, 3rd ed, Birkdale Publishers (2016): 188–189.
37   Thomas R. Dye and Susan A. McManus. *Politics in States and Communities*, 15th ed., Pearson (2015): 291.
38   Elizabeth D. Frederickson, Stephanie L. Witt and David C. Nice, *The Politics of Intergovernmental Relations*, 3rd ed, Birkdale Publishers (2016): 193.

from citizens dissatisfied with their local government's policy responses have also contributed to state-local conflict. Another central issue in state-local conflicts is legislative reallocation that the U.S. Supreme Court resolved through intervention. Their decision led to some improvements in the relations between states and large cities, although its long-term effects were not as extensive as everyone expected it to be.[39] Beyond their relations with state government, local governments have gained political influence largely due to the direct ties that proliferate between them and the national government. Although national-local relations have been a staple feature of American federalism dating back to 1787, they have grown to be more open, expansive, and meaningful during this century.[40] Several factors contributed to the growing national-local connections. These include a growing urban voting population base that has mobilized local political influence in Congressional and presidential elections. The state governments' reluctance and inability to solve costly local problems have pushed local governments to establish direct lines of contact with the national government to pursue national grants by offering themselves as allies willing to pursue federal objectives and spearhead implementation of important federal programs at the local level.[41] Despite conflicts over restrictions, coordination, and regulations associated with federal programs, the growing national-local relations in achieving policy goals have given local government more political weight in shaping intergovernmental relations within the federal system. Finally, local governments are a powerful force within the complex arena of inter-local relations. This complex local arena constituted 350 Metropolitan Statistical Areas (MSAs), with an average ranging from 170 local governments per MSA in the Northeastern region of the country to an average of 57 local government agencies per MSA in the Southern region. Additionally, rural areas hold various special-purpose and general-purpose governments.[42] The challenges and opportunities posed by an abundance of local governments and the extensive nature of inter-local politics have been a topic of great interest among scholars of public administration. Advocates of abundant local governments argue that they are manageable bureaucracies that promote interjurisdictional competition and bring efficiency in service delivery. These governments are more accessible to their communities and more likely to solve grassroot problems. Critics of abundant local governments argue that they lead to lack of coordination, unequal distribution of services, and greater inequities in resources among neighborhood governments.[43]

39   Elizabeth D. Frederickson, Stephanie L. Witt and David C. Nice, *The Politics of Intergovernmental Relations*, 3rd ed, Birkdale Publishers (2016): 218.

40   Elizabeth D. Frederickson, Stephanie L. Witt and David C. Nice, *The Politics of Intergovernmental Relations*, 3rd ed, Birkdale Publishers (2016): 221.

41   Elizabeth D. Frederickson, Stephanie L. Witt and David C. Nice, *The Politics of Intergovernmental Relations*, 3rd ed, Birkdale Publishers (2016): 223.

42   Elizabeth D. Frederickson, Stephanie L. Witt and David C. Nice, *The Politics of Intergovernmental Relations*, 3rd ed, Birkdale Publishers (2016): 251.

43   Elizabeth D. Frederickson, Stephanie L. Witt and David C. Nice, *The Politics of Intergovernmental Relations*, 3rd ed, Birkdale Publishers (2016): 275–276.

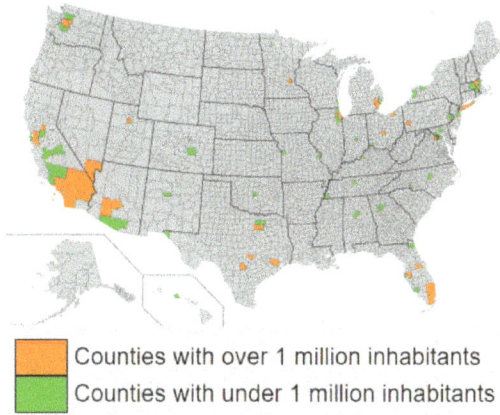

Figure 3.17: Each plot is one county within the United States. The largest counties by population are displayed in green and orange. Each county in the United States has its own local government that interacts with other local (city), regional (state), and the federal government.
Source: Wikimedia Commons
Attribution: User "Fluffy89502"
License: Public Domain

Counties with over 1 million inhabitants
Counties with under 1 million inhabitants

Figure 3.18: Decatur County Board of Education, 103 S West St, Bainbridge, Decatur County, Georgia
Source: Wikimedia Commons
Attribution: Michael Rivera
License: CC BY-SA 3.0

3.2.2.7 Private and Nongovernmental Entities

According to Frederickson, Witt, and Nice, the implementation of public policy in a contemporary context requires intersectoral engagement. This type of engagement usually occurs between federal, state, and local governments and their respective executive, legislative, and judicial branches on one hand and private and nongovernmental entities on the other. Scholars trace the evolution of inter-sector public policy implementation to the growth in citizens' demands for greater government services with tax funds. To meet such growing demands for service delivery, policy makers have sought blended implementation with cooperation from a network of private and nonprofit entities. This type of innovative service delivery through a collaborative multiple-actor network was necessary to avoid any appearance of a corresponding rise in the apparent size of government. However, the type and nature of collaboration and the degree of relational formality varies greatly between network members, leading to a variety of management mechanisms, political implications, and policy outcomes from such multi-actor implementation models.[44] Implementation of public policy in the 21st century,

> **Policy implementation**: It consists of governmental bureaucratic set-up to administer a given public policy or program. Policy implementation is integral part of federal, state, and local governments.

44   Elizabeth D. Frederickson, Stephanie L. Witt and David C. Nice, *The Politics of Intergovernmental Relations*, 3rd ed, Birkdale Publishers (2016): 279. Donald Kettle, "The Job of Government: Interweaving

therefore, has become, unsurprisingly, exceedingly complex. Chapter 6 focuses on understanding the complex web of networked providers and collaborative structures in the context of IGR.

3.3 INTEREST GROUPS AND INTERGOVERNMENTAL POLITICS

The study of interest groups in American politics has a long lineage going back to the early writing of James Madison and Alexis de Tocqueville, who underscored the fundamental importance of organized interests to American political life. Although scholars have held a longstanding debate about whether interest groups enable or harm representative democracy, the centrality of their role in American politics and policymaking remains an undeniable fact.[45] Notwithstanding the historical nature of their influence in American politics, interest groups can be hard to distinguish from other entities, and not much unanimity among scholars prevails regarding how to label and define such groups.[46] As Thomas T. Holyoke notes in *Interest Groups and Lobbying: Pursuing Political Interests in America*, scholars rarely agree on whether terms like "organized interest," "social movement organization," "special interest group," "private interest," "pressure group," "lobby," "nongovernmental organization," or "political organization" are appropriate for use when referring to interest groups and their activities.[47] In his influential book *Interest Groups and the Bureaucracy: The Politics of Energy*, John Chubb defined interest groups as rational and economically self-interested individuals (or firms) who voluntarily come together with an overarching purpose of securing benefits of government policy for its members or leaders (p. 22). While the groups undertake many activities, the most important among them is supplying technical information to government

Interest groups/Public Interest Groups: Interest groups comprise rational and economically self-interested individuals (or firms) who voluntarily come together in securing benefits of government policy for its members or leaders. Put alternately, interest groups are an association of individuals or organizations or a public or private institutions that attempts to influence government decisions. Interest groups are active participants in any political exchange. State and local government associations form a unique type of interest groups, also known as Public Interest Groups (PIGs). They are known as PIGs because they comprise public officials and seek a collective good by appealing to the national government for the interests of the subnational governments, not the constituents of the subnational governments.

Public Functions and Private Hands" *Public Administration Review*, 75, no. 2 (2015): 219.
45   Daniel J. Tichenor and Richard A. Harris, "The Development of Interest Group Politics in America: Beyond the Conceits of Modern Times," *Annual Review of Political Science*, 8 (June 2005): 251–270.
46   Thomas T. Holyoke, *Interest Groups and Lobbying: Pursuing Political Interests in America*, 1st ed. Westview Press (2014). Clive S. Thomas, Ronald J. Hrebenar and Anthony J. Nownes. "Interest group politics in the states: Four decades of developments—The 1960s to the Present" in *The book of the states*, Lexington, KY: Council of State Governments. 40 (2008): 322–331.
47   Thomas T. Holyoke, *Interest Groups and Lobbying: Pursuing Political Interests in America*, 1st ed. Westview Press (2014): 10.

Figure 3.19: President Trump gives remarks at the National Rifle Association Leadership Forum
Source: Wikimedia Commons
Attribution: The White House
License: Public Domain

policy analysts with the ultimate objective of swaying decisions toward group perspectives.[48]

Other scholars have offered similar definitions of interest groups. Clive S. Thomas, Ronald J. Hrebenar, and Anthony J. Nownes, in "Interest group politics in the states: Four decades of developments—The 1960s to the Present," offer a broader definition of interest groups as "an association of individuals or organizations or a public or private institution that attempts to influence government decisions" (p. 99). Thomas T. Holyoke offers a more workable definition of interest groups by integrating the concept of self-interest, a notion that has been fundamental to developing political philosophy and the underlying social contract which dictates western civilization. Interest groups, according to Holyoke, are "collections of people with essentially the same self-interest, about which they feel so strongly that they collectively form an organization to promote

Figure 3.20: Jesse Sharkey President Chicago Teachers Union Chicago Teachers Union Rally
Source: Wikimedia Commons
Attribution: Charles Edward Miller
License: CC BY-SA 2.0

48   John E. Chubb, *Interest Groups and the Bureaucracy: The Politics of Energy*. Stanford, CA. Stanford University Press (1983): 22.

and defend it through the political process."[49] Finally, Virginia Gray, Russell L. Hansen, and Thad Kousser, in *Politics in the American States: A Comparative Analysis*, defined interest groups as associations of individuals, organizations, or a public or private institution that attempts to influence government decisions. In the absence of a single definition for interest groups, many state politics scholars have opted to use the term "organized interests" instead or define the term narrowly to include only those organizations that are required to register under state lobbying laws. However, it should be noted that many states do not require organizations that engage in lobbying to register under state laws.[50]

Figure 3.21: Senate and House democrats along with advocacy groups to urge Senate passage of Paycheck Fairness Act
Source: Wikimedia Commons
Attribution: Senate Democrats
License: CC BY 2.0

Figure 3.22: Senate to take up and pass the Paycheck Fairness Act, legislation which will help close the wage gap between women and men working equivalent jobs, costing women and their families $434,000 over their careers.
Source: Wikimedia Commons
Attribution: Senate Democrats
License: CC BY 2.0

3.3.1 Perspectives on Interest Group Politics

To understand the influential role interest groups have in intergovernmental politics, it is important to trace the development of these groups through various theoretical lenses. Understanding the American political system's informal workings through the activities of organized interests emerged during the 1960s with the Pluralist tradition; unlike the formal constitutional-legalist traditions previously considered more relevant, the Pluralist tradition defined American politics through the lens of group conflict where each group strives to maximize their interests and engages in a continuous process of bargaining over power and influence vis-à-vis competing groups.[51] The Pluralist journey began with the contribution of Arthur Bentley's landmark book *The Process of Government*

49   Thomas T. Holyoke, *Interest Groups and Lobbying: Pursuing Political Interests in America*, 1st ed. Westview Press (2014): 32.
50   Virginia Gray, Russell L. Hansen and Thad, Kousser, *Politics in the American States*. 11th ed. SAGE/CQ Press (2018): 100.
51   David B. Truman. "The Governmental Process", New York, Knopf (1951). Dahl, R. "Who Governs?" New Haven, Conn.: Yale University Press (1961), Charles E. Lindblom. "The Science of 'Muddling Through." *Public Administration Review,* 19 (1959): 79–88.

(1908/1967) and David Truman's *The Governmental Process* (1951). Scholars consider these books the seminal source in studying contemporary interest groups. Bentley's work offered theoretical dimensions in understanding group politics interpretation, earning him the title of group theory's founding father. Like Bentley, Truman interpreted groups broadly, including in its fold institutionalized groups such as the courts, legislatures, executives, and other political institutions, organized churches, manufacturing establishments, transportation systems, and organized markets. In doing so, Truman examined why individuals form groups and studied specific interest groups. [52]

In discussing the Pluralist and Neo-Pluralist traditions on the topic of interest groups in *Neopluralism: The Evolution of Political Process Theory* (2004), Andrew S. McFarland summarizes the various viewpoints within the above two traditions. Pluralists believed that power in American politics is fragmented and the political process is greatly influenced by many agents, who are primarily groups or individuals representing group interests. Each group pursues its own interests and, in the process, interacts with each other and affects one another's behavior. The push and pull of numerous pressure groups representing varied interests against each other in policy making make it adequately representative and effective. Countering the Pluralists' view on organized interests, Robert Dahl argued that interest groups only play a secondary role in policy making and instead introduced "political power" as a causal element in the political process model. Dahl distinguished between "power" and "influence" and defined "political power" more from the point of view of an individual than a group/organization perspective, as put forth by earlier Pluralists such as Arthur Bentley and David Truman.[53] Among other leading Pluralists, Charles Lindblom (1959) also studied the role of interest group bargaining in the policy process and how their influence results in small improvements in decision-making. Unlike Pluralist thinkers, Neo-Pluralists did not believe that the complexities of interest groups automatically lead to policy making that is "representative/fair" and at the same time "effective."[54] However, as Wilson noted, the presence of multiple interest groups on both sides of an issue can sometimes result in administrative agencies that function autonomously. The presence of countervailing groups also prevents bureaucratic "capture" by the policy creators in each policy area.[55] McFarland termed it as a "power triad" comprising producer groups, countervailing power groups, and agencies with some autonomy.[56] The communications among all these groups and coalition formation

---

52   Jordan Grant. "The Process of Government and the Governmental Process." *Political Studies.* Vol.48: 788–801 (2000)

53   Andrew S. McFarland, A. S. *Neopluralism: The Evolution of Political Process Theory*, University Press of Kansas (2004): 4–20.

54   Andrew S. McFarland, A. S. *Neopluralism: The Evolution of Political Process Theory*, University Press of Kansas (2004): 41.

55   James Q. Wilson. *The Politics of Regulation*, New York, Basic Books (1980).

56   Andrew S. McFarland, A. S. *Neopluralism: The Evolution of Political Process Theory*, University Press of Kansas (2004): 48.

occurs within "policy networks."[57] Advocacy coalitions are formed within such networks for the purpose of lobbying on a specific policy issue.[58] More recently in the 1990s, the idea of "interest group niches" emerged as scholars studied interest groups' activities and lobbying efforts in states.[59] As these groups compete for a greater share of resources, they try to occupy a policy niche that has very little or no competition from other groups, the rationale being that a smaller constituency would make them more stable and predictable. This argument is supported by Baumgartner and Leech's work, where they found a lack of conflict in policy areas where very few interest groups are active or where lobbying is undertaken in a secretive process. This structure contrasts with more conflicting policy areas where many groups are involved, including such groups as unions, nonprofits, and citizen groups.[60]

3.3.2 Interest Group Types, Functions, and Tactics

Interest groups can be categorized into several types depending on the interests they represent. Virginia Gray, Russell Hanson, and Thad Kousser (2018) summarized the various interest group typologies. "Traditional membership groups" lobby for social, economic, or political issues on behalf of their members who join voluntarily and pay dues. These groups are sometimes focused on a single-issue or a combination of issues and attempt to influence policy in a way that is advantageous to its members' interests. Examples of traditional membership groups include environmental lobbies, gun lobby groups, abortion rights groups, teacher unions, and professional associations, such as state bar associations. These groups have proliferated so that by concentration of effort they may influence various congressional subcommittees with narrow jurisdictions.[61] The other two categories of interest groups are known as "institutional interests" and "associations" with overlapping characteristics. Institutional interests are not groups but non-membership organizations, such as local governments, state and federal agencies, business firms, universities, and colleges. Most institutional interests are actively engaged in the states. The third category of interest groups are known as associations. Examples include labor unions, state chambers of

Intergovernmental lobbying: The lobbying efforts by PIGs is known as intergovernmental lobbying. Intergovernmental lobbying has emerged as a potent mechanism in IGR with the evolution of American federalism that resulted in redistribution of power and responsibilities among the various layers of governments.

---

57   Andrew S. McFarland, A. S. *Neopluralism: The Evolution of Political Process Theory*, University Press of Kansas (2004): 53.

58   Paul A. Sabatier and Christopher H. Jenkins-Smith. "The Advocacy Coalition Framework: An Assessment" in Paul A. Sabatier (ed.) *Theories of the Policy Process*. Boulder, CO: Westview Press (1999).

59   Virginia Gray and Lowery, David. *The Population Ecology of Interest Representation: Lobbying Communities in the American States*. Ann Arbor: University of Michigan Press (1996).

60   Frank R. Baumgartner and Beth L. Leech. "Interest Niches and Policy Bandwagons: Patterns of Interest Group Involvement in National Politics," *Journal of Politics*, 63 (2001): 191–213. Andrew S. McFarland, *Neopluralism: The Evolution of Political Process Theory*, University Press of Kansas (2004): 58

61   James Anderson. *Public Policymaking: An Introduction*, 8th ed. Cengage Learning (2014): 63

commerce, etc. Associations often consist of institutional interests, such as government agencies or business entities.[62] State and local government associations form a unique type of interest groups, also known as "Public Interest Groups (PIGs)." They are known as PIGs because they comprise public officials and seek a collective good by appealing to the national government not for the interests of the subnational governments but for the interests of their constituents. Examples of PIGs include the National Association of Counties, The National League of Cities, The U.S. Conference of Mayors, The National Conference of State Legislatures, the National Governors' Association (NGA), the National Association of Housing Redevelopment Officials, and the American Public Welfare Association. These PIGs mostly lobby the national government on issues such as administration and public policy funding rather than the substance of policies; they do so with the objective of maintaining or increasing their authority over implementation and control of federally-funded programs.[63] Understanding the lobbying efforts by PIGs, also known as intergovernmental lobbying, is central to our understanding of IGR politics. We discuss this issue below. However, before we discuss intergovernmental lobbying, it is important to highlight some of the functions and tactics that typical interest groups use to advance their group interests.

Thomas R. Dye and Susan A. McManus in *Politics in States and Communities* discuss the typical tactics interest groups use in their lobbying efforts. These efforts usually begin with their testifying before legislative committee hearings, making direct contacts with legislators, and helping to draft legislation. Interest groups also mobilize legislators' constituents by asking them to write to legislators and entering coalitions with legislators' constituent groups to lobby for a legislation. Making monetary contributions directly to legislators or their campaign funds by setting up Political Action Committees (PACs) are also common methods interest groups use, as has been revealed through analyses of campaign contribution records and anecdotal evidence from lobbyists. Filing lawsuits is yet another mechanism that interest groups often use to influence the passage of their preferred legislation. Finally, interest groups sometimes use protests and demonstrations as tactics to build public support, although this strategy is not as common as the others mentioned above. However, as an indirect way of influencing decision-makers, interest groups do invest significant amounts of time, energy, and resources to carry out grassroot lobbying efforts with media and public relations campaigns.[64] In the next section, we discuss intergovernmental lobbying where governments act as interest groups influencing decision-making in a federal system.

---

62 Virginia Gray, Russell L. Hansen and Thad, Kousser, *Politics in the American States*. 11th ed. SAGE/CQ Press (2018): 100.

63 Anne Marie Cammisa, *Governments as Interest Groups: Intergovernmental Lobbying and the Federal System*. Praeger Publishers (1995). Lawrence J. O'Toole, Jr and Robert K. Christensen. *American Intergovernmental Relations Foundations, Perspectives, and Issues*. Sage Congressional Quarterly Press (2013): 127.

64 Thomas R. Dye and Susan A. McManus. *Politics in States and Communities*, 15th ed., Pearson (2015): 116–117

3.3.3 Public Interest Groups and Intergovernmental Lobbying

With the evolution of American federalism resulting in the redistribution of power and responsibilities among the various layers of government, due to various constitutional interpretations and changes to the political environment, intergovernmental lobbying has emerged as a potent mechanism in IGR.[65] As noted by Troy E. Smith in "Intergovernmental Lobbying: How Opportunistic Actors Create a Less Structured and Balanced Federal System," the powers and responsibilities of the state governments, once protected during the 19th century under the dual federalism interpretation of the Constitution, started to get diluted in the 20th century when Congress, with the help of the Supreme Court, reinterpreted its Constitutional grants of power more broadly. This move ushered in a system of cooperative federalism that then transitioned into a system known as process federalism during the latter half of the 20th century. During this phase, not only did the states begin to lose powers once thought reserved to them but also Congress started imposing restrictions and limitations on states through mandates, conditions, and preemptions associated with federal grants. The powers and responsibilities of the federal government increased as state governments' power and autonomy over laws and policies eroded during the 20th century. The federal government assumed growing responsibilities for more domestic programs and policies, justifying such interventions in traditional areas of state authority on the grounds of protecting individual rights denied by state and local governments. Congress granted federal bureaucracy and the courts greater authority over the substance and intricacies of intergovernmental programs. These political circumstances forced state governments to act as interest groups actively lobbying with various branches of federal government for power, access to federal funds, influence over the creation of intergovernmental programs, protection from federal influence, and promotion of their interests more broadly. While growing federal authority over traditional areas of states' influence prompted states to engage in lobbying efforts to protect their interests, an unintended consequence of state lobbying is the federal government's further accumulation of power and authority.[66]

Scholars such as Donald Haider, 1974 (*When Governments Come to Washington: Governors, Mayors, and Intergovernmental Lobbying*) and Anne Marie Cammisa, 1995 (*Governments as Interest Groups: Intergovernmental Lobbying and the Federal System*) have studied the lobbying activities of state

---

65   Smith, Troy E. "Intergovernmental lobbying: How opportunistic actors create a less structured and balanced federal system" in Timothy J. Conlan and Paul L. Posner, (eds.) *Intergovernmental management for the twenty-first century, National Academy of Public Administration.* Washington, DC: Brookings Institution (2008): 310, Anne Marie Cammisa, *Governments as Interest Groups: Intergovernmental Lobbying and the Federal System.* Praeger Publishers (1995).

66   Smith, Troy E. "Intergovernmental lobbying: How opportunistic actors create a less structured and balanced federal system" in Timothy J. Conlan and Paul L. Posner, (eds.) *Intergovernmental management for the twenty-first century, National Academy of Public Administration.* Washington, DC: Brookings Institution (2008): 310–312.

and local government interest groups. The combined work of these scholars captures the various phases of intergovernmental lobbying.[67] The first phase of intergovernmental lobbying, that saw state and local government interest groups begin to act as lobbying organizations, started during the New Deal and continued until the early 1960s. This phase also saw an increase in the prestige of mayors governing cities and an uptake in federal grants to cities. The second phase of intergovernmental lobbying saw state and local governments competing for greater access to the growing federal grants for intergovernmental programs, grants colloquially known as "categorical grants" because they required state and local government to fulfill certain requirements that were attached to spending grant funds. This phase lasted from 1960 to about 1969. By the third phase (1969-1979) of intergovernmental lobbying, state and local governments had adjusted to their roles as powerful lobbying organizations with access to various institutions of the federal government. They were increasingly successful in getting the federal government to share revenues with them and touted such revenue sharing as policy success. During this phase, the Nixon administration benefitted state and local governments by fulfilling their wish for more access to federal funds with fewer strings attached.[68] Funding in this so-called New federalism now came to states in the form of "block" grants—absent strings—that afforded states greater discretion in spending and, hence, policy prioritization. The fourth phase of intergovernmental lobbying saw noticeable changes in the political environment, with a gradual decline in federal grants to subnational governments after 1979. The economic decline noticeable during this phase manifested itself through a decline in the federal government's spending on social programs and the national government's largely hostile response to state and local governments' desire for greater authority. During the intervening period between the end of the Reagan administration and the beginning of the Bush administration in the early 1990s, two things led to a more favorable political environment for intergovernmental lobbying by states and local governments. First, the Bush administration expanded federal grants through new social programs and restricted unfunded mandates in social programs that were unfavorable among the subnational governments. These new programs placed more authority and fewer requirements on subnational governments. Second, although various subnational governments found a favorable ally in the national government during this period, state governors found an uptick in their positions' prestige, with the federal government particularly seeking governors' expertise in program implementation. Consequently, the NGA's position in carrying out intergovernmental lobbying strengthened during this time.[69] Today, this group

67   Lawrence J. O'Toole, Jr and Robert K. Christensen. *American Intergovernmental Relations Foundations, Perspectives, and Issues.* Sage Congressional Quarterly Press (2013): 127–131.
68   Lawrence J. O'Toole, Jr and Robert K. Christensen. *American Intergovernmental Relations Foundations, Perspectives, and Issues.* Sage Congressional Quarterly Press (2013): (129).
69   Lawrence J. O'Toole, Jr and Robert K. Christensen. *American Intergovernmental Relations Foundations, Perspectives, and Issues.* Sage Congressional Quarterly Press (2013): 129. Anne Marie Cammisa, *Governments as Interest Groups: Intergovernmental Lobbying and the Federal System.* Praeger Publishers (1995).

remains a dominant force for carrying out lobbying on behalf of subnational governments, although they face many internal and external constraints. The internal constraint is primarily due to the diverse nature of membership with representation from fifty quite different states, which makes consensus building a difficult endeavor. The NGA also faces competition from other local groups, such as The Conference of Mayors, which is largely democratic. The major external constraints are the growing fiscal deficits faced by federal and state governments. Subnational governments are doubly disadvantaged as the federal deficit limits federal spending on grant programs for states and localities.[70]

Successful lobbying by state governments at the federal level depends on several factors. These factors include (a) the extent of time, energy, and resources that state government officials can spend to monitor and analyze the implications of various policy proposals on states interests well before these proposals reach Congress; (b) their ability to effectively communicate their ideas and preferences to members of Congress, the architect of intergovernmental programs, in a manner that catches congressional attention; (c) interpersonal relationships between state and federal officials, as such relationships often determine whom congressional members will trust and what information they will accept as trustworthy; (d) the extent of inter- and intra-group divisions among various public interest groups engaged in lobbying within states; and (e) the level of unity within a state's congressional delegation. State governors are important players who can help or hurt this unity through their personal relationships with members of Congress and the way they engage with their congressional delegation.[71] Studies have found that similar party affiliation between the governor, representatives, and senators does not guarantee unity, nor does a different party affiliation ensure discord whenever state officials decide to participate in intergovernmental lobbying individually or collectively. Each type of effort has its pros and cons. Collective action on the part of states can be difficult to achieve due to the challenges associated with consensus building, defining common interests, and overcoming the free-rider problem, that is, getting benefits without paying with time and money. Individual lobbying by states, on the other hand, can benefit the specific interests of states, generate less opposition, and require less effort in ensuring coordination. However, political obstacles could thwart state officials' ability to carry out successful lobbying with the national government, as very few states can oppose popular national policies that may be contrary to state interests.[72] In

---

70 Lawrence J. O'Toole, Jr and Robert K. Christensen. *American Intergovernmental Relations Foundations, Perspectives, and Issues.* Sage Congressional Quarterly Press (2013): 130.

71 Smith, Troy E. "Intergovernmental lobbying: How opportunistic actors create a less structured and balanced federal system" in Timothy J. Conlan and Paul L. Posner, (eds.) *Intergovernmental management for the twenty-first century, National Academy of Public Administration.* Washington, DC: Brookings Institution (2008): 322.

72 Smith, Troy E. "Intergovernmental lobbying: How opportunistic actors create a less structured and balanced federal system" in Timothy J. Conlan and Paul L. Posner, (eds.) *Intergovernmental management for the twenty-first century, National Academy of Public Administration.* Washington, DC: Brookings Institution (2008): 328–329.

the next section, we discuss the roles of political parties and the political system in shaping intergovernmental politics.

3.4 INTERGOVERNMENTAL POLITICS: ELECTIONS, VOTING, AND CITIZENSHIP

National, state, and local politics in the U.S. have demonstrable impacts on our daily lives. These intergovernmental politics resolve the provision of public services—including tax administration, roads, private market regulation, law enforcement and fire protection—that shape the social and economic lives of citizens. These governments also prescribe violations of laws and commensurate punishments.[73] Therefore, politics is at the center of democratic governance in the U.S. Such decision-making through intergovernmental relations requires appropriate mechanisms for aggregating diverse preferences for public goods and services among citizens. In contemporary democratic societies, including the U.S., political parties serve as the largest and most influential players among various interest groups in performing this function of interest aggregation. They do so by converting the demands of various interest groups into a slate of policy alternatives.[74] These practical political arrangements are quite pertinent within the federal structure of government in the U.S. The political parties contest democratically over citizen votes in periodic elections for gaining control over various electoral offices at different levels of government. They win votes through political campaigns advocating a slate of policy alternatives that each political party and its candidate presents before the citizens of the U.S. The winning political party and its candidates then legitimately use the various institutions of government at appropriate levels to institute and implement their preferred policies.

Political parties: Political parties serve as the largest and most influential players among various interest groups in performing the function of interest aggregation. They do this by converting the demands of various interest groups into a slate of policy alternatives. The political parties contest democratically over citizen votes in periodic elections for gaining control over various electoral offices at different levels of government.

Elections: It refers to periodic popular exercise of voting rights by eligible citizens for ensuring transfer and continuity of political power at national and subnational governments. The political parties contest democratically over citizen votes in periodic elections for gaining control over various electoral offices at different levels of government.

The federal government and state governments share similar structures of government, with states varying along four factors: state and local sociodemographic, culture and history, economic conditions, and states' geography and topography.[75] Because citizens live nearer to their local and state governments, they tend to trust state government more than they do the federal

---

73   Kevin B Smith and Alan Greenblatt, *Governing States and Localities*. 7th ed. CQ Press (2020).
74   James Anderson. *Public Policymaking: An Introduction*, 8th ed. Cengage Learning (2014).
75   Kevin B Smith and Alan Greenblatt, *Governing States and Localities*. 7th ed. CQ Press (2020).

Figure 3.23: Governor Hogan Virtually Attends the 2020 Electoral College Meeting by Patrick Siebert at 100 State Circle, Annapolis, MD
Source: Wikimedia Commons
Attribution: MDGovpics
License: CC BY 2.0

government. State and local governments directly provide basic services to their respective populations, thereby affecting all aspects of citizens' lives.[76] For many, however, state and local government capture less attention from media than does the national government; therefore, they are perceived as having only minor relevance. Smith and Greenblatt (2020) note in *Governing States and Localities* the paradox of this lack of general understanding, given that the trend toward delegation has increased the discretionary power of states and localities. States are often described as "laboratories of democracy," as they initiate some programs that, with the passage of time, turn out to be successful, thereby attracting the attention of the federal government which then attempts to replicate them nation-wide. Scholars may therefore argue that federal, state, and local governments in the U.S. are all coordinating participants in the politics of intergovernmental lawmaking, in provisioning public goods and services and maintaining the continuity of the democratic federal structure of government.

Chapters 1 and 2 have explained in some detail the constitutional and legal aspects of various government institutions at appropriate levels in the U.S., irrespective of the political and electoral underpinnings of elected officials who are in control of such governments. Here, we discuss political aspects of elected officials who provide leadership to our governments within the federal structure of the U.S. This section begins with a discussion of the electoral college system's stark

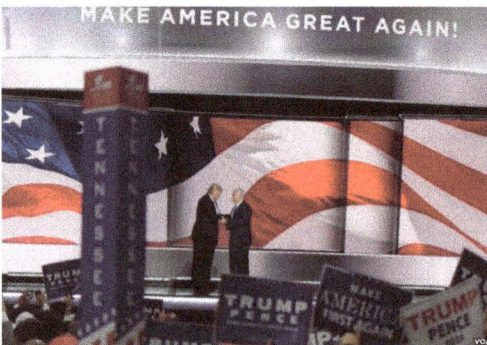

Figure 3.24: Donald Trump and Mike Pence on the third-night of the 2016 RNC
Source: Wikimedia Commons
Attribution: Voice of America
License: Public Domain

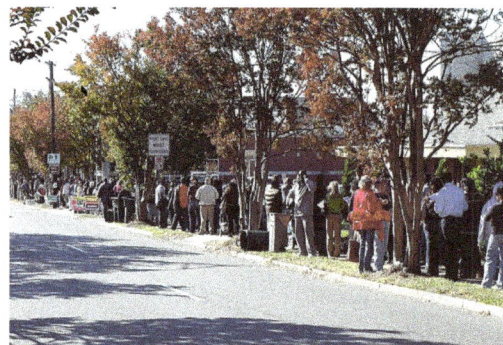

Figure 3.25: 2008 Presidential election early voting lines, Charlotte
Source: Wikimedia Commons
Attribution: James Willamor
License: CC BY-SA 2.0

76   Kevin B Smith and Alan Greenblatt, *Governing States and Localities*. 7th ed. CQ Press (2020).

intergovernmental nature in the U.S., as well as other relevant aspects of elections and electoral reforms, including a discussion of the inter- and intra-political party dimensions intergovernmental relations politics have in the U.S. The chapter also discusses voter participation, instruments of direct democracy, and politics in the context of local U.S governments.

Figure 3.26: Barbara Lee at the National Voting Rights Museum
Source: Wikimedia Commons
Attribution: Barbara Lee
License: Public Domain

3.4.1 Intergovernmental Politics: Electoral College and Political Parties

As noted in Chapters 1 and 2, intergovernmental relations politics conforms to a system of dual constitutionalism in the U.S. According to Smith and Greenblatt (2020), a state's constitution is a state's chief political document. State constitutions are the source of variation among states in terms of distributing political power. This distribution of power within a state tends to reflect public perceptions about the appropriate role of government.[77] State constitutions not only define the institutions by which citizens develop attitudes toward government but also reflect states' political

Electoral College: It consists of federal and state laws and rules that prescribe different manners of voting and elections across states in presidential elections. All but two states allocate pre-assigned electoral votes on a winner-take-all basis. The exceptions are Nebraska and Maine. The Electoral College is one peculiar feature of intergovernmental politics in the selection of the U.S. President.

---

77   Kevin B Smith and Alan Greenblatt, *Governing States and Localities.* 7th ed. CQ Press (2020).

cultures.[78] Daniel Elazar in *American Federalism: A View from the States* bases his cultural theory that explains political cultures and their subtypes on the values that early settlers brought with them as they spread variously across the country, a lack of uniform dispersion largely based on their ethnicities and religious beliefs.[79] Smith and Greenblatt (2020) describe political culture as a reflection of the values and beliefs within an established community that provides an institutionalized legacy of the norms and traditions of the populous. Dye and MacManus (2015) similarly view political culture as historical styles and traditions in states' politics that cannot be directly attributed to socioeconomic factors and the differences across states that consider the values and ways of life of early settler and immigrant groups. State constitutions provide systematic and rigorous means by which to compare political culture across states (Smith and Greenblatt, 2020). Joel Lieske (2010) and Dye and MacManus (2015) identify 11 regional subcultures and emphasize that each state has a unique political culture.[80]

Given the wide variation in political culture across the states in the U.S., the relevant dimensions of intergovernmental relations politics vary across states, too. In particular, each state's constitution and laws not only govern its own elections for various state offices but also administer elections of various national government offices. The U.S. Constitution has explicit provisions in this regard. According to Article I, Section 4 of the Constitution,[81] "The times, places and manner of holding elections for Senators and Representatives, shall be prescribed in each state by the legislature thereof; but the Congress may at any time by law make or alter such regulations." Similarly with regard to the office of the president of the U.S., in Article II, Section 1, Clause 2, the Constitution says:[82]

> Each State shall appoint, in such Manner as the Legislature thereof may direct, a Number of Electors, equal to the whole Number of Senators and Representatives to which the State may be entitled in the Congress: but no Senator or Representative, or Person holding an Office of Trust or Profit under the United States, shall be appointed an Elector.

Consequently, federal and state laws and rules ensure the different manners of voting and elections across states. The Electoral College is one peculiar feature of intergovernmental politics "which plays a significant role in allocating political

---

78   Virginia Gray, "The Socioeconomic and Political Contexts of States" in Virginia Gray, Russell L. Hanson and Thad Kousser (eds.) *Politics in the American States: A Comparative Analysis*, 11th ed. CQ Press (2018). Kevin B Smith and Alan Greenblatt, *Governing States and Localities*. 7th ed. CQ Press (2020).; Daniel J. Elazar. *American Federalism: A View from the States*, 3rd ed. New York: Harper and Row (1984).

79   Virginia Gray, "The Socioeconomic and Political Contexts of States" in Virginia Gray, Russell L. Hanson and Thad Kousser (eds.) *Politics in the American States: A Comparative Analysis*, 11th ed. CQ Press (2018). Daniel J. Elazar, *American Federalism; A View from the States*, 3rd ed. New York: Harper and Row (1984).

80   Lieske, Joel. "The changing regional subcultures of the American states and the utility of a new cultural measure." *Political Research Quarterly* 63, no. 3 (2010): 538–552. Thomas R. Dye and Susan A. McManus. *Politics in States and Communities*, 15th ed., Pearson (2015).

81   https://constitution.congress.gov/browse/essay/artI_S4_C1_1_1_2/. Downloaded on 3/31/2021.

82   https://constitution.congress.gov/browse/article-2/section-1/. Downloaded on 3/31/2021.

influence over the selection of the U.S. President."[83] Because all but two states allocate electoral votes on a winner-take-all basis, presidential candidates have come to focus their attention on competitive states with large electoral vote counts. With the exception of Nebraska and Maine, a winning candidate in popular votes in a state receives all of its electoral votes, irrespective of the margin of victory, thereby creating immense incentive for presidential candidates to allocate their precious campaign resources disproportionately to competitive states where many electoral votes are at stake.[84] Indeed, competitive states with a higher number of electoral votes receive comparably higher amounts of attention from presidential candidates. This has clearly been the case in the last two presidential elections. Large competitive states, such as Pennsylvania, Florida, North Carolina, Michigan, Virginia, and Ohio received disproportionate amounts of attention from presidential candidates of both major political parties in terms of campaign events and television advertisement spending.[85] Another way in which the Electoral College bears on the presidential election is that smaller states find it politically advantageous when compared to large, populous states. This is because no matter how small states are, the U.S. Constitution ensures they each have two senators and at least one representative making up their total count of electoral votes. Therefore, smaller states oppose proposals to abolish the Electoral College.[86] The Electoral College also influences state policies with regard to ballot access. We discuss the Electoral College below.

Although the U.S. Constitution does not mention any political parties, tracing the formation of the U.S. helps explicate the modern two dominant political parties in the nation and their roles in intergovernmental relations politics. Especially illuminating in this formation are the debates over the structure and role of the federal government during the colonies' declaration of independence. At that time, ideological disputes emerged over the ratifications of the Constitution; these debates became known as the Federalists and Anti-Federalists debates (as discussed in Chapter 2).[87] The initial political dispute over the power, structure, and freedom of citizens and businesses under the national government has since taken firm and accepted existence in the U.S.'s two dominant political parties.

According to Dye and MacManus (2015), a political party is an organization that seeks to achieve power by winning public office in elections. Political scientists have developed two broad models to help explain political parties. The Responsible-Party Model is a party system in which each party offers clear

83   Elizabeth D. Frederickson, Stephanie L. Witt and David C. Nice, *The Politics of Intergovernmental Relations*, 3rd ed, Birkdale Publishers (2016): 65.

84   Elizabeth D. Frederickson, Stephanie L. Witt and David C. Nice, *The Politics of Intergovernmental Relations*, 3rd ed, Birkdale Publishers (2016): 65.

85   https://www.nationalpopularvote.com/map-general-election-campaign-events-and-tv-ad-spending-2020-presidential-candidates. Downloaded on 3/31/2021.

86   https://www.nationalpopularvote.com/map-general-election-campaign-events-and-tv-ad-spending-2020-presidential-candidates. Downloaded on 3/31/2021.

87   https://www.loc.gov/exhibits/creating-the-united-states/formation-of-political-parties.html. Downloaded on 3/31/2021.

policy alternatives and holds their elected officials responsible for enacting these policies in office; alternatively, in the Candidate-Centered Model, not parties but individual candidates raise funds, create personal organizations, and rely on professional consultants to direct their campaigns.[88] Primary elections, a decline in party identification, and an increase in split-ticket voting have led to an increased focus on candidates rather than parties. Increasingly, voters are not identifying themselves along party lines but instead are expanding the group of independent voters. These voters pay more attention to candidates and their policies than their parties, resulting in many such voters voting across party lines (or split-ticket voting) in an election. The influence of mass media has further aided this shift, particularly through television and the Web. Other significant factors include a decline in political support and the rise of single-issue interest groups, PACs, and 527s, that is, Political Action Committees that are tax-exempt under Section 527 of the U.S. Internal Revenue Code.[89] As state laws govern political parties,[90] the two dominant national political parties organize in each state according to existing legal requirements. Although the parties are in decline, they still perform important political functions, such as narrowing the choices of political office seekers appealing to voters, creating campaigns, and running primaries. They continue to play an important role in voter choice. Further, the Democratic and Republican parties perform the central task of organizing state legislatures.[91] In like manner, party organizations and activists in the states play an important role in guiding their party and shaping its image with voters. While Smith and Greenblatt (2020) note in *Governing States and Localities* the changing roles and responsibilities of state and local parties over time, they also argue that state political parties have lost strength with the rise of candidate-centered politics. Consequently, they are increasingly taking a consultant and facilitative role in campaigns. Even while voter identification with political parties has also declined, parties nevertheless affect the political process by setting the rules in governments that regulate state electoral provisions for primary elections and third party registration requirements.[92] The latter has greatly contributed to the inability of third or minor parties to achieve electoral success at the federal level while only achieving minimal success at the state level.

3.4.2 Intergovernmental Politics: Voting, Electoral Reforms, and Democracy

Because they govern the regulation of elections and campaign finance, state constitutions and laws are important for understanding political variance across states. Interparty competition within states remains high, though the degree of

88   Thomas R. Dye and Susan A. McManus. *Politics in States and Communities*, 15th ed., Pearson (2015).
89   Thomas R. Dye and Susan A. McManus. *Politics in States and Communities*, 15th ed., Pearson (2015).
90   Thomas R. Dye and Susan A. McManus. *Politics in States and Communities*, 15th ed., Pearson (2015), Kevin B Smith and Alan Greenblatt, *Governing States and Localities*. 7th ed. CQ Press (2020).
91   Thomas R. Dye and Susan A. McManus. *Politics in States and Communities*, 15th ed., Pearson (2015).
92   Kevin B Smith and Alan Greenblatt, *Governing States and Localities*. 7th ed. CQ Press (2020).

interparty competition varies among the states according to political culture.[93] These features shape voter participation, politics around electoral reforms, and direct democracy. The key points discussed here are a brief survey of relevant topics covered by Smith and Greenblatt (2020); Dye and MacManus (2015); and Ronald K. Gaddie and Thomas R. Dye (2020). The common themes these scholars discuss include the existence of structural variation in statewide elections across states. Elections reflect a state's political culture, and low voter turnout leaves much room for greater participation. Each state's rules governing elections ultimately determine the nature and scope of participation and potential candidacies. Active participation in intergovernmental relations politics include eligible citizens running for office, taking part in marches and protests, attending meetings, speeches, and rallies, writing letters, voting, and volunteering in campaigns. But citizen participation in such political activities reaches a maximum only in terms of voting at about half the eligible population.[94] It must be noted that voting rights have not been universal during the greater part of U.S. history since the nation's formation. Between 1800–1840, it took considerable political struggle to eliminate voting based on property qualification. Only after the post-civil war reconstruction and the 15th Amendment in 1870 did the nation extend voting rights to men of color, although states continued to deny them voting rights on the grounds of failed literacy tests and unpaid poll taxes. These practices continued for about a century, between 1870–1964. They ended with the Civil Rights Act, the 24th Amendment, and the Voting Rights Act, 1964–65. Similarly, women could vote only after the 19th Amendment in 1920. The 26th amendment prohibited states and the federal government from using age as a reason to deny the vote to anyone 18 years of age and over. Subsequently, Congress passed the National Voter Registration Act in 1993, now commonly known as the "motor voter" law. This law required states to allow citizens to register to vote when they applied for their drivers' licenses. The law also required states to offer mail-in registration and allow people to register to vote at offices offering public assistance. In the first year of its implementation, more than 30 million people completed their voter registration applications or updated their registration through means that this law made available.[95] After the presidential election controversy and court battle in 2000, Congress passed the Help America Vote Act in 2002. The goal of this law was to streamline election procedures across the nation. States and localities were required to replace outdated voting equipment and create statewide voter registration lists. The law also mandated states to provide provisional ballots to ensure that eligible voters were not turned away if their names did not appear on the registered voters' roll. Further, the law made it easier for people with disabilities to cast private and independent ballots. In a similar vein, the MOVE Act of 2009 significantly expanded

---

93   Kevin B Smith and Alan Greenblatt, *Governing States and Localities*. 7th ed. CQ Press (2020).

94   Ronald K. Gaddie and Thomas R. Dye. *Politics in America, 2018 Elections and Updates Edition*, 11th ed. Pearson (2020).

95   https://www.carnegie.org/topics/topic-articles/voting-rights/voting-rights-timeline/?gclid=CjwKCAjwx 6WDBhBQEiwA_dP8rQg_0qFsh28ALss05JknoX1ucUn6PVTBoV_EzjxNM3kgm0B59YPAJhoCRZEQAvD_ BwE. Downloaded on 3/31/2021.

the Uniformed and Overseas Citizens Absentee Voting Act (UOCAVA) of 1986 to provide greater protections for service members, their families, and other overseas citizens. The MOVE Act requires states to transmit validly-requested absentee ballots to UOCAVA voters no later than 45 days before a federal election, when the request has been received by that date, except where the state has been granted an undue hardship waiver approved by the Department of Defense for that election.[96]

Voting and voter turnout convey how citizens participate in intergovernmental relations politics. Voting is a common method of political involvement and a right in a democracy, yet many people do not vote. Voter turnout comprises the percentage of the voting age population or registered voters that cast ballots in an election. Voter turnout is generally higher in national elections, followed by state elections. Turnout is the lowest in local elections. Political scientists explain these disparities through different theories about voting behavior. A "rational" voter is one who will vote only if the personal benefits outweigh the costs. Per this theory, the young, the poor, the unemployed, and the least educated are the least likely to vote. Nonvoters comprise a wide array of citizens; these include predominantly first-generation immigrants, especially those who are non-English speaking; those who seldom participate in organized religious activities; newcomers to a community; those with little or no interest in politics, little trust in government, no belief that voting is a civic duty, and/ or no belief they can make a difference by voting; persons with physical disabilities; blue-collar and service-sector workers; Asians and Latinos; independents; single parents living in poor neighborhoods; persons who have not been contacted by a candidate or party; renters; and residents of solidly one-party dominated states. Individuals in these groups generally see themselves as gaining little from any outcome of an election and so are unwilling to invest their time, money, effort, etc., in making their way to the polls. On the other hand, voters in high socioeconomic groups with high education and income are more likely to vote. Voters in highly-competitive states also show high turnout. All groups, though, can be adversely affected when the media predicts early winners and so discourages later voters.

More politically controversial issues underlying voter turnout include legal and procedural explanations. States show significant differences in registration procedures that the federally-mandated "motor voter" registration law tried to streamline. States also vary in resources provided to voters in the actual voting experience in terms of time, place, equipment, ballots, and poll workers. The election reforms are still being debated, have become considerably more partisan, and are particularly intense in states with high levels of party competition. The prevalent controversial issues include the following: voter eligibility requirements and verification (IDs) striving to disenfranchise certain people, voting locations and ease of voting, online (Internet) registration, ballot requests, and voting itself. These issues reflect the political power struggle as racial and ethnic minorities are growing in numbers and percentages of the U.S. population and, therefore, in political power. For example, African American voter turnout surpassed white

96   https://www.justice.gov/opa/pr/fact-sheet-move-act. Downloaded on 3/31/2021.

voter turnout for the first time in history in the 2012 presidential election. Hispanics and Blacks are likely to support at higher rates in election those candidates with similar ethnic backgrounds. Asians show relatively low turnouts compared to other minority groups and have a tendency to register as independents.

Active participation in politics is available to citizens at the state level via direct democracy as well. Direct democracy means that the people themselves can initiate and decide policy questions by popular vote. The U.S. Constitution does not provide for direct democracy measures, but many state constitutions allow direct voting in popular initiatives and referenda voting.[97] The different forms of direct democracy include initiative, referendum, and recall. In an initiative, a percentage of voters, using a petition, may have a law or amendment placed on the ballot without legislative involvement. Referendum implies that the electorate must approve legislative decisions before they become law. Recall allows voters to remove an elected official before the end of their term. These processes are now highly professionalized and dominated by special interest groups. Moreover, despite giving citizens a direct voice in the legislative process, direct democracy can also lead to inefficient legislative outcomes, as with Proposition 13 in California.[98] This law imposes the politically burdensome requirement of two thirds majority in contrast to simple majority for making any changes in local property taxes in California. This requirement has been extremely difficult to meet, especially when local governments in California needed extra revenue to fund economic development projects.

3.4.3 Intergovernmental Politics: Politics and Local Governments

Residents live under local governments' jurisdiction and must contend with such governments' roles and decisions in the provision of basic public services, the delivery of which depends on localities; therefore, they reflect local political culture. Local history, culture, style of municipal governance, and state decisions determine the structure, responsibilities, and powers of local officeholders. Mayor-council systems are most prevalent with real executive power, especially in strong mayor systems. On the other hand, Council-manager systems assign policymaking power to an unelected city manager. In both systems, local jurisdictions also have commissions and special districts to lower partisan bias and to provide self-regulatory governance.

As discussed in Chapter 1, Dillon's Rule provides that local governments can exercise only those powers granted by their states, though local governments are charged with many responsibilities that require a lot of money to fulfill. Consequently, local governments are highly dependent upon states for financial support. In addition to facing increasing demands from their citizens for services, local governments contend with the higher governments' issuing mandates for

---

97   Kevin B Smith and Alan Greenblatt, *Governing States and Localities*. 7th ed. CQ Press (2020).

98   See more on Proposition 13 at https://www.taxpolicycenter.org/taxvox/four-decades-after-proposition-13s-tax-revolt-will-california-split-roll-it-back-proposition. Downloaded on 3/31/2021.

providing certain goods and services. These demands are exacerbated by scant levels of political participation, both in terms of voting and supply of well-qualified candidates for office. In an attempt to break away from some state restrictions so they might gain greater control over local affairs, many localities have adopted charters that provide for home rule, or independent self-governance. Despite owing their continued existence to their respective state governments, local governments remain important political actors and are providing a venue for innovation in the administration of public services while enriching citizens' quality of life.

In the context of U.S. urbanization, local governments also confront locality interconnectedness in metropolitan areas and the lack of governmental coordination among them. As these localities have expanded, becoming increasingly economically and socially intertwined, the preexisting boundaries of political jurisdictions have not been modified to reflect these changes, leading to duplicity in service provision and lost opportunities to maximize economies of scale. Some localities have attempted to plug this "hole" through such regional efforts as regional governments, regional councils, government consolidation, and intergovernmental agreements. Not all believe that fragmentation and overlap is bad, however. Smaller communities often resist regional reform efforts, fearing they will lose their voice. Others argue that consolidation is actually an inefficient model. According to the public choice model of politics, and, by extension, the Tiebout Model, fragmented governments that allow for choice through competition are the most efficient means for delivering public goods. States and localities continue to struggle with this debate.

3.5 INTERGOVERNMENTAL POLITICS IN THE COVID-19 HEALTH CRISIS

Public healthcare in the U.S. during both normal times and when under a pandemic like COVID-19 displays political outcomes pertinent to intergovernmental relations, such as roles and responsibilities of different levels of governments, funding arrangements, and addressing the unforeseen problems underlying the issue. Historically, states and local governments provided public healthcare, such as vaccinations and testing in the U.S. Its political culture significantly affects a state's provision of healthcare. The Great Society legislation under President Lyndon B.

Covid-19: It is a public healthcare crisis in the U.S. and around the world and is known as the Corona Virus Disease 2019 (COVID-19). This pandemic has displayed political outcomes pertinent to intergovernmental relations, such as roles and responsibilities of different levels of governments, funding arrangements, and addressing the unforeseen problems underlying the issue.

Johnson created a movement away from state and local control. Subsequently, the federal government's Medicare and Medicaid programs have become the primary healthcare provider in the U.S. These programs are implemented in partnership with state governments, with the latter being responsible for implementation of both programs and sharing some financial burden for the Medicaid program. The Medicaid and Medicare programs serve the poor and elderly, respectively. The Centers for Medicare & Medicaid Services (CMS) is the federal agency that runs the Medicare Program. CMS is housed within the U.S. Department of Health and Human Services (HHS). CMS monitors Medicaid programs offered by each state as well.

Intergovernmental relations politics and public health policy debates in recent decades have centered largely around rising healthcare costs and appropriate healthcare reform responses that can decrease costs. These debates resulted in the highly partisan passage of the national Patient Protection and Affordable Care Act in March, 2010, that mandated healthcare insurance coverage for all Americans. The act, popularly known as Obamacare, took control of public healthcare from state hands but made states responsible for implementing many of the Act's provisions. Several Republican Party-controlled state governments and their officials and nationally elected Republican representatives attempted numerous legislative and legal challenges to Obamacare, so far with little success. For example, the Republican Party-controlled states lost their legal challenge to the individual mandate as the Supreme Court ruled 5-4 in favor of the federal government, upholding that provision of the Act.

Within the context of this strong political dispute between the two governing political parties and cleavage in intergovernmental relations, the COVID-19 pandemic struck. Greg Goelzhauser and David M. Konisky (2021, p. 322) have rightly noted in "The State of American Federalism 2019–2020: Polarized and Punitive Intergovernmental Relations" that

> the pandemic has highlighted nearly every dimension of federalism relevant for understanding how intergovernmental relations influence political outcomes,"…". Moreover, despite noteworthy elements of cooperation, most of the important political decisions are playing out against a backdrop of partisan polarization and punitiveness.

The Center for Disease Control (CDC) confirmed the first U.S. case of 2019 Novel Coronavirus (2019-nCoV) in Washington state on January 21, 2020. Since then, the pandemic has severely impacted individual's lives in the U.S. (and around the world); unsurprisingly, it also had a great impact on the U.S. government.

At the federal level, the Office of the Assistant Secretary of Preparedness and Response (ASPR) within the HHS is responsible for leading the health emergency response after receiving clear direction from the secretary of HHS. The Secretary of HHS declared COVID-19 an emergency on January 31, 2020, thus clearing the way for the ASPR to plan and focus on the pandemic. Since then, the ASPR has developed a COVID-19 medical countermeasure program; deployed personnel to support quarantine facilities, hospitals, and healthcare facilities across the nation; and provided critical equipment in the fight against the virus. HHS/ASPR's

Biomedical Advanced Research and Development Authority (BARDA) increased availability and diversity of COVID-19 diagnostic tests and therapeutics and funded the research and development of vaccines.[99]

Notwithstanding its important and active role, more than a year after the ASPR designated COVID-19 a pandemic that required a national-level coordinated intergovernmental response to contain the spread of this deadly virus and save people's lives, one can argue that COVID-19 has brought a tremendous amount of human suffering, comprising life, health, economy, and social isolation. Per the latest data, more than 550,000 people in the U.S. have died after contracting this virus, with more than 30 million confirmed cases.[100] Among the few top developed countries, these disturbing numbers attest to the U.S.'s having the worst per capita numbers on these two counts.[101] The key question to ask is, how has a public health failure of this magnitude occurred, continuing to disrupt people's daily lives and economic well-being? A complete answer to this question will only be available after this ordeal is fully contained and social scientists critically investigate the pandemic. However, taking stock of the combined intergovernmental response to this pandemic paints a picture of massive failures in leadership, communication, and resource mobilization at all levels of government.

With the exception of the quick turnaround of Operation Warp Speed in vaccine development, authorization, and production, "political polarization and a rejection of science have stymied the United States' ability to control the coronavirus."[102] a *New York Times* (NYT) article *One Year, 400,000 Coronavirus Deaths: How the U.S. Guaranteed Its Own Failure*[103] argues that, faced with the political choice of taking some authoritarian steps such as mask mandates or requiring testing, tracing, and social distancing in a reelection year, the Trump administration ducked leadership. Furthermore, the active administration did not have a federal coordination team in place for distributing vaccine doses and vaccinating people after it succeeded with the Operation Warp Speed vaccine program. Instead, the Trump administration ceded the major leadership role to states in devising responses to this pandemic. The NYT article further noted that "governors and local officials who were left in charge of the crisis squandered the little momentum the country had as they sidelined health experts, ignored warnings from their own advisers and, in some cases, stocked their advisory committees with more business representatives than doctors."[104] According to NYT, each level of government ignored science, with more than 100 state and local health officials having been fired or having resigned since the beginning of the pandemic as their science-based recommendations were overlooked or found inconvenient. This pandemic-focused article highlights some of the challenges of intergovernmental relations and the

---

99   https://www.phe.gov/about/review-2020/Pages/default.aspx. Downloaded on 3/31/2021.
100   https://www.cnn.com/interactive/2020/health/coronavirus-us-maps-and-cases/. Downloaded on 4/4/2021.
101   https://www.cnn.com/interactive/2020/health/coronavirus-us-maps-and-cases/. Downloaded on 4/4/2021.
102   https://www.nytimes.com/2021/01/17/us/covid-deaths-2020.html. Downloaded on 4/4/2021.
103   https://www.nytimes.com/2021/01/17/us/covid-deaths-2020.html. Downloaded on 4/4/2021.
104   https://www.nytimes.com/2021/01/17/us/covid-deaths-2020.html. Downloaded on 4/4/2021.

need for better mechanisms to ensure effective intergovernmental response to a crisis situation.

3.6 CONCLUSION

Intergovernmental relations politics is largely shaped by power dynamics between levels of government in the context of a problem/issue/policy. These politics also influence those power structures. This chapter introduced students to many institutional actors at the national and subnational levels who operate within the federal system to influence how intergovernmental politics are conducted and the decision-making on intergovernmental programs. The institutional actors at the national level are the Office of the President, Congress, the federal courts, and the federal bureaucracy. Numerous government actors operate at the subnational level, trying to influence the national government so as to access federal grants and maintain their interests in various intergovernmental programs. The major subnational actors include the state legislatures, governors, state courts, state bureaucracies, local governments, and regional independent agencies. Private and nongovernmental agencies are also important players within the federal structure. The chapter then discussed the role of interest groups, especially that of PIGs and how they conduct intergovernmental lobbying. Students learned about the many lobbying activities of state and local governments and the factors that influence these entities' successful lobbying efforts. By understanding the phases of intergovernmental lobbying as outlined by scholars, students were able to decipher how state and local governments have been increasingly successful in getting the federal government to share revenues with them, touting such revenue sharing as policy success. The chapter then considered the political system and dynamics that affect political leaders in terms of leading and finding political solutions to thorny intergovernmental problems. The chapter introduced students to political interplay on such topics as the Electoral College, political parties, voter participation, elections, and electoral reforms. Students learned that the Electoral College is a peculiar feature of intergovernmental politics that plays a significant role in allocating political influence over the U.S. President's selection. This section also introduced students to political parties and how they serve as the largest and most influential players among various interest groups in performing interest aggregation. Students learned how political parties convert various interest groups' demands into a slate of policy alternatives. Additionally, this section introduced students to some of the relevant aspects of elections and electoral reforms, including voter participation, instruments of direct democracy, and the inter- and intra-political party dimensions of intergovernmental relations politics in the U.S. Students then learned about politics in the context of local government. The chapter concluded by discussing the COVID-19 pandemic in order to show some of the key features of intergovernmental relations politics.

REFLECTION QUESTIONS

1. Discuss the roles of various players at the national and subnational levels who are involved in intergovernmental relations politics.

2. Define interest groups in an intergovernmental context. Discuss the different types of interest groups that are engaged in intergovernmental politics. Discuss the tactics used by interest groups to influence intergovernmental decisions.

3. Discuss the process of intergovernmental lobbying by subnational government interest groups to influence intergovernmental programs.

4. Discuss the role of political parties and the political system's influence on intergovernmental relations and policy management.

5. Analyze the public policy response to the Covid-19 pandemic through the lens of intergovernmental politics as discussed in this chapter.

BIBLIOGRAPHY

Anderson, James. *Public Policymaking: An Introduction*, 8th ed. Cengage Learning (2014).

Baumgartner, Frank R and Beth L. Leech. "Interest Niches and Policy Bandwagons: Patterns of Interest Group Involvement in National Politics." *Journal of Politics*, 63 (2001): 191–213.

Bowman, Ann O'M. "Trends and Issues in Interstate Cooperation" in Lawrence O'Toole and Robert Christensen, eds. *American Intergovernmental Relations: Foundations, Perspectives, and Issues*. CQ Press (2013).

Bowman, Ann O'M and Richard C. Kearney. *The Resurgence of the States*. Englewood Cliffs, NJ. Prentice Hall (1986).

Cammisa, Anne Marie. *Governments as Interest Groups: Intergovernmental Lobbying and the Federal System*. Praeger Publishers (1995).

Christopher Shortell. "The End of the Federalism Five? Statutory Interpretation and the Roberts Court." *Publius, 42*, no. 3: 516–537.

Chubb, John E. *Interest Groups and the Bureaucracy: The Politics of Energy*. Stanford, CA. Stanford University Press (1983).

Derthick, Martha and Gary Bombardier. *Between States and Nation*, Washington DC: Brookings (1974).

Dye, Thomas, R and Susan A. McManus. *Politics in States and Communities*, 15th ed., Pearson (2015).

Elazar, Daniel J. *American Federalism: A View from the States*, 3rd ed. New York: Harper and Row (1984).

Ferris, Elizabeth and Daniel Petz. *In the neighborhood: the growing role of regional organizations in disaster risk management.* Brookings Institution Press (2013).

Frederickson, Elizabeth D, Stephanie L. Witt and David C. Nice. *The Politics of Intergovernmental Relations*, 3rd ed. Birkdale Publishers (2016).

Gaddie, Ronald K and Thomas R. Dye. *Politics in America, 2018 Elections and Updates Edition*, 11th ed. Pearson (2020).

Glendening, Parris, N and Mavis Mann Reeves. *Pragmatic Federalism*, 2nd ed, Pacific Palisades, CA: Palisades (1984).

Goelzhauser, Greg, and David M. Konisky. "The State of American Federalism 2019–2020: Polarized and Punitive Intergovernmental Relations." *Publius: The Journal of Federalism*, 50, no. 3 (2020): 311–343.

Gray, Virginia and Lowery, David. *The Population Ecology of Interest Representation: Lobbying Communities in the American States.* Ann Arbor: University of Michigan Press (1996).

Gray, Virginia, Russell L. Hansen and Thad, Kousser, *Politics in the American States.* 11th ed. SAGE/CQ Press (2018).

Gray, Virginia. "The Socioeconomic and Political Contexts of States" in Virginia Gray, Russell L. Hanson and Thad Kousser (eds.) *Politics in the American States: A Comparative Analysis*, 11th ed. CQ Press (2018).

Hamilton, Alexander, John Jay and James Madison. *The Federalist*, New York: Modern Library (1937).

Hamman, John A. "Career Experience and Performing Effectively as Governor." *American Review of Public Administration*, 34, no. 2 (2004): 151–163.

Holyoke, Thomas T. *Interest Groups and Lobbying: Pursuing Political Interests in America*, 1st ed. Westview Press (2014).

Joel, Lieske. "The changing regional subcultures of the American states and the utility of a new cultural measure." *Political Research Quarterly* 63, no. 3 (2010): 538–552.

Kettle, Donald. "The Job of Government: Interweaving Public Functions and Private Hands" *Public Administration Review*, 75, no. 2 (2015): 219–229.

Kousser, Thad and Justin H. Phillips. *The Power of American Governors: Winning on Budgets and Losing on Policies.* New York, Cambridge University Press (2012).

Lindblom, Charles E. "The Science of 'Muddling Through." *Public Administration Review*, 19 (1959): 79–88.

Marando, Vincent L, and Patricia S. Florestano. "Intergovernmental Management" in Naomi B. Lynn and Aaron B. Wildavsky, eds., *Public Administration: The State of the Discipline.* Chatham House Publishers, 1990.

McFarland, Andrew S. *Neopluralism: The Evolution of Political Process Theory*, University Press of Kansas (2004).

Moncrief, Gary F and Peverill Squire. *Why States Matter: An Introduction to State Politics.* Lanham, MD. Rowan and Littlefield Publishers (2013).

O'Toole, Jr., Laurence J. and Robert K. Christensen. *American Intergovernmental Relations Foundations, Perspectives, and Issues*. Sage Congressional Quarterly Press (2013).

Rosenbaum, Walter A. *Energy Politics and Public Policy*. CQ Press (1987).

Rosenthal, Alam. *The Best Job In Politics: Exploring How Governors Succeed as Policy Leaders*. Los Angeles, CA. Sage/CQ Press (2013).

Sabatier, Paul A. and Christopher H. Jenkins-Smith. "The Advocacy Coalition Framework: An Assessment" in Paul A. Sabatier (ed.) *Theories of the Policy Process*. Boulder, C): Westview Press (1999).

Schattschneider, Elmer E. *The Semisovereign People*. Hinsdale, IL: Drysdale Press (1975).

Smith, Kevin B and Alan Greenblatt, *Governing States and Localities*. 7th ed. CQ Press (2020).

Smith, Troy E. "Intergovernmental lobbying: How opportunistic actors create a less structured and balanced federal system" in Timothy J. Conlan and Paul L. Posner, (eds.) *Intergovernmental management for the twenty-first century*, National Academy of Public Administration. Washington, DC: Brookings Institution (2008).

Stephanie Lindquist and Pamela Corley. "National Policy Preferences and Judicial Review of State Statutes at the United States Supreme Court." *Publius*, 43, no. 2: 151–178.

Terry, Moe. "The politics of structural choice: toward a theory of public bureaucracy" in Oliver E. Williamson, ed., *Organization Theory: From Chester Barnard to the Present and Beyond*. New York: Oxford University Press (1990).

Thomas, Clive S, Ronald J. Hrebenar and Anthony J. Nownes. "Interest group politics in the states: Four decades of developments—The 1960s to the Present" in *The book of the states*, Lexington, KY: Council of State Governments. 40 (2008): 322–331.

Tichenor, Daniel J. and Richard A. Harris. "The Development of Interest Group Politics in America: Beyond the Conceits of Modern Times." *Annual Review of Political Science*, 8 (June 2005): 251–270.

Wildavsky, Aaron. *The Politics of the Budgetary Process*. 2nd ed. Boston, MA: Little, Brown (1974).

Wilson, James Q. *The Politics of Regulation*, New York, Basic Books (1980).

Wood, Dan. "Federalism and Policy Responsiveness: The Clear Air Case." *Journal of Politics*, 53: 851–859.

4

Fiscal Dimensions of Intergovernmental Relations

Daniel Baracskay

LEARNING OBJECTIVES

- Demonstrate knowledge of how public budgeting and finance principles were institutionalized in the early twentieth century to give rise to the notion of fiscal federalism as a driving force of intergovernmental activity.

Figure 4.1: Handshake.
Source: Pixabay
Attribution: User "Ralphs_Fotos"
License: Pixabay License

- Demonstrate an understanding of how federal grants have shaped the nature of intergovernmental relations over time, allowing for a coordinated and shared implementation structure.

- Demonstrate knowledge of New Deal era's importance as an instrumental stage of intergovernmental relations when new regulations and programs emerged as facets of policy modernization.

- Demonstrate familiarity with various reform initiatives introduced in the decades following the New Deal era (e.g., the Nixon and Reagan administrations) which sought to restructure fiscal processes to generate greater efficiency and effectiveness of intergovernmental activity.

- Demonstrate understanding of recent trends in fiscal federalism and intergovernmental activity, particularly relating to the movement toward greater polarization of views in society, along with ongoing challenges in fiscal austerity and resource constraints as facets of public sector management.

KEY TERMS

Article I

Centralized federalism

Court packing

Elastic Clause

Fiscal federalism

Gramm-Rudman-Hollings (GRH) Act

Grants-in-aid

General revenue sharing

Great Society

Impoundment

New Deal

New Frontier

Progressive Era

Sixteenth Amendment

Unfunded mandates

4.1 INTRODUCTION

As has been the case with many functional areas of American government over time, fiscal operations have been institutionalized based upon practical necessity. Public budgeting and finance in the twentieth century became more formalized arrangements by which revenues have been consistently generated and funds allocated for specific objectives. Today, budgetary and funding considerations drive virtually every aspect of public sector activity (as well as nonprofit operations), having significant ramifications for the study of our ever-changing federal structure and intergovernmental relations (IGR) system. Fiscal considerations have also pervaded the intergovernmental management (IGM) literature, particularly from the standpoint of studying resource usage within organizations and programs. As discussed in Chapter 1, American federalism has progressed through various eras of change, including dual federalism early in our nation's history, to a more cooperative and coordinated structure conducive to IGR, to periods of centralization and competition. The fiscal dimensions of federalism and IGR became more enveloping in the early twentieth century and have endured across eras of change. Consequently, numerous terms have emerged to describe how public finance has become an institutionalized and dynamic component of American politics. Fiscal federalism, financial federalism, categorical federalism, intergovernmental fiscal relations (IFR), and fiscal decentralization are but a few of the many expressions used to emphasize the importance of revenue generation and expenditure distributions in IGR.

The most prevalent expression is fiscal federalism, which addresses how political and economic aspects of governmental structure come together to shape systemic outcomes through financial decision-making and the allocation of funds for various uses. Scholars have regarded fiscal federalism as a subfield of public finance, and it has both normative and positive (empirical)

> *Fiscal Federalism*: the basis for which political and economic aspects of governmental structure come together to shape systemic outcomes through financial decision-making and the allocation of funds for usage.

dimensions, becoming more pertinent under coordinated arrangements in IGR.[1] This segment of the literature has its own associated theoretical bases which this chapter, in the context of the discussion below, will examine from the standpoint of shared responsibilities across levels of government. First, subnational governments have both discretion and autonomy to be able to adapt to changing economic circumstances that affect the nature of operations and programs. This ability includes making regulatory and programmatic adjustments which reflect the dynamics of ever changing political environments and policy priorities. Chapters 6, 7, and 8 will further explore the policy aspects of IGR. Second, governments naturally confront budgetary constraints which affect how spending decisions are shaped. Chapter 2 discussed the political dimensions of IGR, particularly from the standpoint of the many actors involved. Trends in expenditure levels closely parallel changes in revenue generation strategies and are closely tied to policy and programmatic priorities. Third, the existence of a common market prevents barriers from being used in the flow of goods, capital, and labor within subnational boundaries. And fourth, many of fiscal federalism's facets are grounded in an institutionalized structure that the national government may not arbitrarily alter, since routines and long-standing processes provide for procedural consistencies.[2] With these theoretical aspects in mind, this chapter explores several topics. First, it begins by examining the historical background and fiscal dimensions of IGR that established our nation's public finance system and have since then guided how resources are deployed. This investigation includes a discussion on the importance of grants-in-aid as an IGR instrument. Second, this chapter explores the nature of intergovernmental funding, specifically as it relates to specific eras and presidential administrations when IGR evolved as an aspect of American federalism. Third, it details recent trends in fiscal federalism and IGR, giving particular emphasis on the nature of rising costs, scarcity of funding and resources, and economic development. Fourth, it offers final considerations pertaining to fiscal trends.

4.2 HISTORICAL BACKGROUND AND FISCAL DIMENSIONS OF FEDERALISM AND INTERGOVERNMENTAL RELATIONS

Prior to the twentieth century, America had a rudimentary administrative structure grounded in the U.S. Constitution, but it was a fragment of what we have come to realize in terms of the size and scope of our modern government system. Chapter 5 will discuss IGR's administrative dimensions in detail, but suffice it to

1   Wallace E. Oates, "An Essay on Fiscal Federalism," *Journal of Economic Literature, 37, no. 3 (Sep., 1999):* 11–20.
2   See William H. Riker, *Federalism: Origin, Operation, Significance* (Boston, MA: Little, Brown, 1964), 11; Barry R. Weingast, "The Economic Role of Political Institutions: Market-preserving federalism and economic development," *Journal of Law, Economics, and Organization*, 11, no, 1 (1995): 4; Jonathan Rodden, "Comparative Federalism and Decentralization: on meaning and measurement," *Comparative Politics*, 36, no. 4 (2004): 481-500; and Jason Sorens, "The Institutions of Fiscal Federalism," *Publius*, 41, no. 2 (Spring 2011): 208.

say that spending was a small fragment of modern expenditure levels. Early in the twentieth century, the U.S. transitioned away from an isolationist position to become an active participant in global affairs, and policy issues (both old and new) became more complex and wide-ranging. In his book, *American Federalism: A View From the States,* Daniel J. Elazar describes the progression toward intergovernmental collaboration as a "partnership in action," such that there was tremendous growth in the rapidity by which governmental functions were created. This shift naturally had a considerable impact on revenue generation and expenditure levels. The table below shows the history of federal receipts and outlays for selected years, both in nominal dollars and in constant 2020 dollars which account for inflation. Receipts and expenditures most notably began increasing around 1918 when the U.S. entered World War I. Another significant increase occurred in the 1940s and 1960s. For an extended period of our nation's history, outlays have largely outpaced receipts, both in nominal and constant 2020 dollars, causing the deficit to rise steadily over time. As it progresses, this chapter will discuss these and other themes.

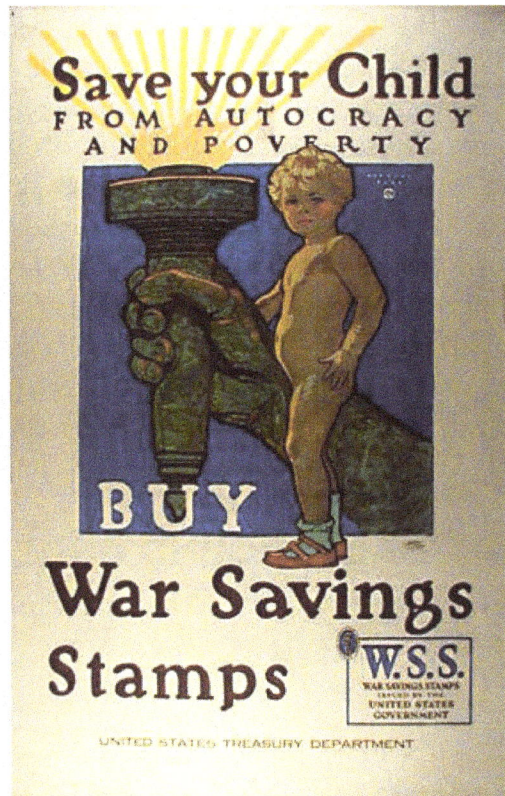

Figure 4.2: A poster for War Savings Certificate Stamps published by the United States Treasury Department between 1914 and 1918. War Savings Stamps were sold by the U.S. government to help mitigate costs incurred in World War I. Purchasers could redeem the stamps for cost plus interest.
Source: Wikimedia Commons
Attribution: Herbert Paus
License: Public Domain

Table 4.1: Historical Trends in Federal Receipts and Outlays (1900-2020) (in millions of dollars)

Year	Receipts	Outlays	Receipts (2020 dollars)	Outlays (2020 dollars)
1901	588	525	--	--
1910	676	694	--	--
1918	3,645	12,677	61,713	214,633
1920	6,649	6,358	84,993	81,273
1930	4,058	3,320	62,123	50,825
1940	6,548	9,468	119,574	172,897
1945	45,159	92,712	641,400	1,316,803
1950	39,443	42,562	418,418	451,505
1955	65,451	68,444	624,365	652,917
1960	92,492	92,191	798,859	796,259
1965	116,817	118,228	948,097	959,549
1970	192,807	195,649	1,270,424	1,289,150
1975	279,090	332,332	1,326,232	1,579,237
1980	517,112	590,941	1,604,409	2,936,158
1985	734,037	946,344	1,744,067	2,248,508
1990	1,031,958	1,252,993	2,018,571	2,450,929
1995	1,351,790	1,515,742	2,267,680	2,542,716
2000	2,025,191	1,788,950	3,006,702	2,655,967
2005	2,151,611	2,471,957	2,816,561	3,235,909
2010	2,162,706	3,457,079	2,535,637	4,053,208
2015	3,249,887	3,671,847	3,505,471	3,960,616
2020	3,644,772	4,745,573	--	--

Source: Office of Management and Budget, "Historical Tables: Summary of Receipts, Outlays, and Surpluses or Deficits," 2020, Accessed at: https://www.whitehouse.gov/omb/historical-tables/.

New functions naturally led to deliberations on how funding would be allocated and how power relationships and jurisdictions would be shaped. The outcome was a vast (and expensive) network of policy areas necessitating an institutionalized system of cooperation across tiers. Localities came to "share the burden" for domestic programs, particularly in terms of implementation. To support domestic policy growth at the rate at which programs were being created, Congress entrusted states with greater shares of responsibility. This choice was especially evident in the public health and safety, environmental protection, consumer protection, agricultural standards, civil rights, and other miscellaneous realms relating to energy usage, employment, land acquisition, election procedures, and transportation. The intergovernmental collaboration system that developed in the twentieth century was in stark contrast to the image of dual federalism, which scholars have used to describe preceding eras of American federalism, where there were relatively exclusive and separate spheres of power. From the IGR perspective, localities had a more vibrant role in the intergovernmental equation, and power sharing occurred upward and downward in the system.[3]

4.2.1 The Early Basis for Funding

In the U.S. Constitution, the Founding Fathers provided the basic structure for our nation's public finance system, associating it largely with legislative powers. Yet, their design also had the flexibility to allow for adjustments and the refinement of funding measures based on the forthcoming generations of leaders' needs. Specifically in terms of public finance, Article I of the Constitution provides broad powers to Congress, including establishing a national money supply and having the authority to levy taxes, borrow and spend money, and regulate commerce. It also grants Congress the ability to pass all laws it deems as "necessary and proper" to execute its functions. As the Founding Fathers originally intended, the Elastic Clause contained in Article I and the ability to amend the Constitution[4] have both afforded opportunities to respond to ambiguities in Constitutional design and permit the system to adapt to social, political, and economic factors over time. For the first one hundred years of our nation's history, the earliest uses of intergovernmental funding were sparse, given dual federalism's nature. The Morrill Act of 1862 provided states with thousands of acres of federal land for constructing higher education institutions. In terms of cash disbursements, support for the National Guard had been realized through cash grants to the states. The Federal Act to Promote the Education of the Blind in 1879 began the most basic form of what would evolve into a complex federal grant system, appropriating

Article I: a section of the Constitution that provides broad powers to Congress, inclusive of establishing a national money supply, and having the authority to levy taxes, borrow and spend money, and regulate commerce. It also grants Congress the ability to pass all laws that it deems as "necessary and proper" in executing its functions.

Elastic Clause: provision contained in Article I of the Constitution that grants Congress the ability to pass laws that it deems as "necessary and proper."

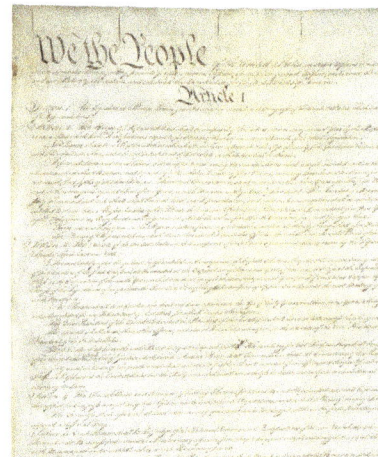

Figure 4.3: US Constitution.
Source: Pixabay
Attribution: User "WikiImages"
License: Public Domain

$250 thousand as a continuing source of funds to the states for the purchase of learning materials for blind students. Annual grants for veterans' benefits to state

---

3   Daniel J. Elazar, *American Federalism: A View From the States,* 3rd ed. (New York: Harper & Row, Publishers, 1984), 53–54.

4   The founding fathers built an amendment process into the Constitution under Article V, where new amendments may be proposed and ratified in order to address societal needs in future generations.

hospitals began in 1888 with a disbursement of $25 thousand. By 1902, five federal grants, comprising the areas of education, agriculture, veterans' benefits, resident instruction at land grant colleges, and money for the District of Columbia, were allocated for disbursement as part of intergovernmental funding in the amount of $7 million, or about 1 percent of total governmental expenditures at the time.[5]

From a public finance perspective, two issues of debate emerged to challenge more extensive uses of intergovernmental disbursements: first, federal income taxes' legality and, second, the constitutionality of using federal grants in a government system where there had been relatively distinctive operational lines (dual federalism) prior to the early 1900s. In understanding the first issue, the power of taxation originated in 1790 to fund the national government under the new Constitution, which then progressed further in 1913 with the passage of

> **Sixteenth Amendment**: granted the national government the power to pass a federal income tax, originally prohibited in the form of a direct tax (head tax) under the Constitution.

the federal income tax after the Sixteenth Amendment's ratification.[6] Under original Constitutional design, Article I, Section 9 prohibited the income tax in the form of a direct tax (head tax), thus necessitating a formal Constitutional amendment in 1913. In 1894, Congress had previously passed an income tax law which levied a two percent tax on income over $4,000, but a 5-4 U.S. Supreme Court decision in 1895 ruled that the income tax was regarded as a direct tax and was therefore unconstitutional. The Sixteenth Amendment institutionalized the income tax as a perpetual funding source for governmental activity, laying the foundations for how to systematize disbursements of funds to lower tiers as a means for promoting policy priorities. Relating to the second issue, the traditional view of dual federalism included critics who charged that grants represented the means by which the national government coerced states into certain patterns of behavior, which

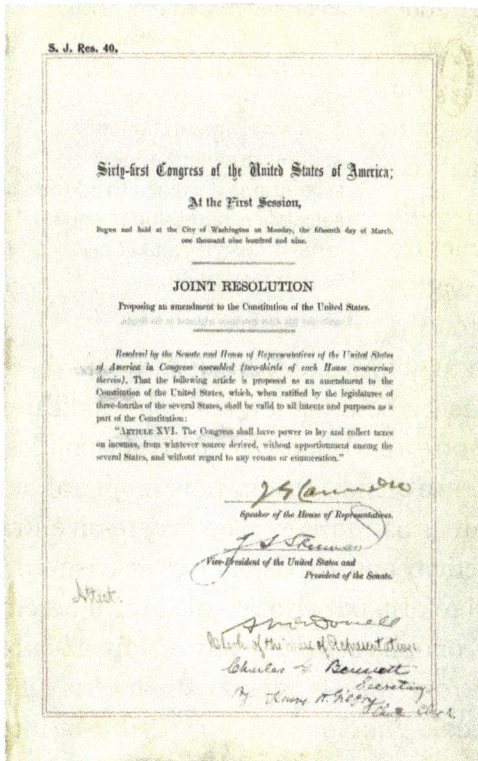

Figure 4.4: First page of the 16th Amendment of the United States Constitution.

Source: Wikimedia Commons

Attribution: NARA

License: Public Domain

---

5   Congressional Research Service, "Federal Grants to State and Local Governments: A Historical Perspective on Contemporary Issues," May 22, 2019, Accessed at: https://fas.org/sgp/crs/misc/R40638.pdf, 16–17.

6   Daniel J. Elazar, American Federalism: A View From the States, 63.

consequently disrupted the separation that existed between the two tiers. This debate was largely settled with two Supreme Court decisions in 1923–*Massachusetts v. Mellon*, and *Frothingham v. Mellon*–which established the judicial precedent that grants were, in fact, constitutional and permissible given that they were voluntary arrangements.[7] As the nation's political structure has evolved toward an intergovernmental arrangement over time, this move has resulted in the need to raise significant revenue to support funding policies and programs across levels of government. The federal government has historically provided large allocations of funding to subnational tiers, though concurrent powers permit taxation and expenditures to occur at lower levels of the system as well so as to provide for infrastructure and essential services.

4.2.2 The Progressive Era's Influence on Governmental Activism and the Direction of IGR

From Constitutional design through the early advancements in our system of public finance via the rise of income taxes and policy expansion through implied powers, spending on intergovernmental activities, including program implementation, has emerged as a formalized practice and means of governmental activism. This shift reflects the progression away from a structure where dual federalism existed with relative independence across tiers of government toward

> *Progressive Era*: a period of intensifying governmental activity and activism which affected the nature of intergovernmental relations and development of new regulations designed to address society's progression toward large industries and complex economic structures.

coordinated (and in many instances cooperative) forms of federalism where there is considerable interaction and interdependence between levels. It also indicates the influence that the Progressive Era (1900–1920) had on American politics, particularly in terms of addressing the influence of industrialization, immigration, and the corresponding growth in large-scale urbanization.[8] The Progressive Era was a period of intensifying governmental activity and activism. Progressivism was not only directed toward social and political reform but also revealed the inherent complexities and shortcomings of resting economic activity solely on laissez-faire principles. Richard Hofstadter frames it from the standpoint of interrelating societal values with political action in his book, *The Age of Reform*. Turn-of-the-century protest movements scrutinized American society's advance from small to medium-sized businesses, strongly individualistic values, and moderately organized private structures, to a more complicated system with large industries and corporations with principles and assumptions grounded in production levels and incentive structures.[9] This transition was inevitable, necessitating both broad

7   Laurence J. O'Toole Jr., and Robert K. Christensen, eds., *American Intergovernmental Relations: An Overview* (Thousand Oaks, CA: Sage Publications, 2013), 11.
8   Frederick R. Lynch, "Social Theory and the Progressive Era," *Theory and Society*, 4, no. 2 (Summer, 1977): 159.
9   Richard Hofstadter, *The Age of Reform* (New York: Vintage Books, 1955), 10–11.

policy guidance from the federal government and funding allocations to implement initiatives downward in the system. Consequently, the progressive movement had a lasting effect which resonated in subsequent eras of American federalism.

4.2.3 The Rise of Grants-in-Aid as an Aspect of IGR

The Progressive movement's emphasis on governmental activism had an enduring effect on American political culture. The evolution toward a more involved and integrated government system necessitated developing a complex array of funding techniques and public finance practices, some

> *Grants-in-aid*: disbursements from the federal government to states and localities for use for specific purposes.

of which have come and gone as part of a trial and error cycle. Federal grants-in-aid, or disbursements from the federal government to states and localities for use in specific areas, have been mechanisms of both cooperation and competition. Monetary allocations from the federal government have provided opportunities for levels of government to work jointly on complex policy areas and programmatic initiatives, though they have also provoked struggles between states and localities to secure funds in times of scarcity (which has become the norm over time, as discussed below). In his work, *American Federalism: A View From the States*, Elazar identifies five broad historical categories traditionally used to classify grants-in-aid: flat grants, proportionate grants, percentage grants, project grants, and entitlement grants. Flat grants provide recipients equal sums of money irrespective of competitive circumstances. While not driven by matching requirements (where recipients must match the amount provided to share in the burden of costs), they do place the burden of administrative costs on the receiving government. These types of allotments were relatively popular in the early to mid-twentieth century, taking the form of land grants or monetary disbursements to local school districts. Proportionate grants have a matching requirement which is calculated to be in proportion to the contribution provided by the program or project's recipient. This structure is based on formulas that consider recipients' needs and capabilities, as was common in highway fund distribution and education grants in the post-World War II era. Percentage grants are similar, but the granting contribution represents a set percentage of the cost that the recipient incurs for maintaining the program, as has been the case with public welfare initiatives started in the past as well as local school district funding. Project grants have specific requirements and may only be applied for specific project use, as was common in periods of urban renewal and redevelopment like the Great Society era. Finally, entitlement grants do not have matching requirements but are issued according to formulae by which recipients are automatically entitled to receive them, as has been the case with revenue sharing in the Nixon era.[10] Funding arrangement systems exist in modern times as a facet of IGR, which will be discussed more below, particularly in terms of block grants.

10   Daniel J. Elazar, American Federalism: A View From the States, 78.

From a macro-level perspective, grants-in-aid were used with less frequency prior to the 1930s. Chapter 1 noted that the New Deal era shifted American federalism toward a more cooperative structure that institutionalized the national-state-local aspects of IGR. As shown in Figure 4.5 below, the 1940s and 1950s onward represented an era of expanding usage in federal grants, such that state and local governments came to rely upon (and expect) disbursements from the national level. The figure provides a nominal dollar amount line and a constant dollar amount line that shows trends in 2020 dollars. As a percentage of total federal outlays, federal grants to states and localities comprised approximately 7.6 percent in 1960, rising to 12.3 percent in 1970, and 15.5 percent in 1980. The percentage was lowered to 11.2 percent in 1985 and dropped further to 10.8 by 1990. It began rebounding in 1995 at 14.9 percent, increasing to 16 percent by 2000, 17.6 percent by 2010, and comprising an estimated 16.5 percent in 2019. When accounting for inflation, the most robust increase period came in the mid-1960s until 1980, with the line's slope naturally approaching actual dollars in recent years. The 1930s era of cooperative federalism transitioned into a more centralized but coordinated arrangement with the Great Society program (1964–1965) and, in the subsequent decades of the 1960s and 1970s, leading to fiscal federalism structure where funding was more closely tied to achieving specific policy and programmatic outcomes as a facet of IGM. The reduction in grants that came in the early 1980s was temporary, being offset by increasing disbursements in succeeding periods. The early 2010s experienced moderate increases in actual dollars, but a slight down-surge in constant dollars.

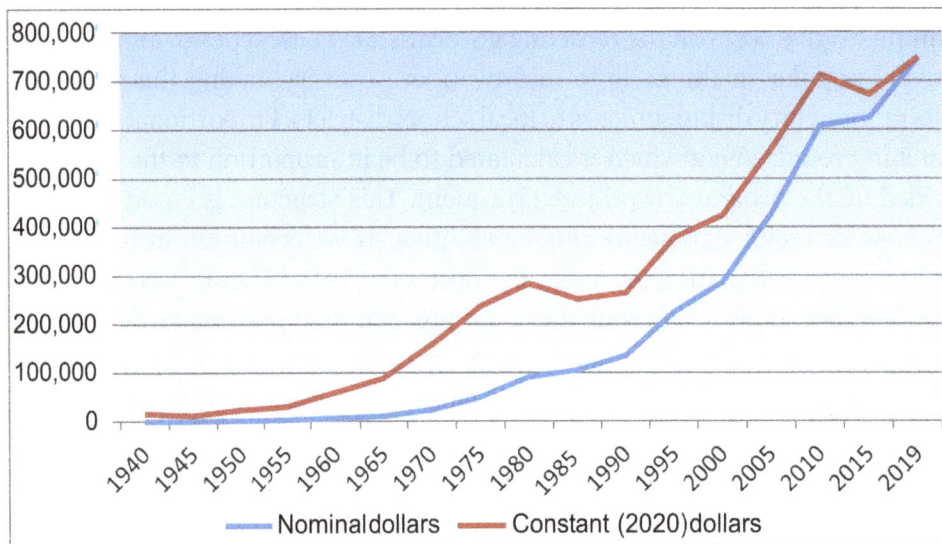

Figure 4.5: Federal Grants-in-Aid to State and Local Governments— 1940 Onward (millions of dollars).

Source: Original Work, adapted from Congressional Research Service, Federal Grants to State and Local Governments: A Historical Perspective on Contemporary Issues, Table 2, May 22, 2019; Accessed at: https://fas.org/sgp/crs/misc/R40638.pdf.

Attribution: Daniel Baracskay

License: CC BY-SA 4.0

4.3 THE EVOLUTION OF INTERGOVERNMENTAL FUNDING

Over time, the basis for how grants-in-aid have been allocated has been a product of many factors pertaining to the availability of resources, areas of usage, expected outcomes and utility to society (including the number of people who benefit), pressures from intergovernmental lobbyists and stakeholders, and competition with recipients. Procedures for funding have generally provided a structured and quantifiable basis for determining need, such as population size and rate or density of residents in a local area where the grant is issued as related to an area of concentration (e.g., poverty levels, public health indicators, unemployment levels, and other need-based qualifiers). Many critics (particularly in lower tiers of government) have contended that federal grants have tended to revolve around "carrot and stick" routines which hold funding in the view of potential recipients but have stringent provisions recipients must satisfy in order for the funding to be awarded. The countervailing perspective draws upon arguments pertaining to accountability and efficiency, where it is the obligation of the funds' issuers to ensure that requirements are met so as to utilize taxpayers' funds as effectively as possible as an aspect of IGM. The discussion below examines specific periods in the progression of fiscal federalism as relevant to the evolving nature of national-state-local relations. It devotes particular attention to the use of federal grants as part of the IGR equation.

4.3.1 Cooperative Federalism and IGR

As Thomas E. Cronin and William R. Hochman remark in their research, "Franklin D. Roosevelt and the American Presidency," Franklin D. Roosevelt is commonly credited with ushering in the era of the modern presidency. The stock market crash of 1929 resulted in the Great Depression; within one year, unemployment rose to over one-quarter of the labor force. This shift marked a transition from laissez-faire economic approaches, which rested private sector activities and industry on a "hidden hand" position, to a stance where Americans demanded that government take a strong role in implementing social and economic policies as a means of relief for deteriorating conditions. In response to national crises and the plethora of societal problems at the time, Roosevelt became a policy leader, making the president's role as chief legislator an expectation for future office holders. This move had significant ramifications for the course of fiscal decision-making as well. Economic crisis was the dominant issue Roosevelt confronted upon taking office, giving rise to initiatives like the Agricultural Adjustment Act and the National Industrial Recovery Act as instruments for forming new regulations designed to revitalize consumer capacity, regulate prices, reform labor conditions and worker wages, and recuperate outputs across industries.[11] In the period from 1930 to 1933, more than 5,500 banks closed, and industry decline experienced a prolonged downward surge that rippled across communities in the nation.

---

11   Bradford A. Lee, "The New Deal Reconsidered," *The Wilson Quarterly*, 6, no. 2 (Spring, 1982): 65–66.

The Roosevelt administration made the executive branch the center of action in the political system, expanded staffing levels, created the Executive Office of the President (EOP), and modernized how the nation viewed the chief executive as an active policy leader and spokesperson.[12] These steps were an important sequence in institutionalizing the administrative capability to implement broad policy initiatives through intergovernmental funding.

4.3.1.1 The New Deal Era

In the 1930s, the executive branch intervened considerably more directly in the nation's economic activities under a new pattern of federalism, which was referred to as "cooperative." A positive American state emerged which saw the initiation of expansive policies in the realms of public assistance, welfare, employment services, public housing, and urban development. The Roosevelt

> *New Deal*: a series of infrastructure projects, financial reforms and new social and economic policies which occurred in the 1930s under the leadership of President Franklin D. Roosevelt.

era of cooperative federalism, in which entities like the Civilian Conservation Corps (CCC) and Tennessee Valley Authority (TVA) were created, was predicated on shared policy responsibilities and coordination across levels of government, dispelling many of the characteristics that scholars identify with the preceding period of dual federalism. Money was allocated by the federal government to help with complex policy challenges at the subnational levels. The concept of IGR rose to fruition in the 1930s under a series of infrastructure projects, financial reforms, and new social and economic policies known as the New Deal. As Deil S. Wright remarks in his book *Understanding Intergovernmental Relations*, intergovernmental activity's focus became effective service delivery in providing aid for large-scale programs such as education and urban growth.[13] The reasons why the number and breadth of social and economic regulations expanded during this period were varied. These causes ranged from the need to police economic competition, to the growing trend in destructive market practices (e.g., price wars, price fixing, monopolies, etc.), to externalities or spillover effects that came in the form of environmental or public health concerns resulting from the advance of industrialization. Also, there was a growing need to provide for special goods and services pertaining to urban development, banking assistance, and agricultural aid which have particular linkages to public sector management and program execution through coordinated efforts.[14]

From the standpoint of fiscal federalism, the New Deal's legacy may be reflected upon from three perspectives. First, the Roosevelt administration introduced

---

12   Thomas E. Cronin and William R. Hochman, "Franklin D. Roosevelt and the American Presidency," *Presidential Studies Quarterly*, 15, no. 2 (Spring, 1985): 277.

13   Deil S. Wright, *Understanding Intergovernmental Relations,* 3rd ed. (Belmont, CA: Wadsworth Publishing Company, 1988), 13.

14   Congressional Quarterly, Inc., *Federal Regulatory Directory*, 8th ed. (Washington, D.C.: Congressional Quarterly, 1997), 2–4.

an unprecedented number of economic regulations which affected the nature of market operations.[15] These necessitated the creation of numerous agencies responsible for implementing Congressional mandates. Second, the New Deal era became synonymous with the introduction of new social welfare programs and associated initiatives, resulting in a considerable expansion of IGM activities as facets of organizational implementation. Social programs have a shared dimension which ties to activity coordination in state and local offices. The Social Security Act of 1935 has been one of the most pronounced ongoing programs from the New Deal era, providing assistance to millions of Americans. Today, social security comprises the largest of the many entitlement programs and includes Old Age and Survivors Insurance (OASI), Disability Insurance, and Supplemental Security Income. OASI was the original program created by the 1935 act and currently pays monthly benefits to 55 million beneficiaries, amounting to approximately $950 billion per fiscal year. The Disability Insurance (DI) program pays monthly benefits to more than 10 million disabled workers and their families, amounting to approximately $150 billion per fiscal year. Lastly, the Supplemental Security Income (SSI) program, later created in 1972, currently provides monthly benefits to eight million aged, blind, and disabled beneficiaries in low income brackets, amounting to $60 billion per fiscal year.[16] Yet, many Roosevelt-era initiatives have also been reformed and restructured over time. For instance, the Clinton administration replaced the preceding welfare design (Aid to Families with Dependent Children [AFDC], Job Opportunities and Basic Skills Training [JOBS] program, and the Emergency Assistance [EA] program), which was created and had evolved after the Great Depression, with the Temporary Assistance for Needy Families (TANF) program. TANF is implemented through a capped block grant which allocates $16.5 billion per year. Unlike the preceding structure, the program places lifetime limitations of five years on the amount of assistance that can be received by recipients, and stipulates work participation rate requirements that states must meet, along with sustaining the "maintenance of effort (MOE) requirement."[17] Third, growth in

---

15   Examples of these included: The Federal Home Loan Bank Board (FHLBB) of 1932 to regulate savings and loan provisions; The Federal Deposit Insurance Corporation (FDIC) of 1933 which was created by the Banking Act introduced earlier that year to regulate and insure funds deposited in our nation's banks; The Securities and Exchange Commission (SEC) which was created in 1934 to protect securities and financial markets against fraudulent activities; The Federal Communications Commission (FCC) of 1934 which was established as an independent agency in charge of regulating radio, telephone, telegraph, and subsequent communication technologies (i.e. television, cable, satellite) across the nation; The National Labor Relations Board (NLRB) established in 1935 from the Wagner Act to safeguard the rights of employees to bargain and to prevent unfair labor practices; The Motor Carrier Act of 1935 which placed the trucking industry under the authority of the Interstate Commerce Commission (ICC); and the U.S. Maritime Administration which was established in 1936 to regulate ship operations during the war, whose functions were ultimately transferred to the Transportation Department and Federal Maritime Commission (FMC). These were largely broad policy spheres that the federal government has had purview over, with some overlapping responsibility at the subnational levels.

16   Social Security Administration, "Fiscal Year 2020 Budget Overview," March 2019, Accessed at: https://www.ssa.gov/budget/FY20Files/2020BO_1.pdf, 4.

17   U.S. Department of Health & Human Services, "Aid to Families with Dependent Children (AFDC) and Temporary Assistance for Needy Families (TANF)– Overview, November 30, 2009, Accessed at: https://aspe.hhs.gov/aid-families-dependent-children-afdc-and- temporary-assistance-needy-families-tanf-overview-0.

a vast number of ancillary agencies facilitated the progression toward a marble cake pattern of intergovernmental activity, where tiers of government were tied together and the federal government was no longer considered a remote entity but instead a fiscal and administrative policy coordinator.[18] While numerous New Deal agencies were created (with many being discontinued at later points), they were nonetheless important in fostering a shared IGR fiscal structure. Examples of these agencies included the following: the Agricultural Adjustment Administration (1933-1942); Civil Works Administration (1933-1934); Civilian Conservation Corps (1933-1942); Farm Security Administration (1937-1946); Federal Emergency Relief Administration (1933-1937); Home Owners Load Corporation (1933-1951); National Recovery Administration (1933-1935); Public Works Administration (1933-1939); and the Works Progress Administration (1935-1943).[19] These offices set the stage for modern organizational structures and the use of IGM as a means for facilitating national policies at the state and local levels of government.

4.3.1.2 Challenges to Fiscal Federalism Under the Roosevelt Administration

President Roosevelt's transition to newer forms of fiscal federalism and administrative capacity were not met with universal support. Despite his popularity with the American public throughout his several terms as president, Roosevelt faced numerous hurdles in moving his policy agendas forward. These hurdles arose most noticeably in battles with the U.S. Supreme Court in executing assorted social welfare programs, and in utilizing IGR more extensively than any other previous chief executive in our nation's history. While the 1923 court cases *Massachusetts v. Mellon* and *Frothingham v. Mellon* allowed federal grants to be constitutionally permissible (see above), there was still ideological resistance to the growing role played by the national government. The conservative majority of justices serving on the Court during the New Deal era upheld a more restrictive ideological view of the federal government's power to expand the realm of administrative law through new regulations. From the initial period when Roosevelt introduced his New Deal program in 1933 until the end of 1936, 16 laws were passed as part of his recovery program, with nine being nullified by the Court.[20] This process had an effect on the ability to revive macro-economic performance in the immediate post-Great Depression period and also stalemated aspects of implementing programmatic mandates from a more intergovernmental approach.

After winning the 1936 presidential election, Roosevelt presented a "court packing" plan to reorganize the Supreme Court and increase the number of justices from nine to upwards of 15 as a means of counterbalancing conservative opposition to his policy objectives. This strategy was a politically-unpopular plan (both within

18   Laurence J. O'Toole Jr., and Robert K. Christensen, eds., *American Intergovernmental Relations: An Overview*, 13.
19   Bradford A. Lee, "The New Deal Reconsidered," 67.
20   Theresa A. Niedziela, "Franklin D. Roosevelt and the Supreme Court," *Presidential Studies Quarterly*, 6, no. 4 (Fall, 1976): 51.

Figure 4.6: On February 5, 1937, Vice President Garner (center) with Senator William H. Dieterich (left) of Illinois; and Senator Henry F. Ashurst of Arizona, Chairman of the Senate Judiciary Committee, reading Judicial Procedures Reform Bill of 1937 (the Court Packing Bill).
Source: Wikimedia Commons
Attribution: Harris & Ewing, Inc.
License: Public Domain

Congress and with the American public) that ultimately became unnecessary after Justice Roberts cast a deciding vote in *NLRB v. Jones & Laughlin Steel Corp.* in 1937 to uphold the constitutionality of New Deal legislation previously challenged by the Court. Roberts' vote was referred to as "the switch in time that saved nine" and occurred around the time that another justice retired, which consequently made the court packing scheme unnecessary. Roosevelt's activist personality and effectiveness in using "fireside chats" in evening radio messages to the nation allowed him to utilize tides of public opinion to push forward programmatic goals under an expansive vision of new federalism where there was a sharing of funds and coordinated implementation of policies.

Scholars do not contest that an activist president was necessary in addressing the problems of the nation at the time. Nor do they disagree that the resulting era of cooperative federalism changed the direction of public budgeting and finance practices by expanding the basis for shared responsibilities through new program initiatives. However, the broadening of intergovernmental activity did not necessarily lead to policy and programmatic efficiency. Hofstadter regarded the New Deal era as a frenzy of random programs and disjointed policies, with some lasting over the long run and others failing in the short-term.[21] That Roosevelt era initiatives had a significant impact on the social, economic, and political structures of the nation is indisputable, but the extent of these impacts is more open to debate. A 25 percent unemployment rate existed when Roosevelt assumed office in 1933, falling to around 17 percent for the remainder of the decade after segments of his reformist agenda were implemented, but not dropping to a lower, more manageable 14 percent until federal spending increased dramatically with the nation's entry in World War II. Some modest shift in national income occurred during the 1930s and 1940s in the years after the New Deal program was initiated, with the share of total national income for the bottom two-fifths of individuals in the nation rising

Court packing plan: a strategy by President Franklin D. Roosevelt to reorganize the Supreme Court and increase the number of justices from nine to upwards of fifteen justices as a means of counterbalancing conservative opposition to his policy objectives.

---

21   Richard Hofstadter, *The American Political Tradition and the Men Who Made It* (New York: Alfred A. Knopf, 1948), XXX.

from 12.5 to 15.7 percent with new social programs.[22] While neither significantly greater wealth equity nor large-scale redistribution of income ensued, the marked expansion of new social programs had an effect on helping to abate poverty levels and revitalize workforce development. This impact represented a shift in public budgeting and finance philosophy, and, at this point, the nation experienced a significant push toward deficit spending, such that the federal government began devoting greater sums to functions and programs that it had been more reluctant to do prior to that point. For instance, David M. Kennedy remarks that deficit spending was five percent of GNP or lower in the 1930s, with the highest level being $4.2 billion in 1936. This point changed when deficit spending enlarged to 28 percent of GNP, approximating $53 billion more than in the 1936 peak year.[23] While war-time revenue legislation expanded federal tax proceeds in order to fund the government's foreign policy activities, it also signaled a progression toward committing large amounts of funding to domestic policy initiatives and deferring costs across years or even generations of tax payers who derive a benefit from spending provisions.

4.3.2 Creative and Centralized Federalism and IGR

The 1960s was a vibrant era that elicited considerable interest from state and local governments pertaining to the expanded use of federal grants. A vast number of new programs had come to fruition since the New Deal era, and grants dispersed downward in the system became the means by which operations were consistently funded. Yet, the thousands of contracts issued to local governments and supporting community-based organizations as the basis for urban renewal had the effect of scattering policies outward and leading to programmatic mismanagement. Coordination problems abounded, causing reflection on how to consolidate the numerous categorical grants that were allocated each year into larger blocks of funding. Reform initiatives were offered during this period as a means for addressing the progression toward excessive use of grants and fragmentation in federal aid.[24] If scholars described federalism in the preceding era as cooperative, from the mid-1960s era until approximately 1980 they described it as creative and centralized. Centralized federalism does not denote a return to the pre-twentieth century's dual federalism era; rather, it signifies the federal government's movement toward taking the lead in broad policy areas and utilizing grants-in-aid more creatively so as to foster desirable outcomes. In essence, the New Deal era had taken its course over a series of three decades; with many initiatives being firmly entrenched as facets of IGR, the focus shifted away from program creation toward programmatic effectiveness.

---

22 Bradford A. Lee, "The New Deal Reconsidered," 66.

23 David M. Kennedy, "What the New Deal Did," *Political Science Quarterly*, 124, no. 2 (Summer 2009): 252.

24 Conlan, Timothy J., From *New Federalism to Devolution: Twenty-Five Years of Intergovernmental Reform* (Washington, D.C.: Brookings Institution Press, 1998), 26.

4.3.2.1 The Great Society Program

The roles played by states and localities were of considerable importance for implementing the series of domestic programs known as the Great Society. Launched by President Lyndon B. Johnson in 1964–1965, these initiatives pertained to education, urban renewal and poverty reduction, transportation, and public health, along with other areas of significance. Johnson regarded his vision for the Great Society not as the progression toward a rich or powerful polity but from the standpoint of creating opportunity equity. This goal had particular relevance for society's most disadvantaged, including minority groups, such that "it demands an end to poverty and racial injustice."[25] The framework for many of these programs originated with the Kennedy administration's New Frontier initiative, which sought to improve local communities through housing, infrastructure, and economic development projects funded by the federal government. From an IGM perspective, the vast increase in the number of New Deal era grants and funding levels had led to an institutionalizing effect at the local levels of government, resulting in a professionalization of personnel, modernization of financial procedures, systematizing of agency functions and programmatic operations, and specialization of personnel responsible for utilizing funds for specific purposes. Consequently, the Johnson administration's focus was on reforming the system which was already in place to better serve the American people with efficient and effective administration.

> ***Centralized federalism***: a progression toward the federal government taking the lead for broad policies areas and utilizing grants-in-aid more creatively so as to foster desirable outcomes.
>
> ***Great Society***: a series of domestic programs launched by President Lyndon B. Johnson in 1964-1965 that related to intergovernmental funding of education, urban renewal and poverty reduction, transportation, and public health, along with other policy areas focused on helping the poor.
>
> ***New Frontier***: an initiative by President John F. Kennedy which sought to improve local communities through housing, infrastructure, and economic development projects funded by the federal government.

From an ideological standpoint, the Democrats had been the support base of social programs originating in the New Deal era, and they remained the means by which such initiatives were sustained. Upon taking office, Johnson had the benefit of a strongly-supportive Congress with a Democratic majority, which he embraced as a means for expanding several intergovernmental initiatives through creative federalism. Aspects of IGM factored into forging relationships (and partnerships) not only between states and localities but also across other segments of community stakeholders, community-based organizations, nonprofit organizations, and even private sector companies. He also had the backing of the Warren Court, which was important from a Constitutional standpoint (recalling the confrontation that Franklin D. Roosevelt had encountered with Supreme Court challenges during the initial years of his presidency), as well as the support of an American public

---

25   Congressional Quarterly, Congress and the Nation, 1965–1968, vol. II (Washington, D.C., 1969), 650.

that enthusiastically embraced his vision, reflecting his high approval ratings.[26] The focus of intergovernmental funding was on efforts to combat poverty, racial discrimination, urban decline, and rural hardship. From the 1960s until 1974, this concentration ushered in a period when grants-in-aid tripled in number, mostly in the form of categorical and project grants.[27] Consequently, a significant increase in public assistance benefits for the elderly and disabled, unemployment compensation, and other forms of income support (e.g., social security, veterans' benefits, worker compensation) occurred during this time.[28]

Figure 4.7: The United States Supreme Court in 1953, known as the Warren Court. Bottom from left: Felix Frankfurter; Hugo Black; Earl Warren (Chief Justice); Stanley Reed; William O. Douglas. Back from left: Tom Clark; Robert H. Jackson; Harold Burton; Sherman Minton
Source: Wikimedia Commons
Attribution: Unknown
License: Public Domain

4.3.2.2 The Changing Scope of Fiscal Federalism Under the Johnson Administration

While it became synonymous with the "war on poverty," the Johnson era also had a broader impact on the affairs of society as a whole. The Great Society included several legislative aspects. First, as an extension of helping to provide opportunity equity, various education and training programs disbursed significant

26   Sar A. Levitan and Robert Taggart, "The Great Society Did Succeed," *Political Science Quarterly*, 91, no. 4 (Winter, 1976–1977): 601–602.
27   Laurence J. O'Toole Jr., and Robert K. Christensen, eds., *American Intergovernmental Relations: An Overview*, 15.
28   Sar A. Levitan and Robert Taggart, "The Great Society Did Succeed," 601–605.

funding from the federal government to states and local school districts. The focus of grants-in-aid under Johnson's Great Society program was on educating the economically disadvantaged. This intentional decision was made by those who recognized that a correlation exists between income and education, and funding designed to address the gap between low-income and moderate-to-high income families was seen as a means to narrow the gap. Head Start legislation during this period allocated funding to public and non-profit organizations that provided education and training to disadvantaged children, particularly in their developmental periods. Institutions of higher education also benefitted from grants that concentrated money on new facility construction. Direct aid to students was based upon need, a procedure formalized by the Economic Opportunity Act of 1964. As part of the act, the Work Study Program included equal opportunity grants focused on assisting previously-disadvantaged groups. Title IV of the Higher Education Act of 1965 provided low-interest loans to students pursuing higher education opportunities. Besides this program, those like the Job Corps represented a facet of the IGR equation by establishing local centers to provide vocational and work training to younger individuals. Subsidies funded manpower policies that had been used since the Area Redevelopment Act of 1961 and the Manpower Development and Training Act of 1962.

Second, in focusing on the residential population, the Housing and Urban Development Act of 1968 established the policies upon which funding for public housing would be based and refocused urban renewal efforts on low income households. It also created the means by which the secondary mortgage market would operate and expanded credit terms for loan insurance in households deemed to be high-risk. Subsidies allowed disadvantaged groups to experience less strain on their income and to be able to purchase larger homes than would otherwise be possible. However, federal funding in this area resulted in high levels of demand, as demonstrated by long waiting lists and low vacancy rates. Subsidized units carry their associated costs, which have potentially higher-than-average expenditures due to union wages, minority contracting requirements, maintenance costs, and other administrative burdens that the government carries to execute the function. Even so, the outcome has been greater suburbanization over time, as well as desegregation of residential populations, representing a staple of court rulings during the era.[29] Third, the passage of the Voting Rights Law of 1965 took a significant step forward in strengthening the earlier Civil Rights Act of 1957 (the first piece of civil rights legislation passed since the Civil Rights Act of 1875). The Civil Rights Act of 1964 is a landmark piece of legislation that outlaws discrimination and prohibits unequal treatment in employment and public facilities.[30] Many of the Johnson era provisions in this area complement the other policy issues discussed above, particularly in terms of securing equal employment

---

29 Sar A. Levitan and Robert Taggart, "The Great Society Did Succeed,"601–607.

30 Elba K. Brown-Collier, "Johnson's Great Society: Its Legacy in the 1990s," *Review of Social Economy*, 56, no. 3 (Fall, 1998): 261–262.

opportunities, school desegregation and access to education and training, and fairness in housing practices. Due process rights under social welfare programs were expanded as part of the era of 1960s legal reform efforts, particularly in terms of equal protection, and in providing the poor with access to legal aid and services.[31]

Fourth, President Johnson made considerable progress in the public health realm, a policy area of increasing consideration since the first Hoover Commission (1947–1949). Accordingly, the 1960s became a fulcrum of several health care initiatives, which reflected the evolving nature of fiscal federalism as a facet of creative funding arrangements where states and localities coordinated broad mandates originating at the national level. For instance, the Comprehensive Health Planning (CHP) and Regional Medical Program (RMP) were two provisions in which funding was distributed to subnational levels to generate a positive expected effect on the health status of the poor and non-poor.[32] These initiatives effected the creation of regional planning agencies and the construction of local neighborhood health centers to provide medical assistance as part of a coordinated and planned process that sought to eliminate duplication and operational inefficiencies. While such activities were designed to benefit all segments of the population, they tended to be of particular assistance to the poor, primarily disadvantaged and low-income groups, like single mothers and children. Intergovernmental financing of health care policies also reflected the demands of a demographically-evolving society that was growing older and more diverse. Medicare spending, for example, addressed the increasing number of the elderly (many of whom were in lower income levels as retirees) as well as the expanding number of individuals in both urban and rural areas who were impoverished and relied upon Medicaid assistance. To address fragmentation and inefficiencies in funding arrangements, the Johnson administration enacted the Partnership for Health Act in 1966, which consolidated nine formula grants into one single block grant.

4.3.3 The Nixon Era, Reform, and IGR

During Richard Nixon's presidency, a centralized form of American federalism continued to evolve through a sequence of reform efforts designed to make government more efficient and effective. By some assessments, the Nixon era began a period of New federalism (which continued into the 1980s with the Reagan administration) which relied less on fiscal tools of intergovernmental policy coordination and more on regulatory tools designed to solidify the national government's supremacy.[33] Competition intensified, particularly as localities sought to secure increasingly-scarce resources in times of budgetary constraints while also focusing their efforts on economic development strategies to promote effective service delivery and so entice residents and businesses into their areas

31   Sar A. Levitan and Robert Taggart, "The Great Society Did Succeed," 609.
32   Anne Mooney, "The Great Society and Health: Policies for Narrowing the Gaps in Health Statues between the Poor and the Nonpoor," *Medical Care*, 15, no. 8 (Aug., 1977): 611.
33   John Kincaid, "From Cooperative to Coercive Federalism," *The Annals of the American Academy of Political and Social Science*, 509, (May, 1990): 139.

Figure 4.8: Richard Nixon being inaugurated as the 37th President of the United States.
Source: Wikimedia Commons
Attribution: Oliver F. Atkins
License: Public Domain

to bolster tax bases. The coordination of broad policy goals set at the national level and implemented at the state and local levels sustained the intergovernmental foundations driving fiscal federalism. The State and Local Fiscal Assistance Act of 1972 exemplified a public finance initiative which allocated significant funds to state and local governments over a five-year period. The act was designed to provide fiscal relief to the subnational tiers and to generate greater balance in intergovernmental financing while decentralizing decision-making authority.[34] More than $30 billion dollars were disbursed during this time, with over 23 thousand special purpose groups and 15 thousand school districts being recipients.[35] Programmatic implementation, as would be expected, depended highly on funding allocation, though the Nixon administration proposed to justify support for intergovernmental coordination by restructuring how all levels of government executed their respective functions. This proposal held significant implications for the IGM side of organizational development—representing a departure from his predecessors—as programmatic assessment and evaluation became a standard measure for validating resource usage. With the 1972 act, which continued into the Ford administration, some programmatic improvements were made based upon fund allocation, and governmental reform facilitated cross-coordination and regional planning. Fiscal disparities moderated, and levels of citizen participation rose in public sector budgeting processes. However, reform neither sparked much interest from the states in pursuing their own revenue-generating approaches so as to lessen their continued reliance on federal assistance nor was funding necessity-driven where localities with the greatest need benefited.[36]

4.3.3.1 Fiscal Aspects of Nixon's Political Reform Efforts: Block Grants and Revenue Sharing

From an IGR perspective, Timothy Conlan notes in his book, *From New Federalism to Devolution: Twenty-Five Years of Intergovernmental Reform,* that Nixon-era approaches to fiscal federalism were designed to bring about greater cross-level coordination and planning.

General revenue sharing: a Nixon era funding arrangement used to provide federal aid with "no strings attached" which lower tiers of government used to respond to pressing problems.

34   Carl W. Stenberg, "Revenue Sharing and Governmental Reform," *The Annals of the American Academy of Political Science*, 419, (May, 1975): 50.
35   William B. Neenan, "General Revenue Sharing and Redistribution," *Review of Social Economy*, vol. 35, no. 2, (April, 1977), 25.
36   Carl W. Stenberg, "Revenue Sharing and Governmental Reform," 50–51.

Most notably, preceding categories of federal grants were consolidated to align with reform initiatives designed to simplify program operations while expanding service delivery and operational responsiveness. Nixon utilized an arrangement known as general revenue sharing to provide federal aid with "no strings attached," which lower tiers of government used to respond to pressing problems.[37] Grant simplification and managerial reforms were interconnected themes of the Nixon era, particularly reflecting the widespread view of the national government as inefficient and detached from the American public, in contrast to the view of state and local governments as more efficient and responsive.[38] In connecting the macro and micro-dimensions of public finance, Nixon-era reforms reinforced the idea that responsibility for far-reaching policy areas like welfare and entitlements, economic development, and social regulation were guided broadly by federal mandates but necessitated effective administrative structures upon which to base their implementation. Restructuring public sector organizations to more efficiently utilize funds and resources is an aspect of IGM that seeks to maximize how taxes are applied as a facet of the public trust.

Consequently, Nixon's vision for fiscal federalism fostered innovation and flexibility for subnational governments to respond to challenges unique to their locations, while promoting programmatic proficiency and accountability. However, Conlan notes that Nixon's approach to

> **Impoundment (of appropriated funds)**: the refusal of a president to employ Congressional appropriations for mandated uses.

federalism became more ideologically charged, if not confrontational, in 1971. At that time, he proposed consolidating 129 categorical programs, which represented approximately one-third of federal aid expenditures. This move created six broad and flexible block grants falling under the designation special revenue sharing, which were coupled with a political strategy designed to build a conservative coalition that would usher in a new era of vast changes in how federal aid was structured.[39] Other segments of the literature likewise note that Nixon introduced a form of new federalism which publicized decentralization and reform as a rationale for policy realignment; in effect, however, fiscal aspects of IGR reflected a neoconservative movement to streamline New Deal programs and their associated funding arrangements.[40] Conlan describes this strategy to "coerce Congress" as high risk. Ultimately, the plan was unsuccessful given the chief executive's unilateral approach, which included using impoundment tactics, that is, refusal to spend congressional appropriations allocated for programmatic usage. The lack of success shifted the president's political style to a more incremental (and restrained) approach grounded in consensus building rather than unilateral

---

37   Timothy Conlan, *From New Federalism to Devolution: Twenty-Five Years of Intergovernmental Reform*, 3.

38   Leonard Robins, "The Plot That Succeeded: The New Federalism as Policy Realignment," *Presidential Studies Quarterly*, 10, no. 1, (Winter, 1980): 102.

39   Timothy Conlan, *From New Federalism to Devolution*, 20.

40   Leonard Robins, "The Plot That Succeeded: The New Federalism as Policy Realignment," *Presidential Studies Quarterly*, vol. 10, no. 1, (Winter, 1980), 99–100.

struggles, which had previously stalemated the reform process. Subsequently, the Nixon administration's objectives for reforming and restructuring the fiscal dimensions of IGR did not falter, particularly after he provided reassurance that allocations of governmental expenditures to lower tiers in the system would remain steady. Instead, the political strategy to achieve these ideological objectives shifted to a more indirect route tied to programmatic intervention and modification and specifically focused on addressing the rate of growth the federal government had experienced under previous administrations as a facet of administrative efficiency and effectiveness. Whether a centralized or decentralized approach was taken depended on the specific policy area being considered. For instance, decentralization was a means for devolving greater responsibility to states and localities for programmatic areas that responded well to significant control at the parochial levels. This strategy prevailed with community development, education and training, and associated fields where programmatic responsibility was guided through federal leadership, but implementation largely resided in communities. In other issue areas where cost containment and uniformity were of concern, nationalization strategies were designed to streamline IGM and bring about greater programmatic effectiveness, as was the case with delivering a more equitable welfare system.

4.3.4 The New Federalism and the Reagan Era

President Ronald Reagan's vision of a new federalism was an extension of Nixon-era reforms for improving how government functions, though his strategies for achieving greater efficiency and effectiveness embraced different approaches. Reagan saw big government as having taken its course from the New Deal and introduced managerial reforms to diminish the national bureaucracy's power and influence. The Reagan approach focused far less on using IGR as a means for improving programmatic and organizational efficiency levels and instead emphasized reducing the national government's scope and justifying responsibility and implementation at lower tiers in the system.[41] This strategy was solidified with two broad legislative initiatives in 1981—the Omnibus Budget Reconciliation Act (OBRA) and the Economic Recovery Tax Act (ERTA)—which advanced fiscal reductionism as a means for addressing high federal tax rates, rising expenditure levels over time, increasing amounts of governmental borrowing, and the many superfluous regulations which stagnate economic growth.[42]

The Reagan presidency was fiscally conservative with domestic policy spending, though it spent large amounts of money in defense policy (spending increased by approximately one-third during his two terms), which escalated debt levels at the time. Many initiatives expanded the Nixon administration's strategy to consolidate categorical grants into broader block grants. From an IGM perspective, the focus went to shifting program responsibilities to lower levels of government as part of a

41 Timothy Conlan, From New Federalism to Devolution, 3–4.
42 David B. Walker, "American Federalism from Johnson to Bush," *Publius*, 21, no. 1 (Winter, 1991): 109.

simplification plan to streamline intergovernmental aid; also, policy responsibility devolved away from the national government to states in selected areas (e.g., health care, infrastructure, education, economic development) as a means of providing greater administrative efficiency.[43] Revenue sharing was eliminated during the Reagan administration, and the number of unfunded mandates increased significantly as subnational governments were forced to fund policies and programs previously supported by grants from the national government.

Figure 4.9: President Reagan during an Oval Office meeting and working visit of Prime Minister Thatcher of the United Kingdom.
Source: Wikimedia Commons
Attribution: Unknown
License: Public Domain

4.3.4.1 Devolution, Unfunded Mandates, and Fiscal Reform

Reagan viewed federalism as having the potential to produce a revitalization effect. Under this vision, the devolution of powers and policy responsibilities to lower levels in the system would counterbalance the negative consequences of big government that began decades earlier under the New Deal, thus resulting in a form of "partnership with the American people."[44] As mentioned above, one example of Reagan's fiscal strategy was the Omnibus Reconciliation Act of 1981, which created nine block grants (through consolidating 77 categorical grants) for distribution to states and localities, but at a much diminished rate of funding than

43   Laurence J. O'Toole Jr., and Robert K. Christensen, eds., *American Intergovernmental Relations: An Overview*, 22.
44   Timothy J. Conlan, "Federalism and Competing Values in the Reagan Administration," *Publius*, 16, no. 1 (Winter, 1986): 29.

had been experienced in the previous three decades. This decision represented his goal to reduce spending by the national government and force subnational governments to incur a greater share of policy responsibility. Block grants had fewer restrictions and requirements than categorical grants, allowing localities to use funding to suit their own diverse and unique needs. Yet, with the elimination of revenue sharing and the decrease of federal appropriations, this dynamic placed a higher level of financial burden on lower levels in the system. From a political perspective, Reagan traded lower funding levels for more significant grants of authority which governors and other local public officials were interested in securing as a means for broader programmatic discretion. Yet, the 10 percent reductions originally posed by governors in actuality averaged around 21 percent less in 1982 than the previous fiscal year spending, representing a significant departure from the Nixon and Ford administrations, which were ideologically conservative though willing to tolerate higher spending levels as a means of bolstering political support.[45] The depth of fiscal cuts was particularly felt in Reagan's first term as he entered office with a contraction strategy to bring spending in line with diminishing authority exercised at the national level of government. Conlan notes in *From New Federalism to Devolution: Twenty-Five Years of Intergovernmental Reform* that this technique was part of the Reagan administration's "swap" and "turnback" approach, in which the federal government assumed financial responsibility for Medicaid's implementation and states assumed accountability for the AFDC and Food Stamp programs, while also devolving responsibility for 40 other federal programs to the states with tax resources by which to fund them. Reagan's vision of federalism contended that the fiscal tradeoffs of shifting policy responsibility between levels would effect a net benefit that would empower states and localities by forcing them to respond with new, innovative funding strategies to maintain their programs' operations.

In addition to funding reductions, the use of unfunded mandates became a decisive factor in national-state-local relations. From the New Deal era forward, subnational governments became accustomed to implementing mandates issued by the federal government that provided policy guidance and programmatic support. Unfunded mandates require state and local governments to assume the financial burden of policy implementation and administrative costs. Part of Reagan's vision for a new federalism decentralized authority and responsibility downward in the system as part of a devolution strategy. Consequently, this move caused considerable fiscal and administrative stress, particularly at lower levels of the system, resulting in additional annually-imposed costs approximating several billion dollars for both cities and counties.[46] While the costs of individual unfunded mandates were typically

> **Unfunded mandates**: requires that state and local governments assume the financial burden of policy implementation and administrative costs.

---

45   Timothy J. Conlan, "Federalism and Competing Values in the Reagan Administration," 31.
46   Timothy Conlan, From New Federalism to Devolution, 260.

low, issuing several hundred such procedures resulted in considerable outlays that were challenging for lower tiers to absorb.[47] The broad results of unfunded mandates' expanded use in many states and localities were higher tax rates and fewer services being provided, though there did exist variation across regions in local governments' abilities to shelter the burden based on tax and revenue-generation capacity. As the course of unfunded mandates unfolded in subsequent years, political pressure mounted to provide fiscal relief for Reagan era directives. The Unfunded Mandates Reform Act (UMRA) of 1995 was passed several years after the Reagan presidency in response to growing intergovernmental pressure to curb the use of such mandates.[48]

4.3.4.2 Outcomes of Reagan's New Federalism Initiatives

Like his predecessors, Reagan was ultimately both successful and unsuccessful in bringing various aspects of his strategies on federalism to fruition. First, Richard L. Cole and Delbert A. Taebel note in their article, "The New Federalism: Promises, Programs, and Performance," that the swap and turnback strategy met with very limited success, though Reagan did achieve some victories in reducing the allocation of federal funds to lower tiers of government, as exemplified in the $6.6 billion reduction in aid linked to the Omnibus Act of 1981 mentioned above.[49] Second—and related—consolidating dozens of categorical grants into nine block grants helped bolster Reagan's plans to streamline government and bring changes to administrative efficiency as a facet of IGM. This move was a continuation of Nixon-era planning, which was successfully applied to several initiatives, like the Job Training Partnership Act in 1982. The act replaced the previously-terminated Comprehensive Employment Training Act passed by the Nixon administration in 1973. The administrative process included linking procedures to address the trend in rising costs.[50] Third, despite granting limited increases of discretionary power to subnational governments, Reagan also centralized authority in many functional areas and signed bills that prevented states from pursuing economic regulations over certain industries. This approach of entrusting states and localities with some limited responsibilities was selectively executed, with concentrated power

47   Janet Kelly, "Unfunded Mandates: The View from the States," *Public Administration Review*, 54, no. 4 (Jul.–Aug. 1994): 405.
48   The reform act was a product of agreement between Republican leaders in Congress who were advancing their Contract with America, and President William Clinton, a Democrat. The bipartisan initiative reinvigorated the perspective that Federalism was an ever-changing facet of American political culture, and shifted the premise of Reagan's vision for unfunded mandates back toward concentration on intergovernmental collaboration and financial assistance. As part of the UMRA, mandates with an unfunded amount of more than $50 million per year for state and local governments could be halted by a House or Senate floor point of order. In doing so, this included Congressional reviews of mandates that required extra spending by state and local units, preemptive measures on the use of state and local revenue sources, and cutbacks of federal authorizations to help cover compliance costs of mandates already in place; see: Paul L. Posner, "Unfunded Mandates Reform Act: 1996 and Beyond," *Publius*, 27, no. 2 (Spring, 1997): 53–54.
49   Richard L. Cole and Delbert A. Taebel, "The New Federalism: Promises, Programs, and Performance," *Publius*, 16, no. 1 (Winter, 1986), 6.
50   Joseph F. Zimmerman, "Federal Preemption under Reagan's New Federalism," *Publius*, 21, no. 1 (Winter, 1991): 11.

Figure 4.10: President Ronald Reagan Signs the 1981 Economic Recovery Tax Act and Omnibus Budget Reconciliation Act at Rancho Del Cielo in California, 8/13/1981.

Source: Wikimedia Commons
Attribution: White House Photographic Collection
License: Public Domain

remaining in functional areas that were politically charged. Consequently, Reagan's style for federalism has been described as a continuation of both "coercive" and "cooperative" measures.[51] This approach represented a new direction in federalism, which continued to use fiscal arrangements to shape power structures.

Finally, Reagan left a permanent mark on how fiscal federalism would be shaped through the politics of the budgetary process. Government spending had been on the rise for decades. As a percentage of Gross Domestic Product (GDP), total government expenditures were 17.3 percent of GDP in 1948. This number increased to 25 percent in 1952, hovering below 30 percent until the mid-1970s. From 1975 through 1997, government expenditures comprised between 31 and 33 percent of GDP.[52] Expenditure levels were particularly high when Reagan assumed office, factoring into his vision of new federalism as a means for reducing the scope and extent of the federal government's expenditure levels.

Consequently, the passage of the Gramm-Rudman-Hollings (GRH) Act in 1985 was a provision which specifically addressed the long-run ramifications of government deficits. From $40 billion in 1979, the federal deficit escalated to $209 billion in 1983, a rise attributable to the economic recession of 1981–1982, tax cuts which had diminished revenue collection at the time, and large increases in defense spending during the initial period when Reagan took office. This increase coupled

> **Gramm-Rudman-Hollings (GRH) Act**: a piece of legislation passed in 1985 which specifically addressed the long-run ramifications of government deficits.

with Congress' resistance toward reducing entitlement program expenditures. The 1985 act established a timetable for successive reductions in the federal deficit to bring about a balanced budget by 1991 (which actually occurred briefly in the Clinton presidency). In fiscal periods when disagreement between Congress

---

51   Daniel J. Elazar, "Opening the Third Century of American Federalism: Issues and Prospects," *The Annals of the American Academy of Political and Social Science*, 509, (May, 1990): 13.

52   Office of Management and Budget, "Historical Tables: Table 14.3— Total Government Expenditures as Percentages of GDP: 1948– 2018, January 2020, Accessed at: https://www.whitehouse.gov/omb/historical-tables/.

and the president fail to generate a reduction as planned, the act allowed for sequestration, or automatic across-the-board cuts in spending that would be applied equally across programs.[53] While Congress did not meet the timetable and political stalemates continued to illustrate the divergence of ideological perspectives which factor into fiscal decisions, the GRH Act accentuated the deficiencies inherent to deficit spending, enlarging budgetary requests, and amplifying policy and program costs, which have led to what has become a permanent schedule of scarcity and shortages.

4.4 RECENT TRENDS IN FISCAL FEDERALISM AND IGR

Summarizing the past 30-plus years of fiscal federalism from the 1990s onward is a challenging endeavor. As discussed in Chapter 1, scholars considerably diverge in how they label the characteristics of era(s) we have encountered or are currently experiencing. They have offered coercive, collaborative, centralized, and even competitive analogies to simplify our understanding of the federal structure's modern evolution. While numerous competing perspectives draw out distinctions in the seemingly ever-shifting power bases of governments (see Chapter 3 in particular), it is plausible to identify several recent trends in IGR that are grounded in the continued relevance of fiscal dimensions of federalism. These movements pertain to the rising costs of intergovernmental activities, the scarcity of funding and resources leading to intensifying levels of competition, and service delivery and economic development aspects of state and local strategies to secure residents and businesses.

4.4.1 Rising Costs of Intergovernmental Activities

The above discussion shows that grants-in-aid disbursements have largely been on the rise for more than a half century, with a few offsetting years. Rising costs within governments have been an enduring facet of fiscal federalism that continues in modern times. Many states have balanced budget provisions which are designed to prevent runaway spending. These allocations take a variety of forms but may be broadly categorized as comprising the following: the governor's budget proposal must be balanced (44 states); the state legislature's budget must be balanced (41 states); and the budget must be balanced at the end of the fiscal year or biennium where no deficit is carried forward (38 states).[54] Figure 4.11 below shows that state and local government receipts and expenditures have been relatively equivalent over the past three decades. Both in terms of nominal and real dollars, receipts

---

53   Sung Deuk Hahm, Mark S. Kamlet, David C. Mowery, and Tsai-Tsu Su, "The Influence of the Gramm-Rudman-Hollings Act on Federal Budgetary Outcomes, 1986-1989," *Journal of Policy Analysis and Management*, 11, no. 2 (spring, 1992): 208.

54   National Conference of State Legislatures, "NCSL Fiscal Brief: State Balanced Budget Provisions," October 2010, Accessed at: https://www.ncsl.org/documents/fiscal/StateBalancedBudgetProvisions2010.pdf., 2–3.

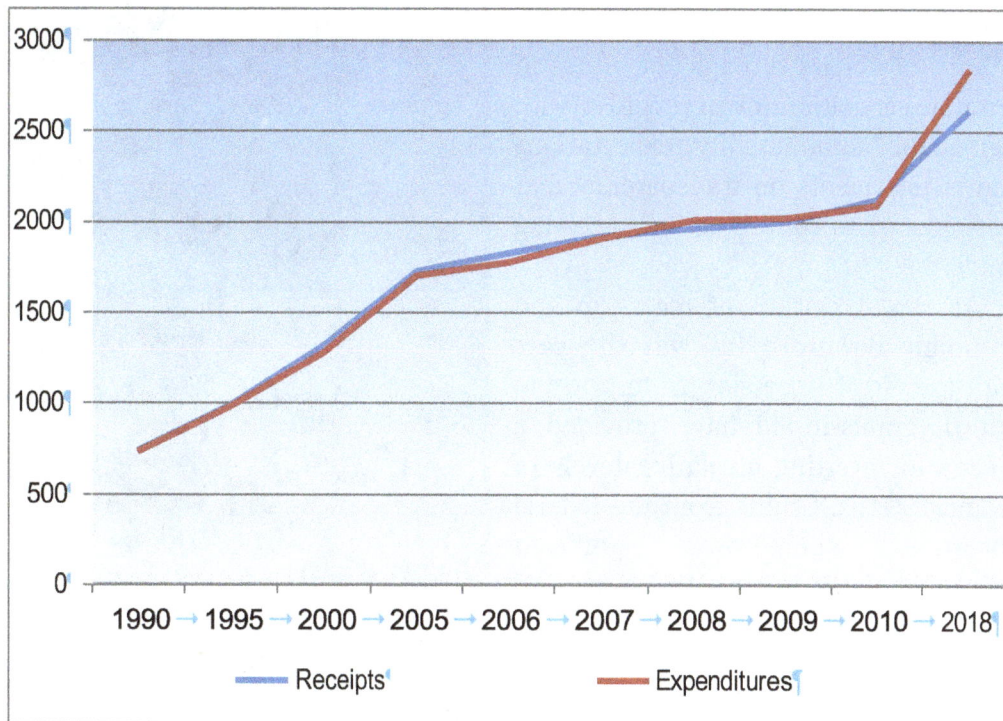

Figure 4.11: State and Local Government Receipts and Expenditures (billions of dollars).

Source: Original Work, adapted from United States Census Bureau, Statistical Abstract of the United States: 2012, "State and Local Government Current Receipts and Expenditures in the National Income and Product Accounts: 1990 to 2010, (Washington, D.C., 2012), 268. Bureau of Economic Analysis, "Government Receipts and Expenditures, 2018," Accessed at: https://apps.bea.gov/scb/2018/12-december/pdf/1218-government-receipts-expenditures.pdf.

Attribution: Daniel Baracskay

License: CC BY-SA 4.0

and expenditures increased at a steady rate in the 1990s during the Clinton administration, intensifying after 9/11 under the administration of President George W. Bush. While his administration centralized some aspects of homeland security policy through passage of the USA PATRIOT Act and its subsequent extensions designed to advance a Global War on Terrorism, Bush also utilized an intergovernmental approach to facilitate stronger state and local preparedness measures to avert future attacks and coordinate efforts by subnational levels (to be discussed more in Chapter 8). Bush also issued the Emergency Economic Stabilization Act of 2008 to avert a deeper financial crisis from affecting many of the nation's top financial institutions, allocating $700 billion of relief. This move coincided with an upsurge in federal grants-in-aid to state and local governments at the beginning of the economic recession. The first term of President Barack Obama coincided with the Great Recession which was in full force. While the Bush administration's stabilization act had some invigorating effect on the national economy, President Obama signed the American Recovery and Reinvestment Act of 2009, which provided an additional $700 billion of economic aid to help the nation recover from what had become a global recession. The act had provisions for tax breaks and incentives, health care, education, and infrastructure as part of the intergovernmental mix. It also allocated billions of dollars through the states to promote economic growth yet did so with significant accountability expectations and requirements on transparency that were placed as conditions for receiving funds.[55]

In recent periods of recession and economic downturn (as was the case with the Great Recession from 2007 to 2009), grants-in-aid have provided a means for averting escalating levels of financial crisis. Grants from the federal government compose a significant portion of states' non-general funds and are treated as designated disbursements that are used for specific purposes. The general funds in each state are revenues generated from taxes and fee collection, which are expended on discrete policy areas. As a rule, non-general funds compose a significant portion of a state's fiscal wellbeing, and cash reserves (rainy day funds) are held to carry governments into subsequent fiscal periods. In many instances, states have used reserves in years of shortfall to abide by balanced budget provisions. The figure above reflects the close proximity of the revenue and expenditure lines. Reserves are a

Figure 4.12: President George W. Bush explained America's plans in the war against terrorism during the ceremony for the George C. Marshall ROTC Award Seminar on National Security at Cameron Hall at the Virginia Military Institute in Lexington, Va., on Wednesday, April 17. "We know that true peace will only be achieved when we give the Afghan people the means to achieve their own aspirations," said President Bush.
Source: Wikimedia Commons
Attribution: Tina Hager
License: Public Domain

percentage of annual expenditures, conventionally set around the five percent level.[56] As a percentage of total federal outlays to state and local governments, grants-in-aid have comprised between five and 18 percent over time. This figure was far lower prior to the post-World War II period, at which time it increased dramatically, as shown in the figure below. The 1960s exhibited an upward trend, starting around the time of the Great Society, that continued with moderate upward gains until 1980 when grant levels subsided for a period. From the 1990s forward, grants have hovered around the 12–15 percent levels.

---

55   Edward T. Jennings Jr., Jeremy L. Hall, and Zhiwei Zhang, "The American Recovery and Reinvestment Act and State Accountability," *Public Performance & Management Review*, 35, no. 3 (March 2012): 528.
56   National Conference of State Legislatures, "NCSL Fiscal Brief: State Balanced Budget Provisions," 7.

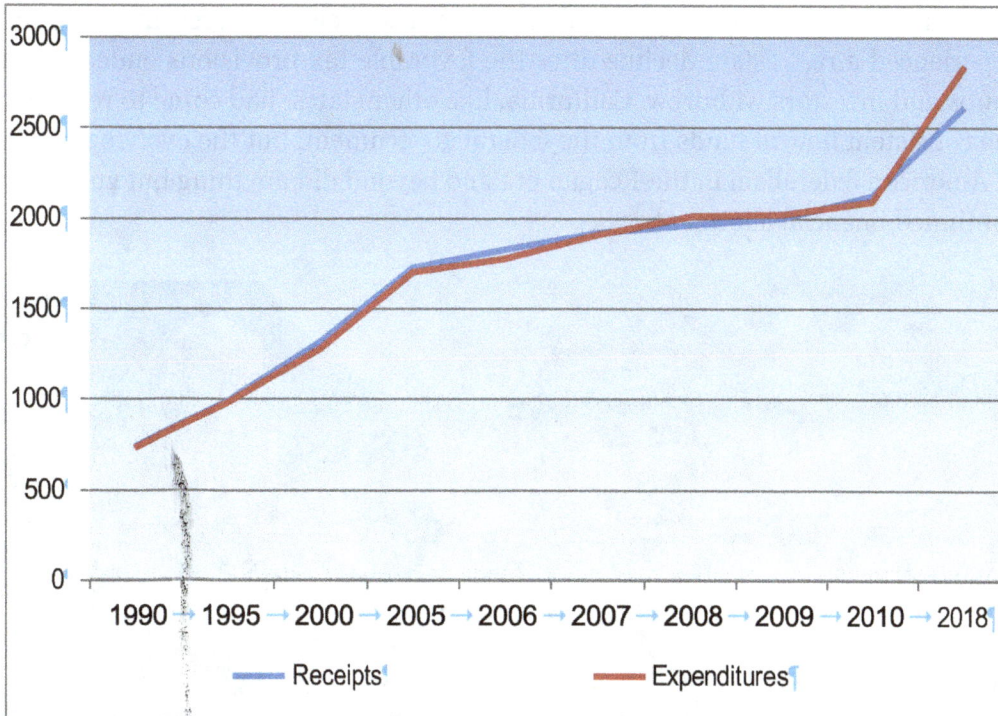

Figure 4.13: Federal Grants-in-Aid as a Percentage of Outlays to State and Local Governments.

Source: Original Work, adapted from United States Census Bureau, "Federal Grants-in-Aid to State and Local Governments," (2010), Accessed at: https://www.census.gov/library/publications/2011/compendia/statab/131ed/state-local-govt-finances-employment.html, and White House, "Aid to State and Local Governments," (2020), Accessed at: https://www.whitehouse.gov/wp-content/uploads/2019/03/ap_17_state_and_local-fy2020.pdf.
Attribution: Daniel Baracskay
License: CC BY-SA 4.0

4.4.2 Scarcity of Funding and Resources: Competition as a Dimension of Fiscal IGR

As discussed above, the use of unfunded mandates became more pronounced in the Reagan era, causing mounting political pressures for reform, as was embodied with bipartisan support of the UMRA passed during the Clinton administration. Many entities were not prepared for this shift in public finance philosophy, and scarcity of funds inherently triggered competition in intergovernmental affairs for those resources that were available. California, for instance, was on the verge of bankruptcy in mid-1992 after its budgetary shortfall increased to more than $14 billion (a doubling from the previous fiscal year). This deficit comprised approximately 25 percent of the state's operating budget resulting both in the state's inability to pay its bills and a decrease in its AAA bond rating.[57] As Paul E. Peterson notes in *The Price of Federalism*, a multitude of factors led up to that point. The California economy had experienced a significant downward slope in revenues after the Cold War concluded, since the defense industry receded from its significant earning levels of earlier decades, and Japanese investments in

57   Paul E. Peterson, *The Price of Federalism* (Washington, D.C.: Brookings Institution, 1995), 2–3.

the housing industry, which took advantage of tax shelters offered in the 1980s, experienced a real estate decline after the favorable tax provisions ended in the 1990s and investors withdrew. California, like other states, had come to rely upon the consistent flow of funds from the federal government, but the evolving nature of American federalism in the Reagan era and beyond did anything but guarantee continued financial allotments.

Figure 4.14: Barack Obama signs American Recovery and Reinvestment Act of 2009.
Source: Wikimedia Commons
Attribution: Pete Souza
License: Public Domain

Consequently, states and localities were instead encouraged to utilize alternative tax provisions which the Reagan administration introduced conterminously with reductions in grants-in-aid, though many states were still not able to react effectively to shifting fiscal conditions. Raising taxes continued to be a politically-risky option for politicians at all levels of government. Voters in California, for instance, had passed Proposition 13 in 1978 to contain taxation levels and place restrictions on the ability of local governments to raise property taxes. The result was that schools and local infrastructures fell into disarray after cuts in federal spending left them without adequate means for generating operating revenues. Peterson notes that what happened in California is symptomatic of what many other states have experienced under changing patterns of intergovernmental financing, where fiscal crises are deepened from changing economic conditions, less support from the federal government, and increasing competition from globalization, among other factors. As the pre-Reagan era of reliable funding came to an abrupt end, states and localities were ill-prepared to assume the burden of programs and services which were previously funded. A similar scenario had occurred in New York in 1974, when the governor pleaded to President Gerald Ford for a federal bailout to avert bankruptcy. Shortly after California's shortfall, Connecticut emulated these conditions with a budgetary gap approximating 37 percent of its operating budget. In fact, three-fifths of states were in the red in 1991, and localities were facing their own shortfalls in light of significant cuts from both the federal government and the states where they were located. Short and long-term debt increased exponentially to $200 billion during the period between 1987 and 1991, a 27 percent increase. Short-term debt alone experienced an increase of 38 percent.[58]

As indicated above, the consolidation of several categorical grants into fewer block grants and the corresponding reduction of aid provided by the federal government was an aspect of the Reagan administration's new federalism. However, Figure 4.16 presented earlier in this chapter shows that federal grants-in-aid moderately rebounded in the 1990s forward. What changed in this brief sequence of years to expand the use of funds as part of the intergovernmental equation? Rising costs, media publicity, intergovernmental lobbyists, and public opinion all factored into the resurgence of federal funding. Conlan notes that the National Unfunded Mandates (NUM) Day initiative promoted by the National League of Cities (NLC), U.S. Conference of Mayors (USCM), National Association of Counties (NACo), and the International City/County Management Association (ICMA) in 1993 had a significant effect in raising nationwide awareness of the costs associated with federal regulations.[59] The initiative generated support from hundreds of cities and counties and was of significant political benefit in pushing unfunded mandates onto the governmental agenda. The widespread publicity that governors, mayors, and other subnational actors focused on the nation's legislature elicited enough support to pass the UMRA of 1995. Consequently, states were granted higher levels of financial relief to ease the stranglehold that federal mandates had on state budgets after the recession of the early 1990s strained revenues and impeded progress for newly-enacted provisions relating to the environment, health care, and handicap requirements. From a public finance standpoint, states and localities benefited from UMRA restrictions on using costly mandates. While the 1990s forward recovery period in grants-in-aid helped to abate severe conditions in many states where bankruptcy seemed inevitable, it has not averted concerns over scarcity and competition. States and localities still have shared fiscal responsibility in many policy and programmatic areas. Further, considerable diversity exists regarding which states win and lose in the competition for intergovernmental revenues from the national government.

As the figure below shows, California and New York rebounded from the fringes of bankruptcy in the 1990s to top the list of states receiving the largest amounts of revenue. They are followed by Texas, Pennsylvania, Florida, and Ohio. Population size and a state's need for funds to promote infrastructure and economic development sustainability represent two driving forces in competition for money.

58   Paul E. Peterson, *The Price of Federalism*, 2–3.
59   Timothy Conlan, *From New Federalism to Devolution*, 260.

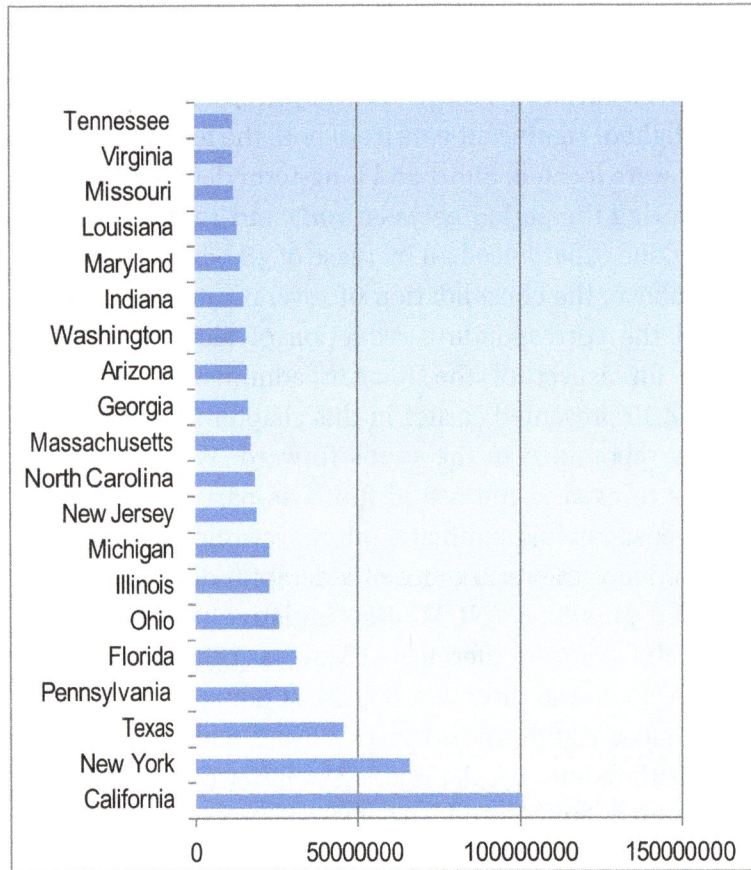

Figure 4.15: Top Twenty States Receiving the Largest Amounts of Intergovernmental Revenue from the National Government (thousands of dollars).

Source: Original Work, adapted from United States Census Bureau, 2017 State & Local Government Finance Historical Databases, https://www.census.gov/data/datasets/2017/econ/local/public-use-datasets.html.

Attribution: Daniel Baracskay

License: CC BY-SA 4.0

4.4.3 Economic Development Tied to Service Delivery and Competing for Residents and Businesses

As mentioned above, fiscal decision making by governments has a considerable relationship with service delivery and outcomes and also factors into how residents and corporations choose where to locate. This approach views the individual as a rational decision maker who seeks to maximize benefits as much as possible while minimizing costs. Organizations of society (public, private, and nonprofit) may likewise be regarded from this perspective as groupings of individuals with shared preferences that are more readily achieved through collective action. This economic perspective closely intertwines with how governments operate in administrative environments that are resource and budget-driven. Consequently, taxation and spending decisions are some of the most politically and fiscally-charged resolutions that government makes. The number of local governments grew significantly in the post-World War II era, changing the dynamics of intergovernmental activity as large urban areas became centers of activity. As indicated in Chapter 1, there are more than 90 thousand governmental units in the U.S. The number of units in each state factors into the intergovernmental funding equation, particularly from the standpoint of localities competing for federal funds to bolster economic development strategies. Yet, having more local governments does not guarantee higher levels of funding. As shown in Figure 4.16 below, considerable variety exists among the number of governmental units (general and special purpose) across the many states. The figure shows the top ten states with the largest number of units, and the ten states with the fewest number of units. This range is a product of American federalism, where considerable diversity exists and localities are "creatures of the state." In comparing Figure 4.16 with Figure 4.15 above, Illinois has the greatest number of governmental units but is sixth in receipts from the federal government. California and New York have fewer local governments at 4,445 and 3,451 respectively, yet they top the list of states receiving the largest allocations of intergovernmental revenue. Texas is second to Illinois in terms of governments and third in terms of revenue receipts. It is interesting to note that while Virginia, Louisiana, and Maryland have far fewer local units than other states, they secured larger amounts of revenue from the national government than counterparts with more localities.

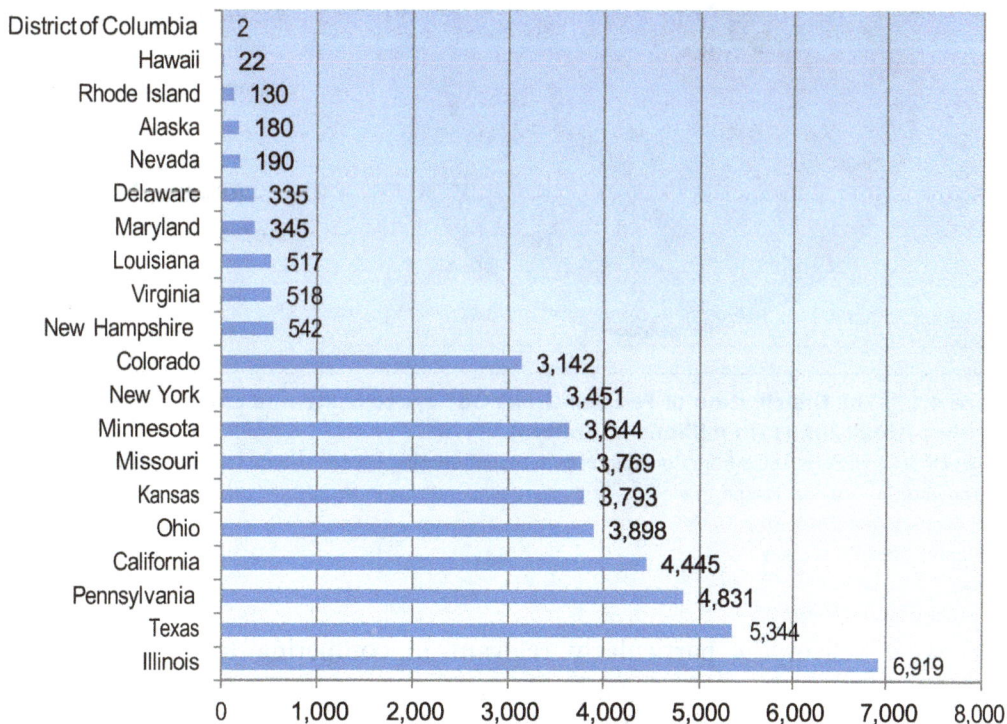

Figure 4.16: States with the Most and Fewest Number of Governments as Part of the IGR Equation.

Source: Original Work, adapted from United States Census Bureau, "Government Units by State, 2017," Accessed at: https://www.census.gov/data/tables/2017/econ/gus/2017-governments.html.
Attribution: Daniel Baracskay
License: CC BY-SA 4.0

This dynamic raises the question, how are federal grant outlays to state and local governments utilized according to the type of policy area? This concept is shown in Figure 4.17 below. In looking at discrete functional areas, spending on health programs represents the largest segment of expenditures in federal grants. National health expenditures have grown significantly over time, representing approximately 17.7 percent of GDP.[60] Medicare and Medicaid represent large segments of total national health expenditures, particularly in terms of Medicare spending for a growing number of senior citizens in the nation. Health spending is followed by income security programs, and education, training, and employment services have expenditure levels approximately half of that allocated for income security, which is also the case with transportation outlays. Finally, community and regional development and other forms of spending receive significant allocations of grant funding, but not to the extent of the other functional categories.

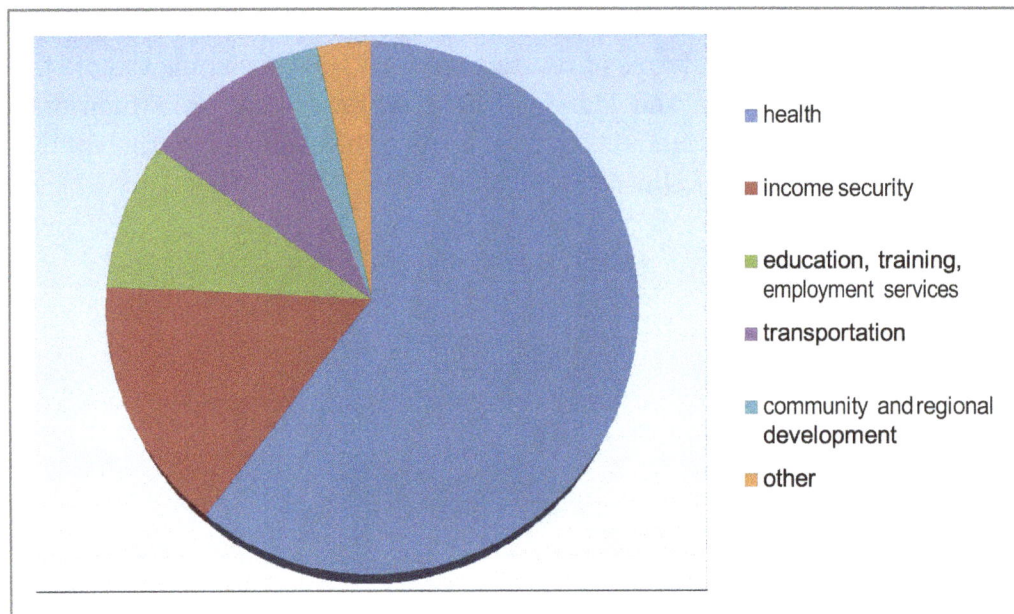

Figure 4.17: The Distribution of Federal Grant Outlays to State and Local Governments by Policy Area (2019) (in millions of dollars).

Source: Original Work, adapted from Congressional Research Service, Federal Grants to State and Local Governments: A Historical Perspective on Contemporary Issues, Table 2, May 22, 2019; Accessed at: https://fas.org/sgp/crs/misc/R40638.pdf.

Attribution: Daniel Baracskay

License: CC BY-SA 4.0

Service delivery is particularly relevant in competing for residents and businesses, especially at the local level where economic development strategies often revolve around providing benefits to the community as a means for enticing inflows of people (and rising tax bases). Decades ago, Charles Tiebout in "A Pure Theory of Expenditures," analyzed a model of prediction grounded in the

---

60   Centers for Medicare & Medicaid Services, "National Health Expenditure Data," 2018, Accessed at: https://www.cms.gov/Research-Statistics-Data-and-Systems/Statistics-Trends-and-Reports/NationalHealthExpendData/NHE-Fact- Sheet.

assumption that, when there is easy mobility and a large number of jurisdictional choices, individuals will rationally select areas to live in that complement their preferences for public goods and taxation levels.[61] Consequently, it follows that jurisdictions will seek high levels of efficiency in the provision of public goods, though centralization at the national level (which has occurred in periods of American federalism) reduces local diversity and increases the costs of moving to another jurisdiction. Consequently, Tiebout's model is useful but rests on many differing assumptions which may not always be applicable, and other intervening factors may affect the outcomes of decisions in uncertain and unpredictable ways. In his *Fiscal Federalism*, Wallace E. Oates augments theories relating to decentralization by showing that, if there is an absence of cost-savings associated with centralizing the provision of a public good and in terms of interjurisdictional externalities, then the benefit will be at least as high (or higher) for each jurisdiction rather than through consumption uniformity under centralized approaches.[62] Yet, there is also the notion that there exist imperfections or asymmetries in information which affect how local outputs are procured as a means for maximizing general welfare, and political pressures also have an effect on the capacity of federal government to generate optimal outcomes.[63] Irrespective of these differences, fiscal federalism continues to represent a significant portion of the literature on IGR. As Oates asserts, fiscal decentralization has been a vibrant strategy in improving the performance of public sector organizations and in vesting confidence in state and local governments as being able to more effectively respond to the preferences of local constituencies.[64]

4.5 FINAL CONSIDERATIONS IN FISCAL FEDERALISM AND IGR

Ann O. M. Bowman, in "Federalism on the Horizon," observes that federalism in the twentieth century was shaped considerably through "system-altering events" relating to global conflict, fluctuating cycles of economic performance, and urbanization. Though the fiscal side of federalism witnessed a dramatic increase in aid to subnational levels of government, this occurred as the relative power of lower tiers lessened.[65] Expanding the scope of programmatic capacity necessitated intergovernmental coordination, but grant programs also inherently produced conflict and competition for scarce funds, as mentioned above. Several traits may be associated with the state of American federalism in recent times. First, consistent with the above discussion on the competitive nature of fiscal federalism, political polarization both within government and across the American electorate has intensified, having an effect on structure. Polarization shapes the sets of

---

61   Charles Tiebout, "A Pure Theory of Expenditures," *Journal of Political Economy*, 64: 416.
62   Wallace E. Oates, *Fiscal Federalism*, (New York: Harcourt Brace Jovanovich, 1972), 54.
63   Wallace E. Oates, "An Essay on Fiscal Federalism," 1123.
64   Wallace E. Oates, "An Essay on Fiscal Federalism," 1120.
65   Ann O'M. Bowman, "Federalism on the Horizon," *Publius*, 32, no. 2 (Spring, 2002): 3–4.

preferences which are tied to changing power arrangements. Timothy J. Conlan and Paul L. Posner, in "American Federalism in an Era of Partisan Polarization: The Intergovernmental Paradox of Obama's 'New Nationalism,'" for instance, note that the polarization of IGR occurred during the Obama administration and became particularly apparent as predominantly Democratic and Republican states took differing courses in implementing policies. This move has led to a diverse sequence of patterns in state action that stand in contrast to the Obama administration's initial objective of shaping federalism around what was intended to be a "new nationalism."[66] Recent considerations involve loosening regulatory requirements, using litigation to defy executive branch mandates, and shifting power structures after elections conclude to reflect newer waves of public officials taking office. Contention over policy areas like immigration, health care, environmental policy, education, and gun control have endured across presidential terms, causing national-state and state-local conflict.[67] The more polarized people are in their views of contentious topics like these, the less likely they are to reach compromise and resolution. These trends recur within the battles that have transpired between the executive, legislative, and judicial branches of government.

Second—and related—governmental gridlock has been the norm even during times when the president and Congress majority are from the same party. Policy areas reflect not only the influence of the electorate, interest groups, and elected officials at all levels of government but also the input of specialists and members of industry who have a stake in the outcome. This dynamic makes standoffs common when legislating and also denotes that conflict does not necessarily end once a piece of legislation has been successfully signed by the president. An example is the Patient Protection and Affordable Care Act (PPACA), which President Obama signed into law early in 2010. At the time, the act represented an ongoing period of significant political battles with Congress, which also reflected growing polarization in the nation. The PPACA was designed to reduce the vast number of uninsured and underinsured people and required that states expand Medicaid coverage to people below a certain percentage of the federal poverty line. Sanctions against states that did not implement the expansion were severe, possibly resulting in a loss of federal funding. The federal government authorized full payment of new enrollees for three years. Medicaid disbursements totaled $265 billion in 2012, representing the largest grant-in-aid to state governments.

In the time following its being mandated, considerable challenges to PPACA have permeated the intergovernmental arena. Initially came a Supreme Court ruling, *National Federation of Independent Businesses v. Sebelius* in 2013, which changed the distribution of grant funding and the expansion requirements that the act had brought to the Medicaid program. While the Court upheld the mandate as constitutional, it also affirmed that Medicaid expansion was not a reasonable

---

66 Timothy J. Conlan and Paul L. Posner, "American Federalism in an Era of Partisan Polarization: The Intergovernmental Paradox of Obama's 'New Nationalism,'" *Publius*, 46, no. 3 (Summer, 2016): 283.

67 Greg Goelzhauser and David M. Konisky, "The State of American Federalism 2018–2019: Litigation, Partisan Polarization, and the Administrative Presidency," *Publius*, 49, no. 3 (Summer, 2019): 379–380.

part of Congress's spending powers, thus allowing states the decision to opt out of expansion mandates, which many did soon after the ruling. In opting out of billions of dollars in federal grants, many states with Republican governors were, in effect, underscoring the embittered partisan quarrel that had encompassed the act's passage.[68] A sequence of other judicial decisions has also affected the direction of the PPACA, including *Stewart v. Azar* (2018), *Texas v. U.S.* (2018), and *Gresham v. Azar* (2019).[69] Next came a series of efforts by the Trump administration to reverse and rescind the PPACA, starting in 2016. Though these actions failed to produce an immediate result in repealing the act, they illustrate that policies are constantly reshaped across presidential administrations, which then has corresponding effects on federal structure. In lieu of the Obama-era health care act, the Trump administration focused more on Medicaid program flexibility through the use of block grants where states are given discretion in distributing coverage to recipients in order to align with cost-savings initiatives. This move responded to the continuous annual increases in Medicaid costs which have resulted in a more significant portion of total health expenditures by the national government. The Trump initiative allows states to cap spending for certain portions of Medicaid and also to scale back benefits for segments of those who are insured. In sum, Trump administration executive actions and the litigation raised by many Republican state governors and attorneys general have sought to block implementation of certain Medicaid requirements by questioning the PPACA's legitimacy, while segments of the electorate and interest groups have raised ballot measures to expand Medicaid in states that resisted expansion, using the election process as a means of counteracting opposition.[70]

Third, besides fiscal federalism's evolution in an increasingly polarized system of government, where policies are constantly under revision through litigation and across presidential administrations, other macro-level considerations factor into the equation. Globalization shifted the nation's focus away from isolationism at the beginning of the last century and became an embedded facet of political, social, and economic structures by the mid-point of the century. The post-World War II era saw the effects of globalization most significantly as having an impact on localities and their economic development strategies to compete for businesses and residents. As part of the intergovernmental equation, fluctuations in economic activity from recessions and downturns (as was the case in 1991 with the discussion above of the California and New York economies) have occurred which have shown that the nation and its many thousands of governments are part of an interconnected world where technology has revolutionized how business operates and governments interact. Fiscal federalism

68   Sean Nicholson-Crotty, *Governors, Grants, and Elections: Fiscal Federalism in the American States* (Baltimore, MD: Johns Hopkins University Press, 2015), 2.
69   Lilliard E. Richardson, Jr., "Medicaid Expansion during the Trump Presidency: The Role of Executive Waivers, State Ballot Measures, and Attorney General Lawsuits in Shaping Intergovernmental Relations," *Publius*, 49, no. 3 (Summer, 2019): 453–454.
70   Lilliard E. Richardson, Jr., "Medicaid Expansion during the Trump Presidency: The Role of Executive Waivers, State Ballot Measures, and Attorney General Lawsuits in Shaping Intergovernmental Relations," *Publius*, vol. 49, no. 3, (Summer, 2019): 437.

continues to involve the public finance dimensions of intergovernmental activity, though there also exists a supra-national level which transcends national boundaries and affects how policies transpire. Globalization has caused federal systems to become both more cooperative and more competitive over time.[71] Competition for business and economic resources has intensified as the internet has opened access to markets, while affording opportunities for non-governmental organizations (NGOs) and governments to work cooperatively on complex and multifaceted policy issues (e.g., health care, environment, and homeland security threats). The nature of IGR in a digital world has revealed a blurring of jurisdictional boundaries which makes identifying and understanding well-defined lines of authority problematic. Because of this issue, the realm of public service has changed considerably as e-government has forged a significant place in fiscal decision-making, and especially in aspects of IGM.[72] Digital technology has been used in concert with IGM as a basis for promoting greater efficiency, though its ramifications for citizen involvement and democracy are still disputed.

Finally, the rationale for reform efforts pertaining to IGR rests in administrative coordination and efficiency. We are now several decades into reform, being well past the basic administrative structure that was built at the turn of the twentieth century. This period coincides with segments of the political science literature which equates the state to an organic and ever-changing entity. Whether reform and change are attained through cooperation or coercion depends upon the leadership style of the president and the willingness of Congress to work with the chief executive on a legislative agenda comprising policies that involve participation by lower tiers. Saving taxpayer money has been a focus of IGM, and is an aspect of fiscal federalism which is in no danger of subsiding in light of limited resources. Public sector organizations must justify their existence as part of the public finance philosophy which has pervaded resource-constrained environments. Technology represents an ever-advancing aspect of government that helps mitigate costs in many areas but also necessitates maintenance in terms of training, infrastructure, and usage, which factor into how levels of government interact.

4.6 CONCLUSION

Across the many eras of American federalism that have transpired from the twentieth century forward, public finance has become an institutionalized facet of IGR. The rise of grants-in-aid as a means for facilitating cross-level cooperation in the Roosevelt era ushered in the notion of fiscal federalism as a feature of American political culture that has persisted over time. Virtually all programs and decisions involve some fiscal aspect that drives how outcomes are pursued, and this is unlikely to subside. Public finance is pervasive, and as the nation has seemingly

---

71   Keith Boeckelman, "Federal Systems in the Global Economy: Research Ideas," *Publius*, 26, no. 1 (Winter, 1996): 6–7.

72   Roger Gibbins, "Federalism in a Digital World," *Canadian Journal of Political Science,* 33, no. 4 (Dec., 2000): 681–682.

grown more intensely polarized in recent times, this structure has affected not only the direction of IGR but also preferences for how scarce resources are allocated. Important and wide-ranging policies span presidential administrations and are shaped and reshaped by chief executives who affect the direction of outcomes and judicial rulings which are established and have a significant impact on the nature of federal structure. As society has progressed toward an information-driven culture, this shift has expanded the forces of globalization such that American federalism includes national-state-local dimensions as well as the influence of NGOs and supra-national entities which interact as part of a world structure.

REFLECTION QUESTIONS

1. Please discuss how early initiatives, particularly the Sixteenth Amendment, helped institutionalize a system of public budgeting and finance upon which fiscal federalism and intergovernmental relations have been based.

2. What influence did the Progressive Era have on governmental activism and the rise of intergovernmental activity? How did this impact relate to the fiscal dimensions of our nation's changing federal structure?

3. Please discuss how the New Deal era led to a significant increase in the use of grants-in-aid. Specifically, how did fiscal federalism in the Roosevelt administration embrace a more cooperative approach that departed from the dual approaches of the past?

4. Please analyze similarities and differences in the visions that Presidents Nixon and Reagan had for using federalism as a means of reform. In particular, how was intergovernmental management viewed as a tool for bringing about greater efficiency and effectiveness?

5. Please discuss how the increasing costs of intergovernmental activities and recent trends in resource scarcity have affected fiscal federalism and intergovernmental relations over the past twenty years.

6. How have changes in the use of grants shaped the evolution of intergovernmental relations over time, specifically in terms of bringing about a more coordinated system of American federalism where there are shared responsibilities and methods of policy implementation?

7. What are ways that globalization, the advancement of technology, and the progression toward extensive communication systems have affected the direction of federalism and IGR over the past twenty years?

BIBLIOGRAPHY

Ann O'M. Bowman, Ann O'M. "Federalism on the Horizon." *Publius,* 32, no. 2 (Spring, 2002): 3–22.

Boeckelman, Keith. "Federal Systems in the Global Economy: Research Ideas." *Publius,* 26, no. 1 (Winter, 1996): 1–10.

Brown-Collier, Elba K. "Johnson's Great Society: Its Legacy in the 1990s." *Review of Social Economy,* 56, no. 3 (Fall, 1998): 259–276.

Centers for Medicare & Medicaid Services. "National Health Expenditure Data," 2018, Accessed at: https://www.cms.gov/Research-Statistics-Data-and-Systems/Statistics-Trends-and- Reports/NationalHealthExpendData/NHE-Fact-Sheet.

Cole, Richard L. and Delbert A. Taebel. "The New Federalism: Promises, Programs, and Performance." *Publius,* 16, no. 1 (Winter, 1986): 3–10.

Congressional Quarterly. *Congress and the Nation, 1965–1968*, vol. II. Washington, D.C., 1969.

Congressional Quarterly, Inc. *Federal Regulatory Directory*, 8th ed. Washington, D.C.: Congressional Quarterly, 1997. Congressional Research Service. "Federal Grants to State and Local Governments: A Historical Perspective on Contemporary Issues," May 22, 2019, Accessed at: https://fas.org/sgp/crs/misc/R40638.pdf, 1–40.

Conlan, Timothy. "Federalism and Competing Values in the Reagan Administration." *Publius* 16, no. 1 (Winter, 1986): 29–47.

Conlan, Timothy J. *From New Federalism to Devolution: Twenty-Five Years of Intergovernmental Reform*. Washington, D.C.: Brookings Institution Press, 1998.

Conlan, Timothy J. and Paul L. Posner. "American Federalism in an Era of Partisan Polarization: The Intergovernmental Paradox of Obama's 'New Nationalism.'" *Publius,* 46, no. 3, (Summer, 2016): 281–307.

Cronin, Thomas E., and William R. Hochman. "Franklin D. Roosevelt and the American Presidency." *Presidential Studies Quarterly,* 15, no. 2 (Spring, 1985): 277–286.

Elazar, Daniel J. *American Federalism: A View From the States*, 3rd ed. New York: Harper & Row, Publishers, 1984.

Elazar, Daniel J. "Opening the Third Century of American Federalism: Issues and Prospects." *The Annals of the American Academy of Political and Social Science,* 509, (May, 1990): 11–21.

Gibbins, Roger. "Federalism in a Digital World." *Canadian Journal of Political Science,* 33, no. 4 (Dec., 2000): 667–689.

Goelzhauser, Greg and David M. Konisky. "The State of American Federalism 2018–2019: Litigation, Partisan Polarization, and the Administrative Presidency." *Publius,* 49, no. 3, (Summer, 2019): 379–406.

Hahm, Sung Deuk, Mark S. Kamlet, David C. Mowery, and Tsai-Tsu Su. "The Influence of the Gramm-Rudman-Hollings Act on Federal Budgetary Outcomes, 1986–1989." *Journal of Policy Analysis and Management,* 11, no. 2 (spring, 1992): 207–234.

Hofstadter, Richard. *The American Political Tradition and the Men Who Made It*. New York: Alfred A. Knopf, 1948.

Hofstadter, Richard. *The Age of Reform.* New York: Vintage Books, 1955.

Jennings Jr., Edward T., Jeremy L. Hall, and Zhiwei Zhang. "The American Recovery and Reinvestment Act and State Accountability." *Public Performance & Management Review,* 35, no. 3 (March 2012): 527–549.

Kennedy, David M. "What the New Deal Did." *Political Science Quarterly,* 124, no. 2 (Summer 2009): 251–268.

Kelly, Janet. "Unfunded Mandates: The View from the States." *Public Administration Review,* 54, no. 4 (Jul.–Aug. 1994): 405–408.

Kincaid, John. "From Cooperative to Coercive Federalism." *The Annals of the American Academy of Political and Social Science,* 509, (May, 1990): 139–152.

Lee, Bradford A. "The New Deal Reconsidered." *The Wilson Quarterly,* 6, no. 2 (Spring, 1982): 62–76.

Levitan, Sar A. and Robert Taggart. "The Great Society Did Succeed." *Political Science Quarterly,* 91, no. 4 (Winter, 1976–1977): 601–618.

Lynch, Frederick R. "Social Theory and the Progressive Era." *Theory and Society,* 4, no. 2 (Summer, 1977): 159–210.

Mooney, Anne. "The Great Society and Health: Policies for Narrowing the Gaps in Health Statues between the Poor and the Nonpoor." *Medical Care,* 15, no. 8 (Aug., 1977): 611–619.

National Conference of State Legislatures. "NCSL Fiscal Brief: State Balanced Budget Provisions." October 2010. Accessed at: https://www.ncsl.org/documents/fiscal/StateBalancedBudgetProvisions2010.pdf: 1–13.

Neenan, William B. "General Revenue Sharing and Redistribution." *Review of Social Economy,* 35, no. 2, (April, 1977): 25–36.

Nicholson-Crotty, Sean. *Governors, Grants, and Elections: Fiscal Federalism in the American States.* Baltimore, MD: Johns Hopkins University Press, 2015.

Niedziela, Theresa A. "Franklin D. Roosevelt and the Supreme Court." *Presidential Studies Quarterly,* 6, no. 4 (Fall, 1976): 51–57.

Oates, Wallace E. "An Essay on Fiscal Federalism." *Journal of Economic Literature,* no. 3 (Sep., 1999): 1120-1149.

Oates, Wallace E. *Fiscal Federalism.* New York: Harcourt Brace Jovanovich, 1972.

Office of Management and Budget. "Historical Tables: Table 14.3— Total Government Expenditures as Percentages of GDP: 1948-2018, (2018), Accessed at: https://www.whitehouse.gov/omb/historical-tables/.

O'Toole Jr., Laurence J., and Robert K. Christensen, eds. *American Intergovernmental Relations: An Overview.* Thousand Oaks, CA: Sage Publications, 2013.

Peterson, Paul E. *The Price of Federalism.* Washington, D.C.: Brookings Institution, 1995.

Posner, Paul L. "Unfunded Mandates Reform Act: 1996 and Beyond." *Publius,* 27, no. 2 (Spring, 1997): 53–71.

Richardson, Jr., Lilliard E. "Medicaid Expansion during the Trump Presidency: The Role of Executive Waivers, State Ballot Measures, and Attorney General Lawsuits in Shaping Intergovernmental Relations." *Publius,* 49, no. 3, (Summer, 2019): 437–464.

Riker, William H. *Federalism: Origin, Operation, Significance.* Boston, MA: Little, Brown, 1964.

Robins, Leonard. "The Plot That Succeeded: The New Federalism as Policy Realignment." *Presidential Studies Quarterly,* 10, no. 1, (Winter, 1980): 99-106.

Rodden, Jonathan. "Comparative Federalism and Decentralization: on meaning and measurement." *Comparative Politics,* 36 (4) (2004): 481–500.

Social Security Administration. "Fiscal Year 2020 Budget Overview," March 2019, Accessed at: https://www.ssa.gov/budget/FY20Files/2020BO_1.pdf, 1–38.

Sorens, Jason. "The Institutions of Fiscal Federalism." *Publius,* 41, no. 2 (Spring 2011): 207–231.

Stenberg, Carl W. "Revenue Sharing and Governmental Reform." *The Annals of the American Academy of Political Science,* 419, (May, 1975): 50–61.

Tiebout, Charles. "A Pure Theory of Expenditures." *Journal of Political Economy,* 64: 416–424.

U.S. Department of Health & Human Services. "Aid to Families with Dependent Children (AFDC) and Temporary Assistance for Needy Families (TANF)– Overview, (November 30, 2009), Accessed at: https://aspe.hhs.gov/aid-families-dependent-children-afdc-and-temporary-assistance-needy-families-tanf-overview-0.

Walker, David B. "American Federalism from Johnson to Bush." *Publius,* 21, no. 1 (Winter, 1991): 105–119.

Weingast, Barry R. "The Economic Role of Political Institutions: Market-preserving federalism and economic development." *Journal of Law, Economics, and Organization,* 11 (1) (1995): 1–31.

Wright, Deil S. *Understanding Intergovernmental Relations*, 3rd ed. Belmont, CA: Wadsworth Publishing Company, 1988.

Zimmerman, Joseph F. "Federal Preemption under Reagan's New Federalism." *Publius,* 21, no. 1 (Winter, 1991): 7–28.

5

Administrative Dimensions of Intergovernmental Relations

Robert (Sherman) Yehl

LEARNING OBJECTIVES

- Demonstrate an understanding of how the structure of American Federalism provides an administrative basis for intergovernmental activities and how governments cooperatively produce and provide services.

- Demonstrate an understanding of mandate use in federal program administration and how funding arrangements have changed over time to include varying levels of unfunded mandates.

- Demonstrate an understanding of the intergovernmental nature of public, private, and nonprofit organizations in services provision at various levels of government as an aspect of programmatic development and implementation.

- Demonstrate an understanding the historical context of the Advisory Commission on Intergovernmental Relations in identifying standards of service.

- Demonstrate an understanding of Georgia's Service Delivery Strategy in encouraging local government consolidation or joint operation of services.

KEY TERMS

Mandates

Direct Orders

Crosscutting Requirements

Crossover Sanctions

Partial Preemption

Unfunded Mandate Reform Act of 1995

Interlocal Agreements

Consent Decree

Settlement Agreement

Interstate Compacts

Uniform Legislation

Networks

National Purpose

5.1. INTRODUCTION

As mentioned in chapter 1, over 90,000 local governmental units exist across the United States, making the U.S. a complex federal system that is unique among Western democracies. Knowing that there are legal and political dimensions which affect how states interact as part of intergovernmental structure, and also considering the complex fiscal realities of public affairs, we now focus on the administrative side of Federalism, which brings together aspects of intergovernmental relations (IGR) and intergovernmental management (IGM). While the national government ensures certain national objectives are met through mandate use, it is ultimately up to state and local governments to implement both mandated programs and scores of operations and planning procedures for programs ranging from airports to zoos—and including other entities, such as counties, independent school districts, special districts, townships, and municipalities. Many governmental and associated programs cross jurisdictions and boundaries, adding complexity to the IGR system. Within this differentiated (or what critics refer to as fragmented) system, there is a tremendous need to coordinate the administrative and fiscal attributes of the various entities while at the same time taking into account the political nature of our federal system.

Intergovernmental relations in the U.S. are both vertical and horizontal. As Ann Bowman notes, the study of Federalism typically concerns the relationships between superior organizations and lower levels, such as the following: national

> **Differentiated system**: The U.S. federal system of multiple local governments. Sometimes referred to as fragmented.

to state, state to local, and local to non-government organizations (NGOs). These are vertical relationships. But horizontal relations—state to state, local to local— may be more numerous and may have a greater impact on citizens. In any event, Bowman notes in "Horizontal Federalism: Exploring Interstate Interactions" that these interfaces have created a "complex network of relationships...linking actors, institutions, and organizations across state boundaries."[1]

---

1   Ann O'M. Bowman, "Horizontal Federalism: Exploring Interstate Interactions," *Journal of Public Administration Research and Theory: J-PART* 14, no. 4 (2004), 535.

As this chapter will discuss, these relationships take any number of configurations, including interstate compacts, a myriad of different state and local service agreements, and the development of uniform laws. Most recently, state attorneys general have joined in multistate lawsuits aimed at big tobacco, big pharma, or the federal government itself.

5.2 THE GROWTH OF INTERGOVERNMENTAL RELATIONS

As previously discussed, the early stages of American Federalism, especially after the adoption of the U.S. Constitution, was marked by a period known as dual Federalism and is frequently referred to as a layer-cake. This was a period when clearer lines of responsibility (separate layers of government) were observed between the federal government and the individual states. The federal government has several enumerated powers which grant it exclusive power to provide for the nation's defense and declare war, coin money, establish rules for naturalization, protect copyrights and patents, regulate interstate and foreign commerce, and create post offices, to name a few. States and local government (when authorized) had jurisdiction of property laws, morality, education, criminal law, elections, professional licensing, and regulation. Under the Tenth Amendment to the Constitution, or the reserve clause, "The powers not delegated to the United States by the Constitution, nor prohibited by it to the States, are reserved to the States respectively, or to the people."[2]

Reserve clause: The 10th Amendment to the U. S. Constitution.

Morrill Act: The federal law that provided land for sale to the states so they could establish agricultural and mechanical colleges; considered the first grants-in-aid for a specific purpose and with conditions.

During the early days of the republic, the administration, Congress, and the president viewed the federal government as having a narrow focus on domestic policy. Even the first efforts of more participatory Federalism which surfaced toward the latter half of the nineteenth-century considered the role of the federal government as being focused more on land grants than on direct cash support. In 1841, nine states were given a minimum of 500,000 acres of federal land that was to be sold at auction for internal transportation projects, such as roads, railroads, and canals. Later, almost 40 million acres of land was provided for railroad improvements.[3] These early grants, though, "were gifts with few or no strings attached, given by a beneficent federal government."[4] As discussed in chapter 4, during the Civil War, Congress enacted the Morrill Act of 1862. Eligible states were provided 30,000 acres of federal land for each member of congress the state had as a result of the 1860 census to "teach such branches of learning as

2   U.S. Constitution.
3   Congressional Research Service, "Unfunded Mandates Reform Act: History, Impact, and Issues," August 28, 2019, R40957. Accessed at: https://crsreports.congress.gov, 14.
4   Jane Perry Clark, *The Rise of a New Federalism*. (New York: Russell & Russell, 1966 reissue), 140.

are related to agriculture and the mechanic arts" without excluding scientific and classical studies.[5] The first Morrill Act (another was enacted in 1890) is considered "a milestone on the road of federal grants-in-aid, for no longer were gifts to be scattered with such benevolent prodigality. As Jane Perry Clark notes in "*The Rise of a New Federalism*," "they were given for a specific purpose..."[6] As a condition of the land grants, colleges established under the acts had to provide annual reports to the federal government.

Figure 5.1: Architect of the Capitol, oil on canvas. According to Wikimedia Commons, "This college building in Kansas was one of the first created under the 1862 Morrill Act, which was meant to ensure higher education for all classes of Americans."
Source: Wikimedia Commons
Attribution: US Capitol
License: Public Domain

Using grants-in-aid as an administrative tool in IGR became common largely in the twentieth century under a more cooperative form of Federalism that had transitioned the nation away from the preceding century's dual Federalism perspective. For instance, with passage of a 1921 highway funding bill, states were required to have a highway department in order to administer the funds. As discussed in chapter 4, Franklin D. Roosevelt's New Deal in the 1930s provided for an expansion into domestic programs as one method to alleviate the economic hardship under the Great Depression.

New Deal: Franklin Roosevelt's national plan to remove the U.S. out of the Great Depression. It fostered numerous new federal grant programs to state and local governments and expanded the domestic policy reach of the federal government.

5   7 U.S.C. § 304.
6   Jane Perry Clark, *The Rise of a New Federalism*, 141.

Between 1933 and 1938, 16 new federal grant programs to both state and local government came into existence.[7] The primary principal for federal aid, then, was whether or not the assistance met a "national purpose" or "national objective." In 1955, the Commission on Intergovernmental Relations emphasized this point as follows:

1. A grant should be made or continued only for a clearly indicated and presently important national objective.

2. Where National participation in an activity is determined to be desirable, the grant-in-aid should be employed only when it is found to be the most suitable form of National participation.

3. Once it is decided that a grant-in-aid should be made, the grant should be carefully designed to achieve its specified objective.[8]

These conditions provided sound advice in what was becoming a complex system of politics and interactions. However, as the Advisory Commission on Intergovernmental Relations (ACIR) lamented, "the Washington tendency has been to treat as a national issue any problem that is emotional, hot, and highly visible."[9] More often than not, this view has forced expenditures that the federal government did not want to fund onto state and local governments. We now have a situation where the federal government monitors local functions, such as establishing the minimum drinking age for drivers, assessing fire and police fitness tests, requiring sidewalk ramps, requiring school asbestos inspections, determining licensing standards for bus and truck drivers, where riders can stand in buses, and many others.[10]

> **ACIR**: The U.S. Advisory Commission on Intergovernmental U.S. Relations which existed from 1959-1996. It was an independent commission that studied intergovernmental relationships within the federal system.

5.2.1 The Golden Rule and Mandates

As discussed in previous chapters, the requirements for granting federal aid have grown over the years. While initially the rules placed on accepting federal grants-in-aid were somewhat benign, upon the dawning of Lyndon Johnson's Great Society in the 1960s, certain compulsory requirements became a new feature of intergovernmental regulation.[11] These requirements are known as mandates

7   Congressional Research Service, "Unfunded Mandates Reform Act: History, Impact, and Issues," 18.

8   The Commission on Intergovernmental Relations, "A Report to the President for Transmittal to the Congress," June, 1955. Accessed at: https://library.unt.edu/gpo/acir/Reports/Y3In87R29.pdf, 123.

9   Advisory Commission on Intergovernmental Relations, "The Role of Federal Mandates in Intergovernmental Relations: A Preliminary ACIR Report," January, 1996. Accessed at: https://library.unt.edu/gpo/acir/mandates.html, 5.

10   Nivola, Pietro S. (2005) *Why Federalism Matters*. The Brookings Institution Policy Brief Series (2005). Accessed at: https://www.brookings.edu/research/why-federalism-matters/.

11   Advisory Commission on Intergovernmental Relations, "The Federal Role in the Federal System: The

and grew from the Golden Rule philosophy: "He who controls the gold makes the rules."[12] When the federal government awards money in support of a program or policy, the funds need to be spent for the stated objective. Mandates are far-reaching policy actions which create the effect of "centralizing effects on the intergovernmental system."[13] While scholars define mandates in any number of ways, this chapter will draw upon Catherine Lovell and Charles Tobin's article, "The Mandate Issue," to define them as "responsibilities, procedures, or activities that are imposed by one sphere of government on another by constitutional, legislative, administrative, executive, or judicial action."[14] This period gave rise to what has been termed "coercive Federalism" (see chapter 1 for more details). The federal "carrot" that had been used to aid state and local efforts in support of broad national purposes was replaced with a "stick" of new federal dictates.[15]

> ***The Golden Rule***: A tongue-in-cheek explanation of the role of the federal government in awarding grants to state and local government.

The magnitude of federal programs created during this period is staggering. From 1960 to 1968, the number of federal grants to state and local governments increased from 132 to almost 400. In addition, these grants had a "number of innovative features...designed purposively by Congress to encourage state and local governments to move into new policy areas, or to expand efforts identified by Congress as national priorities."[16] As the primary donor to these new programs, since many of the new grants had few matching financial requirements, the federal government issued mandatory regulations that were impossible to avoid. As Jane Perry Clark noted more than 80 years ago, while "it is difficult to trace an exact correlation between federal expenditures and federal control, it is generally true that the greater the contribution the higher the control."[17]

Table 5.1 Major Statutes of Intergovernmental Regulation 1960-80[18]

1964	Civil Rights Act (Title VI)
1965	Highway Beautification Act
	Water Quality Act
1966	National Historic Preservation Act

Dynamics of Growth," A-86 (1981). Accessed at: https://library.unt.edu/gpo/acir/Reports/policy/A-86.pdf, 7.

12   Deil S. Wright, "Intergovernmental Games: An Approach to Understanding Intergovernmental Relations." *Southern Review of Public Administration* 3, no. 4 (1980), 389, 390.

13   Congressional Research Service, "Federal Grants to State and Local Governments: A Historical Perspective on Contemporary Issues," May 22, 2019, R40638. Accessed at: https://crsreports.congress.gov, 26.

14   Catherine Lovell and Charles Tobin, "The Mandate Issue," *Public Administration Review* 41, no. 3 (1981) 319.

15   Congressional Research Service, "Federal Grants to State and Local Governments: A Historical Perspective on Contemporary Issues," 27.

16   Congressional Research Service, "Federal Grants to State and Local Governments: A Historical Perspective on Contemporary Issues," 22.

17   Jane Perry Clark, *The Rise of a New Federalism*, 144.

18   Advisory Commission on Intergovernmental Relations, "The Federal Role in the Federal System: The Dynamics of Growth," 6.

1967	Wholesome Meat Act
1968	Civil Rights Act (Title VIII)
	Architectural Barriers Act
	Wholesome Poultry Products Act
1969	National Environmental Policy Act
	Sport Fish Restoration Act
1970	Occupational Safety and Health Act
	Clean Air Act Amendments
	Uniform Relocation Assistance and Real Property Acquisition Policies Act
1972	Federal Water Pollution Control Act Amendments
	Equal Employment Opportunity Act
	Education Act Amendments (Title IX)
	Coastal Zone Management Act
	Federal Insecticide, Fungicide, and Rodenticide Act
1973	Flood Disaster Protection Act
	Rehabilitation Act (Section 504)
	Endangered Species Act
1974	Age Discrimination Employment Act
	Safe Drinking Water Act
	National Health Planning and Resources Development Act
	Emergency Highway Energy Conservation Act
	Family Educational Rights and Privacy Act
	Fair Labor Standards Act Amendments
1975	Education for All Handicapped Children Act
	Age Discrimination Act
1976	Resource Conservation and Recovery Act
1977	Surface Mining Control and Reclamation Act
	Marine Protection Research and Sanctuaries Act Amendments
1978	National Energy Conservation Policy Act
	Public Utility Regulatory Policy Act
	Natural Gas Policy Act

Since this more aggressive era of federal mandates, major laws affecting IGR have continued to be passed by Congress. These include the Superfund Act, the Family and Medical Leave Act of 1993, The Omnibus Transportation Employee Testing Act of 1991, Individuals with Disabilities Education Act, Americans with Disabilities Act, Affordable Care Act, No Child Left Behind, Drug-Free Schools, Community Act, and many others.

Mandates originate from the executive, legislative, or judicial branches of government and, as previously noted, will have as their basis constitutional or federal statutory provisions. Court interpretations have had impacts on several state and local functions, such as schools, free legal assistance to the poor, prisons, and mental institutions.[19] Catherine Lovell and Charles Tobin place mandates into two categories: requirements (procedural and programmatic) and constraints (revenue or expenditure limits).[20]

5.2.2 Four Techniques

The U.S. Advisory Commission on Intergovernmental Regulations (ACIR) further delineated these categories. ACIR identified four regulatory techniques used by the federal government to ensure compliance with mandated obligations: direct orders, crosscutting requirements, crossover sanctions and partial preemption.[21] Direct Orders are legal mandates that state and local governments must comply with or face the peril of civil or criminal actions. The most common example of a direct order is the Equal Employment Opportunity Act of 1972 which prohibits job discrimination on the basis of race, color, religion, gender, or national origin. For public employers, the Equal Opportunity Employment Commission (EEOC) refers cases to the U.S. Attorney General to bring action. While many federal regulations initially applied only to certain businesses and individuals, decades of legal precedents were overturned with the Garcia decision in 1985 (*Garcia v. San Antonio Metropolitan Transit Authority*, 469 U.S., 528). As noted in chapter 2, Garcia argued that the requirements of the Fair Labor Standards Act for minimum wage and overtime requirements did not apply to government employees performing "traditional government functions." These included police, fire and emergency services, public health services, parks services, transportation services and the like. In addition to the minimum wage, the Federal Fair Labor Standards Act (FSLA) required time and one-half pay for employees working in excess of 40 hours per week. The decision had an immediate impact on local government budgets that were going to be faced with paying overtime to a large part of their workforce. While Congress eventually amended the application of the FSLA to governmental units, in several respects the application of the commerce clause to state and local governments had far-reaching budgetary and staffing impacts. The issue of overtime pay resulted in "substantial litigation, with many state or local employees winning retroactive pay for work deemed by a court to qualify as overtime."[22] The Garcia case established that, under the constitution, Congress determines the extent of authority the federal government has over state and local governments and argued that it was up to the political process to resolve the roles within our federal system.[23]

Crosscutting Requirements are requirements applicable "across the board" for all programs receiving financial assistance from the federal government. The

19   Advisory Commission on Intergovernmental Relations, "The Federal Influence on State and Local Roles in the Federal System," A-89, (1981). Accessed at: https://library.unt.edu/gpo/acir/Reports/policy/A-89.pdf, 18.
20   Catherine Lovell and Charles Tobin, "The Mandate Issue," 319.
21   Advisory Commission on Intergovernmental Relations, "The Federal Role in the Federal System: The Dynamics of Growth," 7.
22   Advisory Commission on Intergovernmental Relations, "The Role of Federal Mandates in Intergovernmental Relations: A Preliminary ACIR Report," 10.
23   Advisory Commission on Intergovernmental Relations, "The Role of Federal Mandates in Intergovernmental Relations: A Preliminary ACIR Report," 5.

purpose is to further nationalize policies such as those relating to the handicapped, elderly, women, historic preservation, animal welfare, the environment, and relocation assistance. These are considered to have a "persuasive impact," as they apply to many types of federal assistance programs. The most frequently cited example is the Civil Rights Act of 1964 which requires nondiscrimination in federally-assisted programs and states that "No person in the United States shall, on the ground of race, color, or national origin, be excluded from participation in, be denied benefits of, or be subjected to discrimination under any program or activity receiving Federal financial assistance."[24]As early as 1980, the Office of Management and Budget (OMB) had identified 59 crosscutting requirements to state and local governments eligible for receiving federal funds.[25]

Crossover Sanctions are requirements that provide for financial penalties in one activity to change state or local policy in other areas. Simply stated, if a subnational government fails to comply with the requirements of Activity A, then funds will be reduced or eliminated in Activity B. For example, the Highway Energy Conservation Act of 1974 would not fund highway construction projects in any state with speed limits over 55 mph. All states reduced speed limits within two months of the law going into effect.

Partial Preemption derives from Article VI of the Constitution which states that both the U.S. Constitution itself and subsequent federal laws are the "supreme law of the land." Preemption, then, is the authority to preempt or supersede state and local laws and limits their ability to implement programs outside their policy areas. The Supreme Court has determined that federal law can both expressly and impliedly preempt state or local law.[26] For a century, preemption has been a feature of the regulatory nature of government in industry—including food, drugs, and finance—before it expanded to airlines, auto safety, tobacco, liquor, health insurance, nuclear safety, immigration, and other areas. Preemption of state and local law is now a "ubiquitous feature of the modern regulatory state."[27] Partial preemption, on the other hand, is a variation in that federal laws set up minimum standards, but the administration of that policy may be delegated to appropriate state or local agencies and, to some extent, work as a collaborative exercise. States can choose to enforce standards that meet the national ones or have the federal government take responsibility. The Water Quality Act of 1965 is considered to be the first of such laws establishing minimum standards preemption. Establishing such standards creates a base of national regulatory standards while at the same time reserving some discretion to the state administering the standards.[28]

24   Transcript of Civil Rights Act (1964) retrieved from www.ourdocuments.gov.
25   Congressional Research Service, "Federal Grants to State and Local Governments: A Historical Perspective on Contemporary Issues," 27.
26   Congressional Research Service, "Federal Preemption: A Legal Primer," July 23, 2019, R45825. Accessed at: https://crsreports.congress.gov, 2.
27   Congressional Research Service, "Federal Preemption: A Legal Primer," 2.
28   Joseph F. Zimmerman, "Preemption in the U.S. Federal System," *Publius* 23, no. 4 (1993), 7, 8.

Table 5.2 A Typology of Intergovernmental Regulatory Programs[29]

Program Type	Description	Major Policy Areas Employed
Direct Orders	Mandate state or local action under the threat of criminal or civil penalties	Public employment, environmental protections
Crosscutting Requirements	Apply to all or many federal assistance programs	Nondiscrimination, environmental protection, public employment, assistance management
Crossover Sanctions	Threaten the termination or reduction of aid provided under one or more specified programs unless the requirements of another program are satisfied	Highway safety and beautification, environmental protection, health planning, handicapped education
Partial Preemptions	Establish federal standards, but delegate administration to states if they adopt standards equivalent to the national ones	Environmental protection, natural resources, occupational safety and health, meat and poultry inspection

In state government, full preemption is more likely to pertain to controlling cities, counties, and special district governments. Under state statutory law or provisions and home rule authority, states established standards by which local governments operate. Through efforts by the American Legislative Council (ALEC), which is largely controlled by corporations and their lobby firms, state legislatures are preempting local law in a number of areas. These preemptions include the following: local minimum wage laws (25 states), gun and ammo regulations (43 states), local paid sick days (23 states), e-cigarettes (10 states), and broadband networks (20 states).[30] In addition, some consider certain federal and state tax provisions prohibiting state and local entities from taxing activities or on tax-exempt property as mandates. These provisions create a fiscal impact as onerous as the strategies identified above. For example, under the Internet Tax Freedom Act of 1998, Congress imposed a three-year moratorium precluding state and local governments from efforts to tax Internet access or electronic commerce. The moratorium was extended several times until 2018 when the Supreme Court ruled that states could charge taxes on purchases from out-of-state sellers.[31]

5.3.3 A "Carrot" or a "Stick"

Mandates, of course, have their critics. Since the 1980s when mandate use escalated considerably, state and local governments as well as businesses have been critical of the increase in what scholars term "unfunded mandates." The

29   Advisory Commission on Intergovernmental Relations, "Regulatory Federalism: Policy, Process, Impact And Reform," In Brief, B7, n.d. Accessed at: https://library.unt.edu/gpo/acir/Reports/brief/B-7.pdf, 8.
30   Local Solutions Support Center, "The Growing Shadow of State Interference: Preemption in the 2019 State Legislative Sessions." Accessed at: https://static1.squarespace.com/static/5ce4377caeb1ce00013a02fd/t/5d66a3c36044f700019a7efd/1567007722604/LSSCSiXReportAugust2019.pdf, 6.
31   South Dakota v. Wayfair, Inc. 585 U.S. ___ (2018).

mandates imposed by legislation between 1960 and 1995 created huge financial costs in such areas as managing landfills, wastewater treatment, drinking water, and accessibility under the Americans with Disabilities Act. A coalition of business and government interests were successful in the passage of the Unfunded Mandates Reform Act (UMRA) of 1995. To elaborate on its introduction in chapter 4, UMRA was designed for the following purposes:

> to strengthen the partnership between the Federal Government and State, local, and tribal governments; to end the imposition of certain Federal mandates on State, local, and tribal governments without adequate Federal funding; to assist Congress in its consideration of proposed legislation establishing or revising Federal programs containing Federal mandates; to assist Federal agencies in their consideration of proposed regulations; and to begin consideration of the effect of previously imposed Federal mandates.[32]

Under the original law, the Congressional Budget Office (CBO) is required to estimate intergovernmental mandate costs exceeding a threshold of $50 million in any fiscal year (private-sector mandates were to be reported at $100 million). Federal agencies were required to provide estimated costs and benefits when proposed, and final rules would require an expenditure of $100 million. These amounts are adjusted annually for inflation, and, in 2019, the thresholds for intergovernmental mandates were $82 million (private sector mandates were $164 million).[33]

> *UMRA*: The Unfunded Mandates Reform Act passed in 1995 was the federal government's effort to raise the awareness of the financial obligations of financial and regulatory requirements in federal legislation.

The Congressional Budget Office's analysis of UMRA's impact reports that 15 laws enacted between 1996 and 2018 contained 21 intergovernmental mandates that exceeded the financial threshold. Mandates included requiring schools to meet nutrition standards for all food sold in schools; establishing new standards for driver's licenses, identification cards, and vital statistic documents; requiring health insurance plans to comply with new standards for beneficiary and dependent coverage; and requiring commuter railroads to install train control technology.[34]

5.3.2 Common Issues

The UMRA also directed the ACIR to review and report on the role of federal mandates in intergovernmental relations as well as identify which mandates should be amended or eliminated outright. State and local government officials

---

32   Unfunded Mandates Reform, 2 U.S.C. § 1501.

33   Congressional Research Service, "Unfunded Mandates Reform Act: History, Impact, and Issues," 3.

34   Council of State Governments National Center for Interstate Compacts, "Enacted Intergovernmental Mandates with Estimated Costs That Exceed the Statutory Threshold, 1996 to 2018." Accessed at http://apps.csg.org/ncic/Default.aspx.

identified over 200 mandates in about 170 federal laws supplemented by 3,500 federal court rulings. In early 1996, a preliminary report was released for public review and comment; it created a "firestorm of protest by groups concerned with national commitments and requirements in a whole range of policy sectors."[35] A final report and recommendations were never issued, and ACIR was cut from the budget later that year. However, the draft report included what were termed "common issues" related to the review of mandates that were problematic to the intergovernmental system. These issues included detailed procedural requirements, lack of federal concern about mandate costs, federal failure to recognize state and local governments' public accountability, lawsuits by individuals against state and local governments to enforce mandates, inability of very small local governments to meet mandate standards and timetables, and lack of coordinated federal policy with no federal agency empowered to make binding decisions about a mandate's requirements.

To explicate further, detailed procedural requirements give state and local governments no flexibility to meet national goals in ways that best fit their needs and resources. The imposition of exact standards or detailed requirements, in many instances, merely increase costs and delay achievement of national goals.

The lack of federal concern about mandate costs means that, when the federal government imposes costs on another government without providing federal funds, the magnitude of costs is often not considered. If the federal government has no financial obligation, it has little incentive to weigh costs against benefits or to allow state and local governments to determine the least costly alternatives for reaching national goals.

The federal government can fail to recognize state and local governments' public accountability; indeed, state governments can often be treated as just another interest group, as private entities, or as administrative arms of the federal government rather than as sovereign governments with powers derived from the U.S. Constitution. Local governments, despite the important role they play in delivering government services, have been given even less consideration. Non-governmental advocacy groups' views have sometimes been given more attention than those of state and local governments.

Lawsuits by individuals against state and local governments to enforce federal mandates can place difficult burdens on state and local governments. Many federal laws permit individuals or organizations to sue state and local governments over questions of compliance, even though a federal agency is responsible for enforcement. Federal laws, however, are often written in such broad terms that it is unclear what is required of federal, state, and local officials. In these circumstances, permitting litigation brought by individuals subjects state and local governments to budgetary uncertainties and substantial legal costs. Because the federal agency is not directly involved with the costs and problems

35   Laurence J. O'Toole, Jr., *American Intergovernmental Relations Foundations, Perspectives, and Issues*, 4th edition. (Washington DC: CQ Press 2007), 261.

of this litigation, it has little incentive to propose amendments that would clarify the law's requirements.

Very small local governments are often unable to meet mandate standards and timetables. The requirements for many federal mandates are based on the assumption that all local governments have the financial, administrative, and technical resources that exist in large governments. Many very small local governments have only part-time staff with little technical capability and very limited resource bases. Extending deadlines or modifying requirements for these small governments may have minimal adverse effects on the achievement of overall national goals but may make it possible for such governments eventually to comply.

Issues arise from a lack of coordinated policy with no federal agency empowered to make binding decisions about a mandate's requirements. Some mandates involve several federal agencies. This structure has resulted in confusion about what the law requires and how state and local governments can know when they are in compliance. In addition to making state and local governments aware of mandate requirements, federal agencies should explain the reasons for the mandate and should assist in taking the actions necessary for implementation.[36]

The UMRA was, in several ways, more polish than substance and has resulted in rather mixed outcomes. First, the term "mandate" was narrowly defined and does not target conditions of financial assistance. Under UMRA, an intergovernmental mandate is an enforceable duty, effects certain changes in large entitlement programs, and reduces federal funding for an existing mandate. Regarding an enforceable duty, any provision in legislation, statute, or regulation that would compel or explicitly prohibit actions on the part of state, local, or tribal governments is a mandate unless the provision amounts to a duty that is imposed as a condition for receiving federal aid or that arises from participation in a voluntary federal program.

Intergovernmental mandates effect certain changes in large entitlement programs. Consequently, a new condition on, or a reduction in, federal financial assistance can be a mandate in the case of a large entitlement program (one that provides $500 million or more annually to a state, local, or tribal government), but only if the jurisdiction in question lacks the flexibility either to offset the new costs or to compensate by adjusting other parts of the program. And intergovernmental mandates can reduce federal funding for an existing mandate. A provision to reduce or eliminate federal funding authorized to cover the costs of an existing mandate would itself be considered a mandate under UMRA.[37]

Several types of legislation are excluded from UMRA requirements, including legislation enforcing constitutional or certain statutory rights, emergency or national security legislation, or legislation relating to old-age, survivors, and disability benefits.

36   Advisory Commission on Intergovernmental Relations, "The Role of Federal Mandates in Intergovernmental Relations: A Preliminary ACIR Report," 6–9.
37   Congressional Budget Office, "Intergovernmental Mandates in Federal Legislation," Economic and Budget Issue Brief July 13, 2009. Accessed at: https://www.cbo.gov/sites/default/files/111th-congress-2009-2010/reports/07-14-umra.pdf.

A report by the Congressional Research Services concludes that state and local government officials and Federalism scholars generally view the UMRA as having a limited, though positive, impact on intergovernmental relations. In their view, the federal government has continued to expand its authority through the "carrots" of increased federal assistance and the "sticks" of grant conditions, preemptions, mandates, and administrative rulemaking. Facing what they view as a seemingly ever-growing federal influence in American governance, they generally advocate a broadening of the UMRA's coverage to enhance its impact, emphasizing the need to include conditions of grant assistance and a broader range of federal agency rulemaking, including rules issued by independent regulatory agencies.[38]

Despite the UMRAs good intentions, between 2006 and 2018, over 200 laws were enacted, creating 443 mandates. While most of those mandates did not meet the law's definition, many of these laws did have the effect of imposing a financial impact on state and local governments.[39]

Since its passage in 1995, several attempts have been made to amend the law, the most recent of which occurred in 2019. The H.R.300 the Unfunded Mandates Information and Transparency Act of 20l9 was introduced in early 2019. The bill would expand reporting requirements by independent federal agencies, assess the effects of regulations on state and local governments, and expand the extent of cost statements.[40] However, like previous versions passed in 2014, 2015, and 2018, the Senate never took up the legislation and it appeared to have little chance of passage.[41]

5.4 INTERSTATE COMPACTS

As noted earlier, IGR also exemplify a horizontal arrangement where agreements between equals can be negotiated. These interactions involve a wide variety of service issues and frequently cross state borders, allowing for joint action among two or more separate entities.

One horizontal dimension of IGR is interstate compacts. These are legal, negotiated contracts between two or more states. Rather than comprising a mandate from a higher government to a lower government, compacts take place among equals. Typically, a joint commission of those states involved is established to negotiate the initial agreement. In order to go into effect, they are required to be approved by the state legislatures involved. Article I, §10 of the U.S. Constitution contains explicit language requiring approval of compacts between states. It requires that "No state shall, without the consent of Congress . . . , enter into any agreement or compact with another state, or with a foreign power, or engage in war, unless actually invaded, or in such imminent danger as will not admit of delay."

---

38   Congressional Research Service, "Unfunded Mandates Reform Act: History, Impact, and Issues," 36.
39   Congressional Research Service, "Unfunded Mandates Reform Act: History, Impact, and Issues," 35.
40   Congressional Research Service, "Unfunded Mandates Reform Act: History, Impact, and Issues," 37.
41   United States House of Representatives. "H.R. 300: Unfunded Mandates Information and Transparency Act of 2019." Accessed at: https://www.govtrack.us/congress/bills/116/hr300.

However, in 1893 the Supreme Court opined that such congressional consent is required only if the compact is "directed to the formation of any combination tending to the increase of political power in the States, which may encroach upon or interfere with the just supremacy of the United States."[42] Compacts that are approved by Congress become federal law. Compacts, other than to settle boundary disputes, were little used at the time. However, during the post-World War II period, there was substantial growth in the use of compacts, and today there are almost 200 compacts applicable to a number of different areas, such as emergency management, transportation, law enforcement, and education.[43] Compacts accomplish many goals. They establish a formal, legal relationship among states to address common problems or promote a common agenda. They create independent, multistate governmental authorities (e.g., commissions) that can address issues more effectively than a state agency acting independently, or when no state has the authority to act unilaterally. Compacts establish uniform guidelines, standards, or procedures for agencies in the compact's member states, and they create economies of scale to reduce administrative and other costs. They also respond to national priorities in consultation or in partnership with the federal government, retain state sovereignty in matters traditionally reserved for the states, and settle interstate disputes.[44]

Probably the most famous (or infamous) compact is the Port Authority of New York and New Jersey. In 2016, two aides to New Jersey Governor Chris Christie were convicted of fraud in the "Bridgegate" scandal, where the governor's

Bridgegate: The closing of the George Washington Bridge scandal by the New Jersey Governor's Office.

office shut down the George Washington Bridge connecting New York and New Jersey—one of the world's busiest bridges. The gridlock created was to punish Fort Lee, New Jersey's mayor, who had failed to endorse Christie's re-election bid.

Most compacts are less political than "Bridgegate." For example, Georgia has 31 compacts, including the Civil Defense and Disaster Compact, Interstate Compact for Adult Offender Supervision, National Crime Prevention and Privacy Compact, Southeastern Forest Fire Protection Compact, and the Interstate Library Compact.

5.4.2 Uniform Legislation

Some of the difficulties in operating our federal system, critics argue, are the inconsistencies that exist from state to state and locality to locality in laws and procedures. National businesses, in particular, perceive the need to deal with similar laws and regulations moving from state to state. Another horizontal dimension of IGR can be enhanced by uniform and model laws. A number of organizations promote such legislation.

---

42   U. S. Supreme Court, *Virginia v. Tennessee*, 148 U.S. 503, 519 (1893). Accessed at: https://supreme.justia.com/cases/federal/us/148/503/.
43   Council of State Governments National Center for Interstate Compacts, "Compact Search Results." Accessed at: http://apps.csg.org/ncic/SearchResults.aspx?.
44   Mountjoy, John J., "Interstate Compacts State Solutions—By the states and for the states," Council of State Governments. Accessed at: https://www.csg.org/knowledgecenter/docs/ncic/SolutionsProblems.pdf.ulc.

The Uniform Law Commission (ULC), established in 1892, provides non-partisan draft legislation for state legislators in both areas and tries to ensure "consistency, clarity and stability to state statutory law."[45] Uniform acts develop the same law with the principal objective being uniformity across boundaries. ULC currently has 125 uniform acts on file on such topics as consumer protection, labor, civil procedures, family law, business regulation, and real estate property. Model acts promote some uniformity but allow more flexibility in their enactment, even if not adopted entirely. There are 35 model acts by ULC in areas similar to the uniform acts. These include a controlled substances act, the marriage and divorce act, an eminent domain code, a consumer credit code, and a state administrative procedures act. ULC is largely a volunteer organization, and appointed members are required to be lawyers, including judges, legislators, and law professors. They are appointed by all 50 state governments, the District of Columbia, Puerto Rico, and the U.S. Virgin Islands.

Similar to ULC in writing model legislation, but with a very conservative political view, is the American Legislative Exchange Council (ALEC), founded in 1973. While ALEC claims to be nonpartisan, it is primarily funded by large corporations, and most individual members are conservative Republican state legislators. ALEC is supported by big oil and energy companies, telecom, tobacco and alcohol, transportation, the pharmaceutical trade group Pharmaceutical Research and Manufacturers of America (PhRMA), and the Koch Brothers foundations.[46] Between 2010 and 2018, more than 600 model bills prepared by ALEC became law in Republican-dominated legislatures.[47]

Facilitating IGR, but not promoting the enactment of specific legislation, is the Council on State Governments (COSG). COSG does not draft model legislation but provides a Shared State Legislation program exclusively comprising state officials. It disseminates an annual report sharing legislation that meets the following criteria: the bill addresses a current state issue of national or regional significance and provides a benefit to bill drafters as well as a clear, innovative, and practical structure and approach; also, the legislation needs have become law.[48]

5.4.3 Interlocal Agreements and Contracts

While some bargaining and negotiating occurs among governmental units (even where there are mandates involved), nowhere is this technique more apparent than among local governments. Over 50 years ago, Matthew Holden argued in "The Governance of the Metropolis as a Problem in Diplomacy" that metro and

45   Uniform Law Commission, *2018/2019 Annual Report*. Accessed at: https://www.uniformlaws.org/viewdocument/2018-annual-report, 1.

46   Riestenberg, Jay, "Who Still Funds ALEC?" March 24, 2015. Common Cause. Accessed at: https://www.commoncause.org/democracy-wire/who-still-funds-alec/.

47   Yvonne Wingett Sanchez and Rob O'Dell "What Is ALEC? 'The most effective organization' for conservatives, says Newt Gingrich" USA Today April 3, 2019 Accessed at: https://www.usatoday.com/story/news/investigations/2019/04/03/alec-american-legislative-exchange-council-model-bills-republican-conservative-devos-gingrich/3162357002/.

48   Council of State Governments, *Shared State Legislation*. Accessed at: https://www.csg.org/programs/policyprograms/SSLabout.aspx.

international politics had a "common frame"—the need to conduct diplomacy among governmental units.[49] Local intergovernmental management (IGM) requires interpersonal skills, like that of a good diplomat, in order "to cultivate and exercise the same level of finesse and appreciation for the values of others.[50] Frederickson agrees with this assessment and refers to the system

> **Administrative Conjunction**: The informal system of intergovernmental cooperation that exists in metropolitan areas to facilitate the delivery of services and the exchange of information among professional staff.

of cooperation and agreement in metro areas as resulting from "administrative conjunction." Horizontal relationships develop among local professionals that are based not on formal authority but on professionalism and knowledge. It is common for professional managers, including police and fire chiefs, public works directors, parks and recreation directors, and other key management personnel to have either formal or informal regular meetings or exchanges of information. Such relationships are quite necessary in metro areas, and Frederickson describes the Kansas City area as including "two states, five counties, two central cities, 31 suburban cities, 26 school districts, and a varying number of special districts."[51]

Local governments in the U.S. provide services—local public safety, fire protection, clean water, the safe disposal of wastewater, the provision of green space and recreation opportunities, road repair, snow removal, and others. While most local governments provide many of the same type of services, they do not have to produce them all directly. Over the years, intergovernmental cooperation has addressed particular needs for a community that they were unable to produce for themselves. Modern approaches to IGM have produced organizational outcomes that were previously less attainable. While some argue that local government is too fragmented, efforts to consolidate local governments, particularly in metropolitan areas, have not been very successful. The National League of Cities notes that there have been almost 100 local referenda over the past 40 years for various city-county consolidations, with 75 percent being rejected by voters.[52] Local school districts, on the other hand, have been more successful. In 1942, there were 108,579 school districts while today there are fewer than 13,000[53]. Despite the lack of public support for non-school consolidation, local officials realize the need for the use of intergovernmental agreements.

Cooperation agreements, as they are sometimes called, allow two or more government units to work together. There are three different types of agreements:

49   Matthew Holden, Jr., "The Governance of the Metropolis as a Problem in Diplomacy." *Journal of Politics* 26, no. 3 (1964), 645.

50   Thomas J. Mikulecky, "Intergovernmental Relations Strategies for the Local Manager," *Public Administration Review* 46, no. 4 (1980). 380.

51   H. George Frederickson, "The Repositioning of American Public Administration," *PS: Political Science and Politics* 32, no. 4 (1999), 707. 708.

52   National League of Cities. "Cities 101 — Consolidations." Accessed at: nlc.org/resource/cities-101-consolidations/.

53   U.S. Census Bureau, "Table 4 Special Purposes Local Governments by State Census Years 1942 to 2017." Accessed at: https://www.census.gov/data/tables/2017/econ/gus/2017-governments.html.

service agreements, joint agreements, and mutual aid agreements. When one government contracts to provide a specific service with another government or non-government organization (NGO), this is a service agreement. Sanford, Florida, for example, provides water to the adjacent unincorporated community of Midway. Major capital investments may require the creation of a joint authority. Des Moines, Iowa and surrounding communities operate a wastewater treatment plant through such a joint operating agreement. Many counties and incorporated communities provide mutual aid in case of fires or other emergencies. Small cities, particularly those with populations of 2,500 or less, may find interlocal agreements to be good ways to provide services to their communities without the expense of producing those services directly.

On the extreme end are "contract cities." These cities enter into service contracts for the provision of all or most services, either with other governments or NGOs. The first city to function as a contract city was Lakewood, California. In 1954, Lakewood was an unincorporated community in

> **Contract City:** The name given to local governments that are largely operated through contracts for services with other local governments or NGOs.

Los Angeles County. The adjacent city of Long Beach was interested in a hostile or involuntary annexation of the unincorporated area. To avoid the expense of building an entire governmental infrastructure, including a municipal building, the community incorporated as a municipality but contracted municipal services to Los Angeles County. The Lakewood Plan, as it is known, has become a model for other intergovernmental contracting relationships. While in the case of Lakewood the primary purpose was to avoid annexation, communities today largely contract to achieve economies of scale in service production.[54]

There appears to be some use of what are termed informal intergovernmental agreements, particularly in metropolitan areas. Large metro cities frequently have expertise or equipment that they can share with smaller suburban communities. More often today, however, intergovernmental agreements are formal contracts with mutual obligations. These intergovernmental arrangements are made between all levels of government (including the federal government), but we will focus on agreements between local governments. ACIR noted in 1967 that such contracts were "the most widely used formal method of cooperation..."[55] No national database of the number of intergovernmental agreements exists, but there are thousands of them in the U.S., mostly established by individual state statutes. When applied broadly (and each state is different), joint agreements can be used for service provision in any area that the local government could take on by itself. In 1921, the California state legislature was one of the first to grant wider authority to local governments.[56]

---

54   Falk, Nathan, "Contract Cities: An Alternate Model," Rose Institute of State and Local Government, Claremont McKenna College (2011). Accessed at: http://roseinstitute.org/contract-cities-an-alternative-model/.
55   Advisory Commission on Intergovernmental Relations, *A Handbook for Interlocal Agreements.* (Washington, DC: 1967. Accessed at: https://library.unt.edu/gpo/acir/Reports/information/m-29.pdf, 2.
56   Advisory Commission on Intergovernmental Relations, *A Handbook for Interlocal Agreements.* 4.

In a survey conducted by the International City/County Management Association, 82 percent of respondents reported that they participate in a regional council of governments (COG), metropolitan planning organization (MPO), or regional planning agency.[57] Such agreements are

> **COG**: Regional planning councils of government often times required for the expenditure of federal funds in a metropolitan area.

considered mostly positive by both elected and appointed officials. While they circumvent structural as well as organizational issues, these arrangements "stress consolidation of services, rather than consolidation of governments."[58]

Several core services, such as public safety, support functions, and land use regulation, do not often appear on the list of intergovernmental services. On the other hand, public transit, airport operations, public safety communications (911 systems), jails, animal shelter operations, homeless shelter operations, libraries, solid waste, water and wastewater systems, child welfare programs, and purchasing tend to be managed through contracts for services with another government agency or NGO. A 2001 report in New York state identified 29 separate areas using these types of cooperative agreements.[59]

Federal requirements in the environment and social services led to the regional councils of governments' creation. Also referred to as regional planning commissions, Councils of Governments (COGs) are representative bodies of elected officials from multi-counties and municipalities in metropolitan areas. While COGs are voluntary, certain types of federal funding require a sign-off by the regional COG indicating that there is consensus about certain action or funding. COGs are multi-purpose with limited legal status and assist in planning, coordinating, and administering various state and federal funds. They are involved in regional issues of community and economic development, 911 emergency dispatch, solid waste disposal, criminal justice, emergency preparedness, health and human services, and subsidence. There are currently more than 500 regional councils in all 50 states. Many of the COGs also serve as the metropolitan planning organization. MPOs were created as a result of the Federal-Aid Highway Act of 1962 which required their creation in metropolitan areas with populations in excess of 50,000. The MPOs continue to have responsibility for comprehensive transportation planning and funding in urban areas.[60]

5.4.4 The Georgia Experience

Georgia's efforts to encourage cooperative agreements is twofold. Municipal incorporation in Georgia requires the granting of a local act by the General

---

57   George C. Homsy and Mildred E. Warner, "Intermunicipal Cooperation: The Growing Reform." Accessed at: https://cardi.cals.cornell.edu/sites/cardi.cals.cornell.edu/files/shared/documents/RED/Intermunicipal%20Cooperation.pdf, 58.

58   Advisory Commission on Intergovernmental Relations, *A Handbook for Interlocal Agreements*. 18.

59   Office of the New York State Comptroller, Division of Local Government and School Accountability (n.d.). *Intermunicipal Cooperation and Consolidation*. Accessed at: https://www.osc.state.ny.us/localgov/pubs/research/cooperation1.pdf, 4.

60   National Association of Regional Councils, "Building Regional Communities 2019 Policy Agenda." Accessed at: http://narc.org/wp-content/uploads/2019/08/What-Are-Regional-Councils-Brochure-1.pdf.

Assembly. In addition to population and development requirements, municipal corporations must meet service standards. To be an active municipal corporation they must provide at least three of these services: law enforcement; fire protection and fire safety; road and street construction or maintenance; solid waste management; water supply and/or distribution; wastewater treatment; stormwater collection and disposal; electric or gas utility service; enforcement of building, housing, plumbing, and electrical codes and related codes; and planning and zoning, and recreational facilities[61]

Services can be produced directly or provided under a contract. In order to facilitate service contracting, the Georgia Service Delivery Act was enacted in 1997. While city/county agreements are usually discretionary, in order to receive sales tax revenue and adopt a Service Delivery Strategy (SDS), the agreement is compulsory.

SDS: A requirement by Georgia law for all counties and cities to have an established Service Delivery Strategy to determine the provision of local government services.

In Georgia, for example, all 159 counties are required to develop an SDS. Although somewhat imprecise, cities and counties must agree on service provision and provide the following: an identification of all services presently provided in the county by cities, counties, and authorities; an assignment of which local government will be responsible for providing which service in what area of the county; a description of how all services will be funded; an identification of intergovernmental contracts, ordinances, and resolutions to be used in implementing the strategy, including existing contracts.[62]

The SDS has the following requirements: to provide for eliminating service duplication, or developing an explanation for a similar service's existence; justification for jurisdictions charging water and sewer rate differentials to customers outside their boundaries; the funding of services provided primarily for unincorporated areas derived exclusively from unincorporated areas; the elimination of conflicts in land use plans within a county, between the county, and its cities; and an agreement on a process for resolving land use classification disputes between a county and city over property to be annexed.[63]

Georgia's Department of Community Affairs, the state agency responsible for reviewing and monitoring the SDS, ensures compliance. The law prohibits state-administered financial assistance, grants, loans, or permits to "any local government or authority which is not included in a department verified strategy or for any project which is inconsistent with such strategy."[64]

61   Georgia Municipal Association, "Municipal Incorporation: Requirements under Georgia Law," August 7, 2018. Accessed at: https://www.gacities.com/Resources/Reference-Articles/Municipal-Incorporation-Requirements-under-Georgi.aspx.
62   Georgia Department of Community Affairs "Charting a Course for Cooperation and Collaboration," (1997), Accessed at: https://www.dca.ga.gov/sites/default/files/guide.collaboration.pdf, 1.
63   Georgia Department of Community Affairs "Charting a Course for Cooperation and Collaboration," (1997), 1, 2.
64   O.C.G.A. § 36-70-27. Accessed at: https://law.justia.com/codes/georgia/2010/title-36/provisions/chapter-70/article-2/36-70-27.

Following the adoption and filing of the SDS, cities and counties can then prepare individual intergovernmental agreements. As in most states, these IGAs cover many areas of service delivery: airports, animal control, solid waste, detention, stormwater management, emergency management, libraries, and water supply, to name a few.

Georgia generally has also been more successful than other states in instituting consolidated government. Currently, there are eight city-county governments in the state, with the oldest, Columbus-Muscogee County, established in 1970. As successful as the consolidation is, it took local leaders over two decades to develop a city-county charter that was approved by the public.[65]

5.5 THE "STICK" WITHOUT THE "CARROT"

When enforcing the requirements of the U.S. Constitution or federal statutes, the Department of Justice (DOJ) may enter into a consent decree or settlement agreement with state or local governments. Both arrangement types are negotiated after a response has been submitted to a specific allegation of legal violations. A consent decree is a court order that can be enforced through contempt motions in federal court. A settlement agreement is an out-of-court resolution that mandates certain performance through a memorandum of understanding (MOA) with the state or local government entity. Failure to comply with the MOA requires the Justice Department to file a breach of contract suit. Both potentially place the federal courts or the DOJ in a long-term position to monitor compliance and may require a major financial commitment on the part of the state or local government in order to achieve compliance.[66]

In 2012, Kansas City, Missouri became the 200th city to enter into a settlement agreement under Project Civic Access. The objective of the agreement was for the city to comply with the requirements of the Americans with Disabilities Act (ADA) within a six-year time frame. Some 40,000 violations of the ADA were identified, with the estimated cost in excess of $100 million. The MOA initially required compliance within six years; however, the city has requested additional time to come into compliance.[67]

Ferguson, Missouri entered into a consent decree with the Department of Justice over unlawful conduct, including Title VI of the 1964 Civil Rights Act. The DOJ conducted two investigations. One focused on the killing of Michael Brown by a member of the Ferguson Police Department. While this investigation did not produce evidence of a federal law violation in the killing, the other inquiry

---

65   Carl Vinson Institute of Government. "A Review and Comparison of Georgia's Three Largest Consolidated Governments (2011). Accessed at: cviog.uga.edu.

66   U.S. Department of Justice, "Justice Department Releases Memorandum on Litigation Guidelines for Civil Consent Decrees and Settlement Agreements." November 18, 2018. Accessed at: https://www.justice.gov/opa/pr/justice-department-releases-memorandum-litigation-guidelines-civil-consent-decrees-and.

67   U.S. House of Representatives Committee on Government Oversight and Reform Subcommittee on Intergovernmental Affairs. *Hearing on Unfunded Mandates: Examining Federally Imposed Burdens on State and Local Governments*. Statement by Jermaine Reed, April 26, 2017, 26, 27.

examined the Ferguson Police Department's practices, including the focus on revenue rather than public safety. The investigation revealed violations of the First, Fourth, and Fourteenth Amendments to the U.S. Constitution as well as statutory law. The report concluded there was discriminatory intent regarding racial disparities when enforcing certain laws that adversely affected African Americans. The decree required Ferguson to change police policies, increase its municipal code enforcement, and mandate training and supervision for police officers. The decree will be lifted once the city is in "full and effective" compliance for a two-year period.[68, 69]

Along with Supreme Court decisions—such as *Garcia*—and actions by the Department of Justice, state and local governments can be highly critical of federal intrusion. Debates continue at all levels about the role of the states in light of the 10th Amendment. Taken in context with both the "proper and necessary" clause in the Constitution and the 14th Amendment, the federal government has consistently favored federal supremacy over state and local control. In recent times, the Trump administration conveyed mixed messages on the place of the national government within the federal system. On one hand, DOJ guidelines on consent decrees and settlement agreements appear to protect state governments from onerous interpretations of federal law. In addition, the rollback of federal rules, particularly in the area of clean water, have benefited state and local governments. On the other hand, the Environmental Protection Agency (EPA) and the Department of Transportation (DOT) are being sued for reversing California's authority to set rules on tailpipe emissions. California and about two dozen other states have joined in the lawsuit.70 State and local laws relating to immigration, marijuana businesses, offshore drilling, and sanctuary cities also came under attack during the Trump Administration. Politico noted that the "Trump administration [was] all in favor of states' rights. Except when it's not."[71]

5.6 BARGAINING

Daniel Elazar noted over a half century ago in his book *American Federalism: A View from the States* that intergovernmental collaboration has developed over the course of the Republic to include "virtually every government function."[72] Indeed, for American Federalism to function at all in this day and age, collaboration through

68   U.S. Department of Justice, "Justice Department Announces Findings of Two Civil Rights Investigations in Ferguson, Missouri," March 4, 2015. Accessed at: https://www.justice.gov/opa/pr/justice-department-announces-findings-two-civil-rights-investigations-ferguson-missouri.

69   United States District Court Eastern District of Missouri Eastern Division *United States of America v. The City of Ferguson*, No. 4;16-cv000180-CDP Consent Decree.

70   Davenport, Coral, "California Sues the Trump Administration in Its Escalating War Over Auto Emissions," *New York Times*, September 20, 2019. Accessed at: https://www.nytimes.com/2019/09/20/climate/california-auto-emissions-lawsuit.html.

71   Stratford, Michael, "Trump endorses states' rights—but only when he agrees with the state," *Politico* April 2, 2018. Accessed at: https://www.politico.com/story/2018/04/02/trump-states-rights-education-sanctuary-drilling-492784.

72   Daniel Elazar, *American Federalism: A View from the States*, (New York: Thomas Crowell Company 1966), 53.

IGM is a core requirement. Federal mandates clearly serve as an important "stick" within the intergovernmental system; however, Robert Agranoff and Michael McGuire argue in their article "Another Look at Bargaining and Negotiating in Intergovernmental Management" that Federalism at the administrative level is "highly transactional."[73] This view calls for a less coercive form of Federalism and one where parties negotiate across federal-state-local borders both vertically and horizontally. Even when relationships are unitary under Dillon's Rule (see chapter 1 for further details) between state and local government, there is a fundamental need to practice cooperation and, to some extent, manage through networks. Networks are defined in a number of ways, but R. A. W. Rhodes, in "The New Governance: Governing without Government," describes them as "interorganizational linkages" that involve "several interdependent actors involved in delivering services."[74] Being able to address not only the "wicked" problems that government attempts to resolve but also the day-to-day public policy involving some of the more mundane, but important, services requires the cooperation and collaboration of many. In "The Key to Networked Government," Donald F. Kettl argues that the principal to having such networks is "gathering the players, coordinating their work, and ensuring that the result promotes the public interest."[75] One only has to look at the September 11 response to the attack on the Pentagon to realize it was an "intricate ballet performed by federal, state, regional, and local agencies..."[76] While our federal networked system is not new, it is more complicated than in the past with interconnections between differentiated governmental units as well as both public and private NGOs.

Within our vertical federal system, Agranoff and McGuire have identified four aspects of how governments bargain. The first is the importance of place, with state governments as the base. Under the 10th Amendment, the states became the "primary domestic policy and program engine." Even today, states maintain jurisdictional authority within their boundaries. While local governments remain "creatures of the state," there is a long-held practice of local control in a number of areas, such as public safety, land use, and schools. Jurisdictional boundaries remain important in our federal system. Second, there is a limited national bureaucracy. Most public policy administered in the U.S. remains decentralized and performed by professionals at the state and local levels. Federal agents manage and monitor contracts but have delegated primary responsibility for program administration to state and local agencies. Third, there is typical multi-level, simultaneous action that has replaced dual Federalism, making our system both multilayered and interdependent. This move requires joint action to implement public policy.

---

73   Robert Agranoff and Michael McGuire, "Another Look at Bargaining and Negotiating in Intergovernmental Management," *Journal of Public Administration Research and Theory: J-PART* 14, no. 4 (2004), 485.

74   R. A. W. Rhodes, (1996) "The New Governance: Governing without Government," *Political Studies* 44, 658.

75   Donald F. Kettl, "The Key to Networked Government," *Unlocking the Power of Networks* Stephen Goldsmith and Donald F. Kettl eds. (2009) Accessed at: https://www.brookings.edu/wp-content/uploads/2016/07/unlockingthepowerofnetworks_chapter.pdf, 1.

76   Donald F. Kettl, "The Key to Networked Government," 7.

Finally, there is reciprocal administrative action. Federal laws enacted in the 1930s required the "professionalization" of state and local administrators. You may recall even earlier the federal highway funding bill of 1921 which required states to create a state highway department. The expansion of existing state agencies and the development of new ones and limits on patronage boosted state and local government administration.[77]

5.7 CONCLUSION

As noted in the introduction of this chapter, with 90,000-plus governments in the U.S., intergovernmental administration is both differentiated and excessively complicated. Its function is more than grants-in-aid, regulations, and mandates. Managing local communities today, according to Agranoff and McGuire, "includes contracts, loans, cooperative agreements, reciprocal services agreements, shared or joint investments, procurement of goods and services, personal and political contacts, and lobbying for program and policy changes."[78]

While having only a three percent chance of passage, Congress is once again looking at how intergovernmental relations can be addressed. Reps. Gerry Connolly (D-VA) and Rob Bishop (R-UT) have introduced bi-partisan legislation called the Restore the Partnership Act. The purpose of the act is to reconstitute a new Commission on Intergovernmental Relations and includes several reforms to the defunct ACIR. They include the following: the addition of town and tribal representatives to the Commission as well as expanded membership for state legislatures and counties to reach parity with state executive representation; new responsibilities that include examining Supreme Court decisions and their impact on the intergovernmental relationship; a requirement that Congress hold hearings to examine the Commission's annual report within 90 days of the report's submission to Congress; and new authorities that ensure the Commission receives written responses from agencies on the recommendations it provides to them.

According to the bill's authors, the new provisions generate a fresh approach to accountability to the Commission, placing it on par with the way federal agencies currently engage the Government Accountability Office (GAO).[79]

The proper federal role in administrating intergovernmental relations has been at issue for decades. There are any number of assessment theories, such as developmental, democratic, rational, and administrative models. Forty years ago, ACIR developed five standards of assessment in determining federal involvement levels in domestic policy which are considered to serve as a guide for functional assignments, as per their national purpose, economic efficiency, equity, political accountability, and administrative effectiveness.

77   Robert Agranoff and Michael McGuire, "Another Look at Bargaining and Negotiating in Intergovernmental Management," 497–501.
78   Robert Agranoff and Michael McGuire, "Another Look at Bargaining and Negotiating in Intergovernmental Management," 509.
79   Connolly, Gerry, "Connolly. Bishop Introduce Restore the Partnership Act," July 23, 2019. Accessed at: https://connolly.house.gov/news/documentsingle.aspx?DocumentID=3676.

Regarding national purpose, it has been a long-held view of our federal system that Congress needs to apply limitations in deciding whether a problem that was once the responsibility of the state should be assumed by the federal government. This "traditional Federalist" view holds that the federal government needs to resist its inclination to solve all problems. For economic efficiency, functions should be assigned to jurisdictions that are large enough to realize economies of scale and small enough not to incur diseconomies of scale and are willing to provide alternative service offerings at a price range and level of effectiveness acceptable to local citizenry, and jurisdictions that adopt pricing policies for their functions when appropriate.

To provide equity, functions should be assigned to jurisdictions that are large enough to encompass the costs and benefits of a function or are willing to compensate other jurisdictions for the service costs imposed or benefits received by them, have adequate fiscal capacity to finance their public service responsibilities in a manner which insures interpersonal and interjurisdictional fiscal equalization, and are able to absorb the financial risks involved. To maintain political accountability, functions should be assigned to jurisdictions that are controllable by, accessible to, and accountable to their residents; and jurisdictions that maximize the conditions and opportunities for active and productive citizen participation.

And to achieve administrative effectiveness, functions should be assigned to jurisdictions that are responsible for a sufficient number of functions and that can balance competing functional interests; encompass a logical geographic area for effective performance of a function; explicitly determine the goals and means of discharging assigned public service responsibilities and that periodically reassess program goals in light of performance standards; are willing to pursue intergovernmental means of promoting interlocal functional cooperation and reducing interlocal functional conflict; and have adequate legal authority and management capability to perform a function.[80]

ACIR's advice was sound in the past and is still sound. In many ways, intergovernmental management has few historic antecedents; it has slowly evolved since the first days of the Republic—sometimes with unintended consequences. In the twenty-first century when cooperation is critical for successful policy administration, that lack of planning will limit the effectiveness and efficiency of government operations. Having clearly delineated responsibility within our federal system can only make our Republic more secure.

5.7.1 The Case of COVID-19 and the Administration of IGR in a Time of Crisis

As introduced in chapter 3, the COVID-19 pandemic of 2020 placed a spotlight on the role of state government in our federal system. The following excerpts of a case study from an article by Clay Jenkinson in Governing, *Who's in Charge?*

80   Advisory Commission on Intergovernmental Relations, "The Federal Role in the Federal System: The Dynamics of Growth," 38–99.

Coronavirus and the Tenth Amendment, places an emphasis on the administrative side of IGR. Used with permission.

WHO'S IN CHARGE? CORONAVIRUS AND THE TENTH AMENDMENT

As governors take leading positions on how to manage the pandemic, the nearly forgotten cornerstone of the Constitution is relevant again. It's a reminder of how Federalism and our form of government works.

CLAY JENKINSON, EDITOR-AT-LARGE | APRIL 17, 2020

The global COVID-19 pandemic has raised the question of American Federalism to new levels. It has touched off a fascinating national debate about who's in charge in a global crisis, who must accept responsibility, where the buck stops and what the best governmental authority is to deal with the unprecedented challenges that the coronavirus outbreak represents.

Suddenly the nearly forgotten Tenth Amendment is relevant again! But in a delicious reversal of roles, it is the progressive state governors who are invoking the Tenth Amendment—in desperation—to protect themselves from a national government that is mostly getting in their way as they try to cope with the crisis.

As the Chinese proverb puts it, may you live in interesting times.

Former Speaker of the House of Representatives Tip O'Neill famously said, "all politics is local." The paradox of the coronavirus is that all disease is in many ways local, too. A patient enters a local hospital to be treated by local medical professionals. Absent a national health-care system, medical treatment in the U.S. is delivered by a dizzying range of systems, with widely different results depending on the availability of insurance, affordability, and coverage options, but also social class and regional political philosophies.

The coronavirus has affected some states (New York, Washington, Florida, Louisiana, New Jersey) much more severely than others (North Dakota, Wyoming, Alaska). The social lockdown in a place like New York City or Detroit has to be more draconian than in Nebraska or Utah, if only because of the remarkable differences in population density. Gov. Andrew Cuomo faces challenges that the governor of Montana can scarcely comprehend. Those who wonder why rural states have been more reluctant to adopt strict social distancing protocols than urban states find it hard to conceive of a place like Wyoming, where the largest city, Cheyenne, has a population of only 59,466 people and the next largest population center, Casper, is 178 miles away.

Given how vast, varied, and unevenly populated the U.S. is, it makes sense that state sovereignty would prevail in many coronavirus policy decisions. As the Trump administration rightly understands, a one-size-fits-all national policy is—on some questions—an imprecise tool with which to combat the pandemic. This makes sense. California, with a sixth of the world's economy and a population of 40 million, is a commonwealth unto itself in Jeffersonian terms. New York is still known as the Empire State. With a population of almost 20 million, and one of the five most important cities on the planet, New York has a significance and a set of challenges that sets it apart from most other states.

On the other hand, everyone understands that the coronavirus crisis is an unprecedented chapter in American history. Never before, not even during the Great Depression of the 1930s, has any event brought community life of America to a near-standstill. Never before in the aeronautic era have so few planes flown over American skies (except for one week following the 9/11 attacks). Never in the history of the L.A. freeway system has that vast network of multi-lane highways been essentially empty. Never before have the professional sport leagues been suspended. Never before have all of the nation's schools and colleges and universities canceled onsite classes for the remainder of the school year.

The national economy appears to teeter on the brink of collapse. Unemployment may rise as high as 30 percent, perhaps even higher. Not even the best economists can predict how soon the national economy will rebound and it is universally understood that hundreds of thousands of businesses will never reopen their doors. We are living through a colossal national, and indeed international, crisis. Clearly, states do not have the capacity to get us through the crisis without unprecedented national governmental support.

There is no playbook for sorting out what parts of the coronavirus belong properly to the states and which parts are truly national in scope and urgency. In many respects, America is making it up as it goes along. The Constitution does not provide clear guidelines for elected officials or government functionaries.

Without descending into the blame game, it is perhaps just to acknowledge that the national government of the U.S. has not handled the pandemic very efficiently or with a steady, clear, and centralized voice; and that a crisis of this complexity does not bring out President Trump's strengths as a national leader.

The history of the U.S. has been a roller coaster on the question of state versus national sovereignty. Thomas Jefferson occupied one extreme end of the spectrum, Theodore Roosevelt the other. They served as president exactly 100 years apart. Jefferson, who served between 1801-09, believed that the national government had very few legitimate functions: foreign policy, a common currency, post roads, defense, a judiciary that could serve as the umpire between states at odds with one another. He actually called the national government "the foreign department." Theodore Roosevelt, who served between 1901-09, believed the national government could do anything not specifically prohibited by the Constitution.

Thomas Jefferson was the Founding Father most committed to states' rights. To his old mentor George Wythe, Jefferson wrote in 1787, the year of the constitutional convention, "My own general idea is that the States should severally preserve their sovereignty in whatever concerns themselves alone, and that whatever may concern another State, or any foreign nation, should be made a part of the Federal sovereignty." To Edward Carrington he wrote, "My general plan would be to make the States one as to everything connected with foreign nations, and several as to everything purely domestic."

Theodore Roosevelt was a Hamiltonian who advocated a very strong and proactive national government. Although he was careful not to say it, Roosevelt would have been happy if the concept of state sovereignty was discarded once and for all. Exactly opposite to Jefferson, Roosevelt saw the Constitution as an enabling, not a restraining, document. He famously said, "The Constitution exists for the people, not the people for the Constitution." When Roosevelt tried to set standards for workplace safety, child labor laws, the 40-hour workweek, and environmental protection, he bristled and scoffed at the notion that the national government could only regulate commerce with interstate activities, but not the commerce that occurred entirely within a single state.

You can imagine how differently these two great presidents would have responded to the coronavirus pandemic. Jefferson would have tried to avoid intruding on state sovereignty wherever possible; Roosevelt would have thrust himself into the center of the arena on the principle that it is better to apologize later than to seek permission. But here's what these two statesmen would have shared: clear, rational, consistent, scientifically based national messaging; candor and transparency; a belief that reason is our only oracle and science must be given primacy in its own arena. They would both have told the truth, the whole truth, and nothing but the truth to the American people.

The inefficiency and, in some cases, abdication of the national government in the face of COVID-19 has put the onus on state and local authorities. Some state governors have done such an outstanding—and steady—job of managing the pandemic within their borders that they have emerged as national leaders, almost shadow presidents, in the last two months. California's Gavin Newsom, Washington's Jay Inslee, and New York's Andrew Cuomo have received high marks not only for their management of the crisis, but also for their compassion and empathy, for their calm yet strong demeanor, for their professional deportment, and for the selflessness with which they have performed their roles.

A large number of Americans, hungry for national leadership that seems "presidential," have posited that each of these governors, and a few others, would make good candidates for president. Each of these governors has, in different ways, concluded publicly that in the absence of national leadership, they have no choice but to chart their own destiny. A few of them on both coasts have formed loose regional coalitions with other states to formulate a common approach to the challenge of loosening shelter-in-place restrictions as soon as it is regarded as safe to do so, but not so soon as to jeopardize public health.

One example of government inefficiency has been procurement of masks, swabs, ventilators, and other medical equipment needed by hospitals and medical professionals throughout the U.S. Insisting that the national government is "not a shipping clerk," President Trump urged each state to buy the equipment it needed on the open market. This brought about enormous confusion and inefficiency to the procurement process and forced desperate states to engage in bidding wars for life-saving equipment. In anguish, Cuomo of New York said, "We are all trying to buy the same commodity, literally the same item, so you have 50 states all trying to buy the same item, competing with each other. It's like being on eBay with 50 other states bidding on a ventilator."

This is one of the areas where Jefferson would have wanted federal coordination—to keep the price down and to prevent rivalry between states. Jefferson's government would serve not as a shipping agent but a national referee or umpire to bring order to the process and insist upon distributive justice. In other words, he would wish to make sure a limited supply of ventilators (for example) would be distributed to limit suffering and death to the extent possible. Perhaps each governor would wind up being frustrated in not being able to get all the ventilators she or he needed, but the national government would accept responsibility (and rebuke) to avoid squabbling between the states.

Even when the national government has tried to play a serious role in handling the pandemic, its response has been hampered by confusion, agency infighting, mixed messaging, and what appear to be unkept promises and actual lies. By all accounts, the setting up of a parallel task force led by the president's son-in-law Jared Kushner has decreased the efficiency and messaging of the national government. The daily briefings have mostly lost sight of their original purpose— to provide information to the American people and a sense that the national government is taking appropriate steps to combat the disease—and become an opportunity for President Trump to air his theories and grievances, to spar with reporters, denounce his real or perceived enemies, and to defend himself against the charge that he ignored a range of warnings from top government entities and played down the seriousness of the virus precisely at the time when he should have been marshalling the national government's response.

The Historical Background

State sovereignty has two historic foundations. One is the concept of Federalism, which means that the national government is sovereign in some ways, and state governments in others. This unique dual-sovereignty principle was insisted upon at the constitutional convention of May–September 1787 and though it has been the source of jurisdictional tension and confusion, it is a central fact of American political life. The second principle—one that has emerged mostly in the last hundred years—is the idea of a "laboratory of democracy," in which each of the 50 states addresses public issues in its own way, within some significant limits, so that regional and demographic differences can be factored into public law, and so individual states can undergo policy experiments without committing the entire nation to a one-size-fits-all set of policies. Thus, Montana chooses its judges in one way, Wisconsin in another.

A good example of this in our time is the variety of recreational and medical marijuana laws. Many states decided to observe the logistics, challenges, and opportunities of legalization in Colorado before deciding whether to legalize within their own borders and, if so, under what conditions. Colorado was thus a "laboratory" in which to work out the kinks of legalization in one jurisdiction, from which other states could learn important lessons of what to do and not to do if they chose to follow suit.

The original U.S. Constitution, the Articles of Confederation (1781–1788), created a loose confederation of sovereign nation-states: New Hampshire, New York, South Carolina, Georgia, Virginia. These sovereign states agreed to do a few things in common, but most of the destiny of a citizen living in Pennsylvania would be managed by the state legislature or local authorities (counties, townships, towns). The national government could coin money, provide for the common defense, and manage foreign policy, but almost everything else would be handled at the state level. Under the Articles of Confederation, the national government could not directly tax the people of Virginia or Maryland or any other state. It had to requisition tax funds and hope that the states would voluntarily comply. (They seldom did.) Each state had one vote in the confederation congress. The Articles could only be amended by the unanimous vote of all 13 states.

By 1786, every serious American understood that the Articles of Confederation were a failure. They realized that more authority was needed in a government truly national, including the power to tax. The 55 men who met in Philadelphia in the summer of 1787 tore up the Articles and created a wholly new constitution designed to create enough national authority to permit the U.S. to do the things that a nation must do, but at the same time to preserve to the states whatever sovereignty it could. The result was the Constitution of the U.S. we still use 232 years later, with just 27 amendments in all of that time.

Those who feared so much central authority demanded, and got, the Bill of Rights, drafted by James Madison in the First Congress of the U.S. and adopted on Dec. 15, 1791. From the standpoint of this discussion, the most important of those amendments was the Tenth, which states: "The powers not delegated to the U.S. by the Constitution, nor prohibited by it to the States, are reserved to the States respectively, or to the people." The Constitution-makers had also tried to protect state sovereignty by guaranteeing each state two U.S. senators irrespective of population or geographic size, and by permitting state legislators to choose their own senators (until the Seventeenth Amendment in 1913).

The Paradox in 2020

For a very long time, certainly since the Depression and World War II, Americans have counted on the national government to step up in times of monumental crisis. Nobody (except perhaps Thomas Jefferson) would have expected Louisiana to handle the Hurricane Katrina catastrophe by itself, or Oklahoma the Oklahoma City Bombing (April 19, 1995), or New York the attacks on the World Trade Center on Sept. 11, 2001. Floods, prolonged droughts, tornadoes, hurricanes, tsunamis, the banking collapse of 2008, and other disasters have seemed automatically to call upon the full strength and resources of the national government.

Only the handful of true state's rights conservatives, sometimes including Texas Sen. Ted Cruz, have argued that these are "local concerns." It would seem automatic and inevitable, therefore, that the global pandemic of 2020 would instantly bring the national government of the U.S. to unprecedented prominence. But that is not what has happened—so far. The government of Donald Trump has been oddly detached from the pandemic. Nobody is quite sure why.

The paradox is even more pointed when one considers President Trump's fascination with authoritarianism. He has at various times, perhaps merely in jest, declared his preference for authoritarian powers. His admiration for dictators and strongmen is unmistakable: Vladimir Putin in Russia, Philippine leader Rodrigo Duterte, Xi Jinping of China, Kim Jong Un of North Korea, President Recep Tayyip Erdogan of Turkey, and Saudi Arabia's Crown Prince Mohammed bin Salman, all of whom he says are his good friends.

One might have expected Trump to use the global pandemic to assume unprecedented powers as president, to luxuriate in dictating every response on every level in all 50 states. It is even surprising that President Trump has made his vice president the coronavirus czar and his son-in-law the shadow coronavirus coordinator. Instead, Trump has mostly served as a kind of informal national commentator on the actions of others. When he reads from his script at the daily briefings, he often stumbles on names and pharmaceutical terms (admittedly difficult) and sometimes he appears to be reading his own remarks for the first time. He comes to life mostly during the extended question and answer sessions with reporters in which he often behaves like a cynical tavern know-it-all rather than the presiding officer of a nation of 340 million. Even his supporters find his disruptive approach to the briefings troubling.

Given President Trump's detached approach to leadership in a time of pandemic, it is all the more surprising when he suddenly asserts his mastery and unchallengeable authority. A large number of the nation's governors and all of its constitutional scholars, for example, have rejected Trump's declaration on Monday, April 13, 2020, that he has "absolute power" to determine when to reopen the country for business. Even normally pro-Trump conservatives pushed back hard on this wild claim, including Rep. Liz Cheney of Wyoming, Florida Sen. Marco Rubio, and former G.W. Bush Justice Department official John Yoo.

Most sober commentators who have observed the pandemic crisis from late January until today have concluded, "thank God for Federalism." Most of the states have stepped up in ways that could not have been anticipated in 2019. Some of the state governors have emerged as national heroes and, to a certain extent, alternative national leaders.

Source: Clay Jenkinson, editor-at-large, "Who's in Charge? Coronavirus and the Tenth Amendment," Governing, (April 17, 2020); Accessed at: https://www.governing.com/context/Whos-in-Charge-Coronavirus-and-the-Tenth-Amendment.html.
Author note: Clay S. Jenkinson is a public humanities scholar who lives in Bismarck, North Dakota. He is the author of eleven books, including the recent *Repairing Jefferson's America: A Guide to Civility and Enlightened Citizenship*.The opinion expressed is that of the author and not necessarily the University System of Georgia.

REFLECTIVE QUESTIONS

1. Why is the American federal system so complicated?

2. How do mandates help or hinder intergovernmental management?

3. Local governments need to provide many services but do not have to produce any of them. How, then, is service provision accomplished?

4. What is the purpose of Georgia's Service Delivery Strategies?

5. ACIR at one time identified five standards for functional assignment of service delivery. Which of these standards is the most important and why?

BIBLIOGRAPHY

Advisory Commission on Intergovernmental Relations, "Regulatory Federalism: Policy, Process, Impact And Reform," In Brief, B7, n.d. Accessed at: https://library.unt.edu/gpo/acir/Reports/brief/B-7.pdf.

Advisory Commission on Intergovernmental Relations, *A Handbook for Interlocal Agreements*. (Washington, DC: 1967. Accessed at: https://library.unt.edu/gpo/acir/Reports/information/m-29.pdf.

Advisory Commission on Intergovernmental Relations, "The Federal Role in the Federal System: The Dynamics of Growth," A-86 (1981). Accessed at: https://library.unt.edu/gpo/acir/Reports/policy/A-86.pdf.

Advisory Commission on Intergovernmental Relations, "The Federal Influence on State and Local Roles in the Federal System," A-89, (1981). Accessed at: https://library.unt.edu/gpo/acir/Reports/policy/A-89.pdf.

Advisory Commission on Intergovernmental Relations, "The Role of Federal Mandates in Intergovernmental Relations: A Preliminary ACIR Report," January, 1996. Accessed at: https://library.unt.edu/gpo/acir/mandates.html.

Agranoff, Robert and Michael McGuire, "Another Look at Bargaining and Negotiating in Intergovernmental Management," *Journal of Public Administration Research and Theory: J-PART* 14, no. 4 (2004), 495–512.

Bowman, Ann O'M., "Horizontal Federalism: Exploring Interstate Interactions," *Journal of Public Administration Research and Theory: J-PART* 14, no. 4 (2004), 535–546.

Clark, Jane Perry, *The Rise of a New Federalism*. (New York: Russell & Russell, 1966 reissue).

The Commission on Intergovernmental Relations, "A Report to the President for Transmittal to the Congress," June, 1955. Accessed at: https://library.unt.edu/gpo/acir/Reports/Y3In87R29.pdf.

Congressional Budget Office, "Intergovernmental Mandates in Federal Legislation," Economic and Budget Issue Brief July 13, 2009. Accessed at: https://www.cbo.gov/sites/default/files/111th-congress-2009-2010/reports/07-14-umra.pdf.

Congressional Research Service, "Federal Grants to State and Local Governments: A Historical Perspective on Contemporary Issues," May 22, 2019, R40638. Accessed at: https://crsreports.congress.gov.

Congressional Research Service, "Federal Preemption: A Legal Primer," July 23, 2019, R45825. Accessed at: https://crsreports.congress.gov,.

Congressional Research Service, "Unfunded Mandates Reform Act: History, Impact, and Issues," August 28, 2019, R40957. Accessed at: https://crsreports.congress.gov.

Connolly, Gerry, "Connolly. Bishop Introduce Restore the Partnership Act," July 23, 2019. Accessed at: https://connolly.house.gov/news/documentsingle.aspx?DocumentID=3676.

Council of State Governments National Center for Interstate Compacts, "Compact Search Results." Accessed at: http://apps.csg.org/ncic/SearchResults.aspx?.

Council of State Governments National Center for Interstate Compacts, "Enacted Intergovernmental Mandates with Estimated Costs That Exceed the Statutory Threshold, 1996 to 2018." Accessed at http://apps.csg.org/ncic/Default.aspx.

Council of State Governments, *Shared State Legislation*. Accessed at: https://www.csg.org/programs/policyprograms/SSLabout.aspx.

Davenport, Coral, "California Sues the Trump Administration in Its Escalating War Over Auto Emissions," *New York Times*, September 20, 2019. Accessed at: https://www.nytimes.com/2019/09/20/climate/california-auto-emissions-lawsuit.html.

Elazar, Daniel, *American Federalism: A View from the States*, (New York: Thomas Crowell Company 1966).

Falk, Nathan, "Contract Cities: An Alternate Model," Rose Institute of State and Local Government, Claremont McKenna College (2011). Accessed at: http://roseinstitute.org/contract-cities-an-alternative-model/.

Frederickson, H. George, "The Repositioning of American Public Administration," *PS: Political Science and Politics* 32, no. 4 (1999), 701–711.

Georgia Department of Community Affairs "Charting a Course for Cooperation and Collaboration," (1997), Accessed at: https://www.dca.ga.gov/sites/default/files/guide.collaboration.pdf.

Georgia Municipal Association, "Municipal Incorporation: Requirements under Georgia Law," August 7, 2018. Accessed at: https://www.gacities.com/Resources/Reference-Articles/Municipal-Incorporation-Requirements-under-Georgi.aspx.

Holden, Matthew Jr., "The Governance of the Metropolis as a Problem in Diplomacy."

Journal of Politics 26, no. 3 (1964), 627–647.

Homsy, George C. and Mildred E. Warner, "Intermunicipal Cooperation: The Growing Reform." Accessed at: https://cardi.cals.cornell.edu/sites/cardi.cals.cornell.edu/files/shared/documents/RED/Intermunicipal%20Cooperation.pdf.

Kettl, Donald F. "The Key to Networked Government," *Unlocking the Power of Networks* Stephen Goldsmith and Donald F. Kettl eds. (2009) Accessed at: https://www.brookings.edu/wp-content/uploads/2016/07/unlockingthepowerofnetworks_chapter.pdf.

Local Solutions Support Center, "The Growing Shadow of State Interference: Preemption in the 2019 State Legislative Sessions." Accessed at: https://static1.squarespace.com/static/5ce4377caeb1ce00013a02fd/t/5d66a3c36044f700019a7efd/1567007722604/LSSCSiXReportAugust2019.pdf.

Lovell, Catherine and Charles Tobin, "The Mandate Issue," *Public Administration Review* 41, no. 3 (1981). 318–331.

Mikulecky, Thomas J. "Intergovernmental Relations Strategies for the Local Manager," *Public Administration Review* 46, no. 4 (1980), 379–381.

Mountjoy, John J., "Interstate Compacts State Solutions—By the states and for the states," Council of State Governments. Accessed at: https://www.csg.org/knowledgecenter/docs/ncic/SolutionsProblems.pdf.ulc.

National Association of Regional Councils, "Building Regional Communities 2019 Policy Agenda." Accessed at: http://narc.org/wp-content/uploads/2019/08/What-Are-Regional-Councils-Brochure-1.pdf.

Nivola, Pietro S. (2005) *Why Federalism Matters*. The Brookings Institution Policy Brief Series (2005). Accessed at: https://www.brookings.edu/research/why-federalism-matters/.

O.C.G.A. § 36-70-27. Accessed at: https://law.justia.com/codes/georgia/2010/title-36/provisions/chapter-70/article-2/36-70-27.

Office of the New York State Comptroller, Division of Local Government and School Accountability (n.d.). *Intermunicipal Cooperation and Consolidation.* Accessed at: https://www.osc.state.ny.us/localgov/pubs/research/cooperation1.pdf.

O'Toole, Laurence J. Jr., *American Intergovernmental Relations Foundations, Perspectives, and Issues*, 4th edition. (Washington DC: CQ Press 2007).

Rhodes, R, A. W., "The New Governance: Governing without Government," *Political Studies* 44, (1996), 652–666.

Riestenberg, Jay, "Who Still Funds ALEC?" March 24, 2015. Common Cause. Accessed at: https://www.commoncause.org/democracy-wire/who-still-funds-alec/.

Sanchez, Yvonne Wingett and Rob O'Dell "What Is ALEC? 'The most effective organization' for conservatives, says Newt Gingrich" *USA Today* April 3, 2019 Accessed at: https://www.usatoday.com/story/news/investigations/2019/04/03/alec-american-legislative-exchange-council-model-bills-republican-conservative-devos-gingrich/3162357002/.

South Dakota v. Wayfair, Inc. 585 U.S. ___ (2018).

Stratford, Michael, "Trump endorses states' rights—but only when he agrees with the state," *Politico* April 2, 2018. Accessed at: https://www.politico.com/story/2018/04/02/trump-states-rights-education-sanctuary-drilling-492784.

Uniform Law Commission, *2018/2019 Annual Report*. Accessed at: https://www.uniformlaws.org/viewdocument/2018-annual-report.

Unfunded Mandates Reform, 2 U.S.C. § 1501.

U.S. Census Bureau, "Table 4 Special Purposes Local Governments by State Census Years 1942 to 2017." Accessed at: https://www.census.gov/data/tables/2017/econ/gus/2017-governments.html.

U.S. Department of Justice, "Justice Department Announces Findings of Two Civil Rights Investigations in Ferguson, Missouri," March 4, 2015. Accessed at: https://www.justice.gov/opa/pr/justice-department-announces-findings-two-civil-rights-investigations-ferguson-missouri.

U.S. Department of Justice, "Justice Department Releases Memorandum on Litigation Guidelines for Civil Consent Decrees and Settlement Agreements." November 18, 2018. Accessed at: https://www.justice.gov/opa/pr/justice-department-releases-memorandum-litigation-guidelines-civil-consent-decrees-and.

U. S. District Court Eastern District of Missouri Eastern Division *United States of America v. The City of Ferguson*, No. 4;16-cv000180-CDP Consent Decree.

U.S. House of Representatives Committee on Government Oversight and Reform Subcommittee on Intergovernmental Affairs. *Hearing on Unfunded Mandates: Examining Federally Imposed Burdens on State and Local Governments*. Statement by Jermaine Reed, April 26, 2017.

United States House of Representatives. "H.R. 300: Unfunded Mandates Information and Transparency Act of 2019." Accessed at: https://www.govtrack.us/congress/bills/116/hr300.

United States Supreme Court, *Commonwealth of Virginia v. State of Tennessee*, 148 U.S. 503, 519 (1893). Accessed at: https://supreme.justia.com/cases/federal/us/148/503/.

Wright, Deil S. "Intergovernmental Games: An Approach to Understanding Intergovernmental Relations." *Southern Review of Public Administration* 3, no. 4 (1980), 383-403.

Zimmerman, Joseph F. "Preemption in the U.S. Federal System," *Publius* 23, no. 4 (1993), 1–13.

6

Collaborative Networks as a Dimension of Intergovernmental Relations

Nandan K. Jha

LEARNING OBJECTIVES

- Demonstrate an understanding of how a broader system of networks exists and operates in the American system of government.

- Demonstrate knowledge of the nature of public, private, and nonprofit organizations in various networks and how they interrelate.

- Demonstrate how the network aspect of the federal system reflects changes in the workings of state and local government, and the private and nonprofit sectors.

- Demonstrate an understanding of how policy is formed, implemented, and evaluated in a networked federal system.

KEY TERMS

Collaborative Network Management	Policy Subsystem
Goal-Directed Network	Use Value Exchange Value
Serendipitous Network	Growth Machine
Adaptive Network Management	Urban Regime
Closed Network Management	Industry Cluster
Policy Innovation	Spillover
Policy Invention	Regionalism
Policy Diffusion	The Equivalence Principle
Policy Entrepreneurs	

6.1 INTRODUCTION

Networks are a key aspect of intergovernmental behavior in the context of American government which corresponds to the nature of federalism, intergovernmental relations (IGR), and intergovernmental management (IGM). In various works, Robert Agranoff and Michael McGuire particularly emphasize the distinctiveness and prominence of "collaborative network management" as the fourth governance model in American federalism.[1] As introduced in chapter 1, Agranoff and McGuire define collaborative management as "a concept that describes the process of facilitating and operating in multiorganizational arrangements to solve problems that cannot be solved or easily solved by single organizations."[2] In "An Integrative Framework for Collaborative Governance," Kirk Emerson, Tina Nabatchi, and Stephen Balogh (2012) also provide an expansive definition of collaborative governance as "the processes and structures of public policy decision making and management that engage people constructively across the boundaries of public agencies, levels of government, and/or the public, private and civic spheres in order to carry out a public purpose that could not otherwise be accomplished."[3] This particular definition puts equal emphasis on all components of policy analysis as well as on an analysis of public agencies' involvement and their management. It also addresses H. Brinton Milward's criticism[4] of researchers in the public management field that they display "an overdeveloped capacity for policy analysis and an underdeveloped capacity for administrative analysis."[5]

Collaborative network management: describes the process of assisting and functioning in multiorganizational arrangements to solve problems. These problems cannot be solved or easily solved by single organizations. It engages people constructively across public agencies, levels of government, and/or the public, private and civic spheres in order to carry out a public purpose that cannot be addressed by a single agency.

Figure 6.1: Galveston, TX, September 23, 2008—Steve LeBlanc Galveston City Manager, holds up a corroded electric box while at a press conference with local. state and federal partners about the reentry of citizens into the area after Hurricane Ike.
Source: Wikimedia Commons
Attribution: Jocelyn Augustino
License: Public Domain

1   See Robert Agranoff, and Michael McGuire. "American Federalism and the Search for Models of Management." *Public Administration Review* 61, no. 6 (Nov.–Dec., 2001): 671-677; Robert Agranoff and Michael McGuire. *Collaborative Public Management: New Strategies for Local Governments.* Washington, DC: Georgetown University Press, 2003; and R. Agranoff *Managing within Networks: Adding Value to Public Organizations.* Washington, DC: Georgetown University Press, 2007.
2   Robert Agranoff, and Michael McGuire. *Collaborative Public Management: New Strategies for Local Governments*, 4.
3   Kirk Emerson, Tina Nabatchi, and Stephen Balogh. "An integrative framework for collaborative governance." *Journal of Public Administration Research and Theory* 22, no. 1 (2012): 3.
4   Robert Agranoff, and Michael McGuire. "Managing in network settings." *Review of Policy Research* 16, no. 1 (1999): 19.
5   Refer to H. Brinton Milward. "Mapping the Linkage Structure of Networks", Paper presented at *Conference on Network Analysis on Innovations in Public Programs, LaFollette Institute of Public Affairs,* University of Wisconsin, 1994.

These definitions help in understanding the various dimensions of networks of collaborative public management.

Over at least the last three decades, scholars have identified and studied interorganizational structures within the hierarchy of public organizations.[6] Scholars refer to this modern era as the network era, in which hierarchy of authority in organizations and markets are usefully assisted and served by networks.[7] Building upon the IGM concept introduced in chapter 1, public managers at various government levels must take networks seriously[8] and serve the public through actively participating in an array of collaborative horizontal and vertical networks.[9] However, collaborative networks are one of the several management tools available to public managers.[10] Agranoff argues that some of the other vehicles of collaborative management include informal bilateral and multilateral linkages between local, state, and federal agencies and interagency agreements among organizations within the same government. While agency managers usually discharge the bulk of the responsibility in collaborative management, there may be exceptions such as when public managers are also program specialists and act as liaison with other agencies in their administrative role. Collaborative networks work best when there are incentives/inducements for managers. These incentives include learning new skills in collaborating, networking, and attaining enhanced knowledge that add to technical, informational, and communication skills. There are incentives at the organizational level as well. Although, all agencies participating in a collaborative network accrue some benefits through their participation, home agencies of the participating managers benefit specifically as access to other agencies' information, programs, and resources as well as training of agency staff. Two other advantages accrue to all the collaborative agencies in the network. One is the enhanced collective process skills, such as interagency planning, adaptation of new technology, etc. The other is the set of specific results obtained from the collaborative networking—including an action plan, capacity-building conferences, and new interagency strategies. These benefits indicate that networks share similarities and differences with organizations. They are similar as they require an organizational structure, rules of operation, personnel, etc. They differ from organizations because they lack hierarchy, their participants are equal as organizational representatives, they have consensus-based decision making, their resources are gathered from all participating organizations, and

6   See Robert Agranoff. "Inside collaborative networks: Ten lessons for public managers." *Public Administration Review* 66 (2006): 56–65; Walter W. Powell. "Neither Market nor Hierarchy: Network Forms of Organization." In Barry M. Staww and Larry L. Cummings (eds) *Research in Organizational Behavior*, Vol. 12, 295–336. Greenwich, CT: JAI Press, 1990; Jessica Lipnack, and Jeffrey Stamps. *The Age of the Network*. New York: Wiley, 1994; Robert Agranoff and Michael McGuire. *Collaborative Public Management: New Strategies for Local Governments*; and Laurence J. O'Toole, Jr. "Treating Networks Seriously: Practical and Research-Based Agendas in Public Administration." *Public Administration Review* 57 (1: 1997): 45–52.
7   Robert Agranoff "Inside collaborative networks: Ten lessons for public managers." 56.
8   O'Toole, "Treating Networks Seriously: Practical and Research-Based Agendas in Public Administration." 45.
9   Agranoff "Inside collaborative networks: Ten lessons for public managers." 56.
10   Agranoff "Inside collaborative networks: Ten lessons for public managers." 57–63.

individual participating agencies have the option to back out with little punitive consequences.

Networks are not always directly involved in program and policy adjustments. Agranoff identifies few typical networks in this context. Informational networks forge partnerships to share agency policies and programs, technologies, and potential solutions on which participating agencies can voluntarily make specific changes or actions. Developmental networks are engaged in sharing information and technology, education, and other useful member services that enable member agencies to develop capacities for implementing solutions individually and internally. Outreach networks leave decision making and implementation of program and policy changes to individual agencies, but they employ all developmental network activities, together with a strategies blueprint for agencies undertaking program and policy change. Finally, action networks join all partners together to make adjustments in their programs and policies for officially implementing collaborative courses of action and delivering services.

Figure 6.2: Mayor Bob Fowler of Helen, Georgia, near Robertstown displays a map showing a 100-year flood plain for his small town during a city council meeting held at theater Helen. The plan was received from the Federal Department of Housing and Urban Development. The meeting attracted citizens whose homes and businesses were included in the flood plain zone. A "straw vote" resulted in a 60 to 4 decision against joining the flood insurance program.
Source: Wikimedia Commons
Attribution: Al Stephenson
License: Public Domain

These networks are also engaged in information exchange and increasing members' technology capabilities. These networks promote specific mutual learning and adjustments that lead to decisions and agreements. Because they are co-equals, the participating agencies in a collaborative network invariably base decisions and agreements on consensus. Public sector knowledge management is the most discernible collaborative activity in networks. In the current informational age, knowledge management processes bring together both explicit and tacit knowledge. Whereas the former is codified and communicated easily in words, numbers, charts, or drawings, the latter is conveyed via individual senses, perceptions, physical experiences, intuition, and rules of thumb. Networks do experience occasional tussles over power and other conflicts in spite of the overall environment that fosters a cooperative spirit and accommodation in collaborative efforts. Consensus may elude networks in situations where agencies face turf wars, disagreements over contribution of resources, divisiveness over solutions to the problem at hand, staff time, meeting and conference venues, and threats of withdrawal. Agencies in networks also incur costs and reap benefits from collaborative governance. The costs involved are increases in spending agency resources, reduced agency authority, opportunity cost to the home agency, time and energy costs on slow moving decision-making processes, non-resolution due to vetoes from significant partners, resource hoarding or partial free-riding, public policy barriers, and inclinations toward following consensus and risk-averse decision agendas.

Networks only marginally alter the contours of the traditional government structure in the nation. They definitely have not replaced the traditional public bureaucracy. Networks influence the courses of action taken by government, including new programs and strategies that originated from collaborative activities in those networks. However, in most cases, public institutions make the final call on specific policy decisions. Public administrators at the federal, state, and local levels form the core of every public management network. These actors are also able to influence legislative, regulatory, and budgetary support for the network's activities.

Figure 6.3: Austell, GA, October 26, 2009—After the City Hall Meeting, FEMA Individual Assistance Deputy Branch Director Samuel Lockey and FEMA Intergovernmental Affairs Officer Tom Hardy confer with Mayor Joe Jerkins. FEMA is here as result of severe storms and flooding in September.
Source: Wikimedia Commons
Attribution: George Armstrong
License: Public Domain

Chapter 1 covered the U.S. federal government's structure, theories, and models on federalism, IGR, and IGM features. This chapter focuses on the concept of collaborative network management and its related features. Chapter 1 also explained the composition of collaborators in networks for solving problems. In particular, while introducing the concept of IGR, chapter 1 notes that collaborative management is a complex network of intergovernmental agencies comprising local governments (e.g., city managers, mayors, public administrators, emergency management officials, etc.) nonprofit organizations, community-based organizations, healthcare entities, for-profit firms, utility companies, and various planning agencies.[11] Although, as noted in chapter 1, collaborative management through networks was initially considered one of IGM's components, but works by Agranoff and McGuire have placed it as the fourth and latest model in its own right. In their review chapter, "Historic Relevance Confronting Contemporary Obsolescence?", Deil S. Wright, Carl W. Stenberg, and Chung-Lae Cho aptly note that the terms "FED, IGR, and IGM clearly retained selective usage. But the greater presence and prominence of collaborative, networking, and governance were clear for all to see. Indeed, the latter terms have taken off like rockets from a launchpad in the current decade, while IGM, IGR, and FED have declined sharply in usage over the past three decades."[12]

This chapter brings together the theories and models concerning collaborative network management, including its inherent key characteristics. This chapter also focuses on the U.S.'s intra- and inter-state dimension of intergovernmental networks. It begins with the section on collaborative intergovernmental network management and its features. It then devotes a section on how policy entrepreneurs in various intergovernmental networks bring about public policy innovation and diffusion for solving public problems. The chapter then documents how collaborative networks help local, state, and federal governments by facilitating joint public problem solving. Finally, it explains the role of intergovernmental collaborative networks in solving some of the difficult problems in regional economic development.

6.2 COLLABORATIVE INTERGOVERNMENTAL NETWORK MANAGEMENT AND ITS FEATURES

Public policy making and governance through collaborative intergovernmental networks comprising various actors—individuals, coalitions, bureaus, organizations—is the network model of governance. These actors do not have power and control over the strategies of other actors. In their work, "American Federalism and the Search for Models of Management," Agranoff and McGuire provide an example of an actual network that works to solve a particular economic development problem for a city:[13]

Figure 6.4: Mayor's reception room - Savannah City Hall, Bay and Bull Streets, Savannah, Chatham County, GA.
Source: Wikimedia Commons
Attribution: Historic American Buildings Survey (HABS)
License: Public Domain

11 Refer to Daniel Baracskay (2021, 5-6) in this volume.
12 Deil S.Wright , Carl W. Stenberg, and Chung-Lae Cho. "Historic Relevance Confronting Contemporary Obsolescence?" In Menzel, Donald C., and Jay D. White (eds), *The State of Public Administration: Issues, Challenges, and Opportunities*. Routledge, 2015: 308.
13 Agranoff and McGuire. "American Federalism and the Search for Models of Management." 676.

Figure 6.5: Kyrsten Sinema meeting with the Phoenix Chamber of Commerce in 2016.
Source: Wikimedia Commons
Attribution: Krysten Sinema
License: Public Domain

Figure 6.6: The United States Chamber of Commerce headquarters at 1615 H Street, NW in Washington, D.C.
Source: Wikimedia Commons
Attribution: User "AgnosticPreachersKid"
License: CC BY-SA 3.0

In a small city, for example, the city government, a public-private economic development corporation (EDC), the local chamber of commerce, county government, an investor-owned utility serving the area, three private investors, and a local bank work together as partners to expand an existing industrial park at the edge of town. With the staff support of the EDC, the actors network to make the project a reality by developing a plan that includes pledged business expansions, a private land donation, city government property tax abatements, a county tax contribution, a utility subsidy, and EDC preparation of several business expansion and venture capital grants and loans. The mayor and the EDC director go to the state government and the Economic Development Administration of the U.S. Department of Commerce for intergovernmental assistance to underwrite the remaining costs of the project.

Agranoff and McGuire argue that, in the network model, actors are interdependent and the leadership in intersectoral and intergovernmental relationships is

Figure 6.7: Valdosta Lowndes County Chamber of Commerce, Barber Pittman House, 416 N. Ashley St., Valdosta, Lowndes County, Georgia.
Source: Wikimedia Commons
Attribution: Michael Rivera
License: CC BY-SA 3.0

collaborative. Actors depend on each others' resources in realizing their own goals. Interdependence implies that all actors benefit mutually from their joint interest in a specific activity. Interdependence also propels actors to strategically and collaboratively pursue solutions to a particular problem. Actors' participation in collaborative network is not an administrative choice. For example, merging two departments or streamlining a budgeting process does not constitute a network. Instead, networks are multi-organizational arrangements that characterize many policy-making domains for solving interorganizational problems that are unsolvable by single organizations. A variety of public and private actors constitute networks, each with their own goals and policy strategies.

Aaron Wachhaus (2020) in "Building Health Communities: Local Health Care Networks in Maryland" and Daniela Cristofoli, Benedetta Trivellato, and Stefano Verzillo (2019) in "Network Management as a Contingent Activity: A Configurational Analysis of Managerial Behaviors in Different Network Settings," have both covered some contemporary elements of the collaborative management of public networks and provide details on some new advancements in scholarship on collaborative network management. While the former focuses on structural dimensions of the network,[14] the latter, in addition to emphasizing relevant structural elements, offers strategies and management styles for managers to follow in effective network management in different contexts.[15]

6.2.1 Structure of Collaborative Intergovernmental Networks

Concerning the organizational structure of networks, in *Social Networks and Organizations, M. Kilduff and W. Tsai identify two* types of networks. A goal-directed network[16] originates "with the establishment of a goal." It "exhibits purposive and adaptive movement toward an envisioned end state."[17] Put differently, members

> **Goal-directed network**: exists and revolves around a goal. It purposefully adapts and moves toward achieving an outcome. Members in this network share specific goals and work to achieve it.

share specific goals in goal-directed networks and follow paths around those goals.[18] Wachhaus clarifies that members in goal-directed networks share a common goal and work to achieve it.

A key characteristic of goal-directed networks is the "emergence of an administrative entity that acts as a broker to plan and coordinate the activities of the network as a whole."[19] Goal-directed networks are formalized structures in which members are self-aware that they are in a network, know why they are in that network, and can articulate shared goals and have some processes for coordination.

Serendipitous networks are different and develop from individual actors working independently to establish ties to others.[20] Individual actors in serendipitous

14 See Aaron Wachhaus. "Building Health Communities: Local Health Care Networks in Maryland." *The American Review of Public Administration* 50, no. 1 (2020): 62–76.

15 Daniela Cristofoli, Benedetta Trivellato, and Stefano Verzillo. "Network management as a contingent activity. A configurational analysis of managerial behaviors in different network settings." *Public Management Review*, 21 (12: 2019), 1775-1800, DOI: 10.1080/14719037.2019.1577905.

16 M. Kilduff, and W. Tsai. *Social networks and organizations*. London, England: SAGE, 2003, 93.

17 M. Kilduff, and W. Tsai. *Social networks and organizations*. London, England: SAGE, 2003, 92.

18 M. Kilduff, and W. Tsai. *Social networks and organizations*. London, England: SAGE, 2003, 89.

19 M. Kilduff, and W. Tsai. *Social networks and organizations*. London, England: SAGE, 2003, 89.

20 M. Kilduff, and W. Tsai. *Social networks and organizations*. London, England: SAGE, 2003, 93.

networks "make choices about who to connect with, what to transact, and so on, without guidance from any central network agent concerning goals of strategy."[21] Self-interest motivates actors in initiating partnerships. Serendipitous networking facilitates information and resource sharing. Network-level goals are absent in serendipitous networks, and they develop haphazardly with little formal organization, few communication processes, and little coordination. Thus, "at any point in time, any specific pairs of actors may or may not share goals."[22] Wachhaus credits K. Provan and P. Kenis[23] for coining similar terms in their work, "Towards an Exogenous Theory of Public Network Performance," including "self-initiated" or "voluntary" for serendipitous networks and "mandated" or "contracted" for goal-directed networks. While serendipitous networks are more common, goal-directed networks occur less frequently. The latter, however, are the more-studied form of networks.[24]

Cristofoli et al. (2019) note that an intergovernmental network's age, interconnectedness, and trust are key structural features that play significant roles in its success. A certain minimum age is important for network effectiveness because networks engage in several elementary activities critical for their functioning in the initial years. These activities include building trust between partners and establishing rules to govern interaction. After maturing with a centralized governance structure, overcoming resource paucity, and attaining high levels of system stability, networks can gain internal and external legitimacy and achieve their objectives.

A highly-interconnected network ensures a smooth flow of information, resources, and

Serendipitous networks: develop from individual actors working independently to establish ties to others. Self-interested individual actors in serendipitous networks decide who to connect with, what to transact, and so on, without guidance from any central network agent concerning goals of strategy.

Figure 6.8: Georgia (U.S. state) counties map.
Source: Wikimedia Commons
Attribution: United States Census Bureau
License: Public Domain

Figure 6.9: Cobb County government complex.
Source: Wikimedia Commons
Attribution: Michael Rivera
License: CC BY-SA 3.0

---

21   M. Kilduff, and W. Tsai. *Social networks and organizations*. London, England: SAGE, 2003, 90.
22   M. Kilduff, and W. Tsai. *Social networks and organizations*. London, England: SAGE, 2003, 89-90.
23   See P. Kenis, and K. Provan. "Towards an Exogenous Theory of Public Network Performance." *Public Administration* 87 (3: 2009): 440–456. doi:10.1111/padm.2009.87.issue-3; and K. G. Provan, and P. Kenis. "Modes of Network Governance: Structure, Management and Effectiveness." *Journal of Public Administration Research and Theory* 18 (2: 2008): 229–252. doi:10.1093/jopart/mum015.
24   Provan & Kenis, "Modes of Network Governance: Structure, Management and Effectiveness." 231.

support. Trust can be easily built and maintained in such networks.[25] A network manager's ability to create and manage network relationships is crucial in building trust. The network manager is responsible to act as mediator and moderator among multiple and contrasting interests. These managers encourage partners to trust each other. They also promote knowledge sharing.[26]

The importance of trust for network performance is consequential.[27] Trust is defined as "a more or less stable, positive perception of the intentions of other actors, that is, the perception that other actors will refrain from opportunistic behavior."[28] Trust, therefore, is beneficial for collaboration and network performance. J. Edelenbos and E. Klijn (2006) in "Managing Stakeholder Involvement in Decision Making: A Comparative Analysis of Six Interactive Processes in the Netherlands," and M. Kort and E. Klijn (2011) in "Public-Private Partnerships in Urban Regeneration Projects: Organizational Form or Managerial Capacity?" provide four mechanisms through which trust favors collaboration and the achievement of network success.[29] First, trust increases the predictability of partners' behavior by reducing uncertainty and transaction costs that stimulate actors' investment in the network. Second, by stimulating actors investment in the network, trust also enhances network stability. Third, trust encourages flow of information and learning. Lastly, trust inspires innovation.

6.2.2 Managerial Behavior in Collaborative Intergovernmental Network

In terms of managerial behavior, McGuire and Agranoff distinguish four types of public networks, including activating, framing, mobilizing, and synthesizing in their work, "Managing Networks: Propositions on What Managers Do and

25   See K. G. Provan, K. Huang, and H. B. Milward. "The Evolution of Structural Embeddedness and Organizational Social Outcomes in a Centrally Governed Health and Human Services Network." *Journal of Public Administration Research and Theory* 19 (2009): 873–893. doi:10.1093/jopart/mun036.

26   See Agranoff and McGuire. "American Federalism and the Search for Models of Management." These managers encourage partners to trust each other, see E. H. Klijn, B. Steijn, and J. Edelenbos. "Trust in Governance Networks: Its Impacts on Outcomes." *Administration and Society* 42 (2: 2010b): 193–221. doi:10.1177/0095399710362716. They also promote knowledge sharing, see C. Koliba, S. Wiltshire,S, D. Turner, A. Zia, and E. Campbell. "The Critical Role of Information Sharing to the Value Proposition of a Food Systems Network." *Public Management Review* 19 (3: 2017): 284– 304. doi: 10.1080/14719037.2016.1209235.

27   See J. Edelenbos and E. Klijn. "Managing Stakeholder Involvement in Decision Making: A Comparative Analysis of Six Interactive Processes in the Netherlands." *Journal of Public Administration Research & Theory* 16 (3: 2006): 417. doi:10.1093/jopart/mui049; Klijn et al. (2010b). "Trust in Governance Networks: Its Impacts on Outcomes;" M. Kort and E. Klijn. "Public-Private Partnerships in Urban Regeneration Projects: Organizational Form or Managerial Capacity?" *Public Administration Review* 71 (4: 2011): 618–626. doi:10.1111/puar.2011.71.issue-4; T. Ysa V. Sierra, and M. Esteve. "Determinants of Network Outcomes: The Impact of Management Strategies." *Public Administration* 92 (3: 2014): 636–655; E. H. Klijn , V. Sierra, T. Ysa, E. Berman, J. Edelenbos, and D. Y. Chen. "The Influence of Trust on Network Performance in Taiwan, Spain, and the Netherlands: A Cross-Country Comparison." *International Public Management Journal* 19 (1: 2016): 111–139. doi:10.1080/10967494.2015.1115790.

28   Klijn et al. (2016), "The Influence of Trust on Network Performance in Taiwan, Spain, and the Netherlands: A Cross-Country Comparison."113.

29   See Edelenbos and Klijn, "Managing Stakeholder Involvement in Decision Making: A Comparative Analysis of Six Interactive Processes in the Netherlands;" and Kort and Klijn, "Public-Private Partnerships in Urban Regeneration Projects: Organizational Form or Managerial Capacity?"

Why They Do It."[30] These networks may require different management techniques that vary across time and space. The authors of the discussed work have provided environmental characteristics and formulated a number of propositions about when, how, and why managers choose one behavior over another. Managers' decisions are based on such factors as goal consensus, resource distribution, support, relationships between network partners, policy, and strategic orientation. Activating is a scenario in which managers exhibit the ability to choose when network goals are clear, their resources are not limited, and they rely on policy instruments. In contrast, framing reflects managers' best behavior when faced multiple unclear goals and must rely on subsidies and regulation. Managers use mobilizing when goals are unclear, resources are widely distributed, support from key stakeholders is insufficient, and reliance on policy instruments occurs. Finally, with goal consensus, with the existence of previous relationships between network partners, and reliance on policy instruments and regulations, managers can ensure effective network management through synthetizing. Following a similar approach, S.Verweij, E. H. Klijn, J. Edelenbos, and M. W. Van Buuren (2013) in "What Makes Governance Networks Work? A Fuzzy Set Qualitative Comparative Analysis of 14 Dutch Spatial Planning Projects," identify two types of network management when network complexity and stakeholder involvement

> *Adaptive network management*: is the strategy that ensures high network performance in combination with network complexity, or with high stakeholder involvement.

> *Closed network management*: is the strategy that ensures high network performance when there is low network complexity and stakeholder involvement.

are varied. According to the authors, the adaptive style of network management ensures high network performance in combination with network complexity, or with high stakeholder involvement.[31] In contrast, a closed style of network management works better when there is low network complexity and stakeholder involvement. On their part, S. Hovik and G. S. Hanssen (2015) in "The Impact of Network Management and Complexity on Multi-Level Coordination" identify four types of managerial roles, including conveners, mediators, catalysts, and

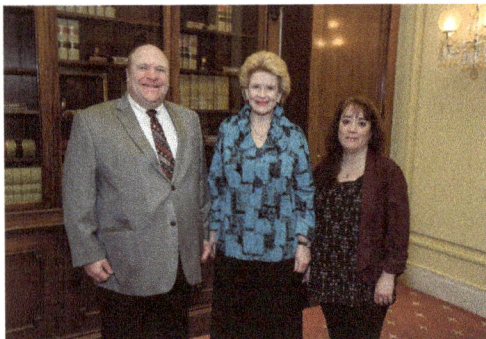

Figure 6.10: Senator Stabenow meets with Mayor Candy Brew and City Manager Roy Anderson of Norway, Michigan.
Source: Wikimedia Commons
Attribution: U.S. Senator Debbie Stabenow
License: CC BY 2.0

---

30   See M. McGuire. "Managing Networks: Propositions on What Managers Do and Why They Do It." *Public Administration Review* 62 (5: 2002): 599–609. doi:10.1111/puar.2002.62.issue-5; and Robert Agranoff, *Managing within Networks: Adding Value to Public Organizations.*

31   See S.Verweij , E. H. Klijn, J. Edelenbos, and M. W. Van Buuren. "What Makes Governance Networks Work? A Fuzzy Set Qualitative Comparative Analysis of 14 Dutch Spatial Planning Projects." *Public Administration: An International Quarterly* 91 (4: 2013): 1035–1055. doi:10.1111/ padm.12007.

bridge-builders.[32] The authors examined these roles in relation to institutional complexity. They argued that bridge-builders help most when institutional complexity is high, and conveners ensure high network performance when institutional complexity is medium-low. And in "How to Make Public Networks Really Work: A Qualitative Comparative Analysis," Daniela Cristofoli and J. Markovic offer three managerial activities of facilitating, mediating, and leading in network management in combination with a selection of contextual, structural, and functioning network mechanisms.[33] Two paths ensure high network performance in contexts where resources are abundant. The strong exercise of managerial activities leads to high performance in centrally-governed networks. Formalized coordination mechanisms ensure high network performance when networks are shared-governed, and network management is not relevant in such a situation.

In order to manage networks effectively, K. G. Provan and P. Kenis (2008) in "Modes of Network Governance: Structure, Management and Effectiveness" consider network management strategies for managers.[34] They suggest that managers should follow the shared governance strategy, when management and governance responsibilities are distributed throughout a network. Managers should follow

Figure 6.11: Councilmember Sally Clark's Final Full Council Meeting, April 6, 2015.
Source: Wikimedia Commons
Attribution: Seattle City Council
License: CC0 1.0

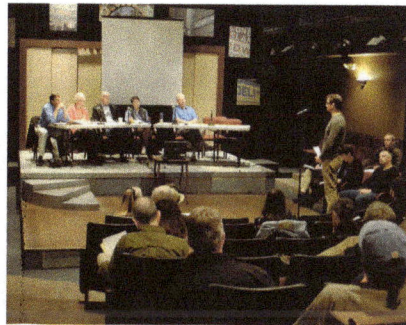

Figure 6.12: Residents joined Councilmembers at Taproot Theatre in Greenwood to discuss how we can encourage the design of quality neighborhood-friendly lowrise buildings in Seattle. 3/20/10.
Source: Wikimedia Commons
Attribution: Seattle City Council
License: CC0 1.0

a lead organization approach, when one organization in the network takes on management duties. Finally, managers should follow a network administrative organization approach when an outside organization is contracted to manage the network. The choice of an appropriate management strategy depends on a number of factors, such as size, network complexity, and the degree of goal alignment among members. Provan and Kenis, therefore, advise managers to understand the network's nature prior to employing one of the three network management strategies effectively. Public managers in collaborative networks do, in fact, show a pattern of behavior that is crucial for network performance. Agranoff and

32   Refer to S. Hovik, and G. S. Hanssen. "The Impact of Network Management and Complexity on Multi-Level Coordination." *Public Administration* 93 (2015): 506–523. doi:10.1111/padm.12135.
33   See D. Cristofoli, and J. Markovic. "How To Make Public Networks Really Work: A Qualitative Comparative Analysis." *Public Administration* 94 (1: 2016): 89–110. doi:10.1111/padm.2016.94.issue-1.
34   Provan and Kenis, "Modes of Network Governance: Structure, Management and Effectiveness."

McGuire argue that network managers are in charge of selecting the best partners and resources for the network, establishing the relevant rules to govern partner interaction, promoting partner commitment, and balancing partners' contrasting goals so as to align them with the network's goal.[35] E. H. Klijn, V. Sierra, T. Ysa, E. Berman, J. Edelenbos, and D. Y. Chen (2016) in "The Influence of Trust on Network Performance in Taiwan, Spain, and the Netherlands: A Cross-Country Comparison" similarly suggest that network managers are responsible for initiating and guiding interactions between actors, including establishing and managing network arrangements for better coordination.[36] Hovik and Hanssen note that managers facilitate collaboration by convening, managing conflicts, identifying and creating value, and moving across the political and administrative authorities.[37] Through an observation of managers' day-to-day activities in their role as network orchestrators, J. A. Bartelings, et al. note in "The Nature of Orchestrational Work" that network managers, as orchestrators, employ their time mostly in bridging,

Figure 6.13: Fernley, NV, January 16, 2008—FEMA Community Relations(CR) Specialist Michael Palmer presents requested information at the City Council Meeting. FEMA works closely with state and local partners and keeps them informed of disaster response and recovery activities.

Source: Wikimedia Commons
Attribution: George Armstrong
License: Public Domain

---

35   Agranoff and McGuire, "American Federalism and the Search for Models of Management."
36   See E. H. Klijn, B. Steijn, and J. Edelenbos. "The Impact of Network Management on Outcomes in Governance Networks." *Public Administration* 88 (4: 2010a): 1063–1082. doi:10.1111/j.14679299.2010.01826.x.
37   See Hovik and Hanssen, "The Impact of Network Management and Complexity on Multi-Level Coordination."

networking, and travelling activities.[38] They devote less time to stabilizing the network, transmitting knowledge, and completing operational activities, such as operational work and preparing documents.

6.3 POLICY INNOVATION AND DIFFUSION: POLICY ENTREPRENEURS IN INTERGOVERNMENTAL NETWORKS

In addition to governance, public policy-making is central to collaborative networks.[39] The former provides public managers with the solutions for addressing public problems. Among public managers and officials, policy entrepreneurs are the agents who bring about policy changes by steering collaborative networks legislatively and administratively. Policy entrepreneurs are critical in formulating policy invention, innovation, and diffusion. This section surveys these topics and explains how a policy, once successfully implemented after its invention, spreads across nations and subnational units of government. This feature of new policy adoption by another government is referred to as policy innovation, and the spread of policy across governments is defined as policy diffusion. Both policy innovation and diffusion are consistent with what scholars emphasize as "not having to reinvent the wheel." After briefly defining these concepts and summarizing their theories, this section also documents how federal, state, and local agencies have undertaken policy innovation and diffusion as facets of IGM.

Policy diffusion: is the spread of the policy across governments. It refers to the process by which an innovation is communicated through certain channels over time among the members of a social system.

Policy innovation: is the adoption of a new policy by another government. Policy innovation refers to the adoption of a policy that is new to the unit adopting it.

Policy entrepreneurs: are political actors within the policy community. They comprise a network of bureaucrats, congressional staff members, academics, and researchers in think tanks who share a common concern in a single policy area. They are advocates for proposals or for the prominence of an idea. They seek to initiate dynamic policy change.

Policy entrepreneurs are political actors within the policy community.[40] They comprise a   network of bureaucrats, congressional staff members, academics, and researchers in think tanks who share a common concern in a single policy area.[41] Policy entrepreneurs' roles as agents of change is key to explaining some of the large-scale, dynamic changes in policy making. Scholars largely

38   Refer to J. A. Bartelings, J. Goedee, J. Raab, and R. Bijl. "The Nature of Orchestrational Work." *Public Management Review* 19 (3: 2017): 342–360. doi:10.1080/14719037.2016.1209233.

39   Agranoff and McGuire, "American Federalism and the Search for Models of Management."

40   See J. W. Kingdon. *Agendas, Alternatives, And Public Policies*. NY: Harper Collins, 1984 & 1995; and Michael Mintrom.. "Policy Entrepreneurs and the Diffusion of Innovation." *American Journal of Political Science*, 41(3: 1997): 738-770.

41   Nikolas Zahariadas. "The Multiple Streams Framework." In Paul A. Sabatier (ed), *Theories of the Policy Process*, 2nd ed. Chapter 3, Boulder, Colorado: Westview Press. 2007, 72.

understand policy making as incremental changes accompanied with long periods of policy stability.[42] In *Agendas, Alternatives, And Public Policies*, John W. Kingdon saw policy entrepreneurs as "advocates for proposals or for the prominence of an idea."[43] These entrepreneurs are always interested in new ideas. They invest their time, resources, and reputations to promote a new idea concerning their preferred policy.[44] Policy entrepreneurs are crucial in identifying and bringing new problems and their possible solutions to the decision table. In addition, in "Policy Entrepreneurs and the Diffusion of Innovation," Michael Mintrom defines policy entrepreneurs as "people who seek to initiate dynamic policy change."[45] Policy entrepreneurs share commonalities with other policy advocates, such as interest groups or lobbyists, as both try to push for the adoption of their preferred policies and changes in marginal policies. However, policy entrepreneurs act differently than most interest groups, as their primary interest is in selling their ideas for bringing sweeping changes in the policy-making process.[46] Kingdon asserts that policy entrepreneurs exist either inside or outside government agencies. When inside, they are in either an appointed or elected position. Interest groups or any other advocacy groups, such as research organizations, also house policy entrepreneurs. Knowing the set of defining characteristics that bind them together is the easiest way to identify policy entrepreneurs.

Figure 6.14: President John F. Kennedy in his historic message to a joint session of the Congress, on May 25, 1961 declared, "...I believe this nation should commit itself to achieving the goal, before this decade is out, of landing a man on the Moon and returning him safely to the Earth." This goal was achieved when astronaut Neil A. Armstrong became the first human to set foot upon the Moon at 10:56 p.m. EDT, July 20, 1969.Shown in the background are, (left) Vice President Lyndon Johnson, and (right) Speaker of the House Sam T. Rayburn.
Source: Wikimedia Commons
Attribution: NASA
License: Public Domain

Figure 6.15: President Obama Signs Health Insurance Legislation Into Law.
Source: Wikimedia Commons
Attribution: Nancy Pelosi
License: CC BY 2.0

42   See Michael Mintrom and Sandra Vergari. "Advocacy Coalitions, Policy Entrepreneurs and Policy Change." *Policy Studies Journal* 24 (1996): 420–438.
43   Kingdon, *Agendas, Alternatives, And Public Policies*, 129.
44   Kingdon, *Agendas, Alternatives, And Public Policies*, 129.
45   Mintrom, "Policy Entrepreneurs and the Diffusion of Innovation." 739.
46   See Paul Sabatier. "The Suitability of Several Models for the Comparative Analysis of the Policy Process." In Robert McKinlay and Louis Imbeau (eds), *Comparing Government Activity*, London: Macmillan, 1996, pp. 101–117.

6.3.1 Policy Entrepreneurs as Agents of Policy Change

Figure 6.16: President Ronald Reagan During a Ceremony with Apollo Astronauts Neil Armstrong, Edwin Buzz Aldrin, James Beggs, and Michael Collins for the 15th Anniversary of The Lunar Landing and Space Exploration Day in The East Room, 7/20/1984.
Source: Wikimedia Commons
Attribution: White House Photographic Collection
License: Public Domain

Figure 6.17: President Bill Clinton plays the saxophone presented to him by Russian President Boris Yeltsin at a private dinner hosted by President Yeltsin at Novoya Ogarova Dacha, Russia.
Source: Wikimedia Commons
Attribution: Bob McNeely
License: Public Domain

Incrementalism in policy-making was first proposed by Charles E. Lindblom in 1959 in the article, "The Science of Muddling Through" and was later taken forward by Aaron Wildavsky in his work, *The Politics of the Budgetary Process*.[47] Incrementalism explains policy change as "continual policy readjustments in pursuit of marginally redefined policy goals."[48] Paul R. Schulman argues in "Nonincremental Policy Making" that changes in policies occur on account of conflicting interests, difficulty in assembling and processing information to evaluate alternative policy solutions, the need to correct for negative feedback, and, finally, the need to establish stable expectations in a complex and uncertain environment. The incremental approach cannot answer how decision makers arrive at these marginal reforms in policies. Some scholars term the incremental approach as "incomplete," as it is unable to explain comprehensive decisions that are characterized by indivisibility and large-scale policy changes.[49] The search for theories in explaining dynamic policy changes during the early 1980s and 90s led scholars to consider the role of policy entrepreneurs. The punctuated equilibrium theory and the agenda setting model put policy entrepreneurs at the forefront.

Policy entrepreneurs are central actors in the Punctuated Equilibrium theory. According to this theory, the shift from stability to sudden change in policy-making lies in the procedure through which issues are formed for policy action.[50] Issue formation and expansion rely on the public's

---

47   First argued by C. E. Lindblom. "The Science of Muddling Through." *Public Administration Review*, vol. 19 (Spring issue, 1959): pp. 79–88; and was later taken forward by Wildavsky, A. *The Politics of the Budgetary Process*. Toronto, Little, Brown and Co., 1964.

48   Paul R. Schulman. "Nonincremental Policy Making." *American Political Science Review*, 69 (4: 1975), 1354.

49   See L. James True, Bryan D. Jones, and Frank R. Baumgartner. "Punctuated-Equilibrium Theory: Explaining Stability and Change in Public Policymaking." In Paul A. Sabatier (ed) *Theories of the Policy Process*, 2nd ed. Chapter 6. Boulder, Colorado: West view Press, 2007.

50   Frank R. Baumgartner, and Bryan D. Jones. *Agendas and Instability in American Politics*. Chicago: University of Chicago Press,1993, 25.

understanding of a policy problem, or "policy image." The second factor behind policy development is "policy venue." Policy venues are institutional locations where authoritative decisions are made on a given issue.[51] Federal government, the market, state or local authorities, and legal institutions constitute policy venues. Different institutional venues favor a different "policy image." A particular policy image may get rejected in one policy venue but be received very well in a different venue. A particular policy image's translating into policy change will depend on which particular policy venue has the final authority to formulate that policy. This interaction between policy image, policy venues, and their implications on issue framing cause sudden policy stopping points. Frank R. Baumgartner and Bryan D. Jones suggest in *Agendas and Instability in American Politics* that policy entrepreneurs use their expertise in acting as a common linkage between an issue, its policy image, and the several policy venues through which the issue traverses before it reaches the agenda table and is transformed into a new policy.

Figure 6.18: Martin Luther King Jr. addresses a crowd from the steps of the Lincoln Memorial where he delivered his famous, "I Have a Dream," speech during the Aug. 28, 1963, march on Washington, D.C.
Source: Wikimedia Commons
Attribution: Unknown
License: Public Domain

Policy entrepreneurs are knowledge brokers in issue framing and issue expansion. As Baumgartner and Jones go on to note, policy entrepreneurs use

51   Frank R. Baumgartner, and Bryan D. Jones. *Agendas and Instability in American Politics*. Chicago: University of Chicago Press,1993, 31.

their specialized knowledge to describe issues in a simple yet attention-catching manner and communicate them to the general public either through symbolic terms (e.g., tax savings, higher wages) or by using emotive appeal (e.g., empathy, charity) with their eye on advancing favorable policy images. The process of creating a favorable image also depends on how the problem is defined. Deborah Stone suggests in her article "Causal stories and the formation of policy agendas" that "problem definition is centrally concerned with attributing bad conditions to human conditions instead of fate, or nature."[52] Baumgartner and Jones argue that policy entrepreneurs change the definition of a problem by altering its image to either bring an issue into the public domain for government intervention for the first time or to raise the ranking of an existing issue on an agenda status list. However, the process is competitive, as there are a number of competing single policy images. These images emerge as proponents and opponents of the policy try to turn public support in their favor and move the issue onto the governmental agenda. Although policy entrepreneurs and other advocates within a policy community push their preferred policies onto the agenda table, the quality of strategy used by each differs and is key to explaining why policy entrepreneurs overcome the problem of too many competing images.

The agenda setting model is particularly useful in this regard[53] and explains what policy entrepreneurs do after they successfully put an issue onto the public agenda table. According to this model, the joining of three independent streams, namely, the "problem stream," the "policy stream," and the "politics stream," results in dynamic changes in policy making. The "problem stream" encompasses an array of

Figure 6.19: President Donald Trump meets with world leaders.
Source: Wikimedia Commons
Attribution: Office of White House Press Secretary
License: Public Domain

Figure 6.20: Vladimir Putin and Donald Trump (2019-06-28).
Source: Wikimedia Commons
Attribution: Presidential Press and Information Office
License: CC BY 4.0

Figure 6.21: President Bush meets with Secretary of Education Rod Paige, left, and Senator Edward Kennedy August 2, 2001, to discuss the education reforms for the country.
Source: Wikimedia Commons
Attribution: Eric Draper
License: Public Domain

---

52   Deborah A. Stone. "Causal stories and the formation of policy agendas." *Political Science Quarterly* 104, no. 2 (1989): 299.
53   As noted by Kingdon, *Agendas, Alternatives, And Public Policies.*

problems facing the society that both citizens and policy makers want to address. The "policy stream" comprises the ideas and solutions that are brought out by specialists within policy communities. The "politics stream" consists of three elements: the national mood, opposition of interest groups, and the legislative and administrative turnover.[54] Nikolas Zahariadas (2007) in "The Multiple Streams Framework" (chapter 3 in Paul A. Sabatier (ed), *Theories of the Policy Process*, 2nd ed., Boulder, Colorado: Westview Press) notes that policy entrepreneurs take the lead in joining three independent streams at decisive moments in time when the "window of opportunity" opens up. Policy windows are "fleeting opportunities for advocates of proposals to push their pet solutions, or to push attention to their special problems."[55] According to Baumgartner and Jones, policy entrepreneurs use these fleeting moments to promote their preferred solutions to the decision makers. Policy entrepreneurs' ability to propose a set of problems and their potential solutions to decision makers differentiates them from other advocates. They are the indisputable experts in making connections between solutions and problems, which is fundamental in policy process. While success may not always materialize, their ability to make clear arguments and potential solutions put them ahead of others in the race.[56] Kingdon argues that when policy entrepreneurs' abilities are matched with other qualities, such as persistence, resources, reputation, and political connections, they surge ahead of others in the policy community.

6.3.2 Policy Entrepreneurs, Networks, and Policy Diffusion

On their path to success, policy entrepreneurs tend to form coalitions around themselves. With time, these coalitions can eventually outweigh all other coalitions. This process is how "Policy Monopolies" are formed. Baumgartner and Jones argue that policy monopolies are structural arrangements that are supported by powerful ideas. The creation of policy monopolies is a gradual process. It occurs when policy entrepreneurs manage to create and maintain a favorable policy image for a long time.

Institutional structures protect policy monopolies and act as gatekeepers to restrict access to outsiders in the policy process. Policy monopolies allow only marginal or incremental changes in policy formulation because they prevent new policy ideas from emerging and reaching the agenda table. The existing policies only marginally incorporate any negative feedback that arises within the system.

Policy monopolies are quite fragile in the long run. Two factors can destroy policy monopolies: the positive feedback originating from a new policy image and the conflict between institutional venues. The punctuated equilibrium theory suggests that disadvantaged policy entrepreneurs may sometimes succeed in bringing a new idea/policy image out of many conflicting images, as it is powerful enough to alter the existing political discourse dramatically. The strength of a new idea at-

54   Zahariadis, "The Multiple Streams Framework." 70.
55   Kingdon, *Agendas, Alternatives, And Public Policies*, 16.
56   See William H. Riker. *The art of political manipulation*. New Haven: Yale University Press, 1986.

tracts keen interest from policy makers and institutions that were earlier ignorant or disinterested. The particular policy image becomes so popular that new groups and multiple venues also favor it. This environment of positive feedback enables the policy idea to move beyond "subsystem politics" to "macro-politics."[57] Subsystem politics is also known as equilibrium politics. L. James True, Bryan D. Jones, and Frank R. Baumgartner (2007) in "Punctuated-Equilibrium Theory: Explaining Stability and Change in Public Policymaking" (in Paul A. Sabatier (ed) *Theories of the Policy Process,* 2nd ed.) argue that policy monopolies, incrementalism, and negative feedback are some of subsystem politics' essential features. Macro-politics is also known as punctuation politics. Large-scale policy change, positive feedback, competing policy images, and political manipulation are some of the essential features of macro-politics. Large-scale changes or stopping points in policy-making happen when an issue moves to macro-politics.

Policy entrepreneurs help bring new ideas and policy innovations for dynamic policy changes or policy punctuations. When they encounter an innovative idea that has the potential to become their preferred policy, they invest their time and resources into it by selling the idea initially to the policy community and later to policy makers in the government.[58] According to the authors, the chances of accepting

> *Policy invention:* is the process by which an original idea is first conceived. is new to the unit adopting it.

an innovative policy depends on the amount of time, energy, and resources devoted by policy entrepreneurs to promoting such policies (True, et al., 2007). "Policy Innovation"[59] refers to adopting a policy that is new to the unit implementing it. Put differently, if a local government adopts a program that already exists in other jurisdictions, it is "innovation." "Policy invention" is the process by which an original idea is first conceived. "Policy diffusion" refers to "the process by which an innovation is communicated through certain channels over time among the members of a social system."[60]

According to Frances Berry and William D. Berry (2007) in "Innovation and Diffusion Models in Policy Research" (in Paul A. Sabatier (ed.) *Theories of the Policy Process*, 2nd edition. Boulder, Colorado: Westview Press), several internal factors and the extent of diffusion at various levels influence policy innovation. The internal factors include economic, social, political, demographic, and motivational issues. Diffusion at various levels ranges from national diffusion to regional, isomorphic, vertical and Leader-Ladder diffusion, defined below. The term "Policy Reinvention" means adoption of an existing policy with some modifications or

57   True et al., "Punctuated-Equilibrium Theory: Explaining Stability and Change in Public Policymaking."162.
58   See Michael Mintrom and Sandra Vergari. "Charter schools as a state policy innovation: Assessing recent developments." *State and Local Government Review* 29, no. 1 (1997): 43–49.
59   Frances Berry and William D. Berry. "Innovation and Diffusion Models in Policy Research." In Paul A. Sabatier (ed.) *Theories of the Policy Process*, 2nd edition, Chapter 6. Boulder, Colorado: Westview Press, 2007, 223.
60   E. M. Rogers. *Diffusion of innovations.* New York: Free Press, 1983 (3rd ed.), 5.

amendments in it.[61] According to Henry R. Glick and Scott P. Hays in "Innovation and Reinvention in State Policymaking: Theory and the Evolution of Living Wills Laws," amendments occur over time due to the social accumulation of experience, information and technology, unit characteristics, and consistent political support. The extent of policy diffusion has a direct bearing on policy innovation. Policy innovation diffusion does not happen automatically; instead, policy entrepreneurs are the primary force behind this process.[62]

Berry and Berry capture the different levels of diffusion undertaken by policy entrepreneurs. According to the authors, national diffusion occurs between state officials who learn about different public programs by interacting with each other through the national communications network. The national diffusion model's underlying assumption is state officials who have already adopted a program do not hide information and interact freely with their counterparts in other states, where such programs are not yet adopted.[63] Another form of diffusion occurs through regional channels. In such cases, diffusion primarily happens between states that are located close to each other. The third form of diffusion occurs through simple emulation. This kind of diffusion is captured by the leader-laggard model, which explains phenomenon where some states happen to be pioneers in adoption, and other states simply emulate them.[64] The isomorphism diffusion model explains diffusion between states that are similar. This type of diffusion is primarily helpful for the late adopter, as they can use information on similar policies, and they are also likely to be aware of the possible consequences of a new policy.[65] The final model of diffusion is the vertical influence model, which suggests that states emulate the national government's policies and not their fellow states. Policy entrepreneurs play an active role in all types of diffusion. It is important, therefore, to understand the mechanisms through which policy entrepreneurs effect innovation and diffusion.

One of the strategies policy entrepreneurs use is networking with other policy actors.[66] Policy networks provide an informal structure where different interests and actors come together, and they are fundamental to policy change. Policy entrepreneurs invest their time in networking, as it helps them understand new policies, identify strategies to sell their policies by talking with a diverse group of people in the network, and, finally, recognize experts that are going to support their ideas at an appropriate time in the future. According to Adam Silke and Hanspeter Kriesi in their work "The Network Approach," policy networks are shaped by transnational contexts, national context, and policy domain specific contexts. The effect of the above three factors in shaping policy networks depends

61   Henry R. Glick and Scott P. Hays. "Innovation and Reinvention in State Policymaking: Theory and the Evolution of Living Wills Laws." *Journal of Politics*, 53 (3: 1991): 537.
62   See Mintrom, "Policy Entrepreneurs and the Diffusion of Innovation."
63   Berry and Berry, "Innovation and Diffusion Models in Policy Research." 226.
64   Berry and Berry, "Innovation and Diffusion Models in Policy Research." 230.
65   Berry and Berry, "Innovation and Diffusion Models in Policy Research." 230.
66   See Kingdon, *Agendas, Alternatives, And Public Policies; and Mintrom*, "Policy Entrepreneurs and the Diffusion of Innovation."

on the distribution and interaction of power. The distribution of power can either be in the hands of a single dominant actor (termed as "concentration"), or it could be collectively shared by a coalition of actors (termed as "fragmentation"). The authors also consider three types of interaction between actors or a coalition of actors. These include conflict, bargaining, and cooperation. The interaction between power distribution and these three interaction types results in six different policy network types. If conflict and power is concentrated, there will be dominance within the policy network. The resulting policy change will be moderate in nature, with the potential for rapid shift. On the other hand, if there is conflict but power is fragmented, there will be competition within the policy network. The possibility of rapid and large-scale policy punctuations is very high in this type of network. If there is cooperation among actors but the power is concentrated in a few hands, policy change will happen at a slower pace with a high probability of retaining the status-quo. On the other hand, if interaction is cooperative and power is fragmented, policy changes will occur at a slower rate and incremental changes will occur over a sequence of years. Finally, if there is bargaining and power is fragmented, there will once again be a high probability of dynamic policy change taking place.[67] The same will not occur if power is concentrated in the hands of a few.[68] Thus any policy change, incremental or punctuated, will depend on the policy network type.

While policy networks are important, their existence cannot be understood in isolation. Policy networks are nested within policy communities, and together they are located within the larger policy subsystem.[69] The larger policy subsystem consists of administrative agencies, legislative committees, and interest groups at various levels of government who are active in policy formulation and implementation, as well as journalists, researchers, and policy analysts who play key roles in dissemination, knowledge generation, and the evaluation of policy ideas. According to Michael Hewlett and M. Ramesh in their work "Policy Subsystem Configurations and Policy Change: Operationalizing the Postpositivist Analysis of the Politics of the Policy Process," while policy communities bring ideas, knowledge, and information to the table, policy networks bring together different interests and actors. At the macro-level, policy-making takes place mostly

> **Policy subsystem**: Policy networks are nested within the policy communities and together they are located within the larger policy subsystem. The larger policy subsystem consists of administrative agencies, legislative committees, interest groups at various levels of government who are active in policy formulation and implementation as well as journalists, researchers, and policy analysts who play key role in dissemination, knowledge generation and evaluation of policy ideas.

67   Adam Silke and Hanspeter Kriesi. "The Network Approach." In Paul A. Sabatier, ed. *Theories of the Policy Process*, 2nd ed. Chapter 5. Boulder, Colorado: Westview Press, 2007, 133–135.
68   Adam Silke and Hanspeter Kriesi. "The Network Approach." In Paul A. Sabatier, ed. *Theories of the Policy Process*, 2nd ed. Chapter 5. Boulder, Colorado: Westview Press, 2007, 135 & 145.
69   See Michael Hewlett and M. Ramesh. "Policy subsystem configurations and policy change: Operationalizing the Postpositivist Analysis of the Politics of the Policy Process." *Policy Studies Journal*, 26 (3: 1998): 466–481.

within the policy subsystem. The main actors in policy subsystems are specialists whose behavior is influenced by the broader political and socioeconomic system.[70] Within the policy subsystem, coalitions are formed by policy entrepreneurs.[71] Michael Mintrom and Sandra Vergari (1996) in "Advocacy Coalitions, Policy Entrepreneurs and Policy Change" argue that policy entrepreneurs frame issues (old and new) in ways that appeal to diverse interests within the policy subsystem and where policy entrepreneurs compete with others and try to change the "image" of a particular policy.[72] Major changes in policy subsystems result as policy entrepreneurs start actively pursuing their strategies of building coalitions. This process causes shifts in subsystem membership and ultimately leads to rapid changes in policy.[73]

In sum, policy entrepreneurs influence policy change in several ways. These include identifying issues, framing issues that appeal to a larger group of people, and taking the issue to the agenda table. Once the issue reaches agenda status, policy entrepreneurs work patiently to find solutions to problems, and, when the right opportunity comes, they put their preferred solution in front of decision makers. Policy entrepreneurs use the policy subsystem to find appropriate solutions to problems at this stage. They bring policy networks and policy communities together to share their ideas and gather support from other experts. Finally, policy entrepreneurs believe in and always welcome innovative ideas. They influence the diffusion of new ideas by communicating with different groups over time. Policy entrepreneurs are active in all stages of the policy process.

6.4 COLLABORATIVE GOVERNANCE FOR ECONOMIC DEVELOPMENT

States and local governments come together to address several economic development issues that have substantial spillover effects built into them. States and local governments address these Economic Development problems through appropriate intergovernmental networks. Such topics include urban growth and management, chamber of commerce, employment, public health, housing and real estate, homelessness, and crime, among several others. This section provides a background on economic development conducted through intergovernmental networks.

---

70   See Paul A. Sabatier and Hank C. Jenkins-Smith. *Policy Change and Learning: An Advocacy Coalition Approach*. Boulder, CO: Westview Press, 1988.

71   See Mintrom and Vergari, "Advocacy Coalitions, Policy Entrepreneurs and Policy Change."

72   See Hewlett and Ramesh, "Policy subsystem configurations and policy change: Operationalizing the Postpositivist Analysis of the Politics of the Policy Process."

73   See Sabatier and Jenkins-Smith, *Policy Change and Learning: An Advocacy Coalition Approach*; Mintrom and Vergari, "Advocacy Coalitions, Policy Entrepreneurs and Policy Change;" and Hewlett and Ramesh, "Policy subsystem configurations and policy change: Operationalizing the Postpositivist Analysis of the Politics of the Policy Process."

Figure 6.22: With fresh ink, representatives from federal, state and local agencies formalized their partnership in a ceremonial Silver Jackets charter signing on Sept. 9, 2016. Silver Jackets is a nationwide flood risk management program that acts as one team to quickly and effectively channel solutions to communities in need.
Source: Wikimedia Commons
Attribution: U.S. Army Corps of Engineers Sacramento District
License: Public Domain

6.4.1 History of Collaborative Governance for Economic Development

In the process of urban evolution, in the late-eighteenth and most of the nineteenth centuries, cities in the U.S. were production centers based on a laissez-faire economic model. Control of production was in private hands. Cities attracted people who needed work, and this labor class settled close to production centers. Cities as production centers were very compact in comparison to today's American cities. Immigration provided cheap labor, and labor had no legal protection.

Working hours were very long. Immigration also provided mass followings for the political machine leaders who came later to govern cities. There was widespread class segregation as well as income disparity. Service provision arose in response to crises as they occurred sporadically, for instance, health problems due to contaminated drinking water, sewage, and trash collection. The private sector was the service provider, and those having the ability to pay could avail such services. Crime was rampant and initial attempts to put a police system in place failed.

In response to these problems, a political machine structure arose as the governing system. Prior to 1830, political power in many American cities was controlled by very small circles of economic elites. The members of these elites belonged to the higher-status Protestant churches in their localities. A powerful

Figure 6.23: Federal, State and local agencies gathered at Metro Nashville's Development Services Center to form a group partnership to help reduce flood reduction Sept. 23, 2014. Silver Jackets is an innovative program that provides an opportunity to consistently bring together multiple state, federal, and local agencies to learn from one another and apply their knowledge to reduce risk.

Source: Wikimedia Commons
Attribution: U.S. Army Corps of Engineers Nashville District
License: CC BY-SA 2.0

individual from this ethnic group rose to power and appointed his close friends to important positions. These friends in turn helped put him in office. This system thrived on buying and selling of contracts for paving streets, installing lighting, and building water and sewage infrastructure. The services provided were fragmented and targeted to meet the demands of more powerful people. This form of local government was, evidently, not very representational, and there was an informal hierarchy as those holding office in many large cities remained in power indefinitely by using this informal hierarchy in political organization. During the economic depressions in 1870 and 1930, riots and ethnic strife were rampant all around as local services weren't available to newly assimilated immigrants and lower-class people when they needed it the most. The political machine, through its network of favored individuals heading different services, was not always able to deliver aid to the working class. However, as the capitalists grew more insecure, they demanded more protections from the political machine that only then provided targeted paved and lighted streets and police protection. This fragmented service structure gave way to a consolidation process, but the mechanism for appointing friends as officials to provide services to the working class under the guise of an election remained the same. The different service departments within this consolidated form of government were headed by individuals owing allegiance to the individual in power. The political machine was an institution which suited the needs of businessmen in a rapidly industrializing society. The government machinery was used in favor of these businessmen in settling factory worker disputes, avoiding unionizing efforts, and so forth. This system of urban governance was mired in electoral corruption as well as corrupt business practices on account of favoritism's prevalence within the structure. The political machine form of government in earlier cities exercised social control to favor a few individuals, rather than promoting social reform and welfare. There was no separation of power. The elected representatives were also bureaucrats.

6.4.2 Contemporary Collaborative Governance for Economic Development

In response to this situation, the struggle for the urban reform movement began. The municipal reformers, comprising businessmen and professional bureaucrats, attempted centralizing local government functions and destroying the political party machines. Specifically, the reformers focused on removing the partisan politics in municipal government and eliminating graft and corruption. They strove for developing accountability for public officials and wanted cities to seek "home rule" charters (see chapter 1). In this system of governance, since the late nineteenth century, politics was separate from administration, and the latter was based on military discipline. In the council manager form, voters elected council members who hired managers to run the city affairs. Alternatively, in the commission model of government, voters directly elected commission heads.

Apart from the reform movement gaining pace, many national events also contributed to the political machine structure's demise. For instance, the U.S. enacted anti-immigration laws in 1920, following which immigrants' economic conditions improved somewhat, allowing immigrants to spread out of their usually-confined poor geographic locations in cities, thus increasing their political power. The evolutionary changes during this period, beginning with the turn of the twentieth century and continuing until the 1970s, effected the emergence of a political organization focused on various functions rather than the ethnic and geographic nature of organizations in the political machine era. The functional organization of power was instrumental in bringing technicians and specialists to the forefront in making important decisions regarding city growth. Specialized agencies, such as water and sanitation, public roads, etc. emerged in place of the previously general-purpose governments. Within the functional area of public activity, the community's most influential individuals were answerable virtually to themselves. The elected politicians consequently had little space to influence decisions made by these agencies.

Figure 6.24: Visit Minister Sigrid Kaag to Atlanta City Hall in Georgia, meeting with Mayor Keisha Lance Bottoms, March 27, 2019.
Source: Wikimedia Commons
Attribution: Netherlands Embassy
License: CC BY 2.0

Since the mid-1960s, cities have undergone another evolutionary phase. Their local autonomy has been challenged by outside economic forces over which local governments have little control. In this scenario, cities have become dependent, as is consistent with what was discussed in chapter 1 pertaining to collaborative and creative forms of American federalism. Local autonomy has been subjected to policy mandates from federal and state governments, such as supply of clean drinking water, public education, environment pollution, affordable housing, etc. that greatly influence the choices cities can make and the way they implement those policies and procedures. Cities have to increasingly depend on state governments for legal authority and on state and federal governments for financial help in the form of grants-in-aid as an aspect of fiscal federalism, examined in chapter 4. Cities have also come to depend on the business community for participation in economic development projects and on surrounding suburbs for cooperation on problems that cross city boundaries. Making such interdependent decisions requires effective political leaders, and, in recent times, this leadership has come from city mayors.

Another significant change in the mid-1960s was happening simultaneously: the innovations in transportation with the wide web of interstate highways facilitating a spreading out of businesses and affluent whites towards city suburbs. Four factors were responsible for this shift: the automobile; the new technology in road and residential construction; the cultural dislike of big cities; and new long-term, low down-payment mortgages. The nexus between the automobile, steel, and rubber industries facilitated the mass production of affordable automobiles. The road networks built by federal and state governments and these cheap cars led to the suburbanization movement in cities during the period between the two world wars. But poor African Americans were flocking to what came to be called the "inner city" in hopes of attaining jobs—which were, ironically, moving out of city centers. This move resulted in the flight of those capital and tax bases essential for growing city centers. As a result, suburban growth surpassed city growth during this period. Private property developers were also seizing the moment and accentuating suburbanization. These entrepreneurs were promoting the increased use of their properties, hence, maximizing their exchange values. The U.S. economy, therefore, shifted from manufacturing to the service sector, following the city-center location model and its impacts on local economies. Service sector jobs did not pay as much to workers with the same level of education who were shifting from manufacturing to the service sector, implying that further reduction would be required from the city's tax base. This unabated city sprawl, along with reduction in their tax base, has continued throughout the twentieth century. Since cities are created by states, cities have had little power to control sprawl.

As discussed in chapter 4, the economic imperatives of cities have shaped their evolution and growth, or lack thereof, during the twentieth century as well. This evolution has been largely within the socio-political and economic structure as described in the city limits, growth machine, and urban regime paradigms.

Declining cities are facing a number of limitations. The limited cities, in order to capture resources for undertaking essential services mandated by laws, such as law and order, public education, public roads, etc., are working in coordination with business elites to attract and retain capital investments. Cities are competing with each other as well. As Paul E. Peterson argues in *City Limits*, cities need to continuously attract capital; in doing so, they are providing many incentives through lower tax rates or subsidies in the form of cheap land.[74] Attracting new businesses as well as encouraging growth in existing businesses are considered essential for promoting employment and for raising incremental revenue for providing additional public goods and services. The city, as a growth machine, has to work with business leaders who control the most important resources needed for economic growth. This economic imperative leads to the formation and evolution of varying regimes in urban politics. The interest group common to all these regimes is the business group, as Stone notes.[75] The interest of the business group is paramount in relation to cities' economic growth imperatives.

6.4.3 Collaborative Governance and Economic Imperative of Growth

Historically, cities and towns sprang up as centers for trade and commerce. The governing coalitions in cities, which have been comprised of capitalists and businessmen traditionally, became aware of the fact that promoting city growth would ensure mutual success. This economic imperative of promoting individual wealth through economic growth in cities above all other goals has led to a situation in which cities could prosper only by gaining a competitive advantage over others as trading centers. The centrality of this economic growth in city politics constitutes an area's political economy. However, scholars who study urban politics have interpreted cities' political economies and economic imperatives in different ways.

Welfare economists approach cities' political economies as microcosms, where individuals are the political system's main components. These individuals are rational, value-maximizing, voting consumers in the political market's competitive environment. In this scenario, political outcomes in cities result from strategic interactions between value-maximizing individuals. This approach is based on the standard assumptions made in the neoclassical economics tradition.[76]

J.R. Logan and Harvey L. Molotch note in *Urban Fortunes: The Political Economy of Place* that the major assumptions underlying the urban social phenomenon's explanations in cities are market centrality and a free market system. In this tradition, the city as a place is a "market-ordered space to which human beings respond."[77] Moreover, the city's interest is the summation of

---

74   See Paul E. Peterson. *City Limits*. University of Chicago Press, 1981.
75   Refer to Clarence Nathan Stone. *Regime Politics: Governing Atlanta, 1946–1988*. University Press of Kansas, 1989.
76   Peterson, *City Limits*, xi.
77   J. R. Logan, and Harvey L. Molotch. *Urban Fortunes: The Political Economy of Place*. Univ of California Press, 1987, 8.

individual interests and policies adopted by cities that reflect those interests. Every significant interest may be represented by some economic firm or voluntary association, which tries to influence public policies serving the associations' vested interests. Such interest groups search for a compromise through debate, and the political leader works out a solution acceptable to every group to the extent possible. It is in the political leader's best interest to arrive at such a conclusion in order to sustain their political power.

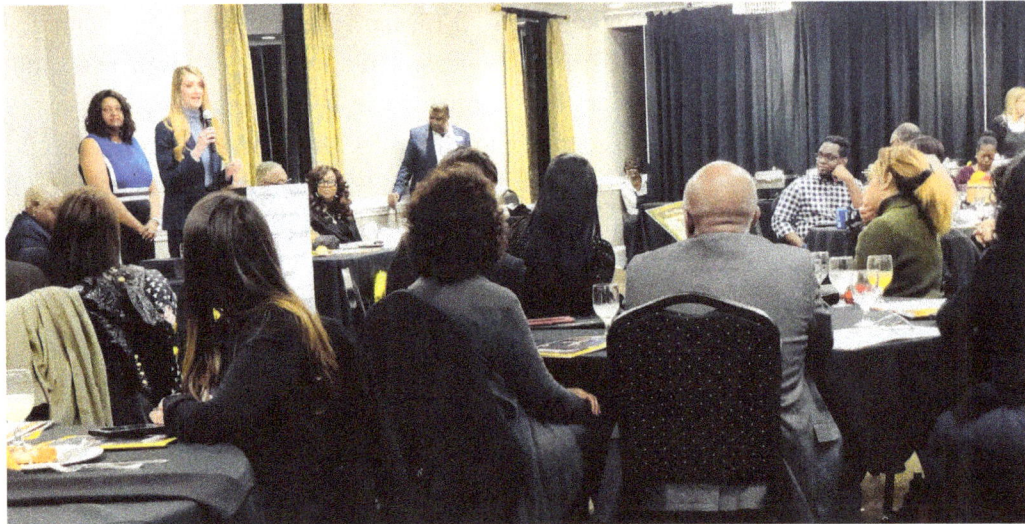

Figure 6.25: Kelly Loeffler speaking at Georgia Greater Black Chamber of Commerce meeting.
Source: Wikimedia Commons
Attribution: Office of Senator Kelly Loeffler
License: Public Domain

As introduced in chapter 4, another approach to promote the economic imperative of cities is in the tradition of Charles Tiebout's optimum city size argument, which he expounded upon in "A Pure Theory of Local Expenditure."[78] The basic argument is that communities in cities seek to attain the optimal size for efficient public goods and services delivery by local city governments. The pursuit of optimal size is essential in order to lower the average cost of public goods and services. Residents reveal their preferences by choosing a package of public goods and services offered by local governments. If the public goods and services are offered efficiently at some optimal size, residential migration will occur until that optimal size has been reached. In this sense, the local government can promote the economic interests of cities by operating local services as efficiently as possible. In these two traditions, city residents consciously choose to live in certain places, and any resulting economic stratification is complimentary and not a cause of conflict.

However, Peterson argues that the interests of cities cannot be represented in terms of either individual summation or pursuit of optimum size. Thus, the

---

78   See Charles Tiebout. "A Pure Theory of Local Expenditure." *Journal of Political Economy*, 64 (1956, October): 416–24.

interests of cities lie in the pursuit of policies and programs undertaken to improve a city's economic standing, social prestige, or political power. Peterson argues that city politics is limited politics. Local governments are creations of respective states, and their powers are limited. He argues that, other than putting land—as a factor of production—to the best possible economic use, there is little that cities as local governments can do. In this respect, too, there are constitutional limits to city authority, though they have considerable autonomy. However, cities cannot control the flow of labor in and out of their boundaries. Paul Peterson argues that cities' competitive advantage is compromised due to lack of skilled, professional managerial talent and highly skilled technicians. Within these limitations, not being able to pursue monetary policies or effective fiscal policies, cities can still do certain things to attract capital or firms to their jurisdictions. According to Peterson, these strategies include minimizing tax on capital, providing low-cost public utilities, and offering public land for free or at subsidized rates, among several other means. When one looks at a city's urban policy in the larger socio-economic and political context, the national political economy affects the policy choices that cities make. Peterson argues that, while making policy decisions in this constrained environment, cities select those policies that are in the city's best interests as a whole. In particular, he notes that internal struggles for power within cities is not the limiting factor, in terms of what policies city governments can adopt.

Logon and Molotch in their previously-mentioned book, provide the Marxian view of political economy of cities. In this view, owners of real estate are considered leftovers from the feudal structure. The capital accumulation process in the productive system is the main tool for explaining urban systems. The Marxists argue that cities form as a result of the tendency in capitalist economies to accumulate capital. City residents constitute labor who are reproduced as production factors, with the exploitation of workers by capitalists. Suburbs develop to provide capitalists with opportunities to invest and stimulate additional demand for consumer goods.

Logan and Molotch believe that local conflicts over growth are central to city organization. Various kinds of people and institutions struggle to achieve their opposing goals in the creation of a metropolis. Logan and Molotch have taken the larger system's economic imperatives into account and contend that, within this system, the business elites make money from development, and ordinary residents make their communities a resource in daily life. From this perspective, the authors derive the concepts of use and exchange value of place. Residents use this concept to satisfy essential needs, whereas entrepreneurs strive for financial returns by trying to intensify the use of their properties. Logan and Molotch argue that the

Use value: refers to a socio-economic and political system of a city in which the ordinary residents make community a resource in their daily life. The residents of a place use it to satisfy essential needs of life.

Exchange value: refers to a socio-economic and political system of a city in which the business elites make money from economic development. The business entrepreneurs strive for financial return by trying to intensify the use of their property in this system.

pursuit of exchange values in cities may not necessarily result in maximized use values for others. In fact, the two goals are contradictory, and this conflict closely determines a city's shape, the distribution of people, and their existence together. The authors believe that this inherent tension can help explain the political dynamics of cities and regions.

This approach reveals how inequalities within and between places and individuals are established and maintained. In this tradition, cities as places grow on account of political action. This political action includes both individual and collective efforts through informal associations and institutions of government and the economy. Markets and individuals are socially structured in hierarchies based on inequality. This differentiation creates a vicious cycle. The issue of growth separates local elite groups from the common people, who mainly consider their city as a place to live and work. Elites on their part view cities as growth machines that can increase aggregate rents and capture wealth for those in the right position to benefit. The desire for growth creates consensus among various groups of elites.

Clarence N. Stone makes similar arguments in his *Regime Politics: Governing Atlanta, 1946-1988*. Along the community power structure propositions, Stone argues that the city is governed through regime politics. This urban regime comprises an informal arrangement between various interest groups that surround and complement the formal working of the government authority. Cities are more limited by the constitutions, national political tradition, and the autonomy of the private sector in comparison to federal and state governments.

Governmental conduct is constrained by the need to promote investment activity for economic growth in cities, which largely hinges on the resources controlled by business elites. In this scenario, Stone notes that local public officials are more than willing to cooperate with those who can provide them with useful resources and opportunities to achieve city interests. The urban regime thus formed enables cities to make and carry out governing decisions. The urban regime of informal groups and political leaders has always had participation from business interests. Cities encourage business investment in order to have an economically thriving

> ***Growth machines***: Markets and individuals in cities are socially structured in hierarchy based on inequality. The issue of growth separates local elite groups from the common people who mainly consider city as a place to live and work. Elites view cities that can increase aggregate rents and capture wealth for those in the right position to benefit. The desire for growth creates consensus among various groups of elites and thus cities become growth machines.
>
> ***Urban regime***: enables cities to make and carry out governing decisions. It includes informal groups and political leaders, and business interests. The urban regime is an informal arrangement between various interest groups that surround and complement the formal working of the government authority. Governmental conduct is constrained by the need to promote investment activity for economic growth in cities, which largely hinges on the resources controlled by business elites. The local public officials are more than willing to cooperate with those who can provide them with useful resources and opportunities to achieve city interests.

community. Businesses control important resources and cannot be left out of the political process of promoting economic growth.

Since the 1980s, economic development theory and practice have undergone major transformation. The earlier conventional approach was to look beyond the internal strengths and weaknesses of local community to promote economic growth and job creation. Within this paradigm, the attraction of external capital investment in the manufacturing sector was considered necessary for economic growth and job creation.[79] In terms of practice, M. Tietz notes in "Changes in Economic Development Theory and Practice," that the local Chamber of Commerce is the principal actor involved in promotional activity for attracting capital investments for local economic development. Most often, the endeavor is to establish large-scale branch plants with a sizeable number of new jobs. The local government and political elites partner with local businesses in forming pro-growth coalitions, according to Tietz. The local and state governments also offer incentives in the form of tax-breaks and cheap land to outside investors.

Within the new local economic development paradigm, however, the emphasis is on utilizing internal resources for economic growth and job creation. Local economic development is an endogenous phenomenon because local entrepreneurs create new firms and the existing local firms augment their capacities. Furthermore, the pro-growth coalition is highly professionalized, whether located within state and local governmental agencies or in nonprofit organizations. The new economic development theory and practice involve local demand management and, in order to do that, governments follow an entrepreneurial approach. The major activities under the new approach include emphasizing import substitutions, promoting local entrepreneurship, providing technical and financial assistance to existing local businesses, and forging private-public partnerships.

The old and new economic development approaches differ significantly in a number of ways. The new economic development initiatives focus growth and employment distribution. The old economic development paradigm was least sensitive to the spatial and demographic distribution of growth and employment. Secondly, it does a comparative evaluation of economic development across urban sub-communities through physical, social, and political lenses. Tietz notes that the old approach did not follow such a micro-level management of economic development. Thirdly, Tietz argues that competition for capital was the hallmark of old economic development theory and practice. However, under the new economic development paradigm, there is more emphasis on seeking cooperation and forming partnerships and networks. The competition has been relegated to a subsidiary role within the new approach. Finally, there are different political views on the two local economic development approaches. The pro-growth political group supports policies for attracting outside capital investments, whereas the new or "progressive" approach supports policies that promote local entrepreneurship and help local businesses grow.

79   See M. Tietz. "Changes in economic development theory and practice." *International Regional Science Review*, vol 16, no 1 (1994), pp 101–6.

6.4.4 Collaborative Governance and Strategies for Economic Development

M.E. Porter's prescription for inner-city development in "New Strategies for Inner-City Economic Development" aligns with the new economic development approach. Porter has emphasized the role of free market mechanisms in sustaining economic development. He argues that sustainable economic development in inner cities would occur "through private, for-profit initiatives, and investments based on economic self-interest and genuine competitive advantage instead of artificial inducements, government mandates, or charity."[80] Porter also contends that the interdependence of sub-regions is crucial in promoting sustainable economic development. He warns that treating inner cities as independent economies while implementing economic development strategies would not produce a sustainable and growing economy. Furthermore, economic development strategies would have to exploit and build on a local economic base and locational advantages of the inner-city. Specifically, the availability of modestly skilled and relatively lower-cost labor, high population density, and substantially large local markets with significant purchasing power offer good economic opportunities for local entrepreneurs and businesses. At the same time, Porter also suggests that the public sector should confine itself to the task of addressing disadvantages in inner cities as business locations. The new economic development school's ideas about enhancing local entrepreneurship and augmenting the capacities of local businesses are very similar to Porter's prescriptions about sustainable economic development, which are led by the private sector and based on local competitive advantage. Furthermore, as implied by the new economic development approach, Porter emphasizes the importance of economic inter-linkages between the inner-city economy and regional economy. He argues that the inner-city private businesses need to capitalize on nearby firm and industry clusters. In this cluster-based economic development strategy, businesses reap the benefits from external economies on account of large common markets, technological spillovers, and the common labor pool. These spillovers are present in regional economies composed of interconnected industry clusters.

> **Industry cluster:** is a group of firms, and related economic actors and institutions. They are located near one another and draw productive advantage from their mutual proximity and connections. The cluster based economic development policies are based on the fact that one firm's growth is tied to the growth of the other firms collectively.

> **Spillovers:** is a situation in a city in which price distortions lead to residents not paying the true costs associated with a particular institutional arrangement. It reflects that the preferences of the residents are not truly captured by the local governments for optimum tax-service package. Urban sprawl, segregation, overlapping infrastructure, and environmental pollution are key examples of spillovers.

---

80   M. E. Porter. "New strategies for inner-city economic development." *Economic Development Quarterly* 11 (1: 1997): 12.

However, the new economic development approach and Porter's prescriptions for inner-city development differ with regard to government and community-based organization (CBO) involvement in promoting local economic growth and job creation. Porter argues that governments and CBOs most often create impediments for the private sector in taking advantage of the economic opportunities in inner cities. He notes that governments have followed poor policies and not addressed disadvantages in terms of poor infrastructure and poorly skilled labor. The governments and CBOs have also created an unreasonable atmosphere of expectations, which tend to make businesses insecure. Porter, therefore, suggests that governments should focus their efforts on addressing local disadvantages and the role of CBOs should remain confined within service delivery. These two institutions should not get directly involved in economic development activities.

In terms of public policy prescriptions, Porter suggests that governments should work towards improving perceptions and the business environment in inner cities. Specifically, crime prevention, improving labor quality, upgrading infrastructure, assembling and improving business sites, and streamlining regulations are vital policy areas where government support is needed. Similarly, CBOs should also work toward facilitating private sector participation, training local residents and linking them to jobs, and improving perceptions about inner cities. Given the largely facilitating and enabling role of governments and CBOs, Porter argues that the private sector would find it profitable to engage in the economic development of inner cities. In their "friendly" critique to Porter's article, Bennett Harrison and Amy K. Glasmeier argue that governments and CBOs cannot play a passive role in promoting local economic development.[81] These authors argue that private-public partnerships and networks are also effective in promoting local economic development.

Many states and cities pursue industry cluster-based economic development strategies. Until the late 1970s, the local development strategy included firm-by-firm recruitment and retention without much consideration given to the strength and structure of local economies.[82] In "Making Sense of Clusters: Regional Competitiveness and Economic Development," Joseph Cortright views an industry cluster as "a group of firms, and related economic actors and institutions, that are located near one another and that draw productive advantage from their mutual proximity and connections."[83] Cluster-based economic development policies are based on the fact that one firm's growth is tied to the growth of the other firms, collectively. Malizia and Feser further note that this correlation occurs because businesses depend on common factors, technological spillovers, and the magnitude

81   See Bennett Harrison and Amy K. Glasmeier. "Response: why business alone won't redevelop the inner city: a friendly critique of Michael Porter's approach to urban revitalization." *Economic Development Quarterly* 11, no. 1 (1997): 28–38.

82   See V. Carlson, and Mattoon, R. "Industry Targeting: A New Approach to Local Economic Development." *Chicago Fed Letter*, Federal Reserve Bank of Chicago, v. 77, 1994; and E. Malizia and Feser, E. *Understanding Local Economic Development.* CUPR Press, 1999.

83   Joseph Cortright. "Making sense of clusters: regional competitiveness and economic development." Brookings Institution, Metropolitan Policy Program, 2006, 3.

of regional economic growth for prosperity. The connected and concentrated firms are most often engaged in the same product chain and have very similar technology and workforce requirements, as well. Economic development strategies based on industrial cluster theory assume the presence of just one economic sector. The product cycle theory, in contrast, predicts a diversified local economy in which standardized product diffusion takes place from developed regions to less developed regions. This product diffusion implies that the local economies attain economic stability based on multi-product and diverse industries.

Economic development under the product cycle theory is viewed as the introduction of new products and the process of diffusing standardized products across geographical spaces. The new products are introduced in more developed regions and then through trade and investment as such products are distributed to less developed regions. Malizia and Feser argue that less-developed regions have real growth opportunities based on product cycle theory propositions. Standardized product availability diversifies the range of consumption opportunities. Establishing new production units for producing standardized products in less developed areas would then lead to increased employment opportunities. There is also a beneficial opportunity for less-developed regions in terms of increased access to investments, loans, and grants from more developed regions. The increase in the number of standardized products would enhance the economic base's diversity. This dynamic is also important for the regional economy's stability. This diversification creates multiplier effects and leads to the establishment of new enterprises. As a result, there is economic growth and job creation.

Cluster-based strategies focus on industry linkages because the individual firm's success is linked to industry. These strategies also link a firm's growth with the common labor pool, other factors of production, technological progress, and overall economic growth. Cluster-based strategies also differ from fierce competition between firms. Cluster-based strategies seek cooperation between firms in bringing technological advancements. The cluster-based strategies recognize that technological advancement drives industry growth.

According to Malizia and Feser, two types of local development policies exist that use cluster-based strategies. One policy goal is to build new clusters and the other is to base economic development policies and programs on existing clusters. In the former, public officials and business leaders try to boost the identified cluster by concentrating on existing or emerging specializations. In the latter, the strategies at the local level focus on modernization. These strategies try to spur the adoption of advanced, flexible-production technologies among regional manufacturers. This is done by providing assistance and information to large regional end-market producers. These regional end-market producers influence the adoption of new and compatible technology by suppliers and contractors in the whole production chain. However, the extent of this diffusion depends on the production chain's strength. Information sharing within the cluster (production chain) may also flow to outside firms.

The goal of diversification strategies, on the other hand, is to attract innovative firms of all sizes that add to the competitive strength of large metropolitan economies in their long-term growth. These regional economies are the developed regions discussed in the product cycle theory that roll out a variety of new products. These products comprise the region's diverse export base and are traded to less-developed areas. After some time, these products mature, become standardized, and are ready to be produced in less-developed regions. A city's size is also very conducive for innovation and industry diversity. The economic development strategy in large cities is to combine entrepreneurship with immobile capital. This technique is used to ensure the flow of innovations and roll out of new products.

Malizia and Feser argue that regional economies differ according to a functional-occupational mix.[84] The functional side of a local economy signifies the mix of industries and specializations. The occupational-functional mix is a much broader concept and conveys the different types of work in cities to attain competitive advantages. These benefits include routine production, precision production, research and development, headquarters administration, and entrepreneurship. Most places possess less than three of these areas. For economic development, the short-term strategy is to exploit existing occupational strengths and specializations. In the long term, the availability and quality of developmental services, such as education, health, cultural activities, and diverse business and professional services, are essential for new products and businesses. The evaluation of a local economy in terms of occupational-functional mix says much about its place in the global economic hierarchy. The long-term development strategy identifies ways to achieve income and skills growth. But educational and infrastructural bottlenecks exist. The strategy is to encourage more innovations and diversify the economy's production base for promoting long-term stability in regions. The cluster-based strategies focus more narrowly on specialized industry growth. However, this exclusivity is not good for the region's economic stability.

There is a possibility of reconciling the strategies based on clusters and economic diversification. The occupational-functional mix analysis provides the relative strength of the local economy. If the economy is based on functional specialization, then the cluster-based strategy in the short-term makes more sense because of the linkages between firms in the product chain for knowledge sharing and improved technologies adoption are strengthened. In the long run, economic developers need to identify ways to improve skills sets, diversify the production base, bring in flexible production practices, and encourage business and financial development services so that the local economy is conducive for innovation. Innovations and entrepreneurship are necessary for economic diversity and long-term economic stability. Thus, the cluster-based strategies are a precursor to economic diversity-based strategies.

---

84   See Malizia and Feser, *Understanding Local Economic Development.*

6.5 COLLABORATIVE NETWORKS IN GOVERNMENTS IN THE AMERICAN FEDERALISM

Governments in the nation significantly rely upon partnerships with other governments at different levels, including the federal government, other countries of the world, states in the nation, and, of course, local governments for providing public goods and services. The non-governmental sector, including for-profit private organizations, also prominently participate in this form of networked governance. According to Russell L. Hanson, some examples of collaborative networks among states in the U.S. and other countries of the world include the Great Lakes-St. Lawrence Water Resources compact, which was

Figure 6.26: Federal, State, and local Manchester, Iowa emergency management officials meet prior to going into the field to initiate a preliminary damage assessment in Delaware county.
Source: Wikimedia Commons
Attribution: Josh deBerge
License: Public Domain

made between American states and Canadian provinces for managing the world's largest surface freshwater system; the North American Clean Air Alliance, between northeastern U.S. states and Canadian provinces for controlling air pollution by promoting the commercial development of emission free vehicles; and the partnership between U.S. and Mexican states along the Rio Grande for checking the spread of tuberculosis, regulating international trucking, and allocating water resources.[85]

6.5.1 Collaborative Networks among State Governments

States manage economic ties with other countries as part of their strategy for promoting economic growth and development. Hanson notes that states focus considerably on foreign trade by promoting overseas markets, providing information and technical assistance to exporting firms, capitalizing on their activities, and conducting trade missions. For resolving new conflicts concerning natural boundaries, pollution, competition for businesses, and moving welfare recipients to other states, states cooperate through interstate compacts, as discussed in chapter 5. The average state has membership in 25 compacts.[86] These compacts span issues including conservation and resource management, pollution management, law enforcement, transportation, interstate waterways, and metropolitan development, among several others. Several of these compacts have federal agencies as members. The Delaware River Compact and the Colorado

---

85 See Russell L. Hanson. "Chapter 2: Intergovernmental Relations." In Gray, Virginia, Russell L. Hanson, and Thad Kousser (eds), *Politics in the American states: A comparative analysis*. CQ Press, 2017. Pp. 28–55.
86 See Russell L. Hanson. "Chapter 2: Intergovernmental Relations." In Gray, Virginia, Russell L. Hanson, and Thad Kousser (eds), *Politics in the American states: A comparative analysis*. CQ Press, 2017. Pp. 28–55.

River Compact are examples in which states come together to share water without Congressional or the Supreme Court's help.[87] States also reciprocate and cooperate in offering in-state tuitions in their public universities to residents of adjacent states. States recognize licensure of teachers, real estate agents, and other professions as part of their cooperative agreements with other states. In addition, state attorney generals come together to fight public welfare lawsuits against powerful corporations, such as tobacco companies. State administrators routinely share information with each other and lobby together on common issues. There are associations that vehemently oppose federal interference in governance issues that fall within state rights and local autonomy. These voices generally arise from the National Governors Association, National Conference of State Legislatures, National League of Cities, U.S. Conference of Mayors, and National Association of Counties.

6.5.2 Collaborative Networks in State and Local Governments

State governments also coordinate relations among a large number of local governments. Although local governments are the creatures of state government, an overwhelming majority of them have home rule charters, as discussed in chapter 1. This implies that local governments enjoy a substantial degree of autonomy, and state governments are generally responsive to the wishes of local governments that have home rule charters. Local governments have been extensively studied in terms of their governing structures, key services, tax sources, two-way relations with states and other local governments, relations with the private and nongovernmental sector, and key associations of the local governments at state, national, and international levels. Public choice theory provides support for the organization of the local government and their optimal level of expenditure on public goods. Tiebout, in his seminal paper, "A Pure Theory of Local Expenditure," responded to the public finance theory propagated by Richard A. Musgrave and Paul A. Samuelson.[88] The basic argument that the two writers agreed on was that the optimal level of expenditure on public goods is indeterminate and the national income allocated on providing such goods is non-optimal when compared with the allocation on private goods. Tiebout argued that the "market failure" in public goods' provision in the national government's case does not hold at the local level of government. He argued that the preferences of residents in a local government's jurisdiction can be captured more adequately than at the national level, and the solution for the level of local expenditure on public goods can be found there.

The basic argument is that residents in local communities consciously choose to live within a local government jurisdiction boundary and thereby ensure efficient delivery of public goods and services. The residents reveal their preferences by

87   See Russell L. Hanson. "Chapter 2: Intergovernmental Relations." In Gray, Virginia, Russell L. Hanson, and Thad Kousser (eds), *Politics in the American states: A comparative analysis.* CQ Press, 2017. Pp. 28–55.
88   See Tiebout, "A Pure Theory of Local Expenditure."

choosing a package of public goods and services offered by local governments. The pursuit of optimum size (the bundle of goods and services) is essential in order to lower the average cost of public goods and services. By choosing to reside in a community, the resident reveals their preferences or willingness to pay, and the local government can tax the community in order to sustain the level of expenditure.

Vincent Ostrom, Charles Tiebout, and R. Warren further expanded this model.[89] Lyons and Lowery note that the "model focuses on the need to maintain numerous units of local governments in each urban area in order to maximize opportunities for individual citizens to choose a tax-service package that best suits their needs."[90] While comparing the central propositions in the debate for metropolitan reform in the traditions of consolidation vs. public choice-based polycentric local governments, Ostrom ascribes a set of propositions to the latter.[91] These are as follows:

A. Whether increasing the size of urban governmental units will be associated with a higher output per capita, more efficient provision of services, more equal distribution of costs to beneficiaries depends upon the type of public good or service being considered.

B. Increasing the size of urban governmental units will be associated with decreased responsibility of local officials and decreased participation by citizens.

C. Increasing the size of the governmental units will be associated with a greater utilization of hierarchy as an organizing principle.

D. Whether reducing the number of public agencies within a metropolitan area will be associated with a higher output per capita, more efficient provision of services, and more equal distribution of costs to beneficiaries depends upon the type of public good or service being considered.

E. Reducing the number of public agencies within a metropolitan area will be associated with less responsibility of public officials.

F. Reducing the number of public agencies within a metropolitan area will increase the reliance upon hierarchy as an organizing principle within the metropolitan area.

G. Whether increasing the reliance upon hierarchy as an organizing principle within the metropolitan area will be associated with higher output per capita and more efficient provision of services depends upon the type of public good or service being considered.

---

89   See V. Ostrom , Tiebout, C. M., and Warren, R. "The Organization of Government in Metropolitan Areas: A Theoretical Inquiry." *American Political Science Review*, 55(4) (1961): 831-842.

90   W. Lyons and Lowery, D. "Governmental Fragmentation Versus Consolidation: Five Public Choice Myths about How To Create Informed, Involved, and Happy Citizens." *Public Administration Review*, 49 (1989): 533.

91   Elinor Ostrom. "Metropolitan reform: Propositions derived from two traditions." *Social Science Quarterly* (1972): 486.

H. Increasing the reliance upon hierarchy as an organizing principle within the metropolitan area is associated with decreased participation by citizens and responsibility of local officials.

Lyons and Lowery have investigated the empirical veracity of five propositions in the public-choice model that advance contrasting arguments about fragmentation versus consolidation of local governments based on the citizens' evaluation of urban governments and the services they provide. The data collected by the authors pertain to citizens' responses from both fragmented and consolidated governments. Lyons and Lowery undertook citizen surveys in two counties. The Louisville-Jefferson county has about 100 municipalities and, hence, has a highly-fragmented system of governments. The Lexington-Fayette county is, by contrast, consolidated. The findings in this paper do not support the basic arguments contained in the public-choice theory.[92] The authors found that citizens living in smaller local jurisdictions located in the more fragmented system were not better informed about the scope and nature of their local tax-service package; they were not more efficacious about their relationships with their local governments; they were not more likely to participate in local affairs; and they were not more satisfied with their local services and the performance of their local governments than their counterparts living in the consolidated setting. Nor did the evidence support the public-choice contention that satisfaction with local services is more widely dispersed across local jurisdictions in more fragmented systems.

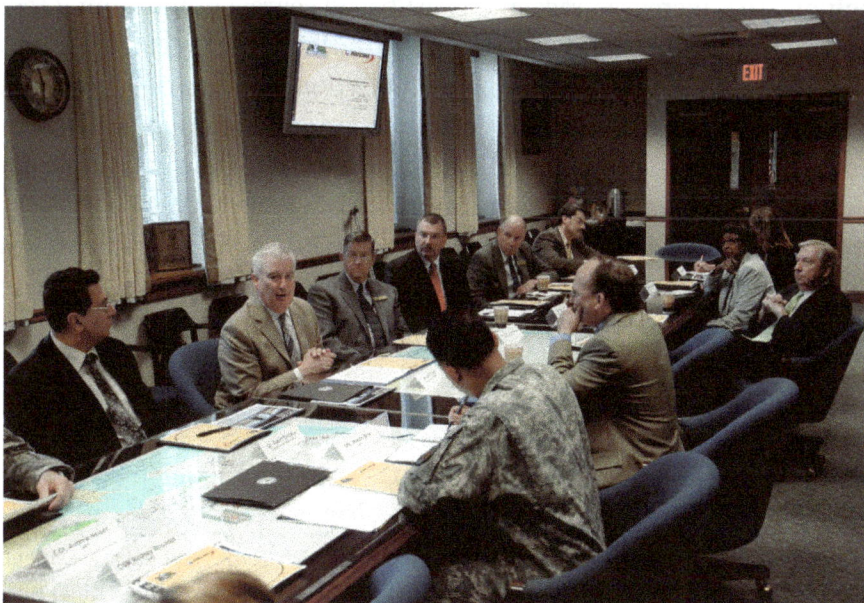

Figure 6.27: Harford County officials met with Aberdeen Proving Ground leaders April 16 to discuss current issues.
Source: Wikimedia Commons
Attribution: U.S. Army RDECOM
License: Public Domain

92   Lyons and Lowery, "Governmental Fragmentation Versus Consolidation: Five Public Choice Myths about How to Create Informed, Involved, and Happy Citizens." 533.

Other than the lack of empirical support for the public-choice theory's central propositions on fragmented governments, as pointed out by Lyons and Lowery, spillovers also exist in fragmented governments. The essential argument is that polycentric governments cause spillover problems and, hence, the solution suggested may no longer be efficient. The criticism from this theoretical angle has brought the polycentric theory of local governments to the initial point from where Tiebout began his seminal work. The free rider problem and spillover effects are well-accepted phenomenon associated with the provision of public goods and services at much larger levels of government. These phenomena make public goods provision inefficient, e.g., there is no market-type solution.

In "The Tiebout Hypothesis 50 Years Later: Lessons and Lingering Challenges for Metropolitan Governance in the 21st Century," Michael Howell-Moroney has brought out such concerns with the central assumptions in the public choice model of fragmented local governments and the ground realities in which such polycentric governments work. He notes that "the residential segregation of people by race and class and the many costs of sprawl are magnified and augmented by arrangements that defer to multiple local jurisdictions."[93] These spillovers lead to price distortions, and people do not pay true costs associated with a particular institutional arrangement. In this way, the preferences of the residents are not truly captured by the local governments for an optimum tax-service package. The important arguments that highlight the problem associated with spillover include the extra costs of urban development borne by other communities in the same metropolitan area, increased race and class-based segregation draining resources from central city areas, cross-municipal subsidization of infrastructure, and sprawl impacting the environment, including air pollution because of high automobile use in low-density American cities. The consolidation reform advocates argue that spillovers are occurring within the metropolitan area, implying that the fragmented local governments are not able to capture costs arising due to the polycentric nature of institutional arrangements within those areas. The implicit argument is that the consolidated metropolitan government can capture these spillovers and costs due to sprawl.[94]

6.5.3 Collaborative Networks, Local Governments, and Regionalism

In response to this conflict of ideas about local governments, considerable interest has arisen in regionalism among public officials and civil society leaders over the last several decades. This interest results from challenges in solving problems that

Regionalism: is governance at the regional scale. It entails shifting authority and functions from local, state or national governments to regional entities.

93 M. Howell-Moroney. "The Tiebout Hypothesis 50 Years Later: Lessons and Lingering Challenges for Metropolitan Governance in the 21st Century." *Public Administration Review* 68 (1: 2008): 100.
94 See Robert E. England, John P. Pelissero, and David R. Morgan. *Managing Urban America*. CQ Press, 2016.

overlap many local political boundaries within a metropolitan region, problems such as urban sprawl, declining regional economies, environmental degradation, incoherent land use policy, inequities in housing, education, and tax policy within the region. Regionalism generally means "ways of thinking and acting at the regional scale."[95] Specifically, regionalism "refer[s] to shifting authority and functions from local, state or national governments to regional entities"[96] Regionalism has various forms, including structure, programs and policies, partnerships and agreements, processes, practices, and cultural expression. In *Regionalism on Purpose*, Kathryn Ann Foster provides an example for each of these forms. City-county consolidation exemplifies structural regionalism; regional fair-share housing policy exemplifies regionalism in the form of programs and policies; inter-local compact is a manifestation of regionalism as partnerships and agreements; regional forums are an expression of regionalism in the form of processes and practices; and regional norms, or logos, are cultural expressions of the same concept.

Regionalism is suitable in conditions including economies of scale, spillover effects, need for cross-border cooperation, residents' preferences, need for standardization, equity, and threshold levels. Foster argues that, although local governments cannot address certain problems in isolation, metropolitan areas can on account of their scale. Complicated problems, such as urban sprawl and environmental pollution, affect more than one locality, requiring a coordinated effort on the part of local governments to tailor solutions for such concerns. Foster further argues that regional governance is more suitable when the goal is to achieve equity and environmental sustainability. The traditional reliance on local governments is preferable if the goal is to ensure political participation and accountability. With regard to efficiency and economic growth, the two systems of governance fare equally well. Summers emphasizes the importance of externalities and service-size optimization in regionalism. The author argues that, even with resource redistribution in the form of intergovernmental aid, the local jurisdiction bears significant costs associated with metropolitan-wide, poverty-related programs, such as public welfare and hospitals, as well as other functions, such as police and education services, because certain services are less costly to provide if they serve a certain threshold limit. Examples of services with optimal threshold limits include public transportation, solid waste disposal, and centralized purchasing.[97] Because he considers federal administration of housing and workforce policy as fragmented and obstacles in regional cooperation, Hughes suggests that these programs could be better administered at the metropolitan level, either through structural consolidation or functional consolidation.[98] R. Voith argues in "Do Suburbs Need Cities?" that suburbs do well in terms of housing

95   Kathryn Ann Foster. *Regionalism on purpose*. Lincoln Institute of Land Policy, 2001, 1.
96   Kathryn Ann Foster. *Regionalism on purpose*. Lincoln Institute of Land Policy, 2001, 7.
97   See A. Summers. "Regionalization Efforts Between Big Cities and Their Suburbs." In R. Greenstein and W. Wiewel (eds), *Urban- Suburban Interdependencies*, pp. 181–193. Cambridge: The Lincoln Institute of Land Policy, 2000.
98   See M.A. Hughes. "Federal Roadblocks to Regional Cooperation." In R. Greenstein and W. Wiewel (eds), *Urban- Suburban Interdependencies*, pp. 161-180. Cambridge: The Lincoln Institute of Land Policy, 2000.

values and family incomes if income in their central cities also rise. This externality supports regionalism and cooperative networks in metropolitan areas.[99]

Foster has listed a comprehensive set of factors that decide whether a service should be provided regionally or locally. Services such as sewer and water, utilities, airports, highways, transit, environment planning, and management require economies of scale, large service areas, narrow preferences, high levels of cross-border cooperation, and standardization in delivery. These considerations favor regionalism in the provision of such services. However, services such as police control, fire, community development, local planning and zoning, schools, parks, libraries, garbage collection, etc., are better suited to local provision. This is due to an absence of economies of scale, no threshold being required, preferences being wide—which require little cross-border cooperation—and no standardization being required.

Foster argues that residents of a metropolitan region come in contact with each other on a regular basis. They share their place-related ideas, problems, and matters of significance for the metropolitan region. This interaction culminates in a broader sense of metropolitan community. Problems such as air pollution, transportation planning, employment, and global competitiveness are viewed at the regional level. Services such as police control, fire, community development, etc., are generally viewed locally. He writes, "As more frequent and durable cross-border links turn once local problems into metropolitan ones, regions gain significance."[100] However, there are philosophical, political, governance, and empirical challenges to regional action, according to Foster. Philosophically, it is imperative to strike a balance between individual freedom and the common good. Regional action creates winners and losers which, in turn, creates political conflict. Normally, residents are more loyal to their local communities than to the whole region. Regional action has to overcome this political challenge. However, regions lack formal structure or authority to realize metropolitan public good. Lastly, a lack of conclusive evidence in support of regionalism's effects on economic development weakens the regionalism argument.

Implementing regional action involves two important issues to consider. First, Foster makes the case that regionalism must conform to the equivalence principle. Second, Benjamin Higgins and Donald Savoie suggest in *Regional Development Theories and Their Application* that development planning and policy should be

The equivalence principle: of governance implies that the decision-making unit(s) of government(s) in solving a problem should share the financing proportionally according to the area affected.

done at the level of the smallest possible decision-making unit. The equivalence principle of governance implies that "the decision-making unit of a problem should equate to both its financing unit and the area affected."[101] These two principles

99   See R. Voith. "Do Suburbs Need Cities?" *Journal of Regional Science*, 38(3) (1998): 445–464
100 Foster, *Regionalism on purpose*, 4.
101 Foster, *Regionalism on purpose*, 4.

together imply that services for solving problems transcending local boundaries should come through regional action. The local provision is more suitable in the absence of any spillover. The equivalence principle is consistent with economies of scale, equity, and standardization of services because these issues have regional reach. Since regional problems involve more than one community, regional action conforms to the bottom-up planning and policy approach suggested by Higgins and Savoie. They have argued that "there are development activities which cannot be handled exclusively at the local level but which need not go to the national level. These are the proper concern of the regional authorities."[102]

Higgins and Savoie also argue that the planning process in development planning and policy must ensure that the measurement of public projects' costs and benefits follow norms and weights suggested by target populations. Professional planners should advise the target population instead of governments. A collective decision-making should occur rather than decisions being made by elected officials. Regional planners should remain at the core of the overall economic, social, and political development process. The authors argue against the system of planning and policymaking by central governments as this type of bureaucratic means for implementing regional programs has not proved successful. Therefore, Higgins and Savoie argue that the collective effort of local communities in solving regional problems is true regionalism and that local communities should manage regional development on their own. According to England, et al., the Metropolitan Planning Organization (MPO) and Council of Governments are two particularly cooperative organizations[103] that exist at the regional scale and provide platforms for intergovernmental networking at the regional level.

6.6 CONCLUSION

This chapter discusses the theories and models concerning collaborative network management, including its key characteristics. As grounded in ideas pertaining to IGM, this chapter also covers intra- and inter-state dimensions of intergovernmental networks. It discusses collaborative intergovernmental network management and its features and covers the behaviors and characteristics of both networks and managers handling those networks. It then considers how policy entrepreneurs in various intergovernmental networks bring about public policy innovation and diffusion for solving public problems. These policy entrepreneurs utilize resources and information within their policy networks to achieve their goals of finding appropriate policy solutions for contemporary problems. The chapter further explains the historical evolution and role of intergovernmental collaborative networks in solving some of the difficult problems in regional economic development. Finally, this chapter documents how collaborative networks help local, state, and federal governments in governance by facilitating

102 Benjamin Higgins and J. Donald Savoie. *Regional Development Theories and their Application.* New Brunswick, US: Transaction Publishers, 1995, 402.
103 England et al., *Managing Urban America*, 61–62.

joint public problem solving. These topics constitute the practical side of performing administrative duties in the public-non-governmental sector. And this chapter also captures the complex empirical side of federalism in the U.S. Grasping the contents of this chapter is, therefore, practically important for aspiring public administrators.

REFLECTION QUESTIONS

9. Consider the structure of and managerial behavior in Collaborative Intergovernmental Networks. Discuss how the various network structures influence different types of managerial behavior. List some of the activities that managers perform in actual network settings.

10. Discuss how policy entrepreneurs act as agents of policy change. Critically analyze and explain how policy entrepreneurs utilize network in policy diffusion. How do policy subsystems help in understanding policy entrepreneurs' roles in policy diffusion?

11. Elaborate on the question concerning how the economic imperative of growth has propelled cities in pursuing collaborative governance. Discuss the "urban regime" and "growth machine" concepts in this context.

12. Consider the new economic development theory. How does it differ from earlier approaches? Discuss the various economic growth and job creation strategies that cities can follow under the new economic development paradigm.

13. Discuss the various collaborative networks that states enter for governance. Given that local governments are creatures of their respective state governments, how do local governments utilize networks and other resources in solving problems that transcend their jurisdictional boundaries? Does regionalism help in this regard, why or why not?

BIBLIOGRAPHY

Agranoff, R. *Managing within Networks: Adding Value to Public Organizations.* Washington, DC: Georgetown University Press, 2007.

Agranoff, Robert, and Michael McGuire. "Managing in network settings." *Review of Policy Research* 16, no. 1 (1999): 18–41.

Agranoff, Robert, and Michael McGuire. "American Federalism and the Search for Models of Management." *Public Administration Review* 61, no. 6 (Nov.-Dec., 2001): 671–677.

Agranoff, Robert, and Michael McGuire. *Collaborative Public Management: New Strategies for Local Governments.* Washington, DC: Georgetown University Press, 2003.

Agranoff, Robert. "Inside collaborative networks: Ten lessons for public managers." *Public Administration Review* 66 (2006): 56–65.

Baracskay, Daniel. "Chapter 1 in Intergovernmental Behavior in American Federalism." University of North Georgia Press, 2021.

Bartelings, J. A., J. Goedee, J. Raab, and R. Bijl. "The Nature of Orchestrational Work." *Public Management Review* 19 (3: 2017): 342–360. doi:10.1080/14719037.2016.120 9233.

Baumgartner, Frank R., and Bryan D. Jones. *Agendas and Instability in American Politics.* Chicago: University of Chicago Press,1993.

Berry, Frances and William D. Berry. "Innovation and Diffusion Models in Policy Research." In Paul A. Sabatier (ed.) *Theories of the Policy Process*, 2nd edition, Chapter 6. Boulder, Colorado: Westview Press, 2007.

Carlson, V., and Mattoon, R. "Industry Targeting: A New Approach to Local Economic Development." *Chicago Fed Letter*, Federal Reserve Bank of Chicago, v. 77, 1994.

Cortright, Joseph. "Making sense of clusters: regional competitiveness and economic development." Brookings Institution, Metropolitan Policy Program, 2006.

Cristofoli, D., and J. Markovic. "How To Make Public Networks Really Work: A Qualitative Comparative Analysis." *Public Administration* 94 (1: 2016): 89–110. doi:10.1111/padm.2016.94.issue-1.

Cristofoli, Daniela, Benedetta Trivellato, and Stefano Verzillo. "Network management as a contingent activity. A configurational analysis of managerial behaviors in different network settings." *Public Management Review*, 21 (12: 2019), 1775–1800, DOI: 10.1080/14719037.2019.1577905

Edelenbos, J., and E. Klijn. "Managing Stakeholder Involvement in Decision Making: A Comparative Analysis of Six Interactive Processes in the Netherlands." *Journal of Public Administration Research & Theory* 16 (3: 2006): 417. doi:10.1093/jopart/mui049.

Emerson, Kirk, Tina Nabatchi, and Stephen Balogh. "An integrative framework for collaborative governance." *Journal of Public Administration Research and Theory* 22, no. 1 (2012): 1–29.

England, Robert E., John P. Pelissero, and David R. Morgan. *Managing Urban America.* CQ Press, 2016. Foster, Kathryn Ann. *Regionalism on purpose.* Lincoln Institute of Land Policy, 2001.

Glick, Henry R. and Scott P. Hays. "Innovation and Reinvention in State Policymaking: Theory and the Evolution of Living Wills Laws." *Journal of Politics*, 53 (3: 1991): 535–550.

Hanson, Russell L. "Chapter 2: Intergovernmental Relations." In Gray, Virginia, Russell L. Hanson, and Thad Kousser (eds), *Politics in the American states: A comparative analysis.* CQ Press, 2017. Pp. 28–55.

Harrison, Bennett, and Amy K. Glasmeler. "Response: why business alone won't redevelop the inner city: a friendly critique of Michael Porter's approach to urban revitalization." *Economic Development Quarterly* 11, no. 1 (1997): 28–38.

Hewlett, Michael and M. Ramesh. "Policy subsystem configurations and policy change: Operationalizing the Postpositivist Analysis of the Politics of the Policy Process." *Policy Studies Journal*, 26 (3: 1998): 466–481.

Higgins, Benjamin, and J. Donald Savoie. *Regional Development Theories and their Application*. New Brunswick, US: Transaction Publishers, 1995.

Hovik, S., and G. S. Hanssen. "The Impact of Network Management and Complexity on Multi-Level Coordination." *Public Administration* 93 (2015): 506–523. doi:10.1111/padm.12135.

Howell-Moroney, M. "The Tiebout Hypothesis 50 Years Later: Lessons and Lingering Challenges for Metropolitan Governance in the 21st Century." Public Administration Review 68 (1: 2008): 97–109.

Hughes, M.A. "Federal Roadblocks to Regional Cooperation." In R. Greenstein and W. Wiewel (eds), *Urban- Suburban Interdependencies*, pp. 161–180. Cambridge: The Lincoln Institute of Land Policy, 2000.

Kenis, P., and K. Provan. "Towards an Exogenous Theory of Public Network Performance." *Public Administration* 87 (3: 2009): 440–456. doi:10.1111/padm.2009.87.issue-3.

Kilduff, M., and Tsai, W. *Social networks and organizations*. London, England: SAGE, 2003.

Kingdon, John W. *Agendas, Alternatives, And Public Policies*. New York: Harper Collins, 1984 & 1995.

Klijn, E. H., B. Steijn, and J. Edelenbos. "The Impact of Network Management on Outcomes in Governance Networks." *Public Administration* 88 (4: 2010a): 1063–1082. doi:10.1111/j.14679299.2010.01826.x.

Klijn, E. H., B. Steijn, and J. Edelenbos. "Trust in Governance Networks: Its Impacts on Outcomes." *Administration and Society* 42 (2: 2010b): 193–221. doi:10.1177/0095399710362716.

Klijn, E. H., V. Sierra, T. Ysa, E. Berman, J. Edelenbos, and D. Y. Chen. "The Influence of Trust on Network Performance in Taiwan, Spain, and the Netherlands: A Cross-Country Comparison." *International Public Management Journal* 19 (1: 2016.): 111–139. doi:10.1080/10967494.2015.1115790.

Koliba, C., S. Wiltshire,S, D. Turner, A. Zia, and E. Campbell. "The Critical Role of Information Sharing to the Value Proposition of a Food Systems Network." *Public Management Review* 19 (3: 2017): 284–304. doi: 10.1080/14719037.2016.1209235.

Kort, M., and E. Klijn. "Public-Private Partnerships in Urban Regeneration Projects: Organizational Form or Managerial Capacity?" *Public Administration Review* 71 (4: 2011): 618–626. doi:10.1111/puar.2011.71.issue-4.

Lindblom, C. E. "The Science of Muddling Through." *Public Administration Review*, vol.

19 (Spring issue, 1959): p 79–88.

Lipnack, Jessica, and Jeffrey Stamps. *The Age of the Network*. New York: Wiley, 1994.

Logan, John R., and Harvey Luskin Molotch. *Urban Fortunes: The Political Economy of Place*. Univ of California Press, 1987.

Lyons, W. and Lowery, D. "Governmental Fragmentation Versus Consolidation: Five Public Choice Myths about How To Create Informed, Involved, and Happy Citizens." *Public Administration Review*, 49 (1989): 533–43.

Majone, Giandomenico. *Evidence Argument and Persuasion in the Policy Process*. Yale University Press, 1989. Malizia, E. and Feser, E. *Understanding Local Economic Development*. CUPR Press, 1999.

McGuire, M. "Managing Networks: Propositions on What Managers Do and Why They Do It." *Public Administration Review* 62 (5: 2002): 599–609. doi:10.1111/puar.2002.62. issue-5.

Milward, H. Brinton. "Mapping the Linkage Structure of Networks", Paper presented at *Conference on Network Analysis on Innovations in Public Programs*, LaFollette Institute of Public Affairs, University of Wisconsin, 1994.

Mintrom, Michael and Sandra Vergari. "Advocacy Coalitions, Policy Entrepreneurs and Policy Change." *Policy Studies Journal* 24 (1996): 420–438.

Mintrom, Michael, and Sandra Vergari. "Charter schools as a state policy innovation: Assessing recent developments." *State and Local Government Review* 29, no. 1 (1997): 43–49.

Mintrom, Michael. "Policy Entrepreneurs and the Diffusion of Innovation." *American Journal of Political Science*, 41(3: 1997): 738–770.

O'Toole, Laurence J., Jr. "Treating Networks Seriously: Practical and Research-Based Agendas in Public Administration." *Public Administration Review* 57 (1: 1997): 45–52.

Ostrom, Elinor. "Metropolitan reform: Propositions derived from two traditions." *Social Science Quarterly* (1972): 474–493.

Ostrom, V., Tiebout, C. M., and Warren, R. "The Organization of Government in Metropolitan Areas: A Theoretical Inquiry." *American Political Science Review*, 55(4) (1961): 831–842.

Paul Sabatier. "The Suitability of Several Models for the Comparative Analysis of the Policy Process." In Robert McKinlay and Louis Imbeau (eds) *Comparing Government Activity*, London: Macmillan, 1996, pp. 101–117.

Peterson, Paul E. *City Limits*. University of Chicago Press, 1981.

Porter, Michael E. "New strategies for inner-city economic development." *Economic Development Quarterly* 11, no. 1 (1997): 11–27.

Powell, Walter W. "Neither Market nor Hierarchy: Network Forms of Organization." In Barry M. Staww and Larry L. Cummings (eds) *Research in Organizational Behavior*,

Vol. 12, 295–336. Greenwich, CT: JAI Press, 1990.

Provan, K. G., and P. Kenis. "Modes of Network Governance: Structure, Management and Effectiveness." *Journal of Public Administration Research and Theory* 18 (2: 2008): 229–252. doi:10.1093/jopart/mum015.

Provan, K. G., K. Huang, and H. B. Milward. "The Evolution of Structural Embeddedness and Organizational Social Outcomes in a Centrally Governed Health and Human Services Network." *Journal of Public Administration Research and Theory* 19 (2009): 873–893. doi:10.1093/jopart/muno36.

Raab, J., R. S. Mannak, and B. Cambré. "Combining Structure, Governance, and Context: A Configurational Approach to Network Effectiveness." *Journal of Public Administration Research and Theory* 25 (2: 2015): 479–511. doi:10.1093/jopart/muto39.

Riker, William H. *The art of political manipulation*. New Haven: Yale University Press, 1986.

Rogers, E. M. *Diffusion of innovations*. New York: Free Press, 1983 (3rd ed.).

Sabatier, Paul A. and Hank C. Jenkins-Smith. *Policy Change and Learning: An Advocacy Coalition Approach*. Boulder, CO: Westview Press, 1988.

Schulman, Paul R. "Nonincremental Policy Making." *American Political Science Review*, 69 (4: 1975): 1354–1370.

Silke, Adam, and Hanspeter Kriesi. "The Network Approach." In Paul A. Sabatier, ed. *Theories of the Policy Process*, 2nd ed. Chapter 5. Boulder, Colorado: Westview Press, 2007.

Stone, Clarence Nathan. *Regime Politics: Governing Atlanta, 1946-1988*. University press of Kansas, 1989.

Stone, Deborah A. "Causal stories and the formation of policy agendas." *Political Science Quarterly* 104, no. 2 (1989): 281–300.

Summers, A. "Regionalization Efforts Between Big Cities and Their Suburbs." In R. Greenstein and W. Wiewel (eds), *Urban- Suburban Interdependencies*, pp. 181–193. Cambridge: The Lincoln Institute of Land Policy, 2000.

Tiebout, Charles. "A Pure Theory of Local Expenditure." *Journal of Political Economy*, 64 (1956, October): 416–24.

Tietz, M. "Changes in economic development theory and practice." *International Regional Science Review*, vol 16, no 1 (1994), pp 101–6.

True, L. James, Bryan D. Jones, and Frank R. Baumgartner. "Punctuated-Equilibrium Theory: Explaining Stability and Change in Public Policymaking." In Paul A. Sabatier (ed) *Theories of the Policy Process*, 2nd ed. Chapter 6. Boulder, Colorado: West view Press, 2007.

Van Raaij, D. P. A. M. "Norms Network Members Use: An Alternative Perspective for Indicating Network Success or Failure." *International Public Management Journal* 9 (3: 2006): 249–270. doi:10.1080/10967490600899549.

Verweij, S., E. H. Klijn, J. Edelenbos, and M. W. Van Buuren. "What Makes Governance Networks Work? A Fuzzy Set Qualitative Comparative Analysis of 14 Dutch Spatial Planning Projects." *Public Administration: An International Quarterly* 91 (4: 2013): 1035–1055. doi:10.1111/ padm.12007.

Voith, R. "Do Suburbs Need Cities?" *Journal of Regional Science*, 38(3) (1998): 445–464.

Wachhaus, Aaron. "Building Health Communities: Local Health Care Networks in Maryland." *The American Review of Public Administration* 50, no. 1 (2020): 62–76.

Wildavsky, A. *The Politics of the Budgetary Process*. Toronto, Little, Brown and Co., 1964.

Wright, Deil S., Carl W. Stenberg, and Chung-Lae Cho. "Historic Relevance Confronting Contemporary Obsolescence?" In Menzel, Donald C., and Jay D. White (eds), *The State of Public Administration: Issues, Challenges, and Opportunities*. Routledge, 2015: 297.

Ysa, T., V. Sierra, and M. Esteve. "Determinants of Network Outcomes: The Impact of Management Strategies." *Public Administration* 92 (3: 2014): 636–655.

Zahariadas, Nikolas. "The Multiple Streams Framework." In Paul A. Sabatier (ed), *Theories of the Policy Process, 2nd ed.* Chapter 3, Boulder, Colorado: Westview Press. 2007.

7

Public Education as a Dimension of Intergovernmental Relations

Neena Banerjee

LEARNING OBJECTIVES

- Develop an understanding of the historic debates surrounding authority and responsibility distribution in education policy and the struggle to balance individual freedom through local control vis-à-vis state authority.

- Demonstrate an understanding of the American federal system's nature concerning decision-making in public education as a facet of intergovernmental relations.

- Develop an understanding of what roles educational institutions play at the federal, state, and local levels as part of intergovernmental relations and management.

- Demonstrate an understanding of the various intergovernmental relations phases in public education through an exploration of prominent education policy initiatives, such as the No Child Left Behind Act, Race to the Top, and Common Core State Standards programs.

- Demonstrate knowledge of the role that courts have played in influencing important education policy initiatives in an intergovernmental context.

- Demonstrate an understanding of non-governmental organizations' roles in public education.

KEY TERMS

Positive Externalities	Distributional Inequity
OECD	Street Level Bureaucrats
Collective Bargaining Laws	Common Schools
Charter Schools	Liberalism

7.1 INTRODUCTION

Figure 7.1: President Obama announces a proposed $1.3 billion investment in Race to the Top, a program to encourage innovation and excellence in education through competitive grants, at an event at Graham Road Elementary School in Falls Church, VA.
Source: Wikimedia Commons
Attribution: White House video
License: Public Domain

Positive externalities: education produces many positive externalities for the society at large. An educated workforce benefits the economy, the society benefits from having responsible citizens willing to participate in the functioning of a democratic society.

Distributional inequity: occurs when there are widespread disparities in funding levels between local school districts and between schools within such districts. Such disparities often lead to unequal access to quality schools for students from lower socioeconomic status and ultimately achievement gaps across socioeconomic and ethno-racial groups.

OECD countries: refers to the Organization for Economic Co-operation and Development. Founded in 1961, it is an intergovernmental economic organization with 37 member countries who work together on global issues to stimulate economic growth and world trade.

We know from preceding chapters that intergovernmental relations (IGR) are politically charged and have significant fiscal and administrative dimensions that affect the nature of policy making. The policy process has been examined throughout this book as being endemic to intergovernmental behavior, with chapter 6 particularly delineating how collaboration has become a strategy of intergovernmental management (IGM) that has allowed governmental and non-governmental organizations in society to work together to achieve common goals. The policy-making theme continues in this chapter with a detailed treatment of education as a core issue area of American government. Notwithstanding Americans' tremendous faith in the power of education to uplift individuals and communities, some have criticized the role of government in educational provision. The government remains the primary provider of public education in the U.S. As Sandra Vergari notes in her article "Safeguarding Federalism in Education Policy in Canada and the United States," government intervention in education has historically been justified on the grounds of many positive externalities that are associated with education as well as its desire to address distributional inequity.[1] The extent of the government's role in K–12 education in the U.S. can be gauged by examining simple statistical data. Public education spending has increased five-fold in real dollars over the last century and

---

1   Sandra Vergari. Safeguarding Federalism in Education Policy in Canada and the United States. *Publius: The Journal of Federalism*. 40, no. 3 (April., 2010), 534–557.

tripled in real terms over the last 50 years, making it the single largest budget item after social security.[2] The U.S. government's domestic expenditures on K–12 education alone constituted about 4.7 percent of the Gross Domestic Product (GDP) in 2010.[3] Internationally, comparisons to other Organization for Economic Co-operation and Development (OECD) countries that have similar GDP per capita show that the U.S government is one of the top spenders in public education.[4] However, concerns about educational excellence, inequities in educational spending, and achievement disparities have continued to dominate the collective

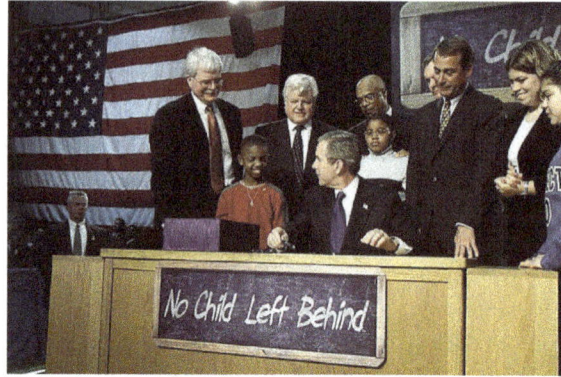

Figure 7.2: President George W. Bush signs into law the No Child Left Behind Act Jan. 8, 2002, at Hamilton High School in Hamilton, Ohio. Pictured from left are: Democratic Rep. George Miller of California, Democratic U.S. Sen. Edward Kennedy of Massachusetts, Secretary of Education Rod Paige, Republican Rep. John Boehner of Ohio, and Republican Sen. Judd Gregg of New Hampshire.

Source: Wikimedia Commons
Attribution: Paul Morse
License: Public Domain

discourse on schooling in America. These concerns generally stem from the fact that American students continue to underperform in reading, mathematics, and science when compared to their international peers.[5] On the domestic front, despite successive reform efforts, student achievement disparities along socioeconomic and ethno-racial lines continue to persist, and unequal schooling remains a troubling reality across the nation. As noted by Diana Ravitch in her book *The Death and the Life of the Great American School System: How Testing and Choice Are Undermining Education*, despite consensus that public schools need reform, the content and mechanisms of such reforms are widely contested.[6]

Intergovernmental relations occupy a central role in the perennial debates on the content and mechanisms of school reform in the nation. Furthermore,

---

2   Bruce D. Baker, *Educational Inequality and School Finance: Why Money Matters for America's Students.* Cambridge, MA: Harvard Education. Press, 2018; Neena Banerjee, Effects of Teacher-Student Ethno-Racial Mismatch and Overall Teacher Diversity in Elementary Schools on Educational Outcomes. *Journal of Research in Childhood Education*, 32, no 1 (2018): 94-118. See also, Paul E. Peterson, *Saving Schools: From Horace Mann to Virtual Learning.* Cambridge: The Belknap Press of Harvard University Press, 2010.

3   Mathew G. Springer, Erik A. Houck, and James W. Guthrie. History and Scholarship Regarding United States Education Finance and Policy. In Helen F. Ladd and Edward B. Fiske, ed., *Handbook of Research in Education Finance and Policy*, New York: Routledge, 2015.

4   Mathew G. Springer, Erik A. Houck, and James W. Guthrie. History and Scholarship Regarding United States Education Finance and Policy. In Helen F. Ladd and Edward B. Fiske, ed., *Handbook of Research in Education Finance and Policy*, New York: Routledge, 2015.

5   The latest round of the Program for International Student Assessment (PISA) that is administered to 15-year-olds in 65 countries shows that students in the United States ranked 14th in Reading, 17th in Science and 25th in Mathematics among Organization for Economic Cooperation and Development (OECD) countries (source: National Center for Education Statistics (NCES) website https://nces.ed.gov/pubsearch/pubsinfo.asp?pubid=2011004; accessed on 17th January, 2010).

6   Diana Ravitch, *The Death and the Life of the Great American School System: How Testing and Choice Are Undermining Education.* New York: Basic Books. 2010.

politics and governance in education cannot be understood in their entirety without situating them within the landscape of intergovernmental relations. Referring to the work by Michael Kirst and Frederick Wirt in their book *The Political Dynamics of American Education*, Jason A. Grissom, and Carolyn D. Herrington in their article "Struggling for Coherence and Control: The New Politics of Intergovernmental Relations in Education" note that "if politics is about group conflict over group differences about using public resources to meet private needs and governance is the process of publicly resolving the group conflict, intergovernmental relations lies at the heart of both politics and governance in education."[7] Schools are an important entity at the local level in the governance of education. Their place in the landscape of IGR stems from their considerable discretionary outreach and the autonomy teachers enjoy within the closed doors of the classroom. Furthermore, some scholars have referred to teachers as "street level bureaucrats,"[8] and, like

> **Street level bureaucrats**: This term was originally coined by Lipsky (1980). Scholars have referred to teachers as "street level bureaucrats" because they are implementers of school-based reforms at the classroom level and in doing so, teachers exercise substantial discretionary powers behind the closed doors of the classroom.
>
> **Collective bargaining laws**: Like other public bureaucrats, teachers are protected by collective bargaining laws. State-level collective bargaining legislation govern collective bargaining agreements at the state and local levels. These laws also regulate the dimensions of union activity and determine the scope of issues that can be negotiated.

other public bureaucrats, teachers in several states are protected by collective bargaining laws of varied strength. The unique place of schools as district and state government reform implementers includes those associated elements, such as budgets, personnel, and relationship building within the community, all of which create an even thicker layer in intergovernmental relationships.[9]

The goal of this chapter is to examine intergovernmental relationships in policymaking in the K–12 education sector. The chapter is organized as follows: it begins by describing the various shades of liberalism to trace the historical origin of debates around authority and responsibility distribution in education and the struggle to balance individual freedom through local control vis-à-vis state authority. Next, it examines federalism and K–12 education policy followed by a discussion of the federal, state, and local government roles and relationships in K–12 public education provision and a description of the intergovernmental relations institutions in public education and a discussion of independent agencies', politics, and interest groups' roles. The chapter then describes the various phases of federal-

---

7   Jason A. Grissom, and Carolyn D. Herrington. Struggling for Coherence and Control: The New Politics of Intergovernmental Relations in Education. *Educational Policy*, 26, no 1 (2012): 5; Also, Michael W. Kirst and Frederick M. Wirt. *The political dynamics of American education* (4th ed.). Richmond, CA: McCutchan. 2009.

8   Kenneth Jeier, Robert D. Wrinkle, and J.L. Polinard. Representative Bureaucracy and Distributional Equity: Addressing the Hard Question. *The Journal of Politics*, 61, no. 4 (Nov 1999): pp. 1025-1039.

9   Jason A. Grissom and Carolyn D. Herrington. *Struggling for Coherence and Control: The New Politics of Intergovernmental Relations in Education.* 6–7.

state relations in education, touching upon three contemporary education policy initiatives to illustrate the dramatic expansion of federal outreach in the education sector and its implications for intergovernmental relations. These three initiatives are the No Child Left Behind Act, Race to the Top, and Common Core State Standards. Next, the chapter focuses on the third branch of government, namely, the courts and how they have influenced important education policy initiatives, including desegregation of public schools and ensuring equity in education funding. The chapter then examines the role of nongovernmental organizations (NGOs) in public education and their influence on intergovernmental relationships.

7.2 HISTORICAL ORIGIN OF THE DEBATES OVER LOCAL CONTROL VIS-À-VIS THE AUTHORITY OF THE STATE

The decentralized system of K–12 public education in today's context is rooted in the larger historical developments in economic, social, and political structures during the Progressive era (see chapter 1), developments that led to the transformation of authority and control over public schools.[10] Drawing from the works on this topic by Kenneth Godwin and Frank Kemerer in their book *School Choice Tradeoffs: Liberty, Equity, and Diversity*; John Chubb and Terry Moe's Politics, Markets, and America's Schools; William Howell's *Besieged: school boards and the future of education politics*; and, more recently, William Fischel's *Making the Grade: The Economic Evolution of American School Districts*, Nandan Jha's study on *Political Economy of Public Education Finance: Equity, Political Institutions, and Inter-School District Competition* offers a detailed overview of the history behind the public education system's transformation in the U.S.[11] The Progressive era saw the transformation of a largely private, local, and religious education system of the early nineteenth century into a more hierarchically-controlled common school system that is modern, professional, and homogenized to meet the needs of a rapidly-industrializing economy. The invention of civil service during this period was intended to remove politics, corruption, and patronage from local and state governments and reward merit and modernity in the government sector. The period also saw the use of penalties in the form of lowered property values to force

> **Common schools**: The term "common school" refers to quasi-public schools that existed in the U.S. during the nineteenth century. These schools originated during the colonial era and subsequently were supported by state governments.

---

10 William G. Howell(ed). *Besieged: school boards and the future of education politics*. Washington, D.C. The Brookings Institution, 2005. 3.

11 Kenneth R. Godwin and Frank R. Kemerer, *School Choice Tradeoffs: Liberty, Equity, and Diversity*. Texas: University of Texas Press, 2002.; William G. Howell(ed). *Besieged: school boards and the future of education politics*, William A. Fischel, *Making the Grade: The Economic Evolution of American School Districts*. Chicago: University of Chicago Press, 2009, Nandan K. Jha, *Political Economy of Public Education Finance: Equity, Political Institutions, and Inter-School District Competition*. Lexington Books/Rowman and Littlefield, 2020.

rural property owners to conform to the idea of a consolidated and age-graded common school system that could prepare children to become informed citizens of a rapidly-modernizing society.[12] During these years, the modern public school system took the shape and form it holds today.

Figure 7.3: Public School, Grapevine, Texas. The postcard features a photo of the school building.
Source: Wikimedia Commons
Attribution: Zeese Co. (Dallas)
License: Public Domain

Figure 7.4: Education Tour in Baltimore.
Source: Wikimedia Commons
Attribution: AmericanSolutions
License: CC BY 2.0

The transformation in control over public education that began during the Progressive era and continued afterwards reflects the changing perceptions about the goals of public education. The conviction a majority of Americans hold about education as the pathway to prosperity for both individuals and the nation can be traced back to the founding icons Benjamin Franklin and Thomas Jefferson, who believed that an educated citizenry

Liberalism: is a philosophical idea that talks about liberty, consent of the governed and equality before the law. The shades of liberalism are useful for understanding the rights of parents versus state rights on the issue of who decides what children will learn in schools.

is key to sustaining the nascent democracy.[13] Over the years, the country has relied upon its public schools to pursue other objectives, including assimilating new immigrants; defeating rivals during the Cold War era; maintaining a competitive advantage in the economy; addressing inequities due to the legacies of racism, slavery, and segregation; and providing equal opportunities to all people.[14]

The various goals of public education and the varying degrees of state and parental control needed to achieve them have evolved in liberal democratic societies, such as the U.S.[15] The various conceptions of liberalism highlight the tension in balancing the rights of parents through local control with the greater

12   Nandan K. ha,. *Political Economy of Public Education Finance: Equity, Political Institutions, and Inter-School District Competition.*
13   Paul Manna, *Collision Course: Federal Education Policy Meets State and Local Realities.* CQ Press. 2011.
14   Paul Manna, *Collision Course: Federal Education Policy Meets State and Local Realities*; Richard Rothstein, Rebecca Jacobson, and Tamara Wilder. *Grading Education: Getting Accountability Right.* Washington, D.C., and New York: Economic Policy Institute and Teachers College Press. 2008; David Tyackand Larry Cuban. *Tinkering Toward Utopia: A Century of Public School Reform.* Cambridge: Mass.: Harvard University Press. 1995.
15   Kenneth R. Godwinand Frank R. Kemerer. *School Choice Tradeoffs: Liberty, Equity, and Diversity.*

Figure 7.5: Students at the 2015 School Choice Week rally at the Arizona State Capitol building in Phoenix, Arizona.
Source: Wikimedia Commons
Attribution: Gage Skidmore
License: CC BY-SA 2.0

control of the state in pursuit of political, social, and economic equity through public education.[16] The classical liberals viewed education as the ability to impart skills for economic self-sufficiency and self-government. To this end, they proposed a minimal role for the state in education and argued against direct educational provision by government. Classical liberals like John Stuart Mill in his book "On Liberty" called on government to administer tests only for literacy and numeracy and to fund education for the poor and needy. Unlike classical liberals, political liberals called for state funding and the regulation of education, viewing educational opportunity as key to achieving social and political equality. However, political liberals were against government's providing education as a monopoly or regulating private schools. Political liberals favored some control in the hands of parents, especially in regards to educating children about what constitutes a good life and a good person. In this way, the role of parents was further diminished in comparison to their role under the classical liberal state.[17] Compared to classical and political liberals, comprehensive liberals argued in favor of state funding and public education provisions. In the view of comprehensive liberals, the state strictly regulates private schools to achieve economic and political equality and end all forms of discrimination. The role of parents and their individual liberty was further diminished under a comprehensive liberal state. The progressive liberals went

16   Kenneth R. Godwin and Frank R. Kemerer. *School Choice Tradeoffs: Liberty, Equity, and Diversity.*
17   Kenneth R. Godwin and Frank R. Kemerer. *School Choice Tradeoffs: Liberty, Equity, and Diversity.*

even further and argued that the state should have total control over education and establish common public schools to socialize students to a common culture so that they become democratic citizens and form a liberal democratic society. As noted by Kenneth R. Godwin and Frank R. Kemerer in *School Choice Tradeoffs: Liberty, Equity, and Diversity*, John Dewey and other progressive liberals viewed the parents as supporters of decisions made by the state and professional educators.[18]

Understanding these various shades of liberalism is important because they offer insights into the evolution of the "local control" concept over public education. Furthermore, one learns that the current federal structure that governs public education did not emerge in a vacuum. Instead, it results from decades of contentious debates over such questions as whether parents or the state have more authority over education and how much control does each get to exercise in such matters as what ought to be taught in public schools across the nation.

As the above discussion reveals, the changing conception about the goals of education led to a diminished role for parents (e.g., local control) and a greater role for the state. Similar arguments have been used in the contemporary context to advocate for significantly greater control of the federal government in public education decision-making over state governments who are constitutionally responsible for public education.

7.3 FEDERALISM AND K–12 PUBLIC EDUCATION

As introduced in chapter 1, federalism is considered an instrument used in a governmental system with more than one layer of government units to ensure smooth functioning and shared decision-making. It is no overstatement to argue that federalism is most profound in the American education sector compared to all the other sectors, with scholars describing education governance as a "tangled web."[19] The complex relations among the federal, state, and local

Figure 7.6: Secretary of Education Betsy DeVos, Dec 2017.

Source: Wikimedia Commons
Attribution: US Department of Education
License: Public Domain

governments in K–12 education governance and policymaking are often captured with metaphors, such as a "layer cake," "marble cake," "fruit cakes," "birthday cakes," "picket fence federalism," and "protean"— all of which are described in chapter 1. In an international context, among all the nations that compete with

18   Kenneth R. Godwin and Frank R. Kemerer. *School Choice Tradeoffs: Liberty, Equity, and Diversity*.
19   Patrick McGuinn and Paul Manna. Education governance in America: Who leads when everyone is in charge? In Patrick McGuinn and Paul Manna (Ed.) *Education governance for the twenty-first century*, pp. 1–17. Washington D.C.: The Brookings Institute, 2013.

America on the educational front, very few have a federal structure as complicated as the one that exists here. As Patrick McGuinn and Paul Manna put it in a recent scholarly piece, a simple question considered by the nation's school principals about who leads the governance of America's nearly 100,000 public schools when "everyone is in charge" can often lead to deeply confusing and dissatisfying answers for many.[20]

7.3.1 The Intergovernmental Landscape for Public Education

Education is not directly mentioned in the U.S. Constitution, but the responsibility for education governance can be discerned in the 10th Amendment which declares that all powers not included in the Constitution are reserved for the states.[21] Constitutions of most states explicitly guarantee free public education,[22] and several state constitutions require equal access to education for all of their children.[23] By custom and with the exception of Hawaii—which has a statewide public education system—

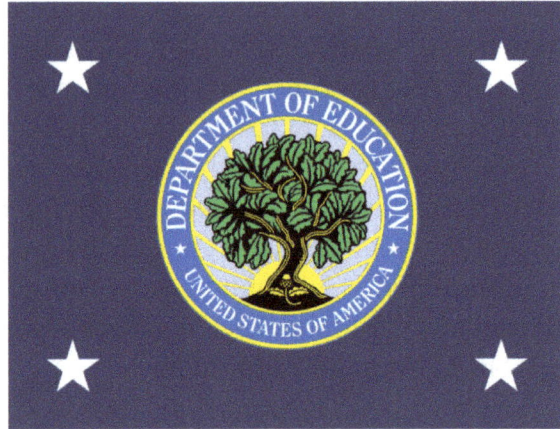

Figure 7.7: Flag of the United States Secretary of Education.
Source: Wikimedia Commons
Attribution: User "Fry1989"
License: CC BY-SA 3.0

most states have delegated the responsibility for public education to local school districts, which are responsible for operating and financing public schools.[24] The federal structure governing K–12 public education can be called a decentralized public education system from a comparatively international perspective.[25] In recent decades, however, public education governance has become more

---

20   Patrick McGuinn and Paul Manna. Education governance in America: Who leads when everyone is in charge? In Patrick McGuinn and Paul Manna (Ed.) *Education governance for the twenty-first century*, pp. 1–17. Washington D.C.: The Brookings Institute, 2013.

21   Julie A. Marsh and Priscilla Wohlstetter. Recent Trends in Intergovernmental Relations: The Resurgence of Local Actors in Education Policy. *Educational Researcher*. 42, no. 5 (2013): 276–283.

22   Michael B. Berkman and Eric Plutzer. *Ten Thousand Democracies: Politics and Public Opinion in America's School Districts*. Washington, DC: Georgetown University Press, 2005.

23   Roslyn A. Mickelson, Achieving the Educational Opportunity in the wake of the judicial retreat from race sensitive remedies: Lessons from North Carolina. *American University Law Review*, 52(6) (2003): 1477–1506.

24   Nora E. Gordon, The Changing Federal Role in Education Finance and Governance." In Helen F. Ladd and Edward B. Fiske (Eds.) *Handbook of Research in Education Finance and Policy*. New York: Routledge, 2015. Also see, Mathew G. Springer, Erik A. Houck, and James W. Guthrie. *History and Scholarship Regarding United States Education Finance and Policy*.

25   Nora E. Gordon, The Changing Federal Role in Education Finance and Governance." In Helen F. Ladd and Edward B. Fiske (Eds.) *Handbook of Research in Education Finance and Policy*. New York: Routledge, 2015. Also see, Mathew G. Springer, Erik A. Houck, and James W. Guthrie. *History and Scholarship Regarding United States Education Finance and Policy*.

centralized with the shifting of power back from local districts to states because states are shouldering more fiscal burdens than are local governments. The federal government's role has also expanded in recent decades.[26]

Figure 7.8: Lowndes County Board of Education, Valdosta, Lowndes County, Georgia.
Source: Wikimedia Commons
Attribution: Michael Rivera
License: CC BY-SA 4.0

The above federal structure in education governance has created an intergovernmental landscape that spans a multi-tiered set of interactions between the federal–state–local, federal–state, state–local, and federal–local levels.[27] The sharing of responsibility in education governance entwines with the fiscal burden shared among the federal, state, and local governments (see Figure 7.9 which shows the fiscal burden shared among federal, state, and local governments in K–12 education). Currently, about 47 percent of funding comes from state governments, 41 percent comes from the local government, and about 12.7 percent comes from the federal government.[28] Although only 41 percent of education funding currently comes from local sources, the figure was more than 80 percent in early 1930. State governments have increased their funding share since the 1980s and currently

26   William G. Howell(ed). *Besieged: school boards and the future of education politics.*
27   Julie A. Marsh and Priscilla Wohlstetter. *Recent Trends in Intergovernmental Relations: The Resurgence of Local Actors in Education Policy.*
28   Bruce D. Baker, *Educational Inequality and School Finance: Why Money Matters for America's Students.* Harvard Education Press, 2018

contribute more than their local government counterparts. Finally, the federal share's growing influence over public education parallels its growing share of the fiscal burden, which shows an increase from about two percent in 1940 to 8.5 percent in 2002 to 12.7 percent in 2009.[29] The turnaround in the federal share of education funding coincided with the passage of the Elementary and Secondary Education Act of 1965 (Title I).[30]

Fiscal Burden Share Between Federal, State and Local Governments in K-12 Education

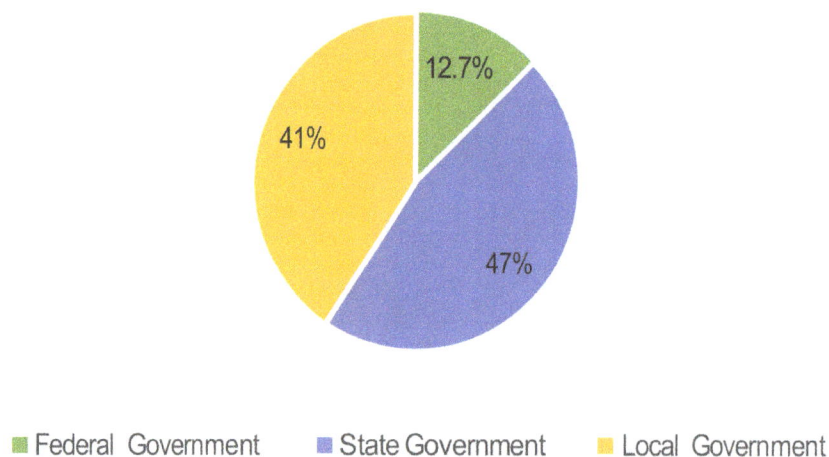

- Federal Government
- State Government
- Local Government

Figure 7.9: Fiscal Burden Share Between Federal, State and Local Governments in K-12 Education. Constructed by author based upon data presented in Bruce D. Baker. *Educational Inequality and School Finance: Why Money Matters for America's Students.* **Harvard Education Press, 2018.**

Source: Original Work

Attribution: Neena Banerjee, based on data compiled by Bruce D. Baker

License: CC BY-SA 4.0

The expansion of federal power in public education parallels state-level shifts, with many states gradually beginning to assert power reactively through implementing federal policy proactively in new policy areas.[31] The federal Race to the Top program (RTTT) launched in 2010 offers a good example of how federal financial incentives to states acted as a catalyst in motivating states to assert more independence in implementing programs and in wielding power to initiate difficult

29   Theresa J. McGuire and Leslie E. Papke. "Local Funding of Schools: The Property Tax and Its Alternatives." In Helen F. Ladd and Edward B. Fiske (Eds.) *Handbook of Research in Education Finance and Policy.* New York: Routledge, 2015. Also, Mathew G. Springer, Erik A. Houck, and James W. Guthrie. *History and Scholarship Regarding United States Education Finance and Policy.*

30   Erik A. Hanushek and Alfred A. Lindseth. *Schoolhouses, Courthouses, and Statehouses: Solving the Funding-Achievement Puzzle in America's Public Schools.* Princeton: Princeton University Press, 2009.

31   Julie A. Marsh and Priscilla Wohlstetter. *Recent Trends in Intergovernmental Relations: The Resurgence of Local Actors in Education Policy.* 277.

reforms in areas that were traditionally out-of-bounds due to resistance from various interest groups. These areas of reform included teacher accountability, compensation, and interventions in low performing schools.[32] Thus, the expansion of federal power in public education has not always led to a unidirectional loss of power from state and local governments. Instead, state and local governments have gained influence in some cases. This indicates the bi-directionality of IGR in public education.

Figure 7.10: Chicago Teachers Union Rally.
Source: Wikimedia Commons
Attribution: Charles Edward Miller
License: CC BY-SA 2.0

Figure 7.11: The National Education Association headquarters.
Source: Wikimedia Commons
Attribution: User "AgnosticPreachersKid"
License: CC BY-SA 3.0

In "Recent Trends in Intergovernmental Relations: The Resurgence of Local Actors in Education Policy," Julie Marsh and Priscilla Wohlstetter note a similar base of evidence in changing state–local relations over the years regarding the bi-directionality of IGR in public education. Two interesting developments can be noted here. On the one hand, local districts have lost significant control over resources due to reforms in state finance systems; at the same time, however, powerful new local players have emerged to weaken state control. The charter school movement is a good example in this regard. It successfully brought many non-traditional players into the public education market, such as charter management organizations (CMOs). These new organizations have empowered citizens by contributing to the rise of charter schools. In many cases, they have also encouraged direct district-charter collaborations, especially in districts that are open to making a diverse set of educational service providers available to their citizens.[33]

School districts and their local government counterparts have also exerted considerable independence over public schooling. Entrepreneurial districts like Denver, Nashville, New York City, and Washington, D.C. exemplify districts that have initiated reforms in teacher incentive and compensation policies and, in

32 Patrick McGuinn, Stimulating reform: Race to the Top, Competitive grants and the Obama Education Agenda. *Educational Policy*, 26, 136–159. 2012.
33 Julie A. Marsh and Priscilla Wohlstetter. *Recent Trends in Intergovernmental Relations: The Resurgence of Local Actors in Education Policy.* 279.

doing so, have set themselves apart from other levels of government.[34] Many school districts in the state of California have cast aside state priorities and opted to move most of the newly flexible "Tier 3" funds into their general funds to avoid teacher layoffs due to the need to balance budgets during difficult economic times.[35] These examples illustrate an intergovernmental landscape for education that is continuously transforming due to the shifting relationships among federal, state,

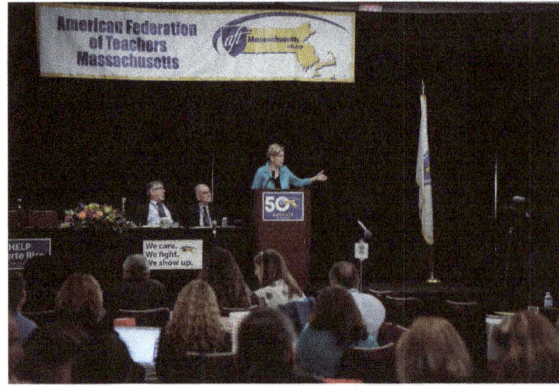

Figure 7.12: American Federation of Teachers Convention.
Source: Wikimedia Commons
Attribution: User "ElizabethForMA"
License: CC BY 2.0

and local governments. While the powers of governments at all levels have grown significantly, what is particularly notable within the education landscape is the growing assertions of that power and an aptitude for confrontational governance among government entities at the lowest levels.[36]

Figure 7.13: Secretary of Homeland Security John Kelly meets with the Council of Governors during the National Governors Association event in Washington, D.C.
Source: Wikimedia Commons
Attribution: Barry Bahler
License: Public Domain

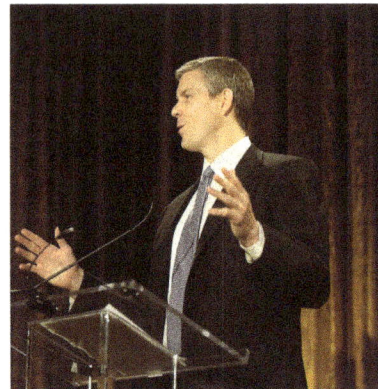

Figure 7.14: Secretary Arne Duncan Speaking at the Council of Chief State School Officers' Teacher of the Year Event.
Source: Wikimedia Commons
Attribution: Department of Education
License: Public Domain

34   Julie E. Koppich and Jessica Rigby. *Alternative teacher compensation: A primer*. Palo Alto, CA: Policy Analysis for California Education. 2009. Also, see Julie A. Marshand Priscilla Wohlstetter. *Recent Trends in Intergovernmental Relations: The Resurgence of Local Actors in Education Policy*. 277.

35   Brian Stecher, Bruce Fuller, Tom Timar, and Julie A. Marsh, *Deregulating school aid in California: How districts responded to flexibility in Tier 3 categorical funds in 2010–11*, technical report. Santa Monica, CA: RAND and Policy Action for California Education. 2012.

36   Julie A. Marsh and Priscilla Wohlstetter. Recent Trends in Intergovernmental Relations: The Resurgence of Local Actors in Education Policy. 277.

7.3.2 Institutions of Intergovernmental Relations in Education

Understanding the institutions at the federal, state, and local levels is important in studies of U.S. federalism. These institutions are important players within the intergovernmental landscape. The evolving landscape of intergovernmental relations in education policy and governance arena is best understood if one has a deeper understanding of the multitude of institutions that operate at various levels of government and outside of these governments. This section looks at each of these agencies, how they were established, the rules within which they operate and their roles in education policymaking and governance. Most of them are part of the executive branch of government and are often extra-constitutional.[37]

7.3.2.1 Institutions at the Federal Level: The Legislature

Although education in America remains the responsibility of state and local governments, the federal government has gradually increased its efforts to intervene in education on the grounds of protecting students' civil rights, to address racial inequalities in educational opportunities, and to close poverty gaps in educational attainment. As the representative face of the federal government, Congress has historically used many of its legislative tools and oversight powers to encourage state governments to pursue policies that have broad support from members of Congress or, at times, to ensure coordination with and compliance from state governments on policies that enjoy partisan support in states.[38] The Elementary and Secondary Education Act (ESEA) of 1965 and The Head Start program, which were initiated by President Lyndon B. Johnson as part of his "War on Poverty" in the 1960s, as well as the No Child Left Behind Act of 2001 are some of the examples of Congress's taking a lead to enact education policy in the nation. Congress has historically used grants-in-aid and loans to encourage state governments and local school districts to enact education policies designed to meet specific societal problems.[39] Examples include the establishment of the National Defense Education Act of 1958 in response to the Soviet Union's successful launch of Sputnik in 1957, with the goal of providing financial aid to states and school districts to help improve the education systems' ability to train students in science, mathematics, and foreign languages.[40]

37   John Phillimore, Understanding Intergovernmental Relations: Key Features and Trends. Australian Journal of Public Administration. 72, no. 3 (2013): 231.

38   William G. Howell and Asya Magazinik. Presidential Prescriptions for State Policy: Obama's Race to the Top Initiative. *Journal of Policy Analysis and Management*. 36, no. 3 (2017): 504.

39   William G. Howell and Asya Magazinik. Presidential Prescriptions for State Policy: Obama's Race to the Top Initiative. *Journal of Policy Analysis and Management*. 36, no. 3 (2017): 504.

40   Thomas R. and Susan A. MacMANUS. *Politics in States and Communities. Pearson* (14th edition). 2012. 537–538.

7.3.2.2 Institutions at the Federal Level: The U.S. Department of Education

Presidents have used the authority vested upon them as the head of the executive branch to lay the groundwork for ambitious education policy initiatives. Often, this happens when Congress is in partisan impasse.[41] In describing the role of the president within American federalism, William Howell and Asya Magazinnik point out that the president possesses a "demonstrably ascendant" role as the primary locus for producing major changes in domestic policy.[42] Still other scholars, like Jal Mehta and Steven Teles in their book chapter titled "Carrots, Sticks and the Bully Pulpit: Lessons From a Half-Century of Federal Efforts to Improve America's Schools," have raised the issue of "jurisdictional competition" in which "the government generally, [and] the president in particular, can empower an alternative governing coalition," and, "leverage decentralized political action by actors sympathetic to its aims."[43] Due to rising polarization within Congress (see chapter 4), recent presidents have turned to states to advance their policy priorities. The Obama administration's Race to the Top (RTTT) is a particular case in point. The Obama administration was able to combine the older model of "interventionist and prescriptive federalism" with the newer model of "funding and administrative support" to ensure voluntary participation from states in adopting policies supported by the Department of Education and the President.[44]

The efforts of the federal government in education are handled through the U.S. Department of Education, founded in 1979. This executive branch agency has evolved into a major policy force in primary, secondary, and higher education, controlling about 45 percent of federal education outlays. The origin of this department, however, goes back to the Reconstruction era when it existed as an Office of Education with a modest portfolio that included gathering statistics about the nation's schools. In offering a brief history of the U.S. Department of Education, D.T. Stallings discusses how Shirley Hufstedler, who was the first Secretary of Education in the Carter administration, envisioned a department that would work to "streamline and strengthen the political workings of the federal/state relationship, reinforce to the public the notion that the department would not supersede local control through imposition of restrictive regulations, address issues of educational inequities, and finally be amenable to change in response to the changing needs of the country."[45] The department managed to demonstrate resilience and survived over the years under many friendly and not-so-friendly

41   Patrick McGuinn, *Stimulating reform: Race to the Top, Competitive grants and the Obama Education Agenda.*
42   William G. Howell and Asya Magazinnik quotes from the work done by Gais, Thomas., and J. Fossett. Federalism and the executive branch. In J. D. Aberbach & M. A. Peterson (Eds.), *The executive branch*, 487. New York, NY: Oxford University Press. 2005.
43   Jal Mehta, J. and Steven Teles, Jurisdictional politics: A new federal role in education. In Frederick. M. Hess & Andrew P. Kelly (Eds.), *Carrots, sticks, and the bully pulpit: Lessons from a half-century of federal efforts to improve America's schools.* Cambridge, MA: Harvard Education Press. 2011. 198.
44   William G. Howell and Asya Magazinnik quotes from the work done by Gais, Thomas., and J. Fossett. *Federalism and the executive branch.* 505.
45   D.T. Stallings, A brief history of the U.S. Department of Education. *Phi Delta Kappan*, 83(9), 678. 2002.

administrations. Although education has always been a responsibility of the states, the U.S. Department of Education has transformed the face of the national education debate and is able to reach the national consciousness as a critical arena for federal support and leadership.[46]

Although education is a state matter, state governments have seen a continuing expansion of control over education policy. Various state level institutions are involved in determining policies for school districts, establishing standards for curriculum, teacher certification, and evaluation of teacher performance. State level institutions are also engaged in designing accountability models to monitor performance of local school districts and schools. Last but not the least, state institutions play an even bigger role in designing education funding frameworks for disbursal of funds to school districts. Thus, it is important to examine some of the prominent state level institutions including how they are formed and their mandate over education issues.

7.3.2.3 Institutions at the State Level: State Boards of Education

State boards of education are entities vested with powers to ensure compliance from local school districts. In most states, the governor appoints these boards. In some states, they are composed of local officials, and, in ten states, citizens directly elect state board members. These ten states are Alabama, Hawaii, Colorado, Kansas, Michigan, Nebraska, Nevada, New Mexico, Texas, and Utah. The state boards of education have the power to decide on matters ranging from teacher certification to textbook selection. In practice, though, they coordinate with the state commissioner of education and the state department of education on all matters.[47]

7.3.2.4 Institutions at the State Level: State Commissioner of Education

State commissioners of education are also known as chief education officers, state school superintendents, or superintendents of public instruction. They can be elected or appointed by either the governor or state education board. The chief education officer plays an influential role in their capacity as the chief spokesperson for education in their respective states by offering testimony before the legislature and by acting as the head of the state department of education.[48]

7.3.2.5 Institutions at the State Level: State Departments of Education

State governments have historically fulfilled their authority over and responsibility of education by (a) establishing local school districts and bestowing

46 D.T. Stallings, A brief history of the U.S. Department of Education. *Phi Delta Kappan*, 83(9), 678. 2002.
47 Thomas R. Dye and Susan A. MacMANUS, *Politics in States and Communities*. 543.
48 Thomas R. Dye and Susan A. MacMANUS, *Politics in States and Communities*. 543.

on them financial and administrative powers to operate local public schools in specific geographic areas and (b) by establishing state level agency or agencies to coordinate with local school districts. Despite appreciation for local control, state level agencies have grown in power and size over the years. Their functions range among disbursal of funds, coordination of services, preparation of statewide curricula, selection of textbooks and materials, determination of teacher qualification policies, establishment and enforcement of school building codes, and supervision of statewide testing. The tool that state agencies use to enforce control over local school districts is the state's education money.[49]

7.3.2.6 Institutions at the Local Level: School District Superintendents

The primary responsibility for public education rests with the 14,000 local school districts. These school districts exercise their control over local public schools by establishing school boards and appointing, or in some cases electing, school superintendents. School superintendents are either appointed by the local school board or elected on a nonpartisan ballot. School superintendents are in charge of the overall management of public schools, including the recruitment and supervision of teachers and principals, planning and organizing the schools, preparing budgets and expenditures, and making policy recommendations to the school board. The three major responsibilities of school superintendents include the following: (a) setting the agenda for school board meetings, (b) implementing school board decisions, and (c) becoming in that role an advocate for policies to the community. In this role, superintendents often provide leadership on important policy matters at the local level. The average tenure of school superintendents is fairly long, approximately eight years.[50]

7.3.2.7 Institutions at the Local Level: School Boards

There are about 80,000 school board members across the nation. School board members have an average tenure of five years and are generally nonpartisan and independently elected. Most members join the board out of a sense of volunteerism and usually do not hold a desire for higher office. Therefore, threat of electoral defeat is not always a mechanism to hold board members accountable. However, in recent times, school board elections have become competitive, especially in large urban, ideologically diverse districts. The influence of interest groups has also increased in these elections.[51]

49   Thomas R. Dye and Susan A. MacMANUS, *Politics in States and Communities*. 543–544.
50   Thomas R. Dye and Susan A. MacMANUS, *Politics in States and Communities*, 548.
51   Thomas R. Dye and Susan A. MacMANUS, *Politics in States and Communities*, 548–549.

7.3.2.8 Institutions at the Local Level: Office of the Mayor

Mayor-appointed school board members are a relatively new phenomenon that started during the 1990s. Considering the effects of mayoral takeovers in his work *Besieged: school boards and the future of education politics*, William Howell talks about the growing number of large urban school districts that initiated this significant change in school governance when they decided to let the mayor take control over school governance by appointing a school board.[52] Currently, 24 states have passed such legislation. The implications of mayoral control over school districts is not fully understood, though. Supporters of "mayoral takeovers" have argued that, since educational systems are well integrated with the economic life of cities, giving mayors authority to manage school districts has potential benefits. Since businesses choose cities that have better educational systems and can supply them with a pool of talented employees, mayors possess the right incentives to solve educational problems in their cities. Mayors can also quickly intervene in failing schools, offering an alternate avenue to district administration to tackle education problems that bypassed a political stalemate. Opponents of "mayoral takeovers" argue that they violate local control and are undemocratic and that the process usually lacks transparency. According to Howell, there are currently three distinct legislative routes that mayors could use to gain authority to appoint school board members. These include the following: (a) work with state legislators and governors to pass laws granting mayors the authority to replace an elected board with an appointed board, (b) have the state legislation call for referendum to allow city residents to vote on whether to give the mayor the authority to appoint the school board, and (c) work to have the city vote to change its charter, allowing mayors more control over the school board. Just as there are different methods that mayors can utilize to gain authority so also can the resulting power structures vary from city to city. In some cities, a mayor can exercise greater control over school boards compared to other cities.[53]

7.3.2.9 Independent Agencies

Independent agencies can also play important roles in IGR regarding education. Many independent agencies have emerged in the education sector as part of the privatization movement that has taken a variety of institutional forms. For example, as part of the movement to

> **Charter schools**: these schools are funded just like public schools but enjoy a lot of independence in day-to-day management and decision-making.

establish charter schools that are publicly authorized and financed but managed by a private board, several for-profit and non-profit educational management organizations have emerged over the years. These organizations enter into contracts with the public school system to operate particular schools within a district

---

52   William G. Howell, *Besieged: school boards and the future of education politics.* 83–84.
53   William G. Howell, *Besieged: school boards and the future of education politics.* 84–85.

independently of conventional district governance and management. As discussed in chapter 6, collaborative arrangements have become much more prevalent in IGR in recent decades. Examples include for-profit educational management organizations (EMOs) and non-profit charter management organizations (CMOs). Proponents of these agencies argue that they provide charter schools much needed financial, human, political, and organizational resources that are often hard to find for stand-alone charters.[54] Opponents worry about adding an extra layer of administration, poor regulation of these agencies, lack of transparency in their functioning, poor management, and underperformance of schools managed by these agencies. Currently, around 36 percent of charters in the nation are managed by CMOs and EMOs.[55]

7.3.2.10 Political Actors

Politics is popularly perceived as "a process that determines who gets what, when or who pays, and who benefits."[56] In "Political Context of Education Finance," James Guthrie and Kenneth Wong describe politics as something that involves various processes, values, interest groups, spheres of policy perceptions, and governmental arrangements.

According to these scholars, the political system comprises "five cultural components through which political actors often view reality and try to shape it." These political cultures "influence the manner in which advocates for a particular change will define a problem or seek predetermined solutions." A "legislative" focused political culture is conventionally associated with policymaking, where legislatures, city councils, and school boards deliberate on issues and make decisions. The making of a policy within a legislative culture is characterized by intense lobbying from political parties and interests and through the process of coalition building. A "regulatory" focused political culture is characterized by "codification, rigidity, specialization, hierarchy, standardization, and efforts to appear objective and independent." For example, school districts operate under many rules that are a product of bureaucratic, but not necessarily political, processes. In a "legally" focused political culture, issues are framed in "keeping with long standing traditions, adherence to precedent, appeals to higher authority and prescribed set of procedural activities." In a "professionally" oriented political culture, "actions are taken to restrict entry into the field, protect clients, enhance standards, advance knowledge in a field, and insulate the profession from overtly partisan or selfish interests." Finally, in a "markets' oriented political culture,

54   Priscilla Wohlstetter, Joanna, Smith, J., Caitlin, Farrell, Guilbert C, Hentschke, and Jennifer, Hirman. How funding shapes the growth of charter management organizations: Is the tail wagging the dog? *Journal of Education Finance*, 37(2), 150–174. 2011.
55   Gary Miron, Jessica L. Urschel Myra A. Yat Aguilar, M. A. and Breanna Dailey, *Profiles of for-profit and nonprofit education management organizations*. Boulder, CO: National Education Policy Center. 2012.
56   James W. Guthrieand Kenneth K. Wong. The Continually Evolving Political Context of Education Finance. In Handbook of Research in Education Finance and Policy, In Helen F. Ladd and Edward B. Fiske (Eds.) *Handbook of Research in Education Finance and Policy*. New York: Routledge, 2015. 60.

the fundamental assumption is that "clients are sufficiently well informed and motivated to operate on their own self-interests, and that, in the process of doing so will, as a collective, promote the public's long-term interests as well."[57] Depending on the political cultures within which political parties operate, they can exercise significant influence on intergovernmental relations. The power of political parties at the national and sub-national levels can determine the extent of administrative cooperation and conflict in intergovernmental relations.[58]

7.3.2.11 Interest Groups

As noted in chapter 3, interest groups play an important role in IGR. Given the resource-intensive nature of K–12 education and its large number of stakeholders, it is no wonder that there are many interest groups and advocates at all levels who are willing to spend considerable resources on lobbying with executive and legislative branch officials.[59] Teacher unions are the single largest interest group in the education sector. The National Education Association (NEA) and the American Federation of Teachers (AFT) are the two major teacher unions that have grown steadily over the years in memberships and resources, and they remain highly visible at the local, state, and national levels. Opponents of teachers' unions believe that their collective bargaining rights are a major hindrance to public education reform because such rights limit the options available to school leadership and district officials in making tough and necessary reforms.[60] Critics fault teachers' unions for being over-protective of teachers' welfare at the cost of students. Proponents of teachers' unions, however, argue that teachers' unions are advocates for teachers' professional rights, development, and collective well-being, which are not necessarily in conflict with policy reforms for better educational outcomes.[61] Due to their growing membership, resources, political contributions, and collective bargaining power, teachers' unions are a powerful force in national and subnational politics. They influence policy at the state and national levels, while also bargaining for the collective good at the local level.[62] However, the power of teachers' unions varies substantially across states and across school districts within states. Data

57   James W. Guthrieand Kenneth K. Wong. The Continually Evolving Political Context of Education Finance. In Handbook of Research in Education Finance and Policy, In Helen F. Ladd and Edward B. Fiske (Eds.) *Handbook of Research in Education Finance and Policy*. New York: Routledge, 2015. 67–69.

58   John Phillimore, Understanding Intergovernmental Relations: Key Features and Trends. *Australian Journal of Public Administration*. 72, no. 3 (2013): 228–238.

59   James W. Guthrie and Kenneth K. Wong. *The Continually Evolving Political Context of Education Finance.* 60.

60   William S. Koski and Eileen L. Horng. Facilitating the teacher quality gap? Collective bargaining agreements, teacher hiring and transfer rules, and teacher assignment among schools in California. *Education Finance and Policy*, 2(3), 262–300. 2007.

61   Nina Bascia, Teachers as Professionals: Salaries, Benefits and Unions. *International Handbook of Research on Teachers and Teaching*, 21, no. 6 (2009): 481–489.

62   Frederick M. Hess and Andrew P. Kelly. Scapegoat, albatross, or what. In J. Hannaway and A. Rotherham (Eds.), *Collective bargaining in education: Negotiating change in today's schools.* Cambridge, MA: Harvard Education Press. 2006. 53–87. Also, see Nandan K. JJha, Neena Banerjee and Stephanie Moller. Assessing the Role of Teachers' Unions in the Adoption of Accountability Policies in Public Education. *The Urban Review*. Pp. 1–32. Springer Netherlands. 2019.

show that teachers' unions were most effective in 31 states, moderately effective in 17 states, and relatively ineffective in two states in 2006-07.[63]

7.4 PHASES OF STATE-FEDERAL RELATIONS IN PUBLIC EDUCATION

The federal government's role has expanded vastly in K–12 education policy making and governance over the past few decades.[64] According to Kenneth Wong in "Public Education as a State-Federal Function in the United States. Federalism and Education: Ongoing Challenges and Policy Strategies in Ten Countries," the complex and evolving nature of the federal-state relationship in public education can be explained by examining three phases. Although there is considerable overlap among the three phases, they illustrate the expanding focus of the federal government from equity to performance-based accountability and school choice as it broadened its control over education policy in the country. Drawing heavily from Kenneth Wong's above work in this area, this section examines several education policy initiatives, such as the No Child Left Behind Act (NCLB), the Race to the Top program (RTTT), and the Common Core State Standards program (CCSS) to contextualize the dynamic nature of interactions between the various layers of government in shaping education governance and policy.[65]

Figure 7.15: George W Bush Presidential Library.

Source: Wikimedia Commons
Attribution: Shannon McGee
License: CC BY-SA 2.0

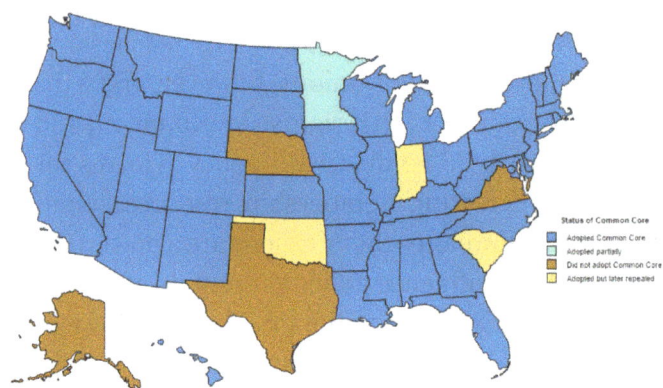

Figure 7.16: A map showing states in the U.S which have either adopted, not adopted, partially adopted, or repealed the Common Core State Standards.

Source: Wikimedia Commons
Attribution: User "MediaKill13"
License: CC BY-SA 4.0

63   Virginia Grayand Russel L. Hanson. *Politics in the American states: A comparative analysis*. Washington, DC: CQ Press. 2008.
64   Kenneth Wong, *Public Education as a State-Federal Function in the United States. Federalism and Education: Ongoing Challenges and Policy Strategies in Ten Countries*. Information Age Publishing. 2018. pp. 231–255. Also, Paul Manna, *Collision Course: Federal Education Policy Meets State and Local Realities*.
65   For a detailed discussion of the various phases of federal-state relations along with various recent education policy initiatives, see Kenneth Wong, *Public Education as a State-Federal Function in the United States. Federalism and Education: Ongoing Challenges and Policy Strategies in Ten Countries* and also Kenneth Wong, The Politics of Education. In Virginia Gray and Russell L. Hanson (Ed.) *Politics in the American States: A Comparative Analysis*.

Figure 7.17: Governor Dannel P. Malloy held a news conference at Annie Fisher STEM Magnet School in Hartford where he announced the launch of the Connecticut Core Initiative to provide additional resources for public schools and a continued dialogue with parents, teachers, administrators, and students as districts work to implement the Common Core State Standards. The initiative is in response to the final report from the Educators' Common Core Implementation Task Force, which lists specific recommendations for successful implementation of the Standards.
Source: Wikimedia Commons
Attribution: Dannel Malloy
License: CC BY 2.0

7.4.1 Focus on Addressing Inequities in Education Since the 1960s (Phase 1)

The 1960s saw a sharp increase in federal involvement in education for the first time. Several events unfolded during the previous decade that helped shift the federal government's role from permissiveness to engagement. These events included the passage of the G.I. Bill in the post-World War-II era enabling veterans to obtain a college education and the passage of the National Defense Education Act in 1958 following the Soviet Union's successful launch of the Sputnik satellite. The latter legislation provided federal funding to all educational institutions to bolster education in fields like science, technology, mathematics, and foreign languages. The previous decade also saw the 1954 landmark Supreme Court ruling Brown v. Board of Education that called on the nation to end institutionalized racism in the form of segregation in public schools. Finally, the eventual passage of the Civil Rights Act in 1964 ended various forms of institutionalized discrimination in the nation. All these events contributed to sharpening federal attention to the needs of disadvantaged students and ultimately culminated with the adoption of the first major federal anti-poverty program, Title 1 of the 1965 Elementary and Secondary Education Act (ESEA). According to Wong, the ESEA program created a complex intergovernmental policy system that occupies a unique position in American history.

The ESEA's passage in 1965 marked a singular transformation in IGR for several reasons. First, many scholars believe that, with the passage of ESEA, the notion of "marble-cake" federalism prevailed over "layer-cake" federalism, giving state and national governments shared responsibilities in the domestic education sector.[66] Prior to the passage of ESEA, the federal government's role was limited because states, especially those in the south, blocked federal funding to segregated school systems out of concern that such funding might trample local autonomy or aid parochial schools.[67] Following the passage of ESEA, there was a significant jump in intergovernmental transfers to finance state and local activities. For example, the number of categorical grant programs, including Title I, increased from 160 to 380 during President Johnson's term and further increased to approximately 500 federally-funded categorical programs by the end of Jimmy Carter's presidency.[68] Second, the redistributive nature of most federal categorical grants was notable in specifically targeting the special education needs of children from lower-income families and deprived neighborhoods, who were also growing up in families with limited English proficiency and/or with disabilities preventing their access to education. Between 1996 and 2005, federal spending under Title 1 increased from $8.9 billion to $14.6 billion in 2005 constant dollars, and over 60 percent of the funds were spent to meet the educational needs of disadvantaged students.[69] The federal government also intervened in early childhood education for the first time during this period by allocating funding for the Head Start early childhood programs in 1965 that promoted school readiness of children from low-income families. Over the years, the federal redistributive grants have taken on several institutional forms. These include the following: (a) the grants-in-aid arrangements whereby the federal government provides funding and sets the programmatic framework but delivery of services is left to the state and local agencies, (b) categorical or single purpose grants with a well-defined target group, namely, eligible students being the sole intended beneficiaries, (c) supplementary and non-supplanting guidelines designed to guard against any local tendency to shift federal resources away from the disadvantaged, and (d) incentivization of local governments to meet anti-poverty objectives by offering compensatory education funds and supplemental resources under the broad umbrella of the Title 1 program.[70]

66   Kenneth Wong, *Public Education as a State-Federal Function in the United States. Federalism and Education: Ongoing Challenges and Policy Strategies in Ten Countries*. Information Age Publishing. 2018. pp. 231–255. . . 351.

67   Kenneth Wong (2008) refers to the work by James L. Sundquist, *Politics and Policy: The Eisenhower, Kennedy, and Johnson Years*. Washington, D.C.: Brookings Institution Press. 1968.

68   Kenneth Wong, *Public Education as a State-Federal Function in the United States. Federalism and Education: Ongoing Challenges and Policy Strategies in Ten Countries*. 234.

69   Kenneth Wong and Gail Sunderman. Education Accountability as a Presidential Priority: No Child Left Behind and the Bush Presidency. Publius: *The Journal of Federalism*. 37 (2007): 333–350.

70   Kenneth Wong, *Public Education as a State-Federal Function in the United States. Federalism and Education: Ongoing Challenges and Policy Strategies in Ten Countries*. 234–235.

7.4.2 The Focus on Performance-Based Federalism Since the 1990s (Phase 2)

Following the publication of the report *A Nation at Risk in 1983*, the issue of rising mediocrity in educational attainment came to the forefront with calls for a series of reforms, including greater demand for accountability, higher standards for performance, improvements in the quality of curriculum, recruitment of qualified teachers, increased teacher salary, and increased instructional time.[71] Thus, the report built momentum for a much broader climate of outcome-based accountability. There were growing concerns about the effectiveness of the federal redistributive grants-in-aid programs, although they continued to garner bipartisan support.[72] In 1994, the Improving America's Schools Act was passed that, for the first time, linked accountability with anti-poverty programs. The legislation encouraged whole-school based reform to prevent isolation of at-risk students and also mandated the use of system-wide standards to assess performance of at-risk students from school districts and states receiving federal funds.[73]

7.4.2.1 The No Child Left Behind Act

The passage of the No Child Left Behind Act (NCLB) in 2001 marked a significant expansion of the federal government's role in K–12 education. The legislation opened up a new era of reform based on accountability and testing for *all* children in public schools. Launched by then President George W. Bush as one of the most ambitious education policies in American history, the overarching goal of NCLB was to raise the achievement levels among all students and thus close the achievement gaps that existed across racial and social class lines.[74] The law also aimed to make all students proficient in reading and mathematics by the end of 2013-2014. Furthermore, the NCLB Act mandated that schools report test score results for students in all demographic subgroups. The law required recruitment of a "Highly Qualified Teacher" in every classroom and gave state and local agencies substantial authority in taking "corrective actions" to turn around failing schools.[75] Some examples of corrective actions included providing supplemental services and transfer options to disadvantaged children and sanctions and closure for schools if they failed to meet the Annual Yearly Progress (AYP) threshold. Finally, the law required that districts participating in the Reading First program follow a scientific and evidence-based curriculum using appropriate teaching methods. This was

71   Diane Ravitch, *The Death and the Life of the Great American School System: How Testing and Choice Are Undermining Education*. 25.
72   Kenneth Wong, *Public Education as a State-Federal Function in the United States. Federalism and Education: Ongoing Challenges and Policy Strategies in Ten Countries*.
73   Kenneth Wong, *Public Education as a State-Federal Function in the United States. Federalism and Education: Ongoing Challenges and Policy Strategies in Ten Countries*. 235.
74   Deborah Meier and George, Wood. *Many Children Left Behind: How No Child Left Behind Act is Damaging Our Children and Our Schools*. Boston: Beacon Press. 2004.
75   George W. Bohrnstedt and Jennifer O'Day, J. (2008). *Introductory Chapter*. Also, Wong, Kenneth. *Public Education as a State-Federal Function in the United States. Federalism and Education: Ongoing Challenges and Policy Strategies in Ten Countries*. 235.

again meant for students from disadvantaged backgrounds, who represent a majority of struggling readers.[76] The legislation addressed the problem of unequal opportunity structure through school choice provision and systematic intervention to reduce interstate and intrastate disparities in resources allocation.[77] The federal Title 1 allocation increased by another $1.7 billion, taking the total allocation to $11 billion during the initial phase of NCLB, with another $900 million allocated for early childhood reading initiatives.[78] Thus, greater federal control during this period did not come in a fiscal sense. On the contrary, federal control came in the form of regulation, accountability, testing, and reporting within a top-down bureaucratic framework. This structure reinforces the complex nature of administration in an IGR system, as discussed in chapter 5.

From a governing perspective, the unusual confluence of political interests that led to the successful passage of NCLB marked a "regime change" that crafted an entirely new framework for the federal role in education.[79] Under the new framework, the federal government could hold states, local districts, and schools accountable for a comprehensive set of standards, including annual academic progress, teacher quality, and achievement gaps. The new framework also allowed the federal government to intervene through state and local districts to close down persistently-failing schools, convert such schools into charters, and allow parents the option of choosing a different school. Thus, the NCLB legislation elevated not only the federal role in education but also educational attainment to the top of the nation's policy agenda.[80]

The new framework under NCLB also created tension in IGR due to implementation challenges at the state and local levels.[81] NCLB allowed states to design their own proficiency standards and assessments in meeting the federal Adequate Yearly Progress as an alternative mechanism to circumvent the existing federal structure in education that did not support a uniform set of accountability measures across all 50 states and the District of Columbia. The states used this provision to their own advantage by lowering test standards and helping students attain higher achievement levels. The result was a wide variation in student proficiencies on state tests and performance on the National Assessment of Educational Progress (NAEP) in many states. The implementation challenges also stemmed from the lack of capacities in many states to hire "highly qualified teachers" as well as the existence of

76   Adam Gamoran, *Standards-based reform and the poverty gap: Lessons for No Child Left Behind.* Washington, DC.: Brookings Institution Press. 2007

77   George W. Bohrnstedt and Jennifer A. O'Day. Introductory Chapter. In Alan R. Sadovnik, Jennifer A. O'Day, George W. Bohrnstedt, and Kathryn M. Borman (Eds.), *No Child Left Behind and the reduction of the achievement gap: Sociological perspectives on federal educational policy.* New York: Routledge. 2008.

78   Kenneth Wong, *Public Education as a State-Federal Function in the United States. Federalism and Education: Ongoing Challenges and Policy Strategies in Ten Countries.* 235.

79   Kenneth Wong, *Public Education as a State-Federal Function in the United States. Federalism and Education: Ongoing Challenges and Policy Strategies in Ten Countries.* 236. Also, see Paul Manna, *Collision Course: Federal Education Policy Meets State and Local Realities.*

80   Kenneth Wong, *Public Education as a State-Federal Function in the United States. Federalism and Education: Ongoing Challenges and Policy Strategies in Ten Countries.* 236.

81   Kenneth Wong, *Public Education as a State-Federal Function in the United States. Federalism and Education: Ongoing Challenges and Policy Strategies in Ten Countries.*

ongoing political stalemate among key stakeholders. Several states resisted federal intervention and took legal actions against mandates, such as the annual testing requirement. These states included Virginia, Connecticut, Utah, and Michigan, along with several other states that registered their opposition with legislative and legal actions. Finally, the unfunded nature of the mandates proposed by NCLB restricted the implementation of the policy at the local level.[82] Thus, intergovernmental conflicts over critical issues, such as annual testing, identification of persistently low-performing schools, intervention in such schools through "corrective actions," and the cost of meeting the new federal mandates weakened the implementation of the NCLB legislation and its overall effectiveness.[83] To relieve the growing pressure created on states and districts and allow some flexibility, the Obama administration introduced waivers to states and districts that failed to comply with the mandates. States like Montana, Idaho, and South Dakota formally notified the federal government of their intention to not implement some of the mandates pertaining to proficiency standards under NCLB.[84] Several other states formally sought waivers from the U.S. Department of Education and came up with ways to comply with the federal policy without sacrificing their authority and interests. California, Pennsylvania, and Texas were some of the states that formally requested NCLB waivers. Interestingly, several districts from states that did not apply for waivers asserted independence by pursuing NCLB amendments and lobbying directly with the federal government. Therefore, from an intergovernmental standpoint, the NCLB not only created dynamic interaction between federal and state governments but also ushered in the resurgence of the federal-local relationship.[85]

7.4.2.2 The Race to the Top Program

Like the federal NCLB legislation, the Race to the Top Program (RTTT) shows the unprecedented reach of the federal government in shaping education policy reforms in states and districts across the nation. Initiated by the Obama administration, it is the largest competitive grant program in education by the federal government in U.S. history.[86] Authorized by the American Recovery and Reinvestment Act of 2009, this federal grant of approximately $4 billion was intended to encourage states to pursue ambitious reforms in areas deemed critical by the federal government and to reward them for raising student achievement. Therefore, understanding the central tenets of the RTTT program is critical to understanding the newly-emergent intergovernmental system in education.[87]

---

82   Kenneth Wong, *Public Education as a State-Federal Function in the United States. Federalism and Education: Ongoing Challenges and Policy Strategies in Ten Countries.*

83   Kenneth Wong, *Public Education as a State-Federal Function in the United States. Federalism and Education: Ongoing Challenges and Policy Strategies in Ten Countries.* 239.

84   Sandra Vergari, *Safeguarding Federalism in Education Policy in Canada and the United States.* 22.

85   Julie A Marsh and Priscilla Wohlstetter. *Recent Trends in Intergovernmental Relations: The Resurgence of Local Actors in Education Policy.* 278.

86   Sandra Vergari, Safeguarding Federalism in Education Policy in Canada and the United States, *Publius: The Journal of Federalism* 40, no. 3 (April., 2010), 22.

87   Sandra Vergari, Safeguarding Federalism in Education Policy in Canada and the United States, *Publius:*

The RTTT program took a different approach to education policy reform from that of the NCLB program. The RTTT relied heavily on incentivizing states to pursue federal reforms in place of the coercive sanctions that were a central feature of the NCLB program.[88] The program was also carefully designed to minimize some of the implementation challenges that were observed during the NCLB era. The intent of the Obama administration was also to send a clear message to the states that the U.S. Department of Education intended to move away from being a "compliance-monitoring organization, to being one focused on capacity building and innovation."[89] The use of a competition grant process, instead of the more traditional need-based categorical grant programs to disburse federal education funds, also underlines the unique approach of the RTTT program within the broader context of federal education policy. Under RTTT, applications from states were graded on a 500-point scale, and states were ranked based on the "rigor of the reforms proposed and their compatibility with four administration priorities: developing common curriculum standards and assessments; improving teacher training, evaluation, and retention policies; creating better data systems; and adopting preferred school- turnaround Strategies."[90] Per Patrick McGuinn's calculations in "Stimulating reform: Race to the Top, Competitive grants and the Obama Education Agenda," 40 states (plus the District of Columbia) applied for the first round of RTTT in January 2010, and the program was successful in generating considerable interest among states and a substantial amount of state policy change in a short period of time. Over its three phases, RTTT attracted applications from all states, except for Alaska, North Dakota, Texas, and Vermont.[91] The U.S. Department of Education's website records a list of applicants and winners of the RTTT grant.[92]

The RTTT program shaped federal-state and state-local relations in fundamental ways. Patrick McGuinn discusses them in "Presidential Policymaking: Race to the Top, Executive Power, and the Obama Education Agenda."[93] First, the program lets states take the lead by allowing them to decide whether to apply for the grant and the type of reform package they will propose in their applications. This design component ensured that (a) states didn't feel that the federal government was being coercive, (b) states knew that their proposals were more likely to win if they proposed reforms that were closely aligned with federal reform approaches, and (c) since states developed

The Journal of Federalism 40, no. 3 (April., 2010), 10.

88   Patrick McGuinn, *Stimulating reform: Race to the Top, Competitive grants and the Obama Education Agenda*. 2012.

89   Patrick McGuinn, *Stimulating reform: Race to the Top, Competitive grants and the Obama Education Agenda*. 2012. 140.

90   Patrick McGuinn, *Stimulating reform: Race to the Top, Competitive grants and the Obama Education Agenda*. 2012. 139. Also, U.S. Department of Education. (n.d.-b). Race to the top program guidance and frequently asked questions. Retrieved from http://www2.ed.gov/programs/racetothetop/faq.pdf.

91   Patrick McGuinn, *Stimulating reform: Race to the Top, Competitive grants and the Obama Education Agenda*. 2012. 139. Also, U.S. Department of Education. (n.d.-b). Race to the top program guidance and frequently asked questions. Retrieved from http://www2.ed.gov/programs/racetothetop/faq.pdf.

92   https://www2.ed.gov/programs/racetothetop/phase1-applications/index.html.

93   Patrick McGuinn, "Presidential Policymaking: Race to the Top, Executive Power, and the Obama Education Agenda." *The Forum*. 12, no. 1: 61–79. 2014.

their own proposals, they retained ownership of the reform approaches proposed in them. Thus, the RTTT was able to contain the damage that occurred in federal-state relations during the NCLB era. RTTT also had an impact on state politics by its pushing many state governors to change/modify state laws to improve their prospects of securing a federal grant under RTTT. It also stimulated state and local conversations on issues of teacher layoffs, collective bargaining, budget cuts, and tax increases during the period of the 2008 economic recession. Further, RTTT shaped federal-state relations in policymaking by paving the way for reform in contentious areas that needed a change in the political climate of states. These included issues of teacher evaluation, performance pay, adoption of common standards, and expansion of charter school reform. RTTT also helped form new political alliances by empowering new actors and organizations at the state level. For example, RTTT put state executives, namely the governors and chief state school officers, in charge of drafting state proposals instead of state legislatures. This strategy of empowering "education executives" ensured a buy-in from governors who generally are more likely to be reform-oriented than state legislatures that are generally more likely to be influenced by various interest groups.[94] Additionally, RTTT spurred a number of private non-profit foundations, private sector philanthropic organizations, and think tanks to get involved in education reform efforts at the state and local level through financial commitment. Agencies like the Gates Foundation provided $250,000 in financial support to 24 states. Their role has generated enthusiasm as well as concern in various quarters.[95] And RTTT shaped state-local relations as well. In many states that won funding, local school districts that were originally set to participate in the program dropped out, foregoing their share of funds due to concerns about the cost of implementation and failed negotiations between state and local governments on controversial matters, such as teacher performance pay policies.[96] Critics of the RTTT program have questioned the program's many management challenges. They have pointed out how administrative discretion that comes with competitive grants like the RTTT could complicate the evaluation of proposals and the distribution of funds to winning states, unlike mostly formula-based grants that involve less administrative discretion. Critics have also raised the possibility of political influence and favoritism by officials in charge of awarding the competitive grants. Even though conclusive evidence of political favoritism has yet to emerge in the scholarly literature, perceptions of such favoritism remain.

7.4.2.3 The Common Core State Standards

The Common Core State Standards program (CCSS) is a state-led initiative launched in 2009 with the objective of bringing consistency to state curricular

---

94   Patrick McGuinn, *Presidential Policymaking: Race to the Top, Executive Power, and the Obama Education Agenda*. 68.
95   Patrick McGuinn, *Presidential Policymaking: Race to the Top, Executive Power, and the Obama Education Agenda*. 66.
96   Sandra Vergari, The Limits of Federal Activism in Education Policy. *Educational Policy*. 26. no. 1(2012): 15–34.

standards and better alignment between state curricular standards and learning expectations for students across the nation.[97] The goal of CCSS is to "ensure that students regardless of where they live, are graduating high school prepared for college, career, and life."[98] Governors and state commissioners from 48 states, two territories, and the District of Columbia worked together to develop the CCSS standards.[99] The National Governors Association Center for Best Practices (NGA Center) and the Council of Chief State School Officers (CCSSO) played key roles in bringing together these state executives under a common cause. The push for state standards that ultimately culminated in the development of CCSS, however, started back in the 1980s when influential organizations such as the National Council of Teachers of Mathematics (NCTM) created standards for each subject that students were supposed to learn in every school in the nation. A decade later, in the 1990s, around 40 states adopted the NCTM standards as a model, and many others acknowledged its influential role in shaping state curricular standards.[100]

The RTTT program was instrumental in the states' rush to adopt the CCSS. Although states were not *required* to adopt CCSS, many voluntarily adopted these standards because they improved these states' chances of obtaining federal funding under RTTT. The eligibility criteria for RTTT funds mentioned in the guidelines indicate that states had to adopt "internationally benchmarked standards and assessments that prepare students for success in college and the work place."[101] The success of CCSS can be recognized from the fact that, in 2010, about 45 states had adopted these standards in their mathematics curriculum, and 46 states had adopted them in their English Language Arts (ELA) curriculum. Several states that have formally adopted the CCSS standards are currently in the process of implementing them, part of which involves generating awareness about these standards among parents, educators, the community-at-large, and all other relevant stakeholders. The implementation process will also involve organizing professional development and training for educators, as they are ultimately the street- level implementers of reform.[102]

In terms of CCSS's effect on IGR and IGM, an interesting dynamic can be noted in the relations between state and local governments. Although states are at the forefront of implementing the CCSS standards, school districts are increasingly

97   Julie A. Marsh and Priscilla Wohlstetter. Recent Trends in Intergovernmental Relations: The Resurgence of Local Actors in Education Policy. 276.

98   http://www.corestandards.org/about-the-standards/.

99   http://www.corestandards.org/about-the-standards/.

100   Julie A. Marsh and Priscilla Wohlstetter. *Recent Trends in Intergovernmental Relations: The Resurgence of Local Actors in Education Policy.* 276-283. Robert Rothman, "How we got here: The emergence of the Common Core State Standards." *The State Education Standard.* Washington, DC: National Association of State Boards of Education. 2012.

101   Julie A.Marsh and Priscilla Wohlstetter. *Recent Trends in Intergovernmental Relations: The Resurgence of Local Actors in Education Policy.* 278. Also see, U. U.S. Department of Education. President Obama, U.S. Secretary of Education Duncan announce national competition to advance school reform. Washington, DC: U. S. Government Press Release July 2009.Retrieved from http://www.ed.gov/news/press-releases/ president-obama-us-secretary-education-duncan-announce- national-competition-adva.

102   Julie A. Marsh and Priscilla Wohlstetter. Recent Trends in Intergovernmental Relations: The Resurgence of Local Actors in Education Policy. 276–283.

playing an influential role in this regard. Alaska decided against adopting CCSS, with the exception of the Anchorage School District (ASD). This school district opted in because it wanted to compare its standards with other districts of the same size and demographics. In some cases, school districts are leading the implementation of CCSS, and states are taking a more supportive role, helping them develop proposals and instructional materials. New York City, Miami-Dade, San Diego, and Chelmsford school districts are some examples in this regard.[103] Similar to that of the RTTT program, implementation remains a challenging problem with the CCSS program as states and school districts struggle to align their assessments, curriculum, professional development programs, and teacher evaluation systems with the CCSS standards.

7.4.3 Reducing Federal Role & Rebalancing Federal-State Relations Since 2015 (Phase 3)

The third phase of federal and state relations in K–12 education saw a significant institutional change that involved a shift from a "federally-defined framework of state reform to a state-defined agenda of education reform."[104] This shift began with the waiver program under NCLB during the second term of the Obama administration. Many states used NCLB waivers to take back control over education by making necessary adjustments to their proposed reform plans for school improvement. However, per the NCLB mandate, their alternate plans had to align with federal requirements for reform. This gradual shift towards a state-defined education agenda continued under the RTTT program but gained significant momentum with the passage of the Every Student Succeeds Act (ESSA) of 2015, which dismantled many of the previous reform requirements mandated by the federal government and restored state control over education.[105] Under ESSA, states were given the primary responsibility for defining academic standards, assessing student proficiency levels using multiple performance measures pertaining to each of those standards, identifying and intervening in schools that fail to meet the proficiency benchmarks, and, finally, deciding the extent and nature of intervention to assist schools in need of improvement. Given that it was passed just four years before this textbook's publication, the ESSA's overall impact cannot yet be judged. Nor will it be possible to know some of the unintended consequences of this legislation on various stakeholder groups.[106]

Several new policy initiatives were proposed in education after the Trump administration took office. In his article "Public Education as a State-Federal

---

103   Julie A. Marsh and Priscilla Wohlstetter. Recent Trends in Intergovernmental Relations: The Resurgence of Local Actors in Education Policy. 278–279.

104   Kenneth Wong, *Public Education as a State-Federal Function in the United States. Federalism and Education: Ongoing Challenges and Policy Strategies in Ten Countries*. Information. 244.

105   Kenneth Wong, *Public Education as a State-Federal Function in the United States. Federalism and Education: Ongoing Challenges and Policy Strategies in Ten Countries*.

106   Kenneth Wong, *Public Education as a State-Federal Function in the United States. Federalism and Education: Ongoing Challenges and Policy Strategies in Ten Countries*.

Function in the United States," Kenneth Wong provides a comprehensive list of these initiatives that have significant implications for intergovernmental relations. These include the following:

> a) scaling back federal direction and shifting substantial decision making power to state and local government, b) proposing substantial budgetary reductions that may result in a reduction of one-fourth of the employees in the U.S. Department of Education, particularly in programs such as college and career access, arts, health, after school, and technology, c) expanding federal support for a broad portfolio of school choice, including charter schools, vouchers for parents to enroll their children in public and private schools, federal tax credit scholarship program, and magnet programs, d) easing possible entry of for profit providers in K–12 education, e) placing limits on federal capacity to promote equal education access, such as taking actions against families of illegal immigrants and limiting the scope of Title IX enforcement, and f) reducing investment in data and research infrastructure that currently stands at less than one percent of the total federal spending in education.[107]

These initiatives taken together illustrate the intent of the Trump administration to critically reassess the nature of federal involvement in K–12 education, including its redistributive focus, without going all out against the long-established traditions of "marble cake" federalism.[108]

7.4.3.1 Reviving School Choice-Based Reforms as a Federal Priority

Although the school choice movement started decades earlier and several administrations have experimented with various forms of school choice as a policy option, under the Trump administration, school choice was heralded as a major catalytic force in the hands of the federal government, with the administration pledging $20 billion in federal funding to promote choice to a new level of prominence.[109] To assess this administration's decision to promote school choice as a reform, it is prudent to delve deeper into the literature on choice and its effectiveness.

In his 1955 classic essay "The Role of Government in Education," Milton Friedman made a case for school choice through voucher programs. He questioned the role of government in educational provision. One of the central points in

107   Kenneth Wong, *Public Education as a State-Federal Function in the United States. Federalism and Education: Ongoing Challenges and Policy Strategies in Ten Countries.* 249.
108   Kenneth Wong, Education Governance in Performance-Based Federalism. In Patrick Manna and Patrick McGuinn (Eds.) *Education Governance for the Twenty-First Century.* Washington D.C.: Brookings Institution Press. 2013.
109   Kenneth Wong, *Public Education as a State-Federal Function in the United States. Federalism and Education: Ongoing Challenges and Policy Strategies in Ten Countries.* 231–255.

Friedman's essay was that the government should restrict itself to funding education through vouchers and ensure that all types of schools, including religious ones, meet certain minimum standards aligned to the social goals of education, such as creating responsible citizens for a democratic society and reducing inequality and crime for a better society. Friedman wrote his essay to advocate for federal aid to private Catholic schools.[110] The choice movement, however, received a boost many years later with the publication of the book *Politics, Markets, and America's Schools* by John E. Chubb and Terry M. Moe. (1990), which called for institutional reform by applying the choice mechanism that, according to them, would bring a new institutional framework within the public school system. However, this choice mechanism would not necessarily "privatize" public schools.[111]

School choice since then has largely taken the form of voucher schools, privately-managed schools, and charter schools.[112] Proponents of school choice argue that competition would increase efficiency by restructuring incentives both within and across schools. Since schools would have to compete in order to attract students and survive in a competitive marketplace, each school would try to operate at a lower cost and become more efficient in the process. Moreover, competition would enhance individual liberty by allowing parents the option to choose an education for their children that best matches their own values. Finally, the matching of consumers (parents and students) and suppliers (schools and districts) would lead to better student achievement.

Two of the central concerns about school choice have been its impact on equity and social cohesion. Opponents believe that school choice would disproportionately benefit children from wealthy families because their parents have the information advantage and can make the most use of it through their well-formed social networks. Furthermore, it would encourage re-segregation as well. This is because, when given a choice, families tend to prefer schools that have students from their own race and socioeconomic background.[113] Moreover, parents with limited resources and education may find it difficult to exercise choice in a timely and appropriate fashion. The non-choosers are likely to suffer academically because they tend to lose their academically-talented peers. A massive outflow of students from a poorly-functioning school due to choice would eventually close down many schools due to higher fixed costs. Limitations in terms of alternatives could seriously undermine the choice program. Denial of admission is yet another issue that opponents have consistently raised.

Scholars like Clive R. Belfield and Henry M. Levin in *Privatizing Educational Choice: Consequences for Parents, Schools, and Public Policy* have also discussed

110 Diana Ravitch, Diana. *The Death and the Life of the Great American School System: How Testing and Choice Are Undermining Education*. 115.

111 John Chubb and Terry, Moe. *Politics, Markets and America's Schools*. Washington, D.C.: The Brookings Institutions. 1990. 225.

112 Clive R. Belfield and Henry M. Levin. *Privatizing Educational Choice: Consequences for Parents, Schools, and Public Policy*. Boulder, CO: Paradigm Publishers, 2005.

113 Mark Schneider, Paul, Teske and Melissa Marshall. *Choosing Schools: Consumer Choice and the Quality of American Schools*. Princeton, NJ.: Princeton University Press. 2000.

the implications of school choice on social cohesion.[114] Belfield and Levin provide a fair assessment of the impact of competition on various educational outcomes by reviewing more than 40 studies conducted between 1972 and 2002. They examined the effects of inter-district and intra-district as well as competition between public and private schools. Although there is a positive relationship between increased competition and a rise in test scores, the effect size is modest at best. The authors did not find any effect on dropout rates related to competition. However, competition from private schools is positively associated with public school graduation rates. The effect of competition on spending is inconclusive, although it has a positive effect on educational efficiency. The authors also note that the additional costs of centralized administration through such services as monitoring, record-keeping, transportation, adjudication, and information sharing are likely to off-set any small gains from competition.[115] Studies on the impact of charter schools have found that these schools are less likely to enroll the neediest students than are regular public schools. Except for a few exceptional charter schools, there is also very little evidence suggesting that charter schools in their entirety perform better in terms of student achievement than do traditional public schools.[116]

In light of the above findings on the effectiveness of school choice as a policy option, it remains to be seen whether the Trump administration will be able to promote choice nationally beyond just Republican-controlled states and also find new service providers to ensure the effective implementation of school choice regionally.[117] The new intergovernmental landscape seems favorable toward an expansion of school choice, as it generally aligns with the goals of the ESSA and allows states extensive authority over policy-making so that they can promote a broader portfolio of school choice programs with federal funding. Currently, school choice is being given active consideration by several states, and with the continued demand for charter schools as a steady preference among parents who exercise choice, the enabling climate is likely to continue and ultimately lead to growth of school choice across several states.[118]

7.4.3.2 Rebalancing of the Federal Role in Addressing Inequity and Accountability

The Trump administration relied on several institutional arrangements to rebalance the federal role in addressing inequities that disproportionately have an impact on the education of various population subgroups. Furthermore, the administration also looked for ways to throttle the growing federal role to ensure

114 Clive R. Belfield and Henry M. Levin. *Privatizing Educational Choice: Consequences for Parents, Schools, and Public Policy*. Boulder, CO: Paradigm Publishers, 2005.
115 Ibid.
116 Diana Ravitch,*The Death and the Life of the Great American School System: How Testing and Choice Are Undermining Education*. 146.
117 Kenneth Wong, *Public Education as a State-Federal Function in the United States. Federalism and Education: Ongoing Challenges and Policy Strategies in Ten Countries*. 251.
118 Kenneth Wong, *Public Education as a State-Federal Function in the United States. Federalism and Education: Ongoing Challenges and Policy Strategies in Ten Countries*.

accountability from schools, districts, and state governments. Kenneth Wong describes these strategies in greater detail in his article "Public Education as a State-Federal Function in the United States. Federalism and Education: Ongoing Challenges and Policy Strategies in Ten Countries."[119] The launch of the ESSA in 2015 started rebalancing federal-state relations by granting states control over standards and other policy issues. Following that, the administration used the Republican majority in both houses of Congress to scale back the federal government's role in monitoring accountability issues under ESSA. For example, the Republican-controlled Congress used the Congressional Review Act to repeal ESSA regulatory guidance that was completed during the last few months of the Obama presidency and included critical issues ranging from civil rights regulation to teacher preparation program accountability as well as the requirement that schools include at least 95% of students in annual assessments.[120] The Secretary of Education, Dr. Betsy DeVos, under the Trump administration, also considered proposals that would weaken/eliminate the Department of Education's current data collection practices allowing it to systematically track schooling opportunities, schooling quality, and civil rights data that has been widely utilized by policy researchers and by states and districts to improve schooling services for all students.[121] Finally, the Trump administration loosened audit regulations on federal categorical grants programs and asked for a bare minimum set of documents from states instead of a comprehensive packet with detailed information. These actions were meant to weaken federal control over equity and accountability and prioritize school choice and state control.[122]

7.5 THE COURTS AND INTERGOVERNMENTAL RELATIONS

A common theme throughout various chapters of this book is that the Supreme Court has played a significant role in shaping American federalism through its landmark rulings (see chapter 2 in particular). This pattern has also been the case over the years in transforming the education sector through judicial precedents. One of the most far-reaching decisions of the Court pertains to the segregation of public schools that continued until 1954. In *Brown v. Board of Education of Topeka, Kansas*, the Court declared segregated public schools unconstitutional due to the overwhelming disparity that schools create in offering

---

119   Kenneth Wong, *Public Education as a State-Federal Function in the United States. Federalism and Education: Ongoing Challenges and Policy Strategies in Ten Countries.* 251–252.

120   Dana Goldstein, (2017, March 9). "Obama education rules are swept aside by Congress." *The New York Times* 9 March 2017. Retrieved from https://www.nytimes.com/2017/03/09/ us/every-student-succeeds-act-essa- congress.html?hpw&rref=education&action=click&pgtype=Homepage&module=well-region&region=bottom-well&WT. nav=bottom-well.

121   Michael Katz, Letting federal data drive state and local policy under Secretary DeVos. Urban Wire. Washington, DC: The Urban Institute. 2017.

122   Kenneth Wong, *Public Education as a State-Federal Function in the United States. Federalism and Education: Ongoing Challenges and Policy Strategies in Ten Countries.* Information 251–252.

quality education to African-American students compared to white students. The landmark ruling gave the U.S. another chance to attain "inclusive citizenship" by ensuring that all its citizens are afforded the opportunity for upward mobility and political participation through access to an equal education.[123] After *Brown v. Board of Education*, the federal government repeatedly intervened in state education matters to ensure racial equality in education, equal educational opportunity, and the separation of religion from public schools. The decision also paved the way for other major rulings on civil rights and voting rights in the early and mid-1960s.

In the last 40 years, the courts at all levels have also played a significant role in shaping the educational finance policy landscape following the 1954 landmark decision. Beginning in the 1960s, legal scholars have used the Equal Protection Clause of the Fourteenth Amendment to address school finance systems in

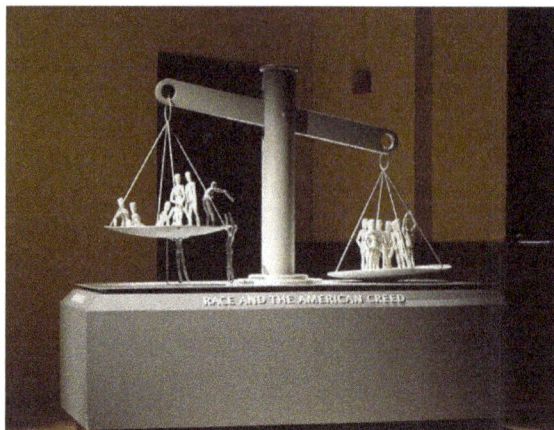

Figure 7.18: Scales of Justice, Brown v. Board of Education National Historic Site, Topeka, Kansas.
Source: Wikimedia Commons
Attribution: Chris Light
License: CC BY-SA 4.0

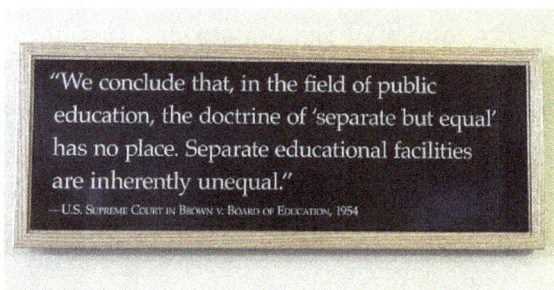

"We conclude that, in the field of public education, the doctrine of 'separate but equal' has no place. Separate educational facilities are inherently unequal."
—U.S. SUPREME COURT IN BROWN V. BOARD OF EDUCATION, 1954

Figure 7.19: Quote on Segregation from Supreme Court Decision, Brown v. Board of Education National Historic Site, Topeka, Kansas.
Source: Wikimedia Commons
Attribution: Adam Jones
License: CC BY-SA 2.0

many states that provided vastly different educational opportunities to children.[124] One of the fundamental reasons for such vastly different educational opportunities experienced by children is the unequal property tax bases that school districts have traditionally relied upon as a primary funding source for public schools. Social activists and education scholars have long recognized inter-district inequality in education financing; however, the *Brown v. Board of Education* decision prompted them to take on the arcane and indeterminate states' constitutional language in this regard. Early school finance legal challenges focused on children's rights to equal per-pupil funding or demanded a school finance system that does not rely on local property wealth. More recent school finance litigations have sought

123   Luis R. Fraga, Nick Rodriguez., and Bari Anhalt Erlichson. Desegregation and School Board Politics: The Limits of Court-Imposed Policy Change. In William G. Howell (Eds.) *Besieged: School Boards and the Future of Educational Politics*. Washington, D.C. Brookings Institution Press. 2005.
124   William S. Koski and Jesse Hahnel, *The Past, Present and Possible Futures of Educational Finance Reform Litigation*.

to "define qualitatively the substantive education to which children are constitutionally entitled."[125] Consequently, state supreme courts have invalidated the educational finance schemes of state legislatures and ordered system reforms. Data up to 2012 reveal that school finance lawsuits have been filed in 45 out of 50 states and, among cases that received a judicial decision, challengers to the state school finance schemes have won in 27 out of 47 such cases.[126]

Figure 7.20: Lets Read Lets Move at The Supreme Court.
Source: Wikimedia Commons
Attribution: US Department of Education
License: CC BY 2.0

Figure 7.21: Judge Robert A. Katzmann (2nd Cir.), Judge Damon J. Keith (6th Cir.), and Judge Sonia Sotomayor (2nd Cir.) at the *Brown V. Board of Education* Exhibit.
Source: Wikimedia Commons
Attribution: Unknown
License: Public Domain

7.6 THE ROLE OF NONGOVERNMENTAL ORGANIZATIONS (NGOS) IN PUBLIC EDUCATION

Although public schools in the U.S. remain overwhelmingly the responsibility of governments, NGOs shoulder a small share of public school revenues. Data from the National Center for Education Statistics show that in 2009-2010, roughly around two percent of public school revenue came from sources other than federal, state, and local governments.[127] Although these sources are often dubbed as NGOs, in reality. they range from school-based organizations, school foundations, local education funds, community foundations, local businesses, private corporate foundations, and corporations.[128] With ever-tightening school budgets, schools and districts are increasingly looking to nongovernmental partners to boost funding and are applying aggressive and sophisticated techniques to attract them.[129]

125 William S. Koski and Jesse Hahnel, *The Past, Present and Possible Futures of Educational Finance Reform Litigation*. 41.
126 William S. Koski and Jesse Hahnel, *The Past, Present and Possible Futures of Educational Finance Reform Litigation*. 41.
127 Janel S. Hansen, Michelle Hall., Dominic Brewer., and Jane Hannaway. The Role of Nongovernmental Organizations in Financing Public Schools. In Helen F. Ladd and Edward B. Fiske (Eds.) *Handbook of Research in Education Finance and Policy*, New York: Routledge, 2015.
128 Janel S. Hansen, Michelle Hall., Dominic Brewer., and Jane Hannaway. The Role of Nongovernmental Organizations in Financing Public Schools. In Helen F. Ladd and Edward B. Fiske (Eds.) *Handbook of Research in Education Finance and Policy*, New York: Routledge, 2015.
129 Scott A. James, Public school's coffers require a private boost. The New York Times. 2011. Ron W.

Figure 7.22: Melinda Gates, Co-founder, Bill and Melinda Gates Foundation.
Source: Wikimedia Commons
Attribution: Chatham House
License: CC BY 2.0

Despite their small share in funding public schools, policymakers and scholars of education also show a growing interest in understanding NGO motives and activities. The two most significant concerns from a school finance standpoint pertain to equity and sustainability. On the equity front, scholars who have researched private funding in public education found that schools that raised $25,000 or above through nonprofit organizations are more likely to be concentrated in high-income districts. Furthermore, high-income school districts spend three times ($135) the average private contribution per student than the state average.[130] Such an uneven growth in private funding at the local level will likely diminish the effects of school finance reforms achieved through decades of court rulings and litigations. In addition to equity concerns, many scholars have also raised sustainability concerns vis-à-vis private giving.

Among all the sources of private giving in public education, the financial support of private philanthropic independent foundations has garnered the maximum level of scrutiny and skepticism. While private foundations have supported ad hoc projects in public education since the early twentieth century, their targeted and reform-oriented giving in recent years have drawn outside scrutiny.[131] Current data shows that, in 2011, the top 1,000 private philanthropic foundations together contributed approximately $1.8 billion in public elementary and secondary education. Among the top 50 K–12 donors, the Bill and Melinda Gates Foundation occupied the number one position and donated $447 million in 2011 followed by the Walton Family Foundation, which donated $160 million. The Marian Community Foundation was ranked 50th and donated $17 million in 2011.[132] Interestingly, foundations that share interests are increasingly collaborating with each other to focus their efforts and maximize impact. Examples of this strategy can be seen in the funding that Teach for America received in 2011 from donors like the Board, Walton, Gates, and Robertson foundations that together donated $73

Zimmer Cathy, Krop and Dominic J. Brewer. Private resources in public schools: Evidence from a pilot study. *Journal of Education Finance*. 28 (2003): 485.

130   Janel S. Hansen, Michelle Hall., Dominic Brewer., and Jane Hannaway. The Role of Nongovernmental Organizations in Financing Public Schools. In Helen F. Ladd and Edward B. Fiske (Eds.) *Handbook of Research in Education Finance and Policy*, New York: Routledge, 2015. 340.

131   Janel S. Hansen, Michelle Hall., Dominic Brewer., and Jane Hannaway. The Role of Nongovernmental Organizations in Financing Public Schools. In Helen F. Ladd and Edward B. Fiske (Eds.) *Handbook of Research in Education Finance and Policy*, New York: Routledge, 2015 341.

132   Janel S. Hansen, Michelle Hall., Dominic Brewer., and Jane Hannaway. The Role of Nongovernmental Organizations in Financing Public Schools. In Helen F. Ladd and Edward B. Fiske (Eds.) *Handbook of Research in Education Finance and Policy*, New York: Routledge, 2015 341.

million to the organization to promote human capital development.[133] Others have highlighted the convergence of the federal Department of Education initiatives and the agendas of private foundations. One such example is the support for Common Core Standards from the Gates Foundation and Hewlett Foundation, which have heavily underwritten the development of standards through their support for the National Governors Association and The Council of Chief State School Officers, two highly influential state-based organizations.[134] Although this topic continues to draw considerable attention in policy circles, the implications of private foundation money on public education remains understudied.

7.7 CONCLUSION

Public schools in the U.S. are currently facing a myriad of challenges in spite of decades of reform. It remains one of the most salient public policy issues confronting American policymakers, academicians, and practitioners, with significant implications for both IGR and IGM. Disparities in educational opportunities and achievement have narrowed over the years, but they have not been eliminated. The apparent failure of reforms to tackle achievement gaps has raised many important questions. One concern that perhaps has not been raised too often in policy discourse pertains to the structure of public education governance in America. Most debates surrounding issues of governance in public education have focused on the ever-expanding role of federal involvement at the cost of state and local control. However, as the discussion in this chapter shows, that is not the full story. In fact, many recent scholars have argued that a greater federal role has in many cases strengthened the influence of state and local actors in governance and policy matters. A greater federal role has also brought in many new players in the education market, along with a host of nongovernmental agencies. Perhaps a more fundamental concern with education governance has to do with the multitude of institutions at every level that are responsible for running schools with overlapping responsibilities. The intergovernmental landscape for education remains highly complex, fragmented, decentralized, politicized, and bureaucratic, and is weakening the effects of well-intended reforms to improve the educational opportunities and academic performance of students. A good starting point is to ask the question that Patrick McGuinn and Paul Manna proposed regarding education governance in America: Where does the buck stop? Who leads when everyone is in charge?

---

133 Janel S. Hansen, Michelle Hall., Dominic Brewer., and Jane Hannaway. The Role of Nongovernmental Organizations in Financing Public Schools. In Helen F. Ladd and Edward B. Fiske (Eds.) *Handbook of Research in Education Finance and Policy*, New York: Routledge, 2015.
134 Janel S. Hansen, Michelle Hall., Dominic Brewer., and Jane Hannaway. The Role of Nongovernmental Organizations in Financing Public Schools. In Helen F. Ladd and Edward B. Fiske (Eds.) *Handbook of Research in Education Finance and Policy*, New York: Routledge, 2015 344.

REFLECTION QUESTIONS

1. Explain how the various conceptions of liberalism offer a useful lens to examine contemporary intergovernmental relations in public education.

2. Discuss the intergovernmental landscape for public education, including how federal- state-local relations have evolved over the years.

3. Please discuss the roles and responsibilities of various institutions in education governance within the intergovernmental landscape.

4. Consider the three recent education policy initiatives, The No Child Left Behind Act, the Race to the Top program, and the Common Core State Standards program. Please discuss whether expansion of federal authority in public education has translated into loss of power from state and local governments.

5. Explain the role of the courts in shaping IGR in public education.

6. Explain the role of NGOs in shaping intergovernmental relations in public education.

BIBLIOGRAPHY

Baker, Bruce D. *Educational Inequality and School Finance: Why Money Matters for America's Students.* Cambridge, MA: Harvard Education Press, 2018.

Banerjee, Neena. "Effects of Teacher-Student Ethno-Racial Mismatch and Overall Teacher Diversity in Elementary Schools on Educational Outcomes." *Journal of Research in Childhood Education*, 32, no 1 (2018): 94–118.

Bascia, Nina. "Teachers as Professionals: Salaries, Benefits and Unions." *International Handbook of Research on Teachers and Teaching*, 21, no. 6 (2009): 481–489.

Belfield, Clive R. and Henry M. Levin. *Privatizing Educational Choice: Consequences for Parents, Schools, and Public Policy.* Boulder, CO: Paradigm Publishers, 2005.

Berkman, Michael B., and Eric Plutzer. *Ten Thousand Democracies: Politics and Public Opinion in America's School Districts.* Washington, DC: Georgetown University Press, 2005.

Bohrnstedt, George W., and Jennifer A. O'Day. "Introductory Chapter." In Alan R. Sadovnik., Jennifer A. O'Day., George W. Bohrnstedt., and Kathryn M. Borman (Eds.), *No Child Left Behind and the reduction of the achievement gap: Sociological perspectives on federal educational policy.* New York: Routledge. 2008.

Chubb, John., and Terry, Moe. *Politics, Markets and America's Schools.* Washington, D.C.: The Brookings Institutions. 1990.

Derthick, Martha. *Keeping the compound republic: Essays on American federalism.* Washington, DC: Brookings Institution Press. 2001.

Dye, Thomas R., and Susan A. MacMANUS. *Politics in States and Communities.* Pearson

(14th edition). 2012.

Fischel, William A. *Making the Grade: The Economic Evolution of American School Districts*. Chicago: University of Chicago Press, 2009.

Fraga, Luis R., Nick Rodriguez., and Bari Anhalt Erlichson. "Desegregation and School Board Politics: The Limits of Court-Imposed Policy Change." In William G. Howell (Eds.) *Besieged: School Boards and the Future of Educational Politics*. Washington, D.C. Brookings Institution Press. 2005.

Franklin, Barry M. Race. "Restructuring, and Educational Reform: The Mayoral Takeover of the Detriot Public Schools." In Edward P. St. John, and Louis F. Miron (Eds.) *Reinterpreting Urban School Reform: Have Urban Schools Failed, Or Has the Reform Movement Failed Urban Schools?* SUNY Press. 2003.

Gais, Thomas., and J. Fossett. "Federalism and the executive branch." In J. D. Aberbach & M. A. Peterson (Eds.), *The executive branch*, 486–524. New York, NY: Oxford University Press. 2005.

Gamoran, Adam. *Standards-based reform and the poverty gap: Lessons for No Child Left Behind*. Washington, DC.: Brookings Institution Press. 2007.

Godwin, Kenneth R., and Frank R. Kemerer. *School Choice Tradeoffs: Liberty, Equity, and Diversity*. Texas: University of Texas Press, 2002.

Goldstein, D. "Obama education rules are swept aside by Congress." The New York Times. March 2017. Retrieved from https://www.nytimes.com/2017/03/09/us/every-student-succeeds-act-essa congress.html?hpw&rref=education&action=click&pgtype=Homepage&module=well-region&region=bottom- well&WT. nav=bottom-well.

Gordon, N.E. "The Changing Federal Role in Education Finance and Governance." In Helen F. Ladd and Edward B. Fiske (Eds.) *Handbook of Research in Education Finance and Policy*. New York: Routledge, 2015.

Gray, Virginia., and Russel L. Hanson. *Politics in the American states: A comparative analysis*. Washington, DC: CQ Press. 2008.

Grissom, Jason A and Carolyn D. Herrington. "Struggling for Coherence and Control: The New Politics of Intergovernmental Relations in Education." *Educational Policy*, 26, no 1 (2012): 3–14.

Grodzins, Morton. *The American system: A New view of government in the United States*. Chicago, IL: Rand McNally. 1966.

Grodzins, Morton. *The federal system. In President's Commission on National Goals, Goals for Americans*. Englewood Cliffs, NJ: Prentice Hall. 1960.

Guthrie, James W and Kenneth K. Wong. "The Continually Evolving Political Context of Education Finance. In Handbook of Research in Education Finance and Policy." In Helen F. Ladd and Edward B. Fiske (Eds.) *Handbook of Research in Education Finance and Policy*. New York: Routledge, 2015.

Hansen, Janel S., Michelle Hall., Dominic Brewer., and Jane Hannaway. "The Role of Nongovernmental Organizations in Financing Public Schools." In Helen F. Ladd and

Edward B. Fiske (Eds.) *Handbook of Research in Education Finance and Policy*, New York: Routledge, 2015.

Hanushek, Erik A and Alfred A. Lindseth. *Schoolhouses, Courthouses, and Statehouses: Solving the Funding-Achievement Puzzle in America's Public Schools*. Princeton: Princeton University Press, 2009.

Hess, Frederick M and Andrew P. Kelly. "Scapegoat, albatross, or what." In J. Hannaway and A. Rotherham (Eds.), *Collective bargaining in education: Negotiating change in today's schools*. Cambridge, MA: Harvard Education Press. 2006.

Hochschild, Jennifer L and Nathan Scovronick. *The American Dream and the Public Schools*. New York: Oxford University Press. 2003.

Howell, William G (ed). *Besieged: school boards and the future of education politics*. Washington, D.C. The Brookings Institution, 2005.

Howell, William G. *Besieged: school boards and the future of education politics*. Washington, D.C. The Brookings Institution, 2005.

Howell, William G., and Asya Magazinik. "Presidential Prescriptions for State Policy: Obama's Race to the Top Initiative." *Journal of Policy Analysis and Management.* 36, no. 3 (2017): 502–531.

James, S. *A public school's coffers require a private boost*. The New York Times. 2011.

Jha, Nandan K. *Political Economy of Public Education Finance: Equity, Political Institutions, and Inter-School District Competition*. Lexington Books/Rowman and Littlefield, 2020.

Jha, Nandan K., Neena Banerjee, and Stephanie Moller. "Assessing the Role of Teachers' Unions in the Adoption of Accountability Policies in Public Education." *The Urban Review*. pp. 1–32. Springer Netherlands. 2019.

Katz, M. *Letting federal data drive state and local policy under Secretary DeVos*. Urban Wire. Washington, DC: The Urban Institute. 2017.

Kirst, Michael W and Frederick M. Wirt. *The political dynamics of American education* (4th ed.). Richmond, CA: McCutchan. 2009.

Kober, Nancy., and Diane Stark Rentmer. *States' Progress and Challenges in Implementing Common Core State Standards*. Center on Education Policy Report, 2011.

Koppich, Julia E and Jessica Rigby. *Alternative teacher compensation: A primer*. Palo Alto, CA: Policy Analysis for California Education. 2009.

Koski, W.S. and Hahnel, J. "The Past, Present and Possible Futures of Educational Finance Reform Litigation." In *Handbook of Research in Education Finance and Policy*, edited by H.F. Ladd and Edward B. Fiske. New York: Routledge, 2015.

Koski, William S and Eileen L. Horng. "Facilitating the teacher quality gap? Collective bargaining agreements, teacher hiring and transfer rules, and teacher assignment among schools in California." *Education Finance and Policy*, 2(3), 262–300. 2007.

Lipsky, Michael. *Street-Level Bureaucracy*. New York: Russell Sage Foundation, 1980.

Manna, Paul. *Collision Course: Federal Education Policy Meets State and Local Realities*. CQ Press. 2011.

Manna, Paul., and Laura L. Ryany. "Competitive Grants and Educational Federalism: President Obama's Race to the Top Program in Theory and Practice." *The Journal of Federalism*, 41, no. 3: 522–546.

Marsh, Julie A., and Priscilla Wohlstetter. "Recent Trends in Intergovernmental Relations: The Resurgence of Local Actors in Education Policy." *Educational Researcher*. 42, no. 5 (2013): 276–283.

McGuinn, Patrick. "Presidential Policymaking: Race to the Top, Executive Power, and the Obama Education Agenda." *The Forum*. 12, no. 1: 61–79. 2014.

McGuinn, Patrick. "Stimulating reform: Race to the Top, Competitive grants and the Obama Education Agenda." *Educational Policy*, 26, 136–159. 2012.

McGuinn, Patrick., and Paul Manna. "Education governance in America: Who leads when everyone is in charge?" In Patrick McGuinn and Paul Manna (Ed.) *Education governance for the twenty-first century*, pp. 1–17. Washington D.C.: The Brookings Institute, 2013.

McGuire, Theresa J. and Leslie E. Papke. "Local Funding of Schools: The Property Tax and Its Alternatives." In Helen F. Ladd and Edward B. Fiske (Eds.) *Handbook of Research in Education Finance and Policy*. New York: Routledge, 2015.

Mehta, J., & Teles, S. "Jurisdictional politics: A new federal role in education." In Frederick. M. Hess & Andrew P. Kelly (Eds.), *Carrots, sticks, and the bully pulpit: Lessons from a half-century of federal efforts to improve America's schools*. Cambridge, MA: Harvard Education Press. 2011.

Meier, Deborah and George, Wood. *Many Children Left Behind: How No Child Left Behind Act is Damaging Our Children and Our Schools*. Boston: Beacon Press. 2004.

Meier, Kenneth J., Robert D. Wrinkle, and J.L. Polinard. "Representative Bureaucracy and Distributional Equity: Addressing the Hard Question." *The Journal of Politics*, 61, no. 4 (Nov 1999): pp. 1025–1039.

Mickelson, Roslyn A. "Achieving the Educational Opportunity in the wake of the judicial retreat from race sensitive remedies: Lessons from North Carolina." *American University Law Review*, 52 (6) (2003): 1477–1506.

Miron, G., Urschel, J. L., Aguilar, M. A., & Dailey, B. *Profiles of for-profit and nonprofit education management organizations*. Boulder, CO: National Education Policy Center. 2012.

Miron, G. "Education management organizations." In H. F. Ladd & E. B. Fiske (Eds.), *Handbook of research on education finance and policy* (pp. 475–496). New York, NY: Routledge. 2008.

O'Toole, Lawrence J., Jr. "American intergovernmental relations: Concluding thoughts." In Lawrence J. O'Toole, Jr. (Ed.), *American intergovernmental relations:*

Foundations, perspectives, and issues (4ᵗʰ ed., pp. 357–360). Washington, DC: CQ. 2007.

Odden, Allan R., and Lawrence, O. Picus. *School Finance: A Policy Perspective*. Boston: McGraw-Hill, 2013.

Peters, B Guy. *American public policy: Promise & performance* (8th ed.). Washington, DC: CQ Press. 2010.

Peterson, Paul E. *Saving Schools: From Horace Mann to Virtual Learning*. Cambridge: The Belknap Press of Harvard University Press, 2010.

Phillimore, J. "Understanding Intergovernmental Relations: Key Features and Trends." *Australian Journal of Public Administration*. 72, no. 3 (2013): 228–238.

Ravitch, Diana. *The Death and the Life of the Great American School System: How Testing and Choice Are Undermining Education*. New York: Basic Books. 2010.

Rothman, Robert. *How we got here: The emergence of the Common Core State Standards. The State Education Standard*. Washington, DC: National Association of State Boards of Education. 2012.

Rothstein, Richard., Rebecca Jacobson, and Tamara Wilder. *Grading Education: Getting Accountability Right*. Washington, D.C., and New York: Economic Policy Institute and Teachers College Press. 2008.

Schneider, Mark., Paul, Teske and Melissa Marschall. *Choosing Schools: Consumer Choice and the Quality of American Schools*. Princeton, NJ: Princeton University Press. 2000.

Springer, Mathew G. *Performance Incentives*. Washington, DC: Brookings Institution Press. 2009.

Springer, Mathew G., Erik A. Houck, and James W. Guthrie. "History and Scholarship Regarding United States Education Finance and Policy." In Helen F. Ladd and Edward B. Fiske, ed., *Handbook of Research in Education Finance and Policy*, New York: Routledge, 2015.

Stallings, D. T. "A brief history of the U.S. Department of Education." *Phi Delta Kappan*, 83(9), 677-683. 2002.

Stecher, B., Fuller, B., Timar, T., & Marsh, J. *Deregulating school aid in California: How districts responded to flexibility in Tier 3 categorical funds in 2010–11*, technical report. Santa Monica, CA: RAND and Policy Action for California Education. 2012.

Sundquist, James L. *Politics and Policy: The Eisenhower, Kennedy, and Johnson Years*. Washington, D.C.: Brookings Institution Press. 1968.

Tyack, David., and Larry Cuban. *Tinkering Toward Utopia: A Century of Public School Reform*. Cambridge: Mass.: Harvard University Press. 1995.

U.S. Department of Education. *President Obama, U.S. Secretary of Education Duncan announce national competition to advance school reform*. Washington, DC: U. S. Government Press Release July 2009.Retrieved from http://www.ed.gov/news/ press-releases/president-obama-us-secretary-education-duncan-announce- national-competition-adva.

Vergari, Sandra, "Safeguarding Federalism in Education Policy in Canada and the United States." *Publius: The Journal of Federalism.* 40, no. 3 (April., 2010), 534–557.

Vergari, Sandra. "The Limits of Federal Activism in Education Policy." *Educational Policy.* 26. no. 1(2012): 15–34.

Wildavsky, A. "Fruitcake federalism or birthday cake federalism?" In D. Schleicher & B. Swedlow (Eds.), *Federalism and political culture* (pp. 55–64). New Brunswick, NJ: Transaction. 1998.

Wohlstetter, Priscilla., Joanna, Smith, J., Caitlin, Farrell, Guilbert C, Hentschke, and Jennifer, Hirman. "How funding shapes the growth of charter management organizations: Is the tail wagging the dog?" *Journal of Education Finance*, 37 (2), 150–174. 2011.

Wong, Kenneth K. "Education Governance in Performance-Based Federalism." In Patrick Manna and Patrick McGuinn (Eds.) *Education Governance for the Twenty-First Century.* Washington D.C.: Brookings Institution Press. 2013.

Wong, Kenneth K., and Gail Sunderman. "Education Accountability as a Presidential Priority: No Child Left Behind and the Bush Presidency." *Publius: The Journal of Federalism.* 37 (2007): 333–350.

Wong, Kenneth. *Public Education as a State-Federal Function in the United States. Federalism and Education: Ongoing Challenges and Policy Strategies in Ten Countries.* Information Age Publishing. 2018. Pp. 231–255.

Wong, Kenneth. "The Politics of Education." In Virginia Gray and Russell L. Hanson (Ed.) *Politics in the American States: A Comparative Analysis.* CQ Press, Washington, D.C. 2008 pp. 350–380.

Zimmer, Ron W., Cathy, Krop and Dominic J. Brewer. "Private resources in public schools: Evidence from a pilot study." *Journal of Education Finance.* 28 (2003): 485–522.

8

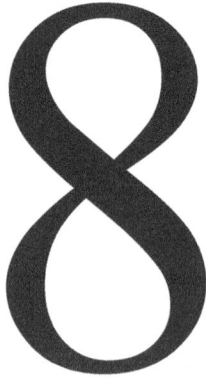

Homeland Security as a Dimension of Intergovernmental Relations

Carol M. Glen

LEARNING OBJECTIVES

- Demonstrate an understanding of the impact that the September 11, 2001 attacks had on intergovernmental relations.

- Demonstrate an understanding of the Department of Homeland Security's primary goals as a crucial agency for coordinating the nation's affairs across government levels.

- Demonstrate an understanding of the threats posed by cyber-attacks at the state and local levels and how responses illustrated the U.S.'s coordinated system of intergovernmental relations.

- Demonstrate knowledge of intergovernmental cooperation in relation to immigration enforcement policy, especially as it pertains to implementing national policies at the subnational levels.

- Demonstrate knowledge of intergovernmental conflicts in relation to immigration enforcement policy.

KEY TERMS

Department of Homeland Security	Anti-commandeering clause
9/11 Commission Report	Immigration and Customs Enforcement
Printz v. United States	Arizona SB 1070
USA PATRIOT Act	287 (g) Agreements
State and Local Fusion Centers	Secure Communities Program
Suspicious Activity Reports	Sanctuary Jurisdictions
Ransomware	Fourth Amendment
Help America Vote Act	Supremacy Clause
Electoral Assistance Commission	

8.1 INTRODUCTION

As we have seen throughout the book, numerous dimensions of intergovernmental relations (IGR) factor into how programs and policies are designed and implemented across levels of government. Not only is our federal system highly politicized but also the policy arena is broader and more complex than ever, drawing in numerous actors and interests seeking attention on the governmental agenda. This final chapter will tie together aspects of intergovernmental behavior to examine the significant role that homeland security plays as a dynamic policy area. Demographic and social change, globalization, and threats to national security continue to test government capacities at all levels to develop effective policy solutions. In some policy areas, greater responsibility centralization may be evident, while in others, decentralization might be the trend. Regardless of which dynamic is present, effective intergovernmental management (IGM) and coordination is crucial if today's complex problems are to be resolved. This chapter continues the examination of intergovernmental policy coordination, which has been a particular focus in chapters 6 and 7, as well as the persistence of intergovernmental tensions in homeland security policy. It specifically focuses on counterterrorism, cyber and election security, and immigration enforcement. Together, these policy domains highlight evolving cooperation and conflicts at the federal, state, and local levels.

8.2 HOMELAND SECURITY

Historically, national security has fundamentally been a federal responsibility. Article I, Section 8 of the U.S. Constitution gives Congress the right to declare war, appropriate funds to raise and support an army and navy, and make rules for the regulation of military forces, while Article II, Section 2 gives the president the role of Commander-in-Chief as well as the power to make treaties, with the advice and consent of the Senate. Scholars widely recognize that power over national security policy has become more centralized in recent decades,

Figure 8.1: September 11 attacks in New York City: View of the World Trade Center and the Statue of Liberty.
Source: Wikimedia Commons
Attribution: National Park Service
License: Public Domain

not only at the federal level but also increasingly within the executive branch. At the same time, it became obvious after September 11, 2001 that securing the homeland requires cooperation and collaboration among all levels of government. After all, if there is an attack on the homeland, it is local police and firefighters as well as other public servants who will be the first responders. Protecting the homeland is, therefore, a national, state, and local concern. As Donald F. Kettl, notes in his work "Homeland Security: The Federalism Challenge," if a homeland security system is going to be effective, it needs to be "at its core, an intergovernmental system."[1]

8.2.1 Department of Homeland Security

The terrorist attacks on September 11, 2001 highlighted disturbing flaws in U.S. national security preparedness. At the time of the attacks, terrorism had not been an overriding national security concern, quite simply because no one believed that such a devastating event could occur. As the 9/11 Commission Report stated, "the most important failure was one of imagination."[2] The report also noted that missed opportunities to prevent the attacks were a symptom of broader failings in the government's capacity to meet the new challenges of the twenty-first century. These flaws included the misallocation of resources, lack of inter-agency information sharing, and generalized bureaucratic rivalries. The devastating 2001 attacks brought two seemingly-contradictory policy responses: a further centralization of authority over national security in the federal government and increased recognition that state and local governments have critical roles to play in homeland security. The National Strategy for Homeland Security (2002) stated, "Our structure of overlapping federal, state, and local governance—our country has more than 87,000 different jurisdictions—provides unique opportunity and challenges for our homeland security efforts... A national strategy requires a national effort."[3]

> **9/11 Commission**: An independent, bipartisan Commission established in 2002. Tasked with giving a complete account of the circumstances surrounding the September 11, 2001 terrorist attacks, and to make recommendations to prevent future attacks.
>
> **USA PATRIOT ACT (2001)**: Significantly increased the surveillance and investigative powers of law enforcement agencies in the U.S. Passed by Congress overwhelmingly on a bipartisan vote, but criticized for undermining civil liberties.

Figure 8.2: Flag of the United States Secretary of Homeland Security.
Source: Wikimedia Commons
Attribution: U.S. Government
License: Public Domain

In addition to the federal national strategy for homeland security, Congress passed both the controversial USA PATRIOT Act (2001) and the Homeland Security Act (2002). The latter created the Department of Homeland Security (DHS), which represented the largest reorganization of the

---

1   Donald F. Kettl, "Homeland Security: The Federalism Challenge" in Laurence J. O'Toole, Jr. and Robert K. Christensen, eds. *American Intergovernmental Relations: Foundations, Perspectives, and Issues* (Washington, D.C.: CQ Press, 2013), 306.
2   National Commission on Terrorist Attacks Upon the United States, "9/11 Report" (New York: W.W. Norton and Company, https://www.9-11commission.gov/report.
3   Office of Homeland Security, "Executive Summary," *National Strategy for Homeland Security* (Washington D.C.: 2002), vii-xiii.

Figure 8.3: Bush signs USA PATRIOT Improvement and Reauthorization Act.
Source: Wikimedia Commons
Attribution: Kimberlee Hewitt
License: Public Domain

federal government in decades. It consolidated 22 government agencies into one large cabinet-level department that employs more than 240,000 people and has a budget of more than $50 billion (2020). The primary goals of the DHS are to counter terrorism; safeguard U.S. borders; and secure transportation, communications, and cyberspace. Figure 8.4 illustrates how the DHS budget for financial year 2020 was allocated.[4]

DHS BUDGET ALLOCATION 2020

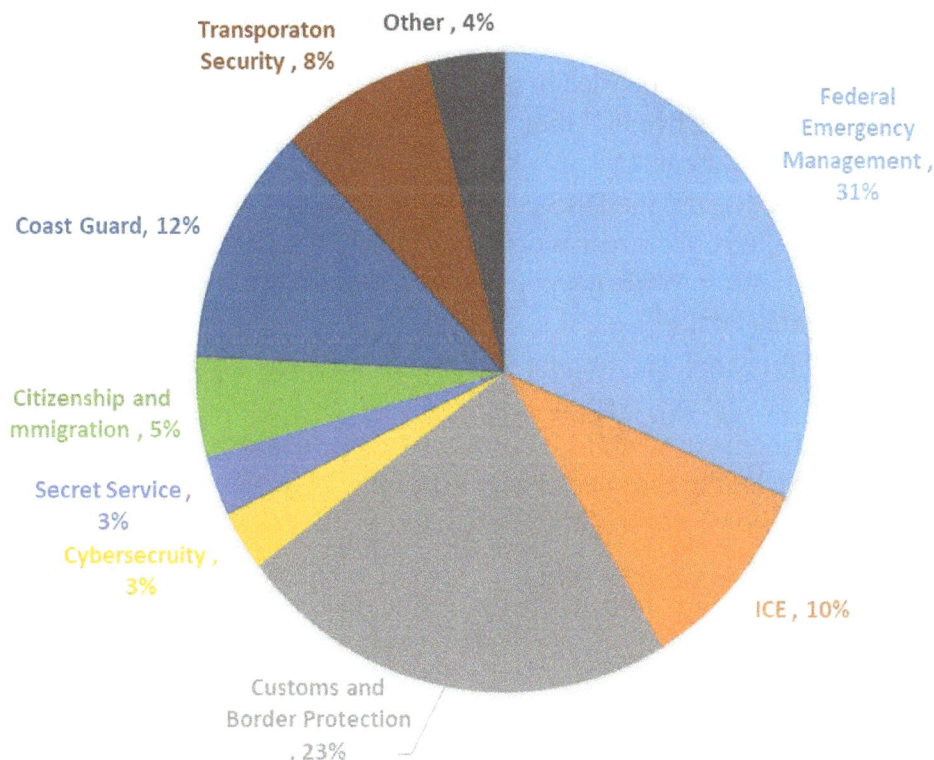

Figure 8.4: Department of Homeland Security Budget Allocation, 2020.
Source: Original Work
Attribution: Carol M. Glen, based on data from US Department of Homeland Security
License: CC BY-SA 4.0

DHS also introduced a Homeland Security Advisory System (HSAS) to disseminate information about terrorist threats to all levels of government and to the American people. The system had a five-level color-coded classification of terrorist

---

4   U.S. Department of Homeland Security, *Budget-in-Brief Fiscal Year 2020*, https://www.dhs.gov.

threats, from "Green," meaning a low risk of terrorist attacks, to "Red," indicating a severe risk of terrorist attacks. Despite its best intentions, the HSAS faced criticism, however, for being too vague and for failing to give guidance on what actions should be taken at each threat level. As Jacob Shapiro and Dara Cohen point out in "Color Bind: Lessons from the Failed Homeland Security Advisory System," an effective alert system must motivate lower levels of government, as well as the private sector, to take protective measures, but they will only do so if they trust the system. In effect, "the federal government must convince them that the desired actions are worthwhile" since national leaders do not have the legal authority to order such actions.[5] Lack of confidence in the HSAS ultimately led to its demise, and it was replaced by the National Terrorism Advisory System (NTAS) in

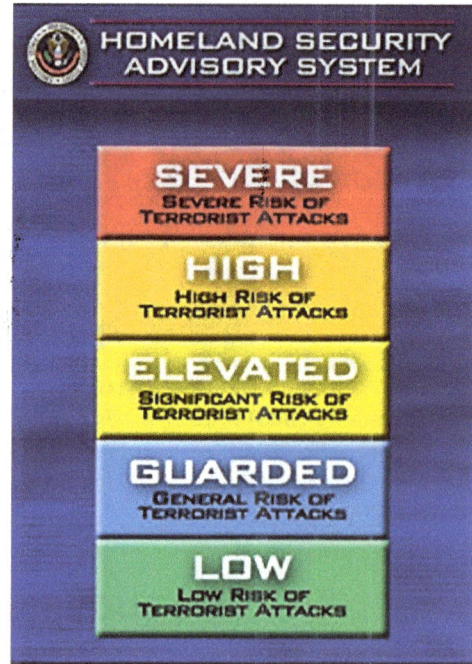

Figure 8.5: Levels of the U.S. Homeland Security Advisory System.
Source: Wikimedia Commons
Attribution: U.S. Navy
License: Public Domain

2011. Under the new system, the DHS issues informational "Bulletins" as well as "Alerts" if a credible terrorist threat is detected. Unlike the HSAS, alerts not only warn of a threat but also provide government agencies and first responders with detailed assessments of risk.

The National Preparedness System represents another federal mechanism for standardizing emergency response activities at all levels of government.[6] The goal of the system is to ensure that disaster response is federally supported, state managed, and locally executed, which can only be achieved with effective intergovernmental coordination. The September 11, 2001 attacks highlighted critical weaknesses in communication and coordination at even the most local level. In his article "Contingent Coordination: Practical and Theoretical Puzzles for Homeland Security," Donald Kettl vividly describes some of the coordination problems in New York City on that day:

> New York City had long divided its public protection functions into the traditional functional lines of police and fire. Over time, functional rivalries had delayed the implementation of new coordination systems, such as improved radio communication in high-rise buildings. Management was so centralized that, when the buildings collapsed, they destroyed the

5   Jacob N. Shapiro and Dara Kay Cohen, "Color Bind: Lessons from the Failed Homeland Security Advisory System" *International Security*, Vol. 32, No. 2 (Fall, 2007), 121.
6   U.S. Department of Homeland Security, *National Preparedness System,* https://www.fema.gov/national-preparedness-system.

operations grid that told fire commanders which crews were working where in which building, so it took hours to determine who was missing and where they might be found. The fire and police commanders did not coordinate their operations, so that warnings from the police helicopter overhead never reached the fire commanders.[7]

Despite heroic efforts to cope with the greatest emergency that first responders in an American city had ever faced to that point, fragmented organizational systems undermined their responses.

8.2.2 Intergovernmental Cooperation through State and Local Fusion Centers

The National Preparedness System is designed to engage all levels of government and local communities to prepare for disasters. To achieve that objective, DHS encourages the establishment of State and Local Fusion Centers (SLFC). A fusion center is a "collaborative effort of two or more Federal, State, local, or tribal government agencies that combines resources, expertise, and information with the goal of maximizing the ability of such agencies to detect, prevent, investigate, apprehend, and respond to criminal and terrorist activity."[8] DHS provides training, grants, and other operational support to SLFC to promote multilevel partnerships and to help facilitate information sharing. Hundreds of representatives from federal agencies have been assigned to fusion centers around the country. The two agencies that provide the most support are DHS's Office of Intelligence and Analysis (I&A) and the Federal Bureau of Investigation (FBI). Within the SLFC, law enforcement personnel comprise the majority of the staff. Currently, there are 79 Fusion Centers, with at least one in each state.[9]

Fusion centers have generated a significant amount of intelligence in support of homeland security. For example, in 2017, SLFC collaborated with other centers and/or federal partners to produce almost 250 "distributable products," including Suspicious Activity Reports (SAR). SARs document behavior that indicates the planning of a terrorist attack or other criminal activity. Gathering

> **Suspicious Activity Reports**: Produced by State and Local Fusion Centers to identify individuals who might be planning a terrorist act. The information is shared with the Department of Homeland Security.

evidence about criminal activity and other threats has, of course, always been the backbone of law enforcement, but the difference now is that such information can be shared nationally through the Homeland Security Data Network. DHS reports that this collaboration has improved the effectiveness of law enforcement. Between

---

7   Donald F. Kettl, "Contingent Coordination: Practical and Theoretical Puzzles for Homeland Security" *American Review of Public Administration*, Vol. 33 No. 3, (September 2003), 260.

8   U.S. Department of Homeland Security, "National Network of Fusion Centers Fact Sheet," last modified August 16, 2019, https://www.dhs.gov/national-network-fusion-centers-fact-sheet.

9   U.S. Department of Homeland Security, "2017 National Network of Fusion Centers Final Report," 24 (October 2018) https://www.dhs.gov/publication/2017-fusion-center-assessment.

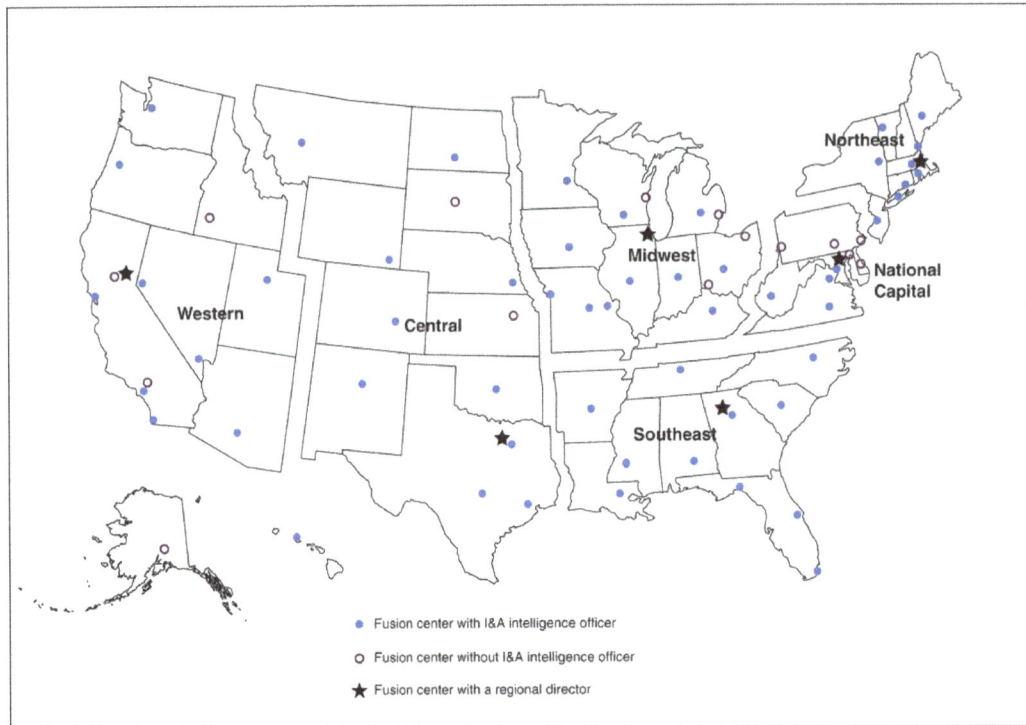

Sources: GAO analysis of I&A data and Map Resources.

Figure 8.6: Locations of State and Local Fusion Centers and Deployed I&A Intelligence Officers and Regional Directors, August 2010.
Source: Wikimedia Commons
Attribution: U.S. Government Accountability Office
License: Public Domain

2015 and 2017, the number of SAR submitted by fusion centers that resulted in the initiation or enhancement of an FBI investigation increased by 95%.[10] Despite successes, SLFC have encountered criticism and continue to face some challenges. A scathing report by the Senate Subcommittee on Investigations in 2012 found that fusion centers often forward intelligence of uneven quality, "oftentimes shoddy, rarely timely, sometimes endangering citizens' civil liberties and Privacy Act protections."[11] The report recommended that DHS improve its oversight of federal grants that support fusion centers and that the department work to strengthen civil liberty protections in SLFC intelligence reporting. To address these criticisms, the DHS conducts annual fusion center assessments to evaluate the performance of SLFC and make recommendations for improvements.

8.3 CYBERSECURITY IN STATE AND LOCAL GOVERNMENTS

One area with an urgent need for more expertise in fusion centers, and in state and local governments generally, is cybersecurity. All levels of government face cyber threats, but states and cities are often less well positioned to address those

10   U.S. Department of Homeland Security, "2017 National Network of Fusion Centers Final Report."
11   U.S. Senate Permanent Subcommittee on Investigations, "Federal Support For and Involvement in State and Local Fusion Centers," (October 3, 2012), 1.

threats than is the federal government. A 2015 survey found that a majority of respondents in federal agencies said they were able to recruit and retain ample expert personnel to minimize cybersecurity risks, but only 31 percent of state and local respondents agreed. In addition, while 55 percent of federal respondents rated their ability to recover from a cyber-attack as very high, only 28 percent of state and local respondents concurred.[12] Numerous examples of cyber-attacks and responses to those attacks bear out this data. For example,

- South Carolina Department of Revenue (2012): A single malicious email sent to workers at the Department of Revenue enabled an international hacker to access state computers and retrieve 3.8 million tax returns, including Social Security numbers and bank account information.[13]

- City of Atlanta (2018): A large-scale cyber attack caused widespread outages in services, including warrant issuances, water service requests, new inmate processing, court fee payments, and other online bill-pay programs. The city was forced to shut down most of its digital services for a period of at least five days, and it took months to fully recover.[14]

- Texas (2019): Twenty-two mostly small local governments were subject to a coordinated cyber attack. The attackers locked up computers and public records, preventing online services and payments. In at least one case, hackers breached an IT company's software program that had been outsourced by the city.[15]

Having less IT expertise and fewer resources, cities have become a favorite target of hackers who extort their governments through installing ransomware. Once hackers gain access to the network (usually through an infected email), they encrypt data and demand bitcoin payments in exchange for a key that would restore city files and services. Although the FBI discourages victims from paying ransom demands, many feel that they have no choice but to do so. The cost of the ransom is typically much less than the total cost of recovery. For instance, the city of Atlanta's refusal to pay a ransom of $51,000 is said to have cost the city $17 million to restore and rebuild their systems.[16] Overall, ransomware attacks

12   Ponemon Institute, "State of Cybersecurity in Local, State & Federal Government," October 2015, https://www.ponemon.org/library/the-state-of-cybersecurity-in-local-state-and-federal-government.
13   David M. Upton and Sadie Creese, "The Danger from Within," Harvard Business Review (September 2014), https://hbr.org/2014/09/the-danger-from-within.
14   Alan Blinder and Nicole Perlroth, "A Cyberattack Hobbles Atlanta, and Security Experts Shudder," *The New York Times,* March 27, 2018.
15   Bobby Allyn, 22 "Texas Towns Hit With Ransomware Attack In 'New Front' Of Cyber assault" *National Public Radio,* (August 20, 2019), https://www.npr.org/2019/08/20/752695554/23-texas-towns-hit-with-ransomware-attack-in-new-front-of-cyberassault.
16   Stephen Deere, "Confidential Report: Atlanta's cyber-attack could cost taxpayers $17 million," *Atlanta Journal-Constitution*, (August 1, 2018), https://www.ajc.com/news/confidential-report-atlanta-cyber-attack-could-hit-million/GAljmndAF3EQdVWlMcXS0K.

increased by over 100 percent in the first quarter of 2019 compared to 2018, and the average payout almost doubled.[17]

Although these attacks are extremely destructive and costly, it is frequently difficult to bring the perpetrators to justice. Many of the hackers are overseas so are immune from U.S. prosecution, even if they can be identified. For example, two Iranians were indicted in December 2018 for the Atlanta ransomware incident, and

> **Ransomware:** A form of cyberattack that is often directed at local government agencies for the purpose of extorting money. Agency data is encrypted until the ransom is paid.

other cyber attacks, under the Computer Fraud and Abuse Act (1986). They will likely never face trial, however, since the U.S. and Iran have not signed an extradition treaty. While the principal motive of ransomware hackers is usually economic gain, these attacks highlight vulnerabilities in government networks and have obvious homeland security implications. Foreign governments could potentially cripple American cities, large and small. DHS has identified ransomware attacks "as the most visible cybersecurity risk playing out across our nation's networks" and strongly urges municipalities "to consider ransomware infections as destructive attacks, not an event where you can simply pay off the

The Nation's Risk Managers

The Cybersecurity and Infrastructure Security Agency (CISA) is the pinnacle of national risk management for cyber and physical infrastructure

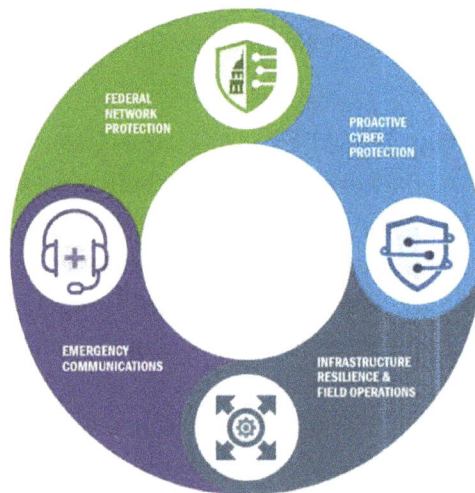

FEDERAL NETWORK PROTECTION

PROACTIVE CYBER PROTECTION

EMERGENCY COMMUNICATIONS

INFRASTRUCTURE RESILIENCE & FIELD OPERATIONS

Figure 8.7: Cybersecurity and Infrastructure Security Agency.
Source: Wikimedia Commons
Attribution: Department of Homeland Security
License: Public Domain

17   Beazly Breach Response Services Team, "Ransomware attacks skyrocket, Q1 2019," *Beazly Breach Insights*, (May 23, 2019), https://www.beazley.com/news/2019/beazley_breach_insights_may_2019.html.

bad guys."[18] The agency provides broad guidance on cyber defense, response, and recovery through its Cybersecurity and Infrastructure Security Agency (CISA) as well as some funding through FEMA, but is it unlikely that this response will be enough to satisfy all demands. To supplement federal efforts, states are building cybersecurity partnerships with lower-levels of government. State assistance in this area is warranted since states typically regulate utility sectors and have a direct obligation to protect this critical infrastructure. A 2019 survey of state IT leaders found that 65 percent of states provided security infrastructure services to local governments. This was an 11 percent increase from 2016, which is not surprising given the increased number of security threats directed at local governments.[19] States provide such services as security management and training, cyber response teams, ransomware response, and election security. Of those states that did not provide services to local governments, the main reason given was lack of funding.

8.3.1 Federal Election Security

Election security is another area that has significant implications for homeland security, especially concerning federal elections. Elections require considerable intergovernmental cooperation and coordination, but this is complicated by the nature of the U.S. electoral system. Rather than one national structure, thousands of state and local systems administer elections. In this highly-decentralized arrangement, responsibilities are divided both within and between states, but there are some commonalities. States typically have primary responsibility for making rules with respect to how elections are managed, while local governments are primarily responsible for conducting elections in accordance with those rules. The county government usually has the responsibility to administer voter rolls, design ballots, select polling places, train poll workers, and report election results. Though most election activity is conducted locally under the supervision of the state, the federal government is far from absent in this policy area.

The Constitution gives the federal government specific responsibilities over campaigns and elections. Table 8.1 outlines the main functions performed by federal and state governments in federal elections.

18   U.S. Department of Homeland Security, "Ransomware Outbreak" *CISI Insights*, (August 21, 2019), https://www.us-cert.gov/sites/default/files/2019-08/CISA_Insights-Ransomware_Outbreak_S508C.pdf.
19   National Association of State Chief Information Officers, "The Responsive State CIO: Connecting to the Customer, 2019 State CIO Survey," https://www.nascio.org/wp-content/uploads/2019/11/2019StateCIOSurvey.pdf.

Table 8.1: Federal and State Responsibilities in Federal Elections

Main Function	Government Responsible	Primary Federal Agency
Campaign Finance	Federal	• Department of Justice • Federal Election Commission
Election Administration	States	• Election Assistance Commission • Department of Justice
Election Security	States	• Department of Homeland Security • Department of Justice
Qualifications and Contested Elections	Federal	• House and Senate
Redistricting	States	• Department of Commerce • Department of Justice
Voting Rights	Federal	• Department of Justice

Source: Congressional Research Service[20]

Prior to 2000, the federal government was primarily concerned with campaign finance; setting contribution limits, disclosure rules, and permissible uses of campaign funds; and requiring disclaimers in political advertising. In addition, since the Voting Rights Act (1965), the federal government has also been deeply involved in ensuring that voters are not discriminated against based on characteristics such as race or disability.

Following the controversial and disputed 2000 election (ultimately decided by the Supreme Court), the federal government directed its attention to the administration of elections. Congress passed the Help America Vote Act (HAVA) in 2002 in direct response to the irregularities that emerged during the 2000 election; HAVA authorized $3.65 billion to be paid to states to improve election security. This sweeping legislation established the Election Assistance Commission (EAC) as an independent bipartisan body charged with bolstering and protecting the nation's voting systems. The EAC supports election officials through the establishment of voluntary voting system guidelines with respect to voting system standards, provisional voting and voting information requirements, computerized statewide voter registration lists, and requirements for voters who register by mail. The EAC also acts as a national clearinghouse for election system information and disseminating information on best practices, as well as other resources aimed at improving elections. In 2017, the DHS designated electoral

> **Voting Rights Act (1965):** Outlawed discriminatory voting practices adopted in many southern states after the Civil War, such as literacy tests as a prerequisite to voting.
>
> **Help America Vote Act (2002):** Created mandatory minimum standards for states to follow in election administration, and provided some funding to help states meet those new standards. The law also established the Election Assistance Commission.

20   R. Sam Garret, "Federal Role in U.S. Campaigns and Elections: An Overview," *Congressional Research Service Report* 5, https://fas.org/sgp/crs/misc/R45302.pdf (September 4, 2018).

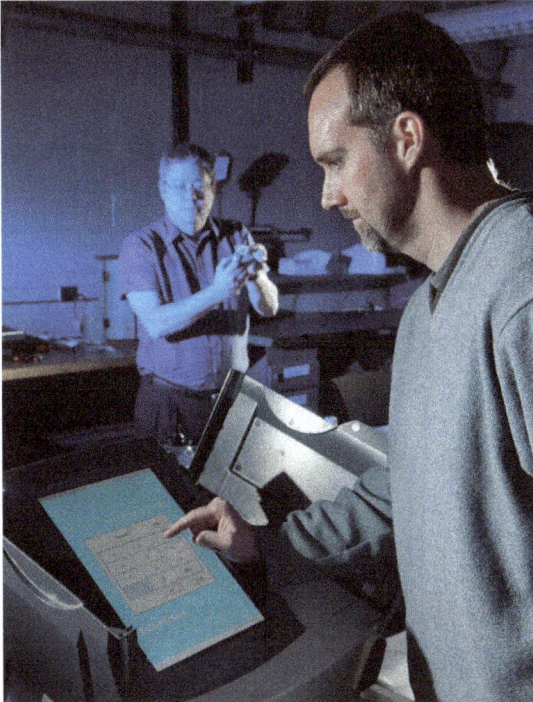

Figure 8.8: The Vulnerability Assessment Team at Argonne National Laboratory, test an electronic voting machine for security.
Source: Wikimedia Commons
Attribution: U.S. Department of Energy
License: Public Domain

systems as critical infrastructure and provided additional funds to secure those systems. During 2018, the EAC distributed $380 million to states, most of which was spent on improving cybersecurity and purchasing new voting machines.[21]

Despite the significant amount of federal funds allocated for elections, states and localities are still primarily responsible for most of the costs associated with conducting federal elections, with states contributing to varying degrees.[22] A Government Accountability Office (GAO) survey in 2018 reported that 11 states covered all of the acquisition costs of voting equipment, while eight states shared the cost with local government. However, in 24 cases, states provided no financial assistance for voting equipment.[23] In some cases, the allocation of funding is disrupted by political conflicts. In Minnesota, for example, election officials were unable to access $6.6 million in HAVA funding until after the 2018 election due to a budget dispute between the state's Democratic governor and the Republican-controlled legislature.[24] Other problems arise because of blurred responsibilities and jurisdictions. Federal statutes generally hold states accountable for ensuring compliance with election laws, but those laws are implemented at the local level. To illustrate, in 2012 the U.S. Department of Justice filed a lawsuit against Alabama for failing to send absentee ballots overseas at least 45 days before the election. The state responded by arguing that it was the responsibility of local officials to comply with this requirement; therefore; the state should have no liability. According to Justin Weinstein-Tull in "Election Law Federalism," "Courts have largely rejected the idea that states may evade liability by delegating responsibility to counties, but questions exist as to whether and how the federal government may force states to

---

21   Election Assistance Commission, "The Impact of HAVA Funding on the 2018 Elections," https://www.eac.gov/sites/default/files/paymentgrants/TheImpactofHAVAFundingonthe2018Elections_EAC.pdf.
22   Congressional Research Service, "The State and Local Role in Election Administration: Duties and Structures" (March 4, 2019), https://fas.org/sgp/crs/misc/R45549.pdf.
23   Government Accountability Office, "ELECTIONS: Observations on Voting Equipment Use and Replacement" (April 2018), https://www.gao.gov/assets/700/691201.pdf.
24   Miles Parks, "Bureaucracy And Politics Slow Election Security Funding To States," *National Public Radio* (June 18, 2018) https://www.npr.org/2018/06/18/617874348/bureaucracy-and-politics-slow-election-security-funding-to-states.

enforce the statutes against their own local governments."[25] The consequence of this "liability mismatch" is widespread non-compliance with some election laws at the state and local levels. The federal government is also limited in its ability to force states to comply with some of its broader national security objectives.

Traditionally, national security was primarily a federal responsibility, as most threats were expected to come from other nation-states abroad. However, terrorism and cyber attacks have changed this calculus. State and local governments are now expected to play key roles in protecting the homeland, and their contributions are vital. Due to constitutional constraints, however, the federal government cannot impose its will on state and local governments. The Supreme Court made this stance clear in *Printz v. the United States* with respect to firearm background checks, stating that "The Federal Government may neither issue directives requiring States to address a particular problem, nor command the State's officers...such commands are fundamentally incompatible with our constitutional system of dual sovereignty."[26] This principle is also known as the anti-commandeering doctrine. The federal government can provide a framework for intergovernmental cooperation and necessary resources, but it cannot create a top-down hierarchy in which state and local governments become its agents. Instead, the federal government must employ other means, such as financial incentives, to induce lower levels of government to act on its priorities. The federal system of government therefore adds complexity to homeland security objectives. If national security goals are to be achieved, then intergovernmental coordination is essential, but difficult. As Donald Ketl notes in "Contingent Coordination: Practical and Theoretical Puzzles for Homeland Security," "Homeland security takes many of the traditional problems of organizational coordination, multiplies them enormously, and vastly raises the stakes for success and failure."[27]

> ***Printz v. United States***: Supreme Court case that reinforced the anti-commandeering doctrine and reaffirmed states' rights.
>
> ***Anti-Commandeering Doctrine***: Principle that the federal government cannot require state officials to enforce federal law.

8.4. IMMIGRATION ENFORCEMENT POLICY

In general, like homeland security policy, immigration policy is a federal responsibility that cannot be achieved without state and local cooperation. However, it is shaped by more intense ideological struggles and partisan conflicts. Although there are certainly intergovernmental tensions over how best to achieve national security, there is broad agreement that this is a worthy objective. By contrast, the goals of immigration policy do not always garner extensive support, and federal administrations of both political parties have had to contend with opposition to their immigration policies at state and local levels. Resistance to federal policy

---

25   Justin Weinstein-Tull, "Election Law Federalism" *Michigan Law Revue, 114* (2016) 747–801.

26   United States Supreme Court, *Pritz v. United States* 854 F.Supp. 1503 (1994).

27   Donald F. Ketll, "Contingent Coordination: Practical and Theoretical Puzzles for Homeland Security," 256.

in this area highlights the difficulties associated with policy implementation in a federal system, even when the federal government has clear authority.

8.4.1 Federal Immigration Authority

Article I, Section 8 of the U.S. Constitution explicitly mentions citizenship, giving Congress the exclusive power to establish a "uniform Rule of Naturalization." Federal authority over citizenship and immigration policy has also been supported by numerous court rulings. In 1976, the Supreme Court stated unequivocally that the "power to regulate immigration, is unquestionably exclusively a federal power."[28] In doing so, the Court applied the doctrine of federal preemption, which asserts that Congress has the power to preempt state legislation as long as it is acting within the powers granted to it under the U.S. Constitution. In another example, a federal district court in California declared that a law designed to deny illegal immigrants access to public benefits is unconstitutional for the same reason: "The State is powerless to enact its own scheme to regulate immigration or to devise immigration regulations which run parallel to or purport to supplement the federal immigration laws."[29]

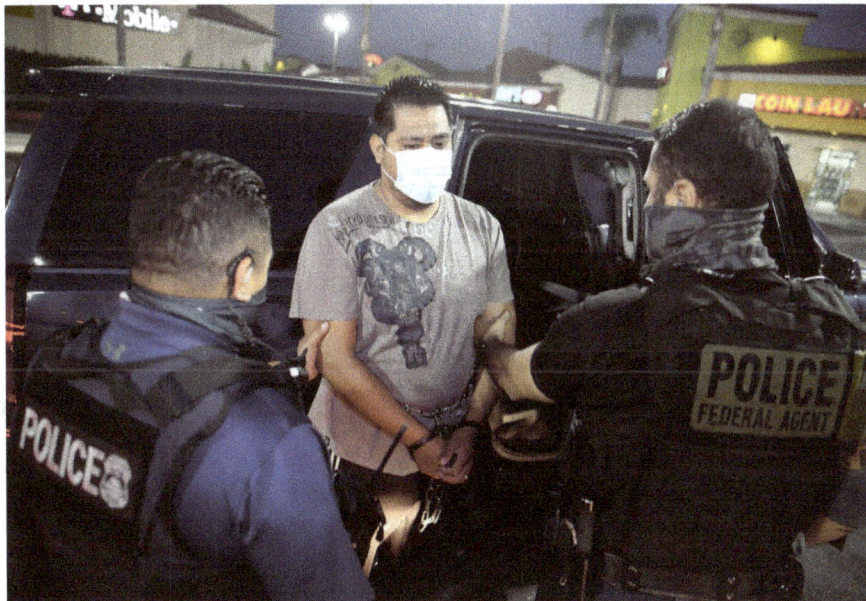

Figure 8.9: 1 October 2020: The Department of Homeland Security (DHS) and U.S. Immigration and Customs Enforcement (ICE) announced the conclusion to a week-long targeted enforcement operation that resulted in the apprehension of over 125 at-large aliens across the state of California, where sanctuary policies have largely prohibited the cooperation of law enforcement agencies in the arrest of criminal aliens.
Source: Wikimedia Commons
Attribution: U.S. Immigration and Customs Enforcement
License: CC BY-SA 4.0

28   U.S. Supreme Court, *De Canas v. Bica*, 424 U.S. 351 (1976).
29   U.S. District Court for the Central District of California, *League of United Latin American Citizens v. Wilson*, 908 F. Supp. 755 (November 20, 1995).

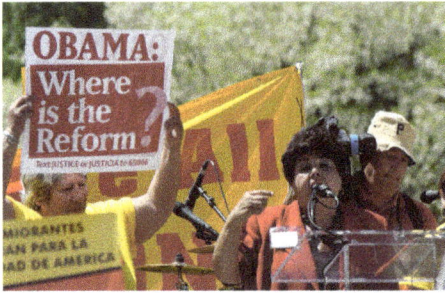

Figure 8.10: On May 1, 2010 leaders of the immigration reform movement were arrested in Washington DC. At the end of a peaceful demonstration at Lafayette Park, leaders of the immigration reform movement were arrested for a sit-in at the railings in front of the White House in what was intended to be an act of civil disobedience. Set against the background of Arizona's adoption of SB1070, the leaders vowed not to move from the railings until either an immigration reform law was passed or they were arrested. Police arrested the volunteers in a very calm and civil pro-forma manner while the surrounding crowds called on President Obama to take the lead in implementing immigration reform.

Source: Wikimedia Commons
Attribution: Arasmus Photo
License: CC BY 2.0

The DHS enforces immigration laws principally through three agencies: U.S. Customs and Border Protection (CBP), U.S. Immigration and Customs Enforcement (ICE), and U.S. Citizenship and Immigration Services (USCIS). CBP enforces immigration laws at and between ports of entry, while ICE is responsible for interior enforcement and for detention and removal operations. Finally, USCIS adjudicates applications and petitions for immigration and naturalization benefits. ICE has more than 200,000 law enforcement officers in more than 400 offices in the U.S. and around the world,[30] while CBP has a workforce of more than 60,000 employees and is one of the world's largest law enforcement organizations.[31]

Despite exclusive federal prerogatives over immigration policy, and the thousands of federal employees devoted to enforcement, the federal government does not have the necessary resources to enforce immigration policy in all locales. To identify, apprehend, and remove illegal immigrants, DHS must therefore rely on the cooperation of local, county, and state police as well as corrections officials. As Cristina Rodriguez notes in "Enforcement, Integration, and the Future of Immigration Federalism," enforcement Federalism is explicitly about IGR, but the system lacks coherence "because federalism's many agents inevitably create intergovernmental friction and pockets of tension between Washington and the local."[32] As a result, implementation of immigration policy will necessitate a combination of centralization and decentralization and "the extent of federal control is always likely to be contested and contingent."[33]

Federal authority over immigration policy has been challenged by state governments regarding the lack of federal enforcement and resources. One of the most controversial state immigration laws was passed by the Arizona legislature

30   Department of Homeland Security "Who we Are," *U.S. Immigration and Customs Enforcement,* (January 8, 2020), https://www.ice.gov/about.
31   Department of Homeland Security, "About CBP" *U.S. Immigration and Customs Enforcement,* (September 18, 2019), https://www.cbp.gov/about.
32   Heather M. Creek and Stephen Yoder, "With a Little Help from Our Feds: Understanding State Immigration Enforcement Policy Adoption in American Federalism," *The Policy Studies Journal,* Vol. 40, No. 4 (2012) 674–697.
33   Cristina Rodriguez, "Enforcement, Integration, and the Future of Immigration Federalism" *Journal on Migration and Human Security,* Vol. 5 No. 2 (2017), 513.

in 2010. Officially named the Support Our Law Enforcement and Safe Neighborhoods Act, it is also known as Arizona SB 1070. The law created new state immigration-related crimes and broadened the authority of the state to enforce immigration laws. The rationale for SB 1070 was an increase in illegal immigration into the state and widespread fear of crime. When Arizona Governor Jan Brewer signed

Arizona SB 1070 (2010): Controversial Arizona law that created new immigrant crimes and strengthened the state's immigration enforcement. Most of the law was deemed unconstitutional by the Supreme Court.

the law, she said that it would be used as a tool to "solve a crisis we did not create and the federal government has refused to fix." She went on to say, "We in Arizona have been more than patient waiting for Washington to act but decades of inaction and misguided policy have created a dangerous and unacceptable situation."[34] The statute contained four main provisions (1) making it a state crime to reside in Arizona without legal permission; (2) making it a state crime to work without legal permission; (3) requiring law enforcement officers to verify the legal status of

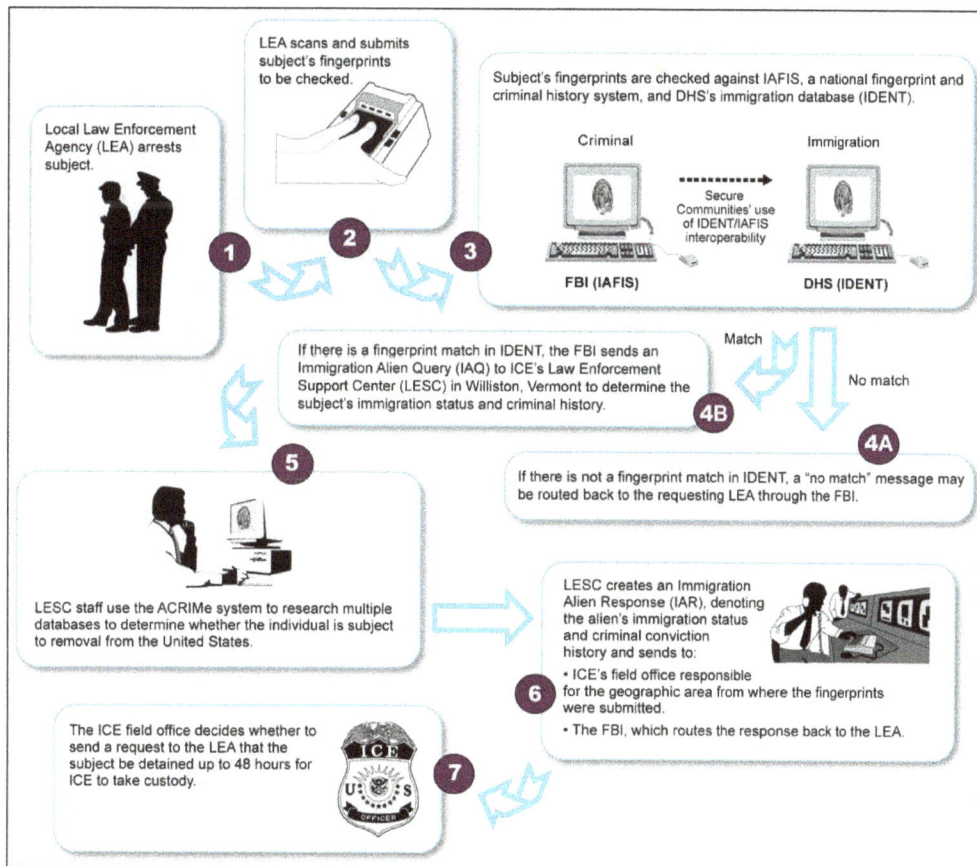

Source: GAO analysis of information provided by ICE

Figure 8.11: This image is excerpted from a U.S. GAO report.
Source: Wikimedia Commons
Attribution: U.S. Government Accountability Office
License: Public Domain

---

34   Devin Dwyer and Huma Khan, "Arizona's Gov. Brewer Signs Controversial Immigration Bill" *ABC News* (April 21, 2010), https://abcnews.go.com/WN/obama-arizona-immigration-bill-misguided/story?id=10457567.

all individuals who were arrested or detained; and (4) allowing law enforcement officers to arrest individuals without a warrant based on probable cause of unlawful presence. The Obama administration immediately sued to block the legislation in federal district court, arguing that the law usurped the federal government's exclusive authority over immigration. The case eventually made its way to the Supreme Court where most of its provisions were determined to be unconstitutional. The Supreme Court noted that, while Arizona was understandably frustrated by problems caused by illegal immigration, it could not introduce polices that undermine federal law.

8.4.2 Federalism and Immigration Enforcement Cooperation

The federal government's court victory over Arizona provided a clear signal to states that they cannot introduce and enforce immigration legislation that goes beyond what is provided in federal statutes. It did not, however, end the role played by state and local authorities in immigration enforcement. Immigration has a direct impact on fiscal well-being, public health, safety, and general welfare, so states have a strong interest in engaging in this policy area. One way to do so is through what are known as "287(g)" cooperation agreements.

> *Section 287(g) Program*: Authorizes the Director of ICE to enter into agreements with state and local law enforcement agencies to allow law enforcement officers to perform some immigration law enforcement functions.

The 287(g) program is named for Section 287(g) of the Immigration and Nationality Act (1952). The program allows the DHS to enter into formal written agreements with state and local police departments and to deputize selected law enforcement officers to perform the functions of federal immigration agents. The agreements are negotiated between DHS and local authorities and delegate authority to a limited number of police officers under the supervision of Immigration and Customs Enforcement. There are two types of agreements in the program: the jail enforcement model and the warrant service officer model. Under the former, police officers can interrogate alleged noncitizens who have been arrested. They can also issue immigration detainers in order to hold individuals for up to 48 business hours beyond the time they would otherwise have been released. Under the warrant service model, ICE trains and authorizes law enforcement officers to execute ICE warrants within state and local jails or correctional facilities. As of April 2019, there were 75 287(g) agreements in 20 states. Considering the thousands of eligible state and local law enforcement agencies around the country, the number of 287(g) agreements remains small. Low levels of interest have been explained by the fact that few concrete benefits accrue to local police departments and that the costs are often too high. Intertwining regular policing with immigration enforcement could have a negative effect on community relations, and it also diverts valuable resources away from the core mission of police departments.[35]

35   Cristina Rodriguez, "Enforcement, Integration, and the Future of Immigration Federalism" 509–540.

A program that is much more extensively used for immigration enforcement is known as Secure Communities (SC). Established in 2008 by the Bush administration, the program identifies immigrants in U.S. jails who are deportable under immigration law. In a typical situation, when an arrest is made, fingerprints are taken and transmitted to a state repository. Then, in the case of felonies and serious misdemeanors, all states voluntarily send that information to the FBI. Under the SC program, the FBI automatically shares fingerprint data with a DHS immigration database system known as IDENT. The database holds tens of millions of records which ICE uses to determine immigration status. In contrast to other ICE-local partnerships, SC provides a technological rather than physical presence in prisons and jails. Also, unlike the 287(g) program, no local law-enforcement agents are deputized to enforce immigration laws. SC was suspended in 2014 by the Obama administration as criticism of the program mounted, but it was subsequently reactivated in 2017 by President Trump.

> **IDENT**: DHS database that holds biometric information and other data on over 200 million people who have entered, attempted to enter, and exited the United States of America.

8.4.3 Federalism and Immigration Enforcement Conflicts

The SC program represented a significant increase in federal-state cooperation, but it also brought controversy and criticism. The system was intended to identify and remove the most dangerous and violent offenders, but DHS data shows otherwise. In 2011, 19 percent of deportees had committed level 1 offences, the most dangerous, while 29 percent had committed minor crimes and misdemeanors. In addition, 26 percent of those deported had immigration violations but no criminal convictions.[36] The SC program was also criticized on the grounds that it could promote racial profiling, that police might arbitrarily arrest someone they suspect of being an illegal immigrant in order to initiate deportation proceedings. As criticism increased, three states—Massachusetts, New York, and Illinois—attempted to opt out of the program by ending their agreement with the federal government. In response, DHS terminated agreements with all states in 2011, stating that they were not required. According to the Director of ICE, once a state submits fingerprint data to the FBI, "no agreement with the state is legally necessary for one part of the federal government to share it with another part."[37]

Through the use of technology, the federal government has reinforced its dominance over immigration policy, and this stance has implications for federal-state relations. Rodriguez argues that the information-sharing component of the SC program reflects "an end-run around federalism."[38] Automated immigration

---

36   American Immigration Council, "Secure Communities: A Fact Sheet" (November 29, 2011), https://www.americanimmigrationcouncil.org/research/secure-communities-fact-sheet.

37   U.S. Department of Homeland Security, *Taskforce on Secure Communities Findings and Recommendations* (September, 2011), 7, https://www.dhs.gov/xlibrary/assets/hsac-task-force-on-secure-communities-findings-and-recommendations-report.pdf.

38   Cristina Rodriguez, "Enforcement, Integration, and the Future of Immigration Federalism," 519.

policing does not allow states to decide how the information they send to the FBI is used. As a result, states indirectly engage in immigration enforcement whether or not they have agreed to cooperate with federal immigration authorities. State and local jurisdictions are not completely powerless in this arrangement, however. In most cases, ICE still needs the cooperation of local authorities in order to facilitate deportation. This typically involves issuing an immigration detainer request to hold the individual for up to 48 hours to give

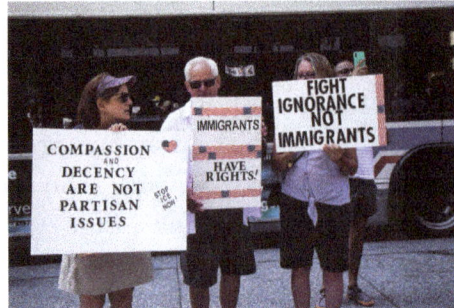

Figure 8.12: People Protesting ICE and Deportation Raids Chicago, Illinois on 7-13-19.

Source: Wikimedia Commons
Attribution: Charles Edward Miller
License: CC BY-SA 2.0

ICE the time to take that person into custody. Since it would be unconstitutional for the federal government to command local governments to enforce federal law, due to the anti-commandeering doctrine, courts have ruled that detainer requests are voluntary. As a result, some local authorities have decided not to cooperate with ICE.

By September 2019, 715 counties had policies against holding people on detainer requests, and 241 counties had policies that limit ICE agents' access to interrogate individuals held in local custody.[39] In some cases, local jurisdictions have argued that detainer requests violate the Fourth Amendment requirement that arrests must be supported by probable cause. Specifically, it requires that ICE must have probable cause to believe an individual is not only a non-citizen but also a non-citizen who is subject to removal.[40] Legislation that limits local cooperation with ICE is referred to as sanctuary law, and locales that refuse to cooperate are called sanctuary jurisdictions.

8.4.3.1 Sanctuary Jurisdictions

Sanctuary jurisdictions refer to cities, towns, and states that have passed ordinances, executive orders, and other legal provisions that are designed to limit enforcement of federal immigration laws. The nature of these laws varies by location, but they fall generally into three approaches: (1) limit

Sanctuary Jurisdictions: Cities, counties, and states that limit their cooperation with federal immigration authorities.

inquiries about a person's immigration status unless investigating another illegal activity ("don't ask"), (2) limit arrests for violation of immigration laws ("don't enforce"), and (3) limit disclosure to federal authorities of immigration status

---

39   Immigrant Legal Resource Center, "Growing the Resistance: How Sanctuary Laws and Policies Have Flourished During the Trump Administration" (December 17, 2019), https://www.ilrc.org/growing-resistance-how-sanctuary-laws-and-policies-have-flourished-during-trump-administration.

40   American Civil Liberties Union, "ICE Detainers and the Fourth Amendment: What do Recent Federal Court Decisions Mean" (November 13, 2014), https://www.aclu.org/other/backgrounder-ice-detainers-and-fourth-amendment-what-do-recent-federal-court-decisions-mean.

information ("don't tell").[41] Sanctuary locales date back to the 1980s when religious groups provided shelter to immigrants who were fleeing civil war in Central America. The federal government successfully prosecuted some of the Americans involved, accusing them of operating a modern-day underground railroad that directed immigrants towards sanctuary churches. A few years later, the federal government addressed the sanctuary movement in the wide-ranging Illegal Immigration Reform and Immigrant Responsibility Act (1996), stating: "no State or local government entity shall prohibit or in any way restrict any government entity or official from sending to or receiving from the INS information regarding the immigration status of any individual in the United States."[42]

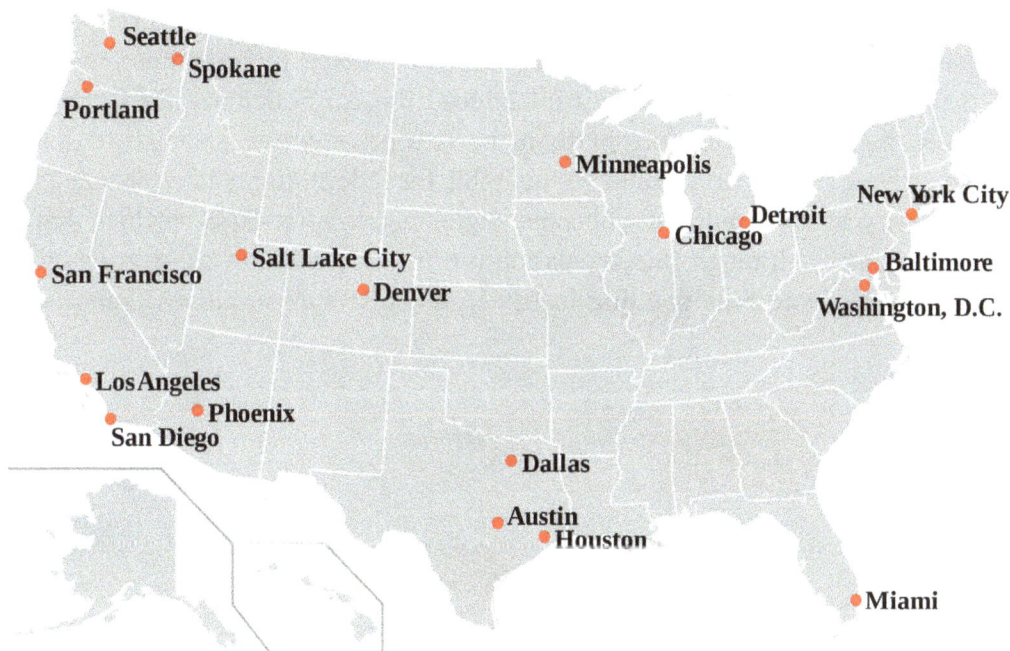

Figure 8.13: U.S. Sanctuary Cities Map: Major cities that had adopted "sanctuary" ordinances by 2017 banning city employees and police officers from asking people about their immigration status.
Source: Wikimedia Commons
Attribution: User "Howpper"
License: CC BY-SA 4.0

Despite this prohibition, it is estimated that there are over 300 sanctuary jurisdictions in the U.S., ranging in size from small towns to large cities, including Los Angeles, Chicago, and New York. By 2019, nine states had declared themselves to be sanctuary states.[43] Several high-profile crimes

> ***Executive Order 13768***: President Trump's order that would make sanctuary jurisdictions ineligible for federal grants.

41   Raina Bhatt, "Pushing an End to Sanctuary Cities: Will it Happen?" *Michigan Journal of Race and Law*, Vol. 22, Issue 1 (2016), 145 https://repository.law.umich.edu/cgi/viewcontent.cgi?article=1068&context=mjrl.
42   U.S. House of Representatives, *Illegal Immigration Reform and Immigrant Responsibility Act of 1996* (September 24), Section 642, https://www.congress.gov/104/crpt/hrpt828/CRPT-104hrpt828.pdf.
43   Bryan Griffith and Jessica M. Vaughan, "Map: Sanctuary Cities, Counties, and States," February 5, 2020, https://cis.org/Map-Sanctuary-Cities-Counties-and-States.

committed by illegal immigrants brought the issue of sanctuary jurisdictions to the fore of public attention, prompting a response by the federal government and some states. On January 25, 2017, President Trump issued Executive Order 13768, Enhancing Public Safety in the Interior of the United States, which declares that sanctuary jurisdictions "willfully violate federal law" and cause "immeasurable harm to the American people." It went on to say that sanctuary jurisdictions will be ineligible to receive federal grants, except as deemed necessary for law enforcement.[44] During June of the following year, however, a federal judge in San Francisco blocked the policy from taking effect. In the ruling, the judge said that, since the U.S. Constitution vests spending powers in Congress, not the president, the Executive Order cannot constitutionally place new conditions on federal funds. At the same time, the Trump Administration put pressure on Congress to introduce legislation to address sanctuary jurisdictions. In June 2017, the House of Representatives introduced the No Sanctuary for Criminals Act (H.R. 3003) that went further than the Executive Order, stipulating that a non-complying jurisdiction would be ineligible for federal financial assistance for at least one year and could only become eligible again after DHS certifies that it is in compliance. Although this legislation did not become law, as of 2019 there were four additional bills pending in the House of Representatives that would

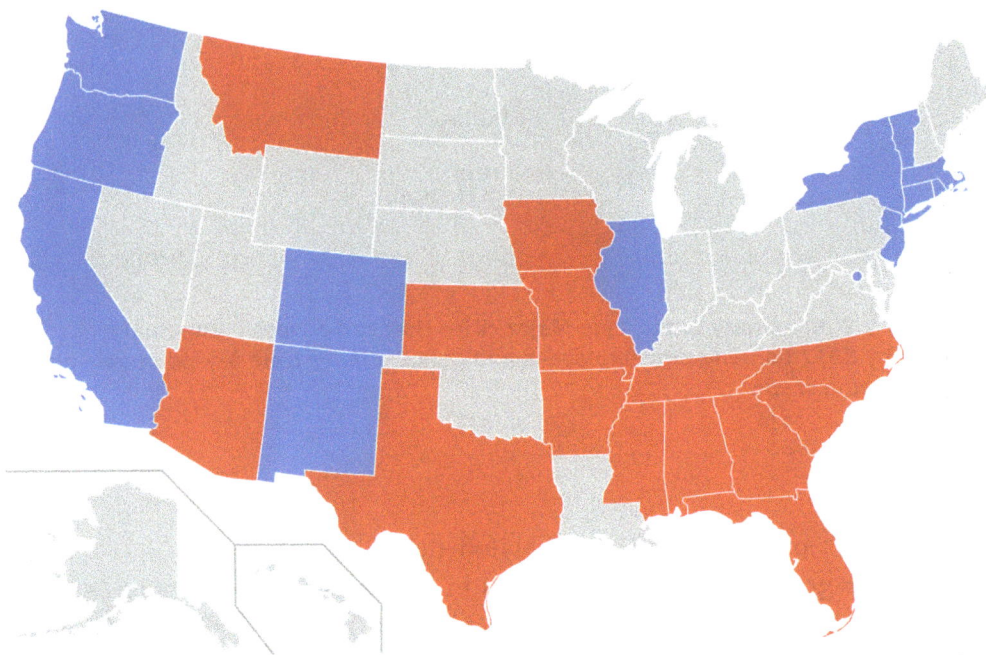

Figure 8.14: Sanctuary Policy by State as of August 2022. Pro-sanctuary states are in blue, states which have banned sanctuary cities are in red, and states in gray have no official policy.
Source: Wikimedia Commons
Attribution: User "TheAmeliaMay"
License: CC BY-SA 4.0

44   President Donald J. Trump, "Executive Order: Enhancing Public Safety in the Interior of the United States" (January 25, 2017), https://www.whitehouse.gov/presidential-actions/executive-order-enhancing-public-safety-interior-united-states.

deny federal funding to any state, locality, or educational institution that impedes immigration enforcement.[45]

There has also been significant legislative activity at the state level concerning sanctuary jurisdictions. As of June 2019, thirty states had pending legislation related to noncompliance with immigration detainers. Of these, 21 states had proposed legislation that would prohibit sanctuary policies, while five states, plus the District of Columbia, had bills supporting sanctuary policies.[46] Some states are also increasing pressure on local government officials by declaring they will be held personally accountable for non-compliance. In Florida, for instance, a 2019 law that bans sanctuary cities includes a provision allowing the Governor to initiate judicial proceedings against officers in order to enforce compliance. This move apparently mirrors the Trump Administration's position. In a 2018 interview, the acting director of ICE stated, "we have got to start charging some of the politicians with crimes."[47] Another development at the state and local levels are citizen initiatives that place, or attempt to place, the issue of sanctuary status on the ballot. These proposals have had mixed results, however. For example, in Humboldt County, California, voters approved a sanctuary city ballot measure in 2018, but a similar measure was defeated in Tucson, Arizona in 2019.

The Supremacy Clause of the Constitution (Article VI, paragraph 2), and specifically the doctrine of preemption, establishes that federal law takes precedence over conflicting state laws. This is especially true with respect to immigration enforcement; courts have also deemed that federal authority in this policy area is preeminent. However, federal power is not unlimited; the anti-commandeering principle holds that state officials cannot be forced to act as agents of the federal government. So, as a substitute for compulsion, the federal government has resorted to financial incentives and penalties in order to elicit compliance. For example, in 1984, Congress passed the National Minimum Drinking Age Act, which withheld five percent of federal highway funding from states that did not maintain a minimum legal drinking age of 21. As discussed in chapter 2, a challenge to that law (*South Dakota v. Dole*) prompted the Supreme Court to rule that Congress has the constitutional right to withhold funds provided it meets certain conditions. Such action must: (1) be in the pursuit of the general welfare, (2) be unambiguous in its conditions, (3) be related to the federal interest in national projects or programs, (d) must not impose unconstitutional conditions, and (e) must not be coercive. The court ruled that the legislation in the *Dole* case did not violate the anti-commandeering doctrine since states still had a choice as to whether or not they accepted federal funds.

Intergovernmental conflicts over the issue of immigration enforcement undoubtedly have greatly intensified in recent years. On one side of the dispute

---

45   National Conference of State Legislators, "Sanctuary Policy FAQ," (June 20, 2019), https://www.ncsl.org/research/immigration/sanctuary-policy-faq635991795.aspx.

46   National Conference of State Legislators, "Sanctuary Policy FAQ."

47   Brandon Conradis, "Trump ICE pick: Politicians who run sanctuary cities should be charged with crimes," *The Hill* (January 2, 2018), https://thehill.com/homenews/administration/367167-trump-ice-pick-politicians-who-run-sanctuary-cities-should-be-charged.

are local jurisdictions that aim to protect undocumented residents and view this conflict as a human rights issue; on the other side are federal and state governments that seek to enforce immigration policies. This intergovernmental clash is neither new nor confined to immigration. As Toni M. Massaro and Shefali Milczarek-Desai contend in "Constitutional Cities: Sanctuary Jurisdictions, Local Voice, And Individual Liberty," local governments have challenged state and federal authority across a range of issues, including LGBT protections, minimum wage increases, gun control, and marijuana legalization.[48] Just as states are not uniform in their policy preferences so also may cities and counties adhere to diametrically opposed positions even within the same state, often due to partisan interests. With respect to immigration, much of this issue remains open to interpretation and has not been legally settled. At the same time, the federal government is taking a firm stand in seeking to enforce its policy. Constitutional scholar Daniel Booth, in "Federalism on Ice: State and Local Enforcement of Federal Immigration Law," notes that "In the context of using state and local authorities to enforce immigration laws, the anti-commandeering doctrine may provide little protection."[49]

8.5 CONCLUSION

The September 11, 2001 attacks proved to be a defining moment for intergovernmental relations. Prior to that date, threats to the homeland emanated largely from international actors outside of the U.S., but today's terrorism has broadened threat perceptions and realities. Traditionally, federal preeminence in national defense policy left state and local governments with a limited role, but it is now widely recognized that homeland security requires cooperation and collaboration at all levels of government. This dynamic has been an appropriate topic upon which to conclude our book. The 9/11 Commission not only highlighted the need for improved information sharing among government

Figure 8.15: Secretary of Defense Donald H. Rumsfeld gives his opening remarks before the 9-11 Commission on March 23, 2004. Rumsfeld testified before the National Commission on Terrorists Attacks that is investigating the formulation of U.S. counterterrorism policy with particular emphasis on the period from the August 1998 embassy bombings in Africa to the September 11, 2001, attacks on America.

Source: Wikimedia Commons

Attribution: Staff Sgt Jerry Morrison

License: Public Domain

48   Toni M. Massaro and Shefali Milczarek-Desai, "Constitutional Cities: Sanctuary Jurisdictions, Local Voice, And Individual Liberty" (January 22, 2019). *50 Columbia Human Rights Law Review* 1 (2018); Arizona Legal Studies Discussion Paper No. 18-31, https://ssrn.com/abstract=3262729.

49   Daniel Booth, "Federalism on Ice: State and Local Enforcement of Federal Immigration Law *Harvard Journal of Law & Public Policy,* Vol. 29, No. 3, 1082.

agencies but also recommended strengthening security intelligence at the state and local levels. Federal, state, and local collaboration is now promoted through fusion centers, as well as a myriad of preparedness programs, designed to identify and address terrorist and cyber threats. For the most part, state and local governments have been willing to cooperate with the federal government in these policy domains, since the latter provides much needed financial and technical resources. By contrast, immigration enforcement policy has been considerably more conflicted. A host of sanctuary jurisdictions, both state and local, continue to resist federal demands by pursuing legal challenges in court. These disputes involve principles that lie at the very heart of the Constitution and are likely to generate clashes over the nature and scope of federalism for some time to come.

REFLECTIVE QUESTIONS

1. What were the national security weaknesses that led to the establishment of the Department of Homeland Security (DHS)? Do you think that the DHS has been successful in addressing those weaknesses?

2. What are the main cybersecurity challenges faced by state and local governments?

3. How does the system of Federalism affect election security?

4. Why has the USA PATRIOT Act been criticized?

5. Discuss sanctuary jurisdictions in relation to the anti-commandeering doctrine, the Supremacy Clause, and the Fourth Amendment to the Constitution.

BIBLIOGRAPHY

American Civil Liberties Union, *ICE Detainers and the Fourth Amendment: What do Recent Federal Court Decisions Mean*, November 13, 2014, https://www.aclu.org/other/backgrounder-ice-detainers-and-fourth-amendment-what-do-recent-federal-court-decisions-mean.

American Immigration Council, *Secure Communities: A Fact Sheet*, November 29, 2011, https://www.americanimmigrationcouncil.org/research/secure-communities-fact-sheet.

Bhatt, Raina, "Pushing an End to Sanctuary Cities: Will it Happen?" *Michigan Journal of Race and Law*, Vol. 22, Issue 1 (2016), 139-162.

Beazly Breach Response Services Team, "Ransomware attacks skyrocket, Q1 2019," *Beazly Breach Insights*, May 23, 2019.

Blinder, Alan and Nicole Perlroth, "A Cyberattack Hobbles Atlanta, and Security Experts Shudder," *The New York Times*, March 27, 2018.

Bobby Allyn, 22 "Texas Towns Hit with Ransomware Attack In 'New Front' Of Cyber assault" *National Public Radio*, August 20, 2019, https://www.npr.org/2019/08/20/752695554/23-texas-towns-hit-with-ransomware-attack-in-new-front-of-cyberassault.

Booth, Daniel, "Federalism on Ice: State and Local Enforcement of Federal Immigration Law *Harvard Journal of Law & Public Policy*, 1063–1083.

Congressional Research Service, *The State and Local Role in Election Administration: Duties and Structures*, March 4, 2019, https://fas.org/sgp/crs/misc/R45549.pdf.

Conradis, Brandon, "Trump ICE pick: Politicians who run sanctuary cities should be charged with crimes," *The Hill*, January 2, 2018, https://thehill.com/homenews/administration/367167-trump-ice-pick-politicians-who-run-sanctuary-cities-should-be-charged.

Creek, Heather M. and Stephen Yoder, "With a Little Help from Our Feds: Understanding State Immigration Enforcement Policy Adoption in American Federalism," *The Policy Studies Journal*, Vol. 40, No. 4 (2012) 674–697.

Deere, Stephen, "Confidential Report: Atlanta's cyber-attack could cost taxpayers $17 million," *Atlanta Journal-Constitution*, August 1, 2018.

Dwyer, Devin and Huma Khan, "Arizona's Gov. Brewer Signs Controversial Immigration Bill" *ABC News*, April 21, 2010, https://abcnews.go.com/WN/obama-arizona-immigration-bill-misguided/story?id=10457567.

Election Assistance Commission, "The Impact of HAVA Funding on the 2018 Elections," https://www.eac.gov/sites/default/files/paymentgrants/TheImpactofHAVAFundingonthe2018Elections_EAC.pdf.

Garret R. Sam, "Federal Role in U.S. Campaigns and Elections: An Overview," *Congressional Research Service Report* 5," September 4, 2018, https://fas.org/sgp/crs/misc/R45302.pdf.

Government Accountability Office, *ELECTIONS: Observations on Voting Equipment Use and Replacement,* April 2018, https://www.gao.gov/assets/700/691201.pdf.

Griffith, Bryan and Jessica M. Vaughan, *Map: Sanctuary Cities, Counties, and States*, February 5, 2020, https://cis.org/Map-Sanctuary-Cities-Counties-and-States.

Immigrant Legal Resource Center, *Growing the Resistance: How Sanctuary Laws and Policies Have Flourished during the Trump Administration,* December 17, 2019, https://www.ilrc.org/growing-resistance-how-sanctuary-laws-and-policies-have-flourished-during-trump-administration.

Kettl, Donald F. "Contingent Coordination: Practical and Theoretical Puzzles for Homeland Security" *American Review of Public Administration*, Vol. 33 No. 3, September 2003, 253–277.

Kettl, Donald F. "Homeland Security: The Federalism Challenge" in Laurence J. O'Toole, Jr. and Robert K. Christensen, eds. *American Intergovernmental Relations: Foundations, Perspectives, and Issues,* Washington, D.C.: CQ Press, 2013, 306–315.

Massaro, Toni M. and Shefali Milczarek-Desai, "Constitutional Cities: Sanctuary Jurisdictions, Local Voice, And Individual Liberty," January 22, 2019, *50 Columbia Human Rights Law Review* 1 (2018); *Arizona Legal Studies Discussion Paper* No. 18–31, https://ssrn.com/abstract=3262729.

National Association of State Chief Information Officers, *The Responsive State CIO: Connecting to the Customer, 2019 State CIO Surve,* https://www.nascio.org/wp-content/uploads/2019/11/2019StateCIOSurvey.pdf.

National Commission on Terrorist Attacks Upon the United States, *9/11 Report,* New York: W. W. Norton & Company, July 17, 2004.

National Conference of State Legislators, *Sanctuary Policy FAQ,* June 20, 2019, https://www.ncsl.org/research/immigration/sanctuary-policy-faq635991795.aspx.

Office of Homeland Security, *National Strategy for Homeland Security,* Washington D.C.: 2002.

Parks, Miles, "Bureaucracy and Politics Slow Election Security Funding To States," *National Public Radio,* June 18, 2018, https://www.npr.org/2018/06/18/617874348/bureaucracy-and-politics-slow-election-security-funding-to-states.

Ponemon Institute, "State of Cybersecurity in Local, State & Federal Government," October 2015, https://www.ponemon.org/library/the-state-of-cybersecurity-in-local-state-and-federal-government.

Rodriguez, Cristina, "Enforcement, Integration, and the Future of Immigration Federalism" *Journal on Migration and Human Security,* Vol. 5 No. 2, 2017, 509–540.

Shapiro, Jacob N. Shapiro and Dara Kay Cohen, "Color Bind: Lessons from the Failed Homeland Security Advisory System" *International Security*, Vol. 32, No. 2, Fall, 2007. 121-154.

Trump, Donald J. Trump, *Executive Order: Enhancing Public Safety in the Interior of the United States,* January 25, 2017, https://www.whitehouse.gov/presidential-actions/executive-order-enhancing-public-safety-interior-united-states.

Upton, David M. and Sadie Creese, "The Danger from Within," *Harvard Business Review* September 2014, https://hbr.org/2014/09/the-danger-from-within.

U.S. Department of Homeland Security, *Taskforce on Secure Communities Findings and Recommendations,* September 2011, https://www.dhs.gov/xlibrary/assets/hsac-task-force-on-secure-communities-findings-and-recommendations-report.pdf.

U.S. Department of Homeland Security, "About CBP" *US Immigration and Customs Enforcement,* September 18, 2019, https://www.cbp.gov/about.

U.S. Department of Homeland Security, *2017 National Network of Fusion Centers Final Report*, 24 October 2018, https://www.dhs.gov/publication/2017-fusion-center-assessment.

U.S. Department of Homeland Security, *National Preparedness System,* January 29

2019, https://www.fema.gov/national-preparedness-system.

U.S. Department of Homeland Security, *National Network of Fusion Centers Fact Sheet*, August 16, 2019, https://www.dhs.gov/national-network-fusion-centers-fact-sheet.

U.S. Department of Homeland Security, "Ransomware Outbreak" *CISI Insights,* August 21, 2019, https://www.us-cert.gov/sites/default/files/2019-08/CISA_Insights-ransomware_Outbreak_S508C.pdf.

U.S. Department of Homeland Security "Who we Are," *US Immigration and Customs Enforcement,* January, 8, 2020, https://www.ice.gov/about.

U.S. Department of Homeland Security, *Budget-in-Brief Fiscal Year 2020,* https://www.dhs.gov.

U.S. District Court for the Central District of California, *League of United Latin American Citizens v. Wilson,* 908 F. Supp. 755, November 20, 1995.

U.S. House of Representatives, *Illegal Immigration Reform and Immigrant Responsibility Act of 1996,* September 24, Section 642, https://www.congress.gov/104/crpt/hrpt828/CRPT-104hrpt828.pdf.

U.S. Senate Permanent Subcommittee on Investigations, *Federal Support for and Involvement in State and Local Fusion Centers*, October 3, 2012.

U.S. Supreme Court, *Pritz v. United States* 854 F.Supp. 1503, 1994.

U.S. Supreme Court, *De Canas v. Bica*, 424 U.S. 351, 1976.

www.ingramcontent.com/pod-product-compliance
Lightning Source LLC
Chambersburg PA
CBHW080549270326
41929CB00019B/3242

* 9 7 8 1 9 4 0 7 7 1 9 9 1 *